A Facsimile Reprint
Published by Cornmarket Press
London 1970

Published by Cornmarket Press Limited
42/43 Conduit Street, London WIR ONL
Printed in Switzerland
7191 2104 3

SUMMARY OF AND INDEX TO WAAGEN

L. Kraus. del.

Dr. Gustav Friedrich Waagen

From the original picture by
Ludwig Kraus in the Berlin
National Gallery

SUMMARY OF AND INDEX TO

WAAGEN

BY

ALGERNON GRAVES, F.S.A.

AUTHOR OF THE "ROYAL ACADEMY EXHIBITORS," AND "THE SOCIETY OF ARTISTS
EXHIBITORS," AND "THE BRITISH INSTITUTION EXHIBITORS, 1806-1867"

DEDICATED BY GRACIOUS PERMISSION TO

HIS MAJESTY THE KING

LONDON
PUBLISHED BY ALGERNON GRAVES
42 OLD BOND STREET, W.

MCMXII

PREFACE

THE name of Dr. WAAGEN is well known among Art Collectors in connection with his four volumes of " TREASURES OF ART IN GREAT BRITAIN " published in three volumes in 1854 and followed by a supplement in 1857. This work is valuable as containing his criticisms of those works of art that came under his notice during his journey through England and part of Scotland, and as giving a description of the finest pictures in the various private galleries. The only drawback to this work is its most imperfect and confused Index which has deprived it of its principal value. The compiler, two years ago, decided to make a new and complete Index; of that decision the present volume is the outcome. To those collectors who possess Dr. Waagen's work this Summary and Index will be of special value as it gives an easy reference to the page on which the picture is described or criticised, and to those who have not got the work it will be useful in giving the titles of the pictures and the owner's names at the time when Dr. Waagen wrote. Indeed, for many purposes this Summary and Index will render unnecessary actual reference to the volumes of Waagen; it is complete in itself.

The number of pictures mentioned in Waagen's four volumes, including the collections of King Charles I and the Orleans Gallery, is over 9,200, all of which are included in this Summary.

The second portion of this volume consists of a list of those pictures mentioned by Dr. Waagen in his tour of 1835, and not repeated in the later work.

The third portion consists of a special Index of all the 1,130 portraits mentioned by Dr. Waagen, followed by an Index of Owners.

Dr. Gustave Friedrich Waagen was born in 1794 and died in 1868; he held the appointment of Director of the Royal Gallery of Pictures at Berlin.

ALGERNON GRAVES.

42, OLD BOND STREET,
    November 1912.

LIST OF SUBSCRIBERS TO TIME OF PUBLICATION

ABRAHAM, W., 11, King Street, S.W.

AGNEW & SONS, 43, Old Bond Street.

ASHER & CO., 14, Bedford Street, Covent Garden.

BEDFORD, HIS GRACE THE DUKE OF, Woburn Abbey.

BERLIN KÖNIGLICHE LIBRARY, Berlin.

BLAKESLEY, T. J., 358, Fifth Avenue, New York.

COLNAGHI, P. & D., & OBACH, 14, Pall Mall East.

CREMETTI, EUGENE, 7, Haymarket.

DAVIS, CHARLES, 147, New Bond Street.

DUVEEN BROS. (2 *copies*), 26, Place Vendome, Paris.

EDWARD GALLERY, 26, King Street, St. James's.

FORTESCUE, HON. J. W., Royal Library, Windsor Castle.

KNOEDLER & CO. (3 *copies*), 15, Old Bond Street.

LANE, JOHN, Bodley Head, Vigo Street.

LEGGATT BROS., 30, St. James's Street.

MCCORMICK, R. HALL, ESQ., 332, Michigan Avenue, Chicago.

NATIONAL GALLERY, Trafalgar Square.

NATIONAL PORTRAIT GALLERY, St. Martin's Place.

NEWBERRY LIBRARY, CHICAGO, per Stevens & Brown.

NORTHBROOK, THE RT. HON. THE EARL OF, Stratton Park, Hants.

NORTHUMBERLAND, HIS GRACE THE DUKE OF, Syon House.

PARSONS, E., & SONS, 45, Brompton Road.

POLLARD, FREDERICK, 16, Panton Street, Haymarket.

QUARITCH, BERNARD (3 *copies*), 11, Grafton Street, Bond Street.

ROTHSCHILD, ALFRED DE, ESQ.

SABIN, FRANK T., 172, New Bond Street.

SALOMONS, SIR DAVID, BART., Brawnhill, Tunbridge Wells.

SCOTT & FOWLES, 590, Fifth Avenue, New York.

STEVENS & BROWN, 4, Trafalgar Square.

SULLEY & CO., 159, New Bond Street.

VICARS, BROS., 12, Old Bond Street.

VICTORIA & ALBERT MUSEUM, South Kensington.

WALKER ART GALLERY, Liverpool.

WALLIS, SIR WHITWORTH, Corporation Art Gallery, Birmingham.

WEARDALE, RT. HON. LORD, 3, Carlton Gardens.

WERTHEIMER, ASHER, 158, New Bond Street.

WALLIS & SON, French Gallery, 120, Pall Mall.

WILLIAMSON, DR., Burgh House, Well Walk, Hampstead.

WILLSON, BROS., 48, Pall Mall.

YARRELL & CO., 19, Ryder Street, St. James's.

SUMMARY OF WAAGEN

B

	VOL. & PAGE		OWNER
ARETINO, Spinello			
St. Catherine before Judges	3.	2	W. Fuller Maitland
St. Catherine Praying in Prison	3.	2	W. Fuller Maitland
ARPINO, Cavaliere D'			
The Falling Angels	2.	63	Duke of Sutherland
Christ on Mount of Olives	3.	192	Mr. Harford
Sketch for Large Battle Piece	3.	225	Mr. Martin
St. Michael Subduing Satan	3.	288	M'Lellan Gallery
His Own Portrait	4.	336	Duke of Bedford
A Pietà. Virgin and 4 Figures	4.	467	Duke of Northumberland
The Virgin in Glory, and Angels	4.	497	W. Drury Lowe
ARTOIS, Jacob van			
A Picture	2.	42	Bridgewater House
Landscape with Herd of Cattle	2.	69	Duke of Sutherland
Landscape, Figures by Teniers	3.	31	Duke of Norfolk
Landscape, Figures by Teniers	3.	31	Duke of Norfolk
Landscape and Figures	3.	293	Sir A. Campbell
Large Landscape	3.	460	Duke of Buccleuch
Landscape	4.	149	Earl of Caledon
Landscape	4.	149	Earl of Caledon
A Large Landscape	4.	438	Earl of Wemyss
Two Men and Woman, painted with Rubens	4.	496	W. Drury Lowe
ASHFIELD, Edmund (1680)			
Lady Pembroke. After Vandyck	3.	408	Marquis of Exeter
Lady Warwick. After Vandyck	3.	408	Marquis of Exeter
ASSELYN, Jan			
A Picture	2.	52	Bridgewater House
Cattle and Female before Cavern	2.	186	Thomas Baring
Bridge of Avignon	2.	284	Duke of Bedford
A Harbour with a Smithy	2.	308	Mr. Wombwell
Landscape with a Bridge	2.	499	Orleans Gallery
A Large Picture, 1646	3.	333	Meynell Ingram
Landscape	3.	459	Earl Spencer
Landscape	3.	459	Earl Spencer
Landscape	3.	481	Marquis of Bute
Landscape, Buildings, and Gray Horse	4.	318	Rev. Mr. Heath
Landscape, Broken Bridge, and Figures	4.	351	Vernon Harcourt
Ruins, Sportsman in Red Jacket	4.	427	Rev. Thos. Staniforth
ASSERATO, Giovachino			
Christ Disputing in Temple	3.	240	Liverpool R.I.

	VOL. & PAGE	OWNER
AUBRY		
A Fox Hunt	4. 264	Duc D'Aumale
A Wolf Hunt	4. 264	Duc D'Aumale
AVERKAMP, Hendrik van (called " De Stomme van Campen ")		
A Winter Piece	4. 361	Lord Folkestone

BACKHUYSEN, Ludolph

	VOL. & PAGE	OWNER
Landscape	1. 358	National Gallery
Mouth of the Thames	1. 413	Sir Robert Peel
Brisk Gale, a Ship on Beach	1. 413	Sir Robert Peel
Mouth of River Brille	2. 22	Buckingham Palace
View of the Texel, 1670	2. 51	Bridgewater House
View on the Y near Amsterdam	2. 51	Bridgewater House
Coast Scene and Yacht	2. 111	Lord Ashburton
Seapiece, and 6 Vessels	2. 111	Lord Ashburton
Boat Taking in Cargo	2. 123	Henry Thomas Hope
Mouth of the Bril, Man-of-War, etc.	2. 123	,,
View on the Y, with Amsterdam	2. 123	,,
Agitated Sea, Boat in Front	2. 139	H. A. J. Munro
A Storm	2. 139	H. A. J. Monro
Vessels in Brisk Breeze	2. 188	Thos. Baring
Agitated Sea, Boat being Launched	2. 188	Thos. Baring
Agitated Sea, Large Ship, etc.	2. 203	R. S. Holford
Agitated Sea, Large Ship, etc.	2. 203	R. S. Holford
A Storm	2. 228	Hon. E. Phipps
Sea Coast, Man in Blue Dress	2. 256	F. Heusch
Agitated Sea, Large Vessel, etc.	2. 292	Charles Bredel
Agitated Sea, 3 Vessels, etc.	2. 297	Wynn Ellis
A Storm	2. 309	Mr. Wombwell
Agitated Sea, etc.	2. 312	Earl of Listowel
Slightly Agitated Sea	3. 40	Petworth
Seapiece	3. 134	James Morrison
A Quiet Sea	3. 163	Marquis of Lansdowne
Agitated Sea with Vessels	3. 209	Lord Northwick
A Male Portrait	3. 209	,,
A Seapiece, Red Figures	3. 209	,,
A Storm	3. 253	Blundell Weld
Small Boats Driving into Harbour	3. 275	Edinburgh R.I.
Sea Coast, Woman on Horseback	3. 287	M'Lellan Gallery
A Storm	3. 290	,,
Small Seapiece	3. 290	,,
Seapiece with a Pier	3. 311	Earl of Hopetoun
Storm, 2 Large Ships, etc.	3. 443	Mr. Tomline
Agitated Sea, numerous Vessels	4. 102	R. S. Holford
Stormy Sea, Boat in Foreground	4. 132	Lord Overstone
Agitated Sea, Boat in Foreground	4. 145	Lord Overstone

	VOL. & PAGE		OWNER
BACKHUYSEN, Ludolph—*continued*			
Sea Coast, Gentleman, Lady, and Greyhound	4.	157	St. John Mildmay
Harbour and many Ships	4.	160	Abraham Robarts
Agitated Sea, Boat with White Flag	4.	165	Abraham Robarts
Agitated Sea, 2 Large Boats	4.	212	Mr. Henderson
A Seapiece	4.	278	Sir C. Eardley
Agitated Sea, Boats in Front	4.	309	J. Morrison
Agitated Sea, 2 Large Vessels	4.	365	Earl of Normanton
Dutch Coast, Boat full of Figures	4.	443	Sir Hugh Campbell
Vessels in a Storm, Rocky Coast	4.	477	W. W. Bardon
Agitated Sea, Vessels Signed LB	4.	482	Matthew Anderson
Agitated Sea, Large Vessels	4.	483	Matthew Anderson
BAGNACAVALLO			
Virgin Carried by Four Angels	3.	169	Earl of Suffolk
The Visitation (Altar Piece)	3.	378	Davenport Bromley
St. Augustin	4.	103	Lord Ward
BANDINELLI, Baccio			
An Old Man Holding Letter	4.	498	W. Drury Lowe
BARNA			
Three Gothic Pediments, Virgin and Child	2.	462	Rev. Mr. Russell
BARNABA da Modena			
Coronation of Virgin, 1374	4.	169	Lord Wensleydale
The Trinity, 1374	4.	169	,,
Virgin and Child Enthroned, 1374	4.	169	,,
The Crucifixion, 1374	4.	169	,,
BAROCCIO, Federigo			
Madonna del Ghetto	1.	324	National Gallery
A Holy Family	2.	91	Devonshire House
A Holy Family	2.	242	H. Danby Seymour
The Entombment	2.	270	Miss Rogers
Holy Family	2.	486	Orleans Gallery
Flight into Egypt	2.	486	,,
Holy Family, " La Vierge au Chat "	2.	486	,,
Destruction of Troy	2.	486	,,
Marriage of St. Catherine	3.	172	Colt Hoare
Virgin and Child in Clouds	3.	289	M'Lellan Gallery
A Madonna	3.	383	Earl of Shrewsbury
Virgin and Child	3.	390	M. A. Whyte

	VOL. & PAGE	OWNER
A Magdalen	3. 404	Marquis of Exeter
The Nativity	3. 456	Earl Spencer
The Nativity	4. 494	Lord Feversham
Magdalen with a Skull	4. 505	Earl of Yarborough

BARRY, James, R.A.

Five Pictures	2. 321	Society of Arts
Pandora in Assembly of Gods	4. 201	James Tulloch
First Duke of Northumberland	4. 266	Duke of Northumberland

BARTHOLOMEW, Valentine

Peonies	2. 352	E. Bicknell

BARTOLINI

Venus de Medici (copy)	3. 222	Howard Galton

BARTOLO, Taddeo di

Virgin and Child	3. 436	Earl of Orford
A Diptych, Crucifixion, etc.	4. 284	Rev. J. Fuller Russell

BARTOLOMMEO, Fra

Virgin and Child	2. 82	Lord Elcho
Virgin Enthroned (Altar Piece)	2. 194	R. S. Holford
Virgin Caressed by Child	2. 314	Earl Brownlow
Virgin and Child and Two Saints	2. 418	Henry Labouchere
Christ in Lap giving Cross to John	3. 10	Earl Cowper
Holy Family	3. 172	Colt Hoare
Virgin and Child	3. 183	J. P. Miles
Virgin with Child in Lap and John	4. 93	Thos. Baring
Virgin and Child	4. 101	R. S. Holford
Virgin Nursing the Child	4. 321	Lord Enfield
Virgin and Child	4. 397	Lord Methuen
Virgin and Child (School of)	4. 446	Lord Kinnaird
A Large Picture	4. 456	Earl of Dunmore

BASAITI, Marco

St. Jerome Kneeling	4. 58	National Gallery

BASSANO, Francesco

Good Samaritan	2. 77	Samuel Rogers
Adoration of Kings	2. 267	Miss Rogers
Noah's Ark	2. 486	Orleans Gallery
A Farmyard	2. 486	,,
A Sleeping Shepherd	2. 486	,,
The Prodigal Son	2. 486	,,

C

	VOL. & PAGE	OWNER
Good Samaritan	4. 60	National Gallery
Landscape and Cattle	4. 96	Thomas Baring
Giacomo Bassano	4. 335	Duke of Bedford
Spring	4. 361	Lord Folkestone
Summer	4. 361	„
Autumn	4. 361	,,
Winter	4. 361	„
Saint Adoring Virgin	4. 412	Mr. Barry
Christ on the Mount of Olives	4. 425	Earl of Burlington
Christ and Money Changers	4. 477	W. W. Bardon
Annunciation to Shepherds	4. 493	Lord Feversham
Annunciation to Shepherds	4. 503	Earl of Yarborough
A Picture	4. 515	Duke of Portland
A Picture	4. 515	Duke of Portland

BASSANO, Leandro

The Last Judgment	2. 487	Orleans Gallery
Adoration of Shepherds	4. 108	J. Morrison
Exodus of Israelites	4. 148	Earl of Caledon
Christ with Martha and Mary	4. 158	St. John Mildmay
Adoration of the Kings	4. 158	St. John Mildmay
A Dominican	4. 173	E. Cheney
Old Man in White Collar	4. 175	E. Cheney
A Vintage	4. 281	Sir C. Eardley
A Smithy	4. 281	Sir C. Eardley
Man in Black Dress and Brown Fur	4. 326	Sir Thomas Sebright
Leandro Bassano	4. 336	Duke of Bedford
Woman on a Horse Receiving Child	4. 408	Smith Barry
Holy Family and St. John	4. 413	Smith Barry

BASSANO Family

Five pictures	2. 482	Charles I
Landscape with Cattle	3. 314	Duke of Buccleuch
Two pictures	3. 465	Duke of Bedford
The Four Seasons	4. 459	M'Lellan Gallery

BATTONI, Pompeo

Lord Eardley and his tutor	4. 284	Sir C. Eardley
The Sacrifice of Iphigenia	4. 505	Earl of Yarborough

BAUERSTADT

Street of Dutch Town, figures by Lingelbach	3. 165	Marquis of Lansdowne

	VOL. & PAGE	OWNER
BAUMANN, Miss (Madame Steinhauser)		
A Polish Family in Exile	2. 152	Marquis of Lansdowne
BECCAFUMI		
Marriage of the Virgin	4. 459	M'Lellan Gallery
BEELDEMAKER, Jan		
Pointers	3. 253	Blundel Weld
BEERESTRAATEN		
A Town in Winter	3. 222	Howard Galton
BEGA, Cornelius		
A Picture	2. 52	Bridgewater House
A Man and his Wife	3. 478	Marquis of Bute
Peasant Woman and Girl with basket	4. 208	Mr. Henderson
Peasants in a Room	4. 269	Duke of Northumberland
BEGYN, Abraham		
View of Trieste	4. 200	J. Tulloch
Landscape and Figures	4. 211	Mr. Henderson
BELLINI, Gentile		
A Doge in his robes of office	4. 172	E. Cheney
Portrait of a Doge	4. 352	Vernon Harcourt
BELLINI, Giovanni		
A Doge	1. 316	National Gallery
Warrior kneeling before Virgin (school of)	1. 317	National Gallery
Virgin and Child and Six Saints	2. 59	Duke of Sutherland
Virgin and Child	2. 178	Thomas Baring
A young Man " Non Aliter "	2. 196	R. S. Holford
A Male Portrait	2. 235	Lord Ward
Virgin with Child with four Saints	2. 265	Sir C. Eastlake
His own Portrait	2. 362	Hampton Court
A Concert	2. 368	Hampton Court
The Circumcision	2. 487	Orleans Gallery
The Wise Men's Offering	2. 487	Orleans Gallery
Portrait in Peruke	3. 32	Petworth
Adoration of the Kings	3. 185	J. P. Miles
A Riposo	3. 201	Lord Northwick

	VOL. & PAGE	OWNER
Virgin with Child on Parapet	3. 201	Lord Northwick
Virgin and Child Adored by St. John	3. 234	Liverpool R.I.
Giovanni Bellini	3. 234	Liverpool R.I.
A Picture	3. 314	Captain Stirling
The Circumcision	3. 319	Earl of Carlisle
Christ on Mount of Olives	3. 376	Davenport Bromley
Christ giving Keys to Peter	3. 403	Marquis of Exeter
Virgin and Child with Pomegranate	4. 58	National Gallery
Landscape, Death of Peter Martyr	4. 114	Sir C. Eastlake
Virgin seated, Child with White Cap	4. 147	Earl of Caledon
Gods assembled in Landscape	4. 467	Duke of Northumberland
Presentation in Temple	4. 494	Lord Feversham
Holy Family (school of)	4. 512	Duke of Portland

BELLOTTO, Bernardo (pupil of Canaletto)

An Architectural Piece	3. 159	Marquis of Lansdowne
An Architectural Piece	3. 159	Marquis of Lansdowne
Architectural View	3. 203	Lord Northwick
Architectural View	3. 203	Lord Northwick
Arsenal at Venice	3. 240	Liverpool R.I.
Piazza of St. Mark	3. 248	Blundell Weld
Church of the Salute	3. 248	Blundell Weld
An Architectural Piece	3. 337	Charles Wynn
Piazza of St. Mark	4. 134	Lord Overstone
Canal in Venice	4. 210	Mr. Henderson

BELTRAFFIO (see also BOLTRAFFIO)

An Altar-piece, Virgin and Child, etc.	4. 409	Smith Barry

BERGHEM, Nicholas

Peasant and Cattle, Gray Horse, 1655	2. 16	Buckingham Palace
Landscape, Three Women with Rushes, etc.	2. 16	,,
Three Shepherds and Flocks	2. 17	,,
Herdsman on Horseback, etc.	2. 17	,,
Shepherdess, Goat and Dog, 1650	2. 17	,,
Woman on Horseback, Drover and Cows	2. 17	,,
Cattle Reposing, Shepherd and Woman	2. 17	,,
Man with an Ass, etc.	2. 17	,,
Bridge and Hawking Party	2. 46	Bridgewater House
Landscape, Woman on Ass	2. 47	,,
Satyr and two nymphs	2. 47	,,
Herdsman and Cattle, Woman on Ass	2. 47	,,
Woman on Ass near River	2. 47	,,

	VOL. & PAGE		OWNER
BERGHEM, Nicholas—*continued*			
Two Gentlemen on Horseback, Girl on Ass	2.	95	Devonshire House
Seaport, Gentleman and Lady, Falcons	2.	95	Devonshire House
Herdsman and Cows by Water	2.	108	Lord Ashburton
Lobster Catchers	2.	108	,,
"Le Fagot," Woman Driving Cows	2.	108	,,
Waterfall, Temple of Sibyl	2.	121	Henry Thomas Hope
Jupiter deceiving Calisto	2.	138	H. A. J. Munro
A Small Picture	2.	159	Marquis of Hertford
Rocky Landscape, Women Dancing	2.	167	Marquis of Westminster
Drove of Cattle Passing Ford	2.	186	Thos. Baring
Hunting Party, Lady on White Mule	2.	186	,,
Drover on Horseback with Wallet	2.	186	,,
Shepherd Playing Pipe and Flock	2.	201	R. S. Holford
Several Drawings	2.	204	R. S. Holford
High Hills and Cattle	2.	228	Hon. E. Phipps
Cattle and Herdsmen at Ford	2.	240	Lord Colborne
Herdsman seated on Cow with Flute	2.	240	Lord Colborne
A Picture	2.	252	Henry Bevan
A Picture	2.	286	Duke of Bedford
Woman with Spindle and Cows	2.	290	Charles Bredal
Herdsman and Woman, Two Cows	2.	296	Wynn Ellis
Men and Animals	2.	309	Mr. Wombwell
Landscape, Shepherds, and Cattle	2.	336	Haywood Hawkins
Peasants and Cattle, White Cow	2.	343	Dulwich Gallery
Shepherdess and Flock Wading	2.	344	Dulwich Gallery
Landscape, Herd of Cattle	2.	435	Windsor Castle
Man in Red Jacket on Horse	2.	452	Richard Forster
Stream, Houses, and Cattle	3.	160	Marquis of Lansdowne
Landscape	3.	208	Lord Northwick
Landscape, Woman Dancing	3.	208	Lord Northwick
Landscape, Numerous Animals	3.	223	Howard Galton
Landscape, Two Cows, and Goat	3.	275	Edinburgh R.I.
Shepherd, Two Cows, and a Dog	3.	287	M'Lellan Gallery
Landscape, Herd of Cattle, Water	3.	299	Duke of Hamilton
Seaport, Lady and Gentleman, and Falcons	3.	347	Duke of Devonshire
River at Foot of Mountains, etc.	3.	350	,,
Landscape, Rider and Cattle	3.	351	,,
Landscape, Peasant Ploughing	3.	396	Duke of Rutland
Cattle and Herdsman at Ford	3.	396	,,
A Large Picture	3.	399	,,
Landscape procession of animals	3.	434	Earl of Orford
Landscape, Herdsman, and Cattle	3.	442	Mr. Tomline

	VOL. & PAGE		OWNER
Landscape, Woman on Mule, etc.	3.	479	Marquis of Bute
Waterfall, Figures, and Cattle	3.	479	,,
Figures and Horses on the Ice	3.	479	,,
Herdsmen and Cattle, *see* Vol. 2, 239	4.	62	National Gallery
His Own Portrait as Huntsman	4.	69	Earl of Yarborough
Shepherdess on Horseback and Herd	4.	89	Marquis of Hertford
Woman on Mule and Cattle	4.	109	J. Morrison
Shepherdess Carrying Lamb, etc.	4.	157	St. John Mildmay
Ox, Cow, and Sheep in Water	4.	162	Abraham Robarts
Girl Milking a Goat, etc.	4.	194	G. Field
White Cow, etc., Cart Passing	4.	207	Mr. Henderson
Merrymaking, An Interior	4.	289	J. Sanders
Shepherd, Two Cows, and Two Sheep	4.	291	J. Sanders
Woman on Grey Horse, etc.	4.	294	J. Walter
Winter Landscape, Men, and Horses	4.	295	J. Walter
Shepherdess, and Basket of Vegetables	4.	320	Lord Enfield
Three Oxen and an Ass	4.	340	Knole
A Dark Picture	4.	350	Vernon Harcourt
Landscape and Cattle	4.	364	Earl of Normanton
Hilly Landscape, Cavern	4.	379	Kingston Lacy
Figure on a Mule with Ass	4.	439	Earl of Wemyss
Winter Landscape	4.	458	M'Lellan Gallery
Woman on Mule and Cattle	4.	480	Matthew Anderson
Shepherd Leaning on White Cow	4.	482	Matthew Anderson
Herd Crossing a Ford	4.	496	Earl of Harrington
Annunciation to Shepherds	4.	522	Earl of Hardwick

BERKHEYDEN, Job

Four Views	2.	123	Henry Thomas Hope
A Dutch Town, Figures in a Square	2.	188	T. Baring
Dutch Town with Canal	3.	209	Lord Northwick
Exterior of a Church	3.	303	Duke of Hamilton
Architecture	3.	482	Marquis of Bute
Two Huntsmen before a Tavern	4.	235	Earl of Harrington
Companion Picture	4.	235	,,
Picture like Wouverman	4.	237	,,
Hotel de Ville, Amsterdam	4.	482	Matthew Anderson

BERNASIO

A Landscape	3.	270	Edinburgh R.I.

BERNINI, Cavalier (Sculptor)

A Monk	2.	487	Orleans Gallery
A Student	2.	487	Orleans Gallery
Neptune	4.	71	Earl of Yarborough

	VOL. & PAGE		OWNER
BICCI, Neri de'			
Assumption of the Virgin	2.	126	A. Barker
BIRD, Edward, R.A.			
The Raffle for the Watch	1.	379	Marlborough House
BISCAINO			
A Picture	2.	93	Devonshire House
Noli me tangere	4.	503	Earl of Yarborough
Christ and Woman of Samaria	4.	503	Earl of Yarborough
BISSOLO			
A Picture	4.	374	Sir W. Knighton
BLIECK, D. D.			
Interior of a Church, 1656	4.	458	M'Lellan Gallery
BLOEMART, Abraham			
Altar Piece, a Pietà, etc.	3.	206	Lord Northwick
BOEL, Peter			
Poultry and Dogs	3.	387	Earl of Shrewsbury
BOL, Ferdinand			
Man in Chair, Wife with Necklace	2.	182	T. Baring
Five Women and Negress	2.	183	T. Baring
Esther before Ahasuerus	2.	308	Mr. Wombwell
Angel Appearing to Hagar	3.	240	Liverpool R.I.
A Professor	3.	271	Edinburgh R.I.
Boy Holding a Goblet	3.	326	Earl of Carlisle
Young Man in Hat and Feather	4.	164	Abraham Robarts
BOLTRAFFIO, Antonio (*see also* **BELTRAFFIO**)			
Man in Red Dress	2.	346	Dulwich Gallery
Virgin and Child	3.	122	Duke of Marlborough
Virgin and Child	3.	201	Lord Northwick
BONIFAZIO			
Allegorical Subject	2.	252	Henry Bevan
Allegorical Subject	2.	252	Henry Bevan
A Picture	2.	258	Sir C. Coote
Virgin with Child on Lap	2.	265	Sir C. Eastlake
Woman of Samaria	2.	365	Hampton Court
Adoration of The Kings	3.	42	Petworth

	VOL. & PAGE	OWNER
Exposure of Romulus and Remus	3. 203	Lord Northwick
Finding of Moses	3. 261	Earl of Lonsdale
The Last Supper	3. 271	Edinburgh R.I.
Resurrection of Christ	3. 300	Duke of Hamilton
A Picture	3. 314	Captain Stirling
Return of Prodigal Son	3. 383	Earl of Shrewsbury
St. Jerome in the Desert	3. 482	Marquis of Bute
Destruction of Pharaoh	4. 171	E. Cheney
Moses Striking the Rock	4. 171	,,
Baptism of Christ	4. 172	,,
Virgin Nursing Child, and Angels	4. 172	,,
Virgin and Child, St. Joseph, etc.	4. 291	J. Sanders
Virgin and Child in Glory	4. 325	Lord Enfield
Marriage of St. Catharine	4. 408	Smith Barry
Susannah and the Elders	4. 410	Smith Barry
Woman Taken in Adultery	4. 459	M'Lellan Gallery
Virgin with Book and Sleeping Child	4. 468	Duke of Northumberland
Virgin Holding Child on Her Lap	4. 469	Duke of Northumberland
A Holy Family	4. 491	Archdeacon of Durham

BONINGTON, R. P.

The Dogana at Venice	1. 385	Marlborough House
Turk Asleep over Pipe	2. 75	Samuel Rogers
A Female Portrait	2. 128	A. Barker
View in Venice	2. 141	H. A. J. Munro
Misty Morning, Selling Fish	2. 141	,,
Francis I and his Sister	2. 141	,,
Seashore, Two Fish Women, etc.	2. 174	Marquis of Westminster
The Doge's Palace	2. 190	T. Baring
Three People on Balcony	2. 190	T. Baring
Italian Sea coast	2. 268	Miss Rogers
Italian Sea coast	2. 268	Miss Rogers
Seashore with a Cart	3. 211	Lord Northwick
Sea coast, Grey and Brown Horse	4. 92	Marquis of Hertford
Sea coast in France	4. 332	Duke of Bedford
Piece of Water with Cows	4. 369	Earl of Normanton

BORDONE, Paris

Repose of Holy Family	2. 32	Bridgewater House
Two Old Women and Nude Woman	2. 235	Lord Ward
A Lady at her Toilet	3. 269	Edinburgh R.I.
Virgin and Child and St. George	3. 288	M'Lellan Gallery
Mother, Father, and Daughter	3. 351	Duke of Devonshire
Man in Chair with Letter	3. 378	Davenport Bromley

D

	VOL. & PAGE		OWNER
BORDONE, Paris—*continued*			
Virgin, Elizabeth, and Joseph Asleep	3.	383	Earl of Shrewsbury
A good Male Portrait	3.	384	Earl of Shrewsbury
Young Woman, Hand on Breast	3.	456	Earl Spencer
Titian with his Mistress	3.	456	Earl Spencer
The Centurion of Capernaum	3.	483	Marquis of Bute
A Young Woman	3.	483	Marquis of Bute
Venus Reposing	4.	63	Lord Elcho
Stately Lady in Purple Dress	4.	172	E. Cheney
Virgin and Child and Saints	4.	411	Smith Barry
Venus, Mars, and Cupid	4.	411	Smith Barry
Woman with right Breast bare	4.	469	Duke of Northumberland
BORGOGNONE, Il (Ambrogio di Fossano)			
Virgin and Child on Throne	4.	167	Davenport Bromley
Dead Christ and Angels	4.	284	Rev. John Russell
BORRAS			
St. Rock	2.	259	G. A. Hoskins
BOSCH, Jerome			
Adoration of the Kings	2.	243	H. Danby Seymour
Scene of a Conspiracy	2.	413	Hampton Court
St. John in Profile	3.	5	W. Fuller Maitland
Adoration of Kings	3.	39	Petworth
Temptation of St. Anthony	3.	251	Blundell Weld
BOTH, Andreas			
Rocky Landscape	3.	272	Edinburgh R.I.
BOTH, Jan and Andreas			
Waterfall and five Horsemen	2.	187	T. Baring
Figures and Cattle under Tree	2.	187	T. Baring
Woman on Mule, etc.	4.	161	A. Robarts
BOTH, Jan			
Mountainous Landscape	1.	357	National Gallery
Judgment of Paris, with Polemberg	1.	358	National Gallery
St. Philip Baptizing Eunuch	2.	21	Buckingham Palace
Cavern in a Rock	2.	50	Bridgewater House
Four Figures Bathing	2.	50	Bridgewater House
Mountain Chain	2.	111	Lord Ashburton
Stream between Two Hills	2.	122	H. T. Hope

	VOL. & PAGE		OWNER
Ponte Molle, Woman on Mule, etc.	2.	139	H. A. J. Munro
Landscape, Man and Ass, etc.	2.	139	H. A. J. Munro
A Landscape	2.	153	Marquis of Lansdowne
Pilgrim Conversing with Shepherd	2.	166	Marquis of Westminster
Philip Baptizing Eunuch	2.	203	R. S. Holford
Several Drawings	2.	205	R. S. Holford
Hilly Landscape with Herdsmen	2.	242	H. Danby Seymour
Landscape, Evening	2.	248	Mr. Neeld
Landscape, Figures on a Road	2.	255	Mr. Hensch
Evening, Landscape, large Trees	2.	292	Charles Bredel
Man Drinking out of Hat	2.	297	Wynn Ellis
Small Landscape	2.	297	Wynn Ellis
Three Landscapes	2.	331	C. S. Bale
Landscape, Figures by Andreas	2.	336	James Gray
Travellers Passing a Ford	2.	344	Dulwich Gallery
Waterfall in Rocky Landscape	3.	17	Earl Cowper
A Landscape	3.	43	Petworth
Falls of Terni	3.	134	James Morrison
A Landscape	3.	134	James Morrison
Buildings with Ninepin Players	3.	165	Marquis of Lansdowne
Large Landscape	3.	224	Mr. Martin
A Landscape	3.	270	Edinburgh R.I.
A Landscape	3.	274	Edinburgh R.I.
A Landscape	3.	289	M'Lellan Gallery
The Tiber Winding through Woods	3.	449	Fitzwilliam Museum
Two Laden Mules, Driver and Dog	4.	135	Lord Overstone
Landscape, Rocks, and Waterfall	4.	138	„
Rocks, Bridge, and Oxen Cart	4.	139	„
Waterfall, Drivers with Loaded Mules	4.	151	Earl of Caledon
Rocky Landscape with Water	4.	268	Duke of Northumberland
Waterfall and high Rock, Woman on Mule	4.	287	E. Foster
Rocky Cavern, two Grey Horses	4.	292	J. Sanders
Two Men by Water	4.	295	J. Walter
Stream, three laden Mules	4.	309	J. Morrison
Waterfall, three Figures	4.	311	J. Morrison
Trees with lofty trunks, etc.	4.	323	Lord Enfield
Travellers with Asses	4.	324	„
Landscape	4.	325	„
Waterfall, Road with Figures	4.	342	Humphrey Mildmay
Waterfall between high Rocks	4.	346	Earl Cowper
Landscape, Trees and Hills	4.	350	Vernon Harcourt
Waterfall, three Figures	4.	365	Earl of Normanton
Traveller Resting with laden Ass	4.	384	H. D. Seymour
Woman on a Donkey	4.	421	Jacob Fletcher

	VOL. & PAGE	OWNER
BOTH, Jan—*continued*		
Landscape, Figures by Andreas	4. 483	Matthew Anderson
Landscape, Figures by Andreas	4. 483	Matthew Anderson
Rock and Waterfall	4. 492	Lord Feversham
Landscape with high Hill	4. 497	W. Drury Lowe
Landscape with Fir Trees	4. 506	Sir John Nelthorpe
Landscape with Water	4. 513	Duke of Portland
BOTTICELLI, Sandro		
Virgin and Child and St. John	2. 127	A. Barker
Virgin and Child, Joseph, etc.	2. 231	Lord Ward
Virgin and St. John Adoring	3. 3	W. Fuller Maitland
The Nativity, 1511	3. 3	W. Fuller Maitland
Virgin Adoring Child	3. 196	Lord Northwick
Apostles and Tomb of Virgin	3. 296	Duke of Hamilton
A Picture	3. 314	Captain Stirling
Venus in Blue Drapery	3. 374	Davenport Bromley
Taking a Town	3. 374	„
David Coming to Samuel (School of)	3. 374	„
Virgin Adoring the Child	3. 376	„
Virgin and Child with Pomegranate	3. 376	„
Virgin and Child and St. John	4. 54	National Gallery
Virgin Standing with Child	4. 72	Alexander Barker
Venus on a Couch	4. 72	Alexander Barker
Study for Calumny of Apelles	4. 117	C. S. Bale
Venus, full length	4. 167	Davenport Bromley
Virgin Looking down on Child	4. 260	Duc d'Aumale
The Annunciation	4. 459	M'Lellan Gallery
BOUCHER, François		
Venus and Adonis	2. 128	A. Barker
Madame Montespan	2. 128	A. Barker
Madame de Pompadour	4. 432	John Gibson Craig
Leda and the Swan	4. 462	M'Lellan Gallery
Boy teaching Girl to play the Flute	4. 462	M'Lellan Gallery
BOURDON, Sebastian		
Philistines Sending back the Ark	1. 346	National Gallery
A Portrait	2. 487	Orleans Gallery
Christina, Queen of Sweden	2. 487	„
A Portrait	2. 487	„
A Portrait	2. 487	„
The Sentence of Midas	3. 172	Colt Hoare
A Bacchanalian Scene	3. 240	Liverpool R.I.

	VOL. & PAGE	OWNER
Moses Striking the Rock	3. 332	Meynell Ingram
A Rich Landscape	3. 484	Marquis of Bute
Christ and Samaritan Woman	4. 199	James Tulloch
Holy Family and St. Joseph	4. 348	Vernon Harcourt
Judgment of Midas	4. 378	Kingston Lacy
Europa and the Bull	4. 379	Kingston Lacy
The Child Sleeping	4. 493	Lord Feversham
The Seven Works of Mercy (7 pictures)	4. 505	Earl of Yarborough

BOURGUIGNON, Le

	VOL. & PAGE	OWNER
Skirmish of Cavalry	2. 93	Devonshire House
Sea piece	2. 93	,,
Sea piece	2. 93	,,
Battle piece	2. 93	,,
Battle piece	2. 93	,,
Two Horsemen Fighting	2. 270	Miss Rogers
Winter Landscape	3. 36	Petworth
A Battle piece	3. 172	Colt Hoare
Skirmish of Cavalry	3. 275	Edinburgh R.I.
Skirmish of Cavalry	3. 275	Edinburgh R.I.
Skirmish of Cavalry	3. 333	Meynell Ingram
His Own Portrait	3. 333	,,
Sea piece	3. 334	,,
Landscape with a Bridge	3. 399	Duke of Rutland
Large Battle Piece	3. 459	Earl Spencer
Landscape	3. 485	Marquis of Bute
Horsemen	4. 329	Sir T. Sebright
A Battle piece	4. 362	Lord Folkestone
Landscape with Robbers	4. 395	Lord Methuen
Landscape	4. 423	Earl of Burlington
Landscape	4. 423	,,
Horsemen	4. 425	,,
Horsemen	4. 425	,,
View in the Apennines	4. 497	W. Drury Lowe
A Fierce Combat	4. 497	,,
A Fight of Horsemen	4. 498	,,

BOYERMANS, Theodor

	VOL. & PAGE	OWNER
Continence of Scipio	4. 235	Earl of Harrington

BRACHELAER

	VOL. & PAGE	OWNER
Thief Stealing Grapes	4. 479	J. Anderson

	VOL. & PAGE		OWNER
BRACKENBURG, Regnier			
A Sick Chamber	2.	228	Hon. E. Phipps
Artist's Studio	2.	430	Windsor Castle
Artist's Studio	2.	430	Windsor Castle
A large Picture	3.	154	Earl of Pembroke
St. Nicholas Day, etc.	3.	478	Marquis of Bute
People in a Room	4.	518	Lady Galway
People in a Room	4.	518	Lady Galway
BRAMANTINO			
Adoration of the Kings	3.	372	Davenport Bromley
BREENBERG, Bartholomew			
Finding of Moses	1.	358	National Gallery
Large Rocky Landscape	2.	122	H. T. Hope
Two Pictures	2.	482	Charles I
Landscape with Round Tower	2.	499	Orleans Gallery
Large Landscape, 1630	3.	388	Earl of Shrewsbury
Travellers Asking their Way	4.	458	M'Lellan Gallery
BREKLENKAMP, Quirinus			
A Picture	2.	52	Bridgewater House
An Old Woman at Breakfast	2.	71	Duke of Sutherland
A Woman Threading a Needle	2.	280	Earl of Carlisle
A Man and Woman at a Meal	3.	223	Howard Galton
Mother and Daughter in Conversation	4.	238	Earl of Harrington
BREUGHEL, Jan			
A Picture	2.	42	Bridgewater House
A Picture	2.	311	Earl of Listowel
Two Pictures	2.	482	Charles I
St. John Preaching	3.	206	Lord Northwick
The Crucifixion	3.	264	Earl of Lonsdale
Landscape, Figures by Van Balen	3.	289	M'Lellan Gallery
Landscape, Figures by Van Balen	3.	289	M'Lellan Gallery
A Picture	3.	476	Marquis of Bute
Dutch Canal, Houses, Ships, etc.	4.	201	J. Tulloch
High Road, Carts and Horses	4.	235	Earl of Harrington
The Garden of Eden	4.	279	Sir C. Eardley
Animals, Fruit, and Flowers, with Rothenhammer	4.	279	Sir C. Eardley
Landscape	4.	356	Lord Folkestone
Bunch of Flowers in a vessel	4.	424	Earl of Burlington
Paradise, signed	4.	471	Duke of Northumberland
Temptation of St. Anthony	4.	471	Duke of Northumberland
Spring, Flora, with Rothenhammer	4.	509	Duke of Newcastle

	VOL. & PAGE		OWNER
BREUGHEL, Peter			
Murder of the Innocents	2.	413	Hampton Court
A Picture	2.	482	Charles I
A Kitchen	4.	268	Duke of Northumberland
Tournament, Old Woman and Man	4.	515	Duke of Portland
BREUGHEL, Velvet			
Landscape with high Road	2.	500	Orleans Gallery
Destruction of Babylon	2.	500	„
A Circular Landscape	2.	500	„
Sheep-shearing	2.	500	„
The Queen of Sheba	3.	462	Glandon Hall
Flower piece	4.	356	Lord Folkestone
BRILL, Paul			
A Picture	2.	42	Bridgewater House
Landscape, lofty Mountains	2.	500	Orleans Gallery
Tower of Babel	2.	500	„
Flight into Egypt	2.	500	„
A large Landscape	3.	35	Petworth
Landscape	3.	123	Duke of Marlborough
Landscape	3.	170	Earl of Suffolk
Landscape	3.	260	Earl of Lonsdale
The Campagna from Tivoli	3.	326	Earl of Carlisle
Landscape, Figures by Elzheimer	3.	347	Duke of Devonshire
Waterfall with Hunting Party	4.	202	J. Tulloch
Waterfall, Diana and Nymphs	4.	324	Lord Enfield
Small Landscape	4.	367	Earl of Normanton
Landscape with piece of Water	4.	514	Duke of Portland
BRONZINO, Angelo			
Cosmo I, Duke of Tuscany	2.	195	R. S. Holford
Leonora di Toledo	2.	269	Miss Rogers
Four Pictures	2.	482	Charles I
A Youth of agreeable physiognomy	3.	41	Petworth
Young Standard Bearer	3.	158	Marquis of Lansdowne
Boy with a Book	3.	160	Marquis of Lansdowne
Boy with a Dog	3.	197	Lord Northwick
Woman with Vase in hand	3.	248	Blundell Weld
Cosmo I and Wife	3.	302	Duke of Hamilton
Isabella, Wife of Cosmo I	3.	305	Duke of Hamilton
Pope Paul V	3.	382	Earl of Shrewsbury
A Holy Family	3.	382	Earl of Shrewsbury
Cosmo I, Duke of Tuscany	4.	223	Prince Consort
Cardinal Soderini	4.	456	Earl of Dunmore

	VOL. & PAGE		OWNER
BROUWER			
Farmhouse and Pollard Trees	2.	45	Bridgewater House
A Picture	2.	95	Devonshire House
Swineherd Driving Pigs	2.	138	H. A. J. Munro
Three Boors in a Room	2.	277	Duke of Wellington
Two quarrelling Boors with Knives	2.	280	Earl of Carlisle
Peasants Smoking and Drinking	3.	177	Mr. Vivian
Boors Playing Cards	3.	263	Earl of Lonsdale
Peasant Playing Guitar, etc.	3.	300	Duke of Hamilton
Card Players	3.	478	Marquis of Bute
Party Merrymaking	3.	478	Marquis of Bute
Peasant Seated Asleep	4.	88	Marquis of Hertford
BUCHTENSCHILD			
Sea piece	4.	425	Earl of Burlington
Sea piece	4.	425	Earl of Burlington
BURCKMAIR, Hans			
Adoration of Infant Christ	4.	227	Prince Consort
St. Natalitia	4.	317	Rev. Mr. Heath
St. Adrian with Sword	4.	461	M'Lellan Gallery
BYZANTINE SCHOOL			
Death of St. Ephraim	3.	1	W. Fuller Maitland
The Sudarium (King Abgarus)	4.	220	Prince Consort
The Nativity	4.	221	Prince Consort

E

	VOL. & PAGE	OWNER
CALCOTT, Sir A. W., R.A.—*continued*		
On the Scheldt	2. 258	Sir Charles Coote
Six Pictures	2. 307	J. Sheepshanks
A large Water Scene	2. 321	Sir J. Soane
Large Landscape with Cattle	2. 349	E. Bicknell
Rochester Bridge	2. 353	E. Bicknell
An Agitated Sea	3. 37	Petworth
Seaport and Part of Town	3. 165	Marquis of Lansdowne
A large Sea piece and Figures	3. 466	Duke of Bedford
On the Maas by Rotterdam	4. 136	Lord Overstone
The Pool on the Thames	4. 136	Lord Overstone
The Tomb of Cicero and distant Sea	4. 184	W. Marshall
A Young Girl	4. 185	W. Marshall
View of the Scheldt	4. 331	Duke of Bedford
A Sea piece	4. 416	S. Ashton
A Sea coast like Claude	4. 419	J. Chapman
CALLOT, J.		
Troop of Players Riding, etc.	2. 182	T. Baring
CALVART, Denys		
Virgin Presenting Child to Francis	3. 384	Earl of Shrewsbury
The Annunciation	3. 405	Marquis of Exeter
CAMALDOLESE, Don Silvestro		
Birth of John the Baptist	3. 232	Liverpool R.I.
Death of the Virgin	4. 284	Rev. J. F. Russell
A Royal Saint and 6 smaller Saints	4. 284	Rev. J. F. Russell
CAMBIASI, Luca		
Venus and Adonis	2. 65	Duke of Sutherland
Five Pictures	2. 482	Charles I
Death of Adonis	2. 487	Orleans Gallery
Judith	2. 487	Orleans Gallery
CAMPANA		
Magdalen Taking off her Pearls	2. 259	G. A. Hoskins
CAMPBELL, Thomas (Sculptor)		
Statue of Pauline Borghese	3. 367	Duke of Devonshire
Statue, Duke of Wellington	4. 435	Duke of Buccleuch
A Shepherd Boy Seated	4. 445	Lord Kinnaird
CAMPHUYSEN, Theodor		
Large Cattle piece	3. 209	Lord Northwick

	VOL. & PAGE	OWNER
CAMPI, Giulio		
Marriage of St. Catherine	2. 260	G. A. Hoskins
CANALETTO, Antonio		
Landscape	2. 101	Lord Ashburton
Landscape	2. 101	Lord Ashburton
Four Pictures	2. 155	Marquis of Hertford
The Rialto at Venice	2. 179	T. Baring
Doge's Palace and Piazzetta	2. 198	R. S. Holford
Riva dei Schiavoni	2. 294	Wynn Ellis
Grand Canal, Venice	2. 321	Sir J. Soane
A View of Buildings	2. 331	C. S. Bale
The Colosseum	2. 355	Hampton Court
Three Pictures	3. 172	Colt Hoare
Doge's Palace, Figures	3. 216	Earl of Warwick
Two Pictures	3. 219	Earl of Craven
View in Venice	3. 314	Duke of Buccleuch
Six Views of Venice	3. 314	„
Whitehall	3. 314	„
Large View of Venice	3. 323	Earl of Carlisle
Seventeen Pictures	3. 324	Earl of Carlisle
View of the Rialto	3. 422	Earl of Leicester
Twenty-four Pictures	3. 466	Duke of Bedford
View of the Piazzetta	4. 80	Marquis of Hertford
Bridge of the Rialto	4. 80	„
Two Venetian Views	4. 80	„
Two Pictures	4. 80	„
Two Views of Venice	4. 80	„
The Capitol from the Forum	4. 150	Earl of Caledon
View from Rome	4. 150	Earl of Caledon
Church of S. Francesco	4. 210	Mr. Henderson
Church of S. Pietro di Castello	4. 210	„
The Canale Regio	4. 211	„
View in Venice	4. 234	Earl of Harrington
View in Venice	4. 234	„
View in Venice	4. 238	„
View in Venice	4. 238	„
The Doge's Palace	4. 282	Sir C. Eardley
View of Venice	4. 282	Sir C. Eardley
Piazzetta of Venice	4. 325	Lord Enfield
The Doge's Palace	4. 367	Earl of Normanton
Grand Canal, Venice	4. 409	S. Barry
View of the Piazzetta	4. 424	Earl of Burlington
Six Views in Venice	4. 437	Duke of Buccleuch
Montague House, Whitehall	4. 437	Duke of Buccleuch

	VOL. & PAGE	OWNER
CANALETTO, Antonio—*continued*		
View of the Piazzetta	4. 460	M'Lellan Gallery
View of the Giudecca	4. 478	J. Anderson
The Doge's Palace	4. 478	,,
The Piazza and Canal	4. 479	,,
The Grand Canal	4. 479	,,
Campo S. Giacomo	4. 497	W. Drury Lowe
CANO, Alonso		
St. Agatha enchained	2. 136	H. A. J. Munro
An Ecclesiastic with Hour Glass	2. 242	H. D. Seymour
A General to the Knees	2. 242	H. D. Seymour
Madonna and Child	2. 259	G. A. Hoskins
St Anthony of Padua, etc.	3. 385	Earl of Shrewsbury
The Virgin and Child	4. 96	T. Baring
Portrait of Calderon	4. 104	Henry Labouchere
Child Sleeping on White Couch	4. 383	Kingston Lacy
The Magdalen Repentant	4. 390	Lord Heytesbury
Painted Statue of the Virgin	4. 450	W. Stirling
Two Angels, Red Chalk	4. 451	W. Stirling
The Poet, Lope di Vega	4. 520	Earl of Hardwicke
CANOVA (Sculptor)		
Napoleon I, colossal	2. 272	Duke of Wellington
Sleeping Endymion, and Dog	3. 365	Duke of Devonshire
Madame Letitia	3. 365	,,
Napoleon, Bust	3. 365	,,
Hebe, Statue	3. 366	,,
Canova, Bust	3. 366	,,
Several Designs	3. 366	,,
Perseus and the Graces	3. 411	Earl of Westmoreland
CARAVAGGIO, Polidoro da		
Egyptians in Red Sea	2. 29	Bridgewater House
St. Peter	2. 169	Marquis of Westminster
St. Paul	2. 169	Marquis of Westminster
Boy with Boat and Swans	2. 355	Hampton Court
The Three Graces	2. 489	Orleans Gallery
CARAVAGGIO, Michael Angelo da		
Christ and Disciples	1. 338	National Gallery
Guitar and Flute Players	2. 92	Devonshire House
Old Man Playing the Lute	2. 101	Lord Ashburton
A Young Man in Profile	2. 101	Lord Ashburton
A Cardinal as a Monk	2. 284	Duke of Bedford

	VOL. & PAGE	OWNER
A Portrait	2. 355	Hampton Court
Dorcas Lying Dead	2. 468	Charles I
A Holy Family	2. 468	Charles I
Dream of Caravaggio	2. 489	Orleans Gallery
Abraham Offering up Isaac	2. 489	„
The Transfiguration	2. 489	„
Esau Selling his Birthright	3. 22	Earl of Darnley
Card players and Soothsayers	3. 172	Colt Hoare
St. Christopher	3. 270	Edinburgh R.I.
Woman Taken in Adultery	3. 292	Sir A. Campbell
Gipsy Woman Telling Fortunes	3. 400	Duke of Rutland
Expulsion of Hagar	3. 401	Duke of Rutland
Susannah and the Elders	3. 405	Marquis of Exeter
Peter Denying Christ	3. 405	Marquis of Exeter
Abel Seated and Holding Flute	4. 272	Earl of Jersey
The Unbelieving Thomas	4. 323	Lord Enfield
Shepherd with Dog and Ass	4. 393	Lord Arundel
Christ and the Doctors	4. 410	Smith Barry
Body of St. Stephen Lamented	4. 471	Duke of Northumberland
Drinking Subject	4. 485	Lord Ravensworth
Gambling Subject	4. 485	„
Achilles and Daughters of Lycomedes	4. 485	„
Alexander and Aristotle	4. 485	„
The Crowning with Thorns	4. 497	Drury Lowe

CARENNO
Male Portrait in Black dress with Letter	4. 449	W. Stirling
Immaculate Conception	4. 481	Matthew Anderson

CARRACCI, School of
Virgin and Child and 6 Saints (by Ludovico Carracci)	2. 77	S. Rogers

CARRACCI, Agostino
Triumph of Galatea	1. 336	National Gallery
Cephalus and Aurora	1. 336	„
Susanna and the Elders	1. 336	„
Martyrdom of St. Bartholomew	2. 64	Duke of Sutherland
Apostles round Tomb of Virgin	2. 179	T. Baring
Christ Appearing to Magdalen	2. 489	Orleans Gallery
Martyrdom of St. Bartholomew	2. 489	Orleans Gallery
Baptism of Christ, Landscape	3. 169	Earl of Suffolk
Bacchus and Ariadne after Titian	3. 200	Lord Northwick
Virgin and Child Presenting Cross to St. John	3. 325	Earl of Carlisle

	VOL. & PAGE		OWNER
CARRACCI, Agostino—*continued*			
Christ and Angel Appearing to Virgin	3.	447	Fitzwilliam Museum
Christ Raising Widow's Son	4.	101	R. S. Holford
Tancred Baptising Chloinda	4.	470	Duke of Northumberland
Pan Bound by Cupid	4.	492	Lord Feversham
CARRACCI, Annibale			
Temptation of St. Anthony	1.	317	National Gallery
St. John the Baptist	1.	335	,,
St. Peter Flying from Rome	1.	335	,,
Pan and Apollo	1.	335	,,
Two Satyrs and Silenus	1.	335	,,
Landscape, Hunting Party	1.	336	,,
Landscape, with Water Party	1.	336	,,
Triumph of Bacchus (copy)	1.	394	Duke of Northumberland
St. Gregory at Prayer, etc.	2.	34	Bridgewater House
St. Francis Adoring Infant Christ	2.	34	,,
Danaë Receiving Golden Shower	2.	34	,,
St. John Pointing to Christ	2.	35	,,
St. John Baptist as a Child	2.	35	,,
Collection of Drawings	2.	54	,,
Repose in Egypt	2.	64	Duke of Sutherland
St. Stephen and Angels	2.	64	Duke of Sutherland
A Pietà	2.	87	Earl of Yarborough
Infant Christ Asleep and Angels	2.	101	Lord Ashburton
Venus Adorned by Graces	2.	135	H. A. J. Munro
A Repose in Egypt	2.	135	H. A. J. Munro
Christ and Woman of Samaria	2.	179	T. Baring
Christ and Woman of Samaria (smaller)	2.	179	,,
Christ on Cross, and St. Francis	2.	179	,,
St. John the Evangelist Kneeling	2.	198	R. S. Holford
Susanna and the Elders	2.	198	R. S. Holford
Christ Walking on Sea	2.	293	Wynn Ellis
Landscape	2.	293	Wynn Ellis
Virgin and Child	2.	468	Charles I
St. Bartholomew	2.	468	Charles I
St. John Pointing to Christ	2.	487	Orleans Gallery
Child Jesus Appearing to St. Francis	2.	488	,,
John the Baptist Asleep	2.	488	,,
Christ on the Cross	2.	488	,,
Danaë Receiving Golden Shower	2.	488	,,
St. Jerome, after Correggio	2.	488	,,
Diana and Calisto	2.	488	,,
Landscape called " Les Bateliers "	2.	488	,,
Dead Christ and Three Maries	2.	488	,,

	VOL. & PAGE		OWNER
Landscape "La Chasse au Vol"	2.	488	Orleans Gallery
Portrait of Himself	2.	488	,,
Repose in Egypt	2.	488	,,
St. Stephen and Angels	2.	488	,,
St. John in the Wilderness	2.	488	,,
The Toilette of Venus	2.	488	,,
Martyrdom of St. Stephen	2.	488	,,
St. Roque and Angel	2.	488	,,
Christ and Woman of Samaria	2.	488	,,
Landscape "Procession of Host"	2.	488	,,
Descent from the Cross	2.	488	,,
Holy Family, called "Le Raboteur"	2.	488	,,
St. John Evangelist and Angels	2.	488	,,
St. Roque Worshipping Virgin	2.	488	,,
A Portrait	2.	488	,,
The Toilet of Venus	3.	21	Earl of Darnley
Family of Butchers	3.	47	Ch. Ch., Oxford
Virgin and Child and Saint	3.	127	Duke of Marlborough
A Landscape, 15 × 21	3.	160	Marquis of Lansdowne
Landscape, Flight into Egypt	3.	169	Earl of Suffolk
A Male Portrait	3.	170	Earl of Suffolk
A Holy Family	3.	172	Colt Hoare
St. John in the Wilderness	3.	179	J. P. Miles
Diana and Actæon	3.	180	,,
St. Francis in Ecstacy, etc.	3.	184	,,
Two Franciscans	3.	186	,,
A Riposo	3.	190	Mr. Harford
Polyphemus and Galatea	3.	200	Lord Northwick
St. John in the Desert	3.	200	,,
A Riposo	3.	200	,,
A Pietà. Angels by Torchlight	3.	216	Earl of Warwick
The Crucifixion (copy)	3.	239	Liverpool R.I.
Virgin and Child, St. John and Joseph	3.	292	Sir A. Campbell
Virgin and Child, St. Peter, Paul, etc.	3.	292	Sir A. Campbell
The Penitent Magdalen	3.	302	Duke of Hamilton
Mountainous Country	3.	319	Earl of Carlisle
Boat and large Figures	3.	319	,,
Dead Christ and three Maries	3.	324	,,
His Own Portrait	3.	324	,,
A Boy and Girl with Cat	3.	325	,,
Dead Christ and Disciples	3.	332	Meynell Ingram
Christ Crowned with Thorns	3.	341	Earl Fitzwilliam
Orlando Delivering Olympia	3.	393	Lord Scarsdale
Mary Magdalen in the Desert	3.	393	Lord Scarsdale
Polyphemus and Galatea	3.	421	Earl of Leicester

	VOL. & PAGE		OWNER
CARRACCI, Annibale—*continued*			
Christ and Magdalen in Garden	3.	440	Mr. Tomline
Large Scriptural Subject	3.	465	Duke of Bedford
St. John the Baptist Seated	4.	65	Earl of Yarborough
Christ Mourned by 6 Figures	4.	66	Earl of Yarborough
Dead Christ Lamented by Magdalen	4.	144	Lord Overstone
Venus Sleeping, with Cupids	4.	261	Duc D'Aumale
Landscape, Boat and 3 Figures, etc.	4.	319	Lord Enfield
Virgin and Child with Apple	4.	329	Sir T. Sebright
Christ Appearing to Magdalen	4.	333	Duke of Bedford
Four Pictures, the Elements	4.	380	Kingston Lacy
Silenus on the Ass	4.	411	Smith Barry
St. Francis Contemplating Crucifix	4.	444	Lord Elgin
A Pietà	4.	448	Lord Kinnaird
A Pietà, with Virgin, St. John and Magdalen	4.	456	Earl of Dunmore
Susannah and the Elders	4.	470	Duke of Northumberland
Giulio Cesare Scaligero	4.	470	,,
John the Baptist Kneeling	4.	470	,,
Pilate Washing his Hands	4.	496	Earl of Harrington
St. John the Baptist Pointing to Christ	4.	514	Duke of Portland
Portrait of a Monk	4.	520	Earl of Hardwicke
CARRACCI, Antonio			
Virgin and Child	2.	151	Marquis of Lansdowne
CARRACCI, Ludovico			
Descent from the Cross	2.	34	Bridgewater House
Virgin and Child and St. Catherine	2.	34	,,
A Pietà	2.	34	,,
Virgin and Child	2.	64	Duke of Sutherland
The Crucifixion	2.	91	Devonshire House
Christ on Mount of Olives	2.	150	Marquis of Lansdowne
A Holy Family	2.	150	Marquis of Lansdowne
A Holy Family	2.	170	Marquis of Westminster
The Entombment	2.	179	T. Baring
Adoration of the Shepherds	2.	179	T. Baring
Virgin Borne to Heaven	2.	198	R. S. Holford
Venus and Cupid	2.	224	Richard Ford
Christ Derided	2.	236	Lord Ward
A Magdalen	2.	244	Mr. Neeld
A Magdalen	2.	313	Earl of Listowel
A Holy Family	2.	330	C. S. Bale
Marriage of St. Catherine	2.	489	Orleans Gallery
Descent from the Cross	2.	489	,,

	VOL. & PAGE	OWNER
Virgin and Child and St. Catherine	2. 489	Orleans Gallery
The Entombment	2. 489	,,
Christ with Crown of Thorns	2. 489	,,
Ecce Homo	2. 489	,,
Susanna and Elders	2. 489	,,
Virgin and Child, and 4 Saints	3. 158	Marquis of Lansdowne
A Holy Family	3. 186	J. P. Miles
Copy of Correggio's St. Jerome	3. 189	Mr. Harford
Death of Abel	3. 270	Edinburgh R.I.
The Cumæan Sibyl	3. 300	Duke of Hamilton
The Entombment	3. 319	Earl of Carlisle
The Crucifixion	3. 348	Duke of Devonshire
The Virgin and Child	3. 430	A. Fountaine
Our Saviour Healing Blind Man	4. 101	R. S. Holford
The Holy Family	4. 356	Lord Folkestone
The Holy Family	4. 360	,,
A Charity	4. 362	,,
The Annunciation	4. 398	Lord Methuen
St. Francis Praying before Crucifix	4. 409	Smith Barry
St. Francis in Ecstasy	4. 446	Lord Kinnaird
The Repentant Magdalen	4. 447	Lord Kinnaird
The Visitation	4. 455	Earl of Dunmore
Herminia and the Shepherds	4. 469	Duke of Northumberland
St. Francis Receiving the Stigmata	4. 470	Duke of Northumberland
The Assumption of the Virgin	4. 498	W. Drury Lowe

CASTIGLIONE, Benedetto

Cattle	3. 131	Duke of Marlborough
A Grey Horse and Shepherd and Flock	3. 240	Liverpool R.I.
A Caravan	3. 385	Earl of Shrewsbury
Virgin and Child	3. 405	Marquis of Exeter
Passage of Israelites, Red Sea	3. 405	Marquis of Exeter
Abraham Journeying to Canaan	3. 447	Fitzwilliam Museum
Departure of Israelites	4. 333	Duke of Bedford
A Caravan, Leopards, etc.	4. 506	Earl of Yarborough
The Finding of Cyrus	4. 511	Duke of Newcastle

CATENA, Vincenzo

Venus and Cupid in Landscape	3. 202	Lord Northwick
Virgin and Child Blessing Donor	3. 238	Liverpool R.I.
Christ at Emmaus	4. 497	W. Drury Lowe

CATTERMOLE, George

The Quarrel	Drawing	4. 203	Mr. Henderson
The Warning	,,	4. 203	,,

F

		VOL. & PAGE		OWNER
CATTERMOLE, George—*continued*				
Conspirators of Holyrood	Drawing	4.	203	Mr. Henderson
Venice	„	4.	203	„
Christ Preaching	„	4.	203	„
The Betrayer Betrayed	„	4.	203	„
Festival of the Monastery	„	4.	204	„
The Knotty Point	„	4.	204	„
Pilgrims at the Gate	„	4.	204	„
The Baron's Chapel	„	4.	204	„
Columbus at the Convent	„	4.	204	„
The Refectory	„	4.	205	„
Reading the Fathers	„	4.	205	„
The Cardinal's Study	„	4.	205	„
Rocky Fortress	„	4.	205	„
A Piece of Still Water	„	4.	205	„
The Baron's Chapel	„	4.	205	„
Pilgrims at Vespers	„	4.	205	„
A Prior Instructing Monks	„	4.	205	„
Falls of the Tummel	„	4.	206	„
Moonlight March	„	4.	206	„
Lady Macbeth and Daggers	„	4.	414	Mr. Cooke
Horse Being Watered	„	4.	415	Mr. Cooke
Two Drawings		4.	415	Samuel Ashton
CENNINO, di Drea Cennini				
Virgin and Child Enthroned		4.	299	Higford Burr
CENNO, di Ser Cenni				
Adoration of True Cross, etc.		4.	299	Higford Burr
CEREZO, Mateo				
Virgin and Child and St. Joseph		4.	173	Edward Cheney
CERQUOZZI (called Michael Angelo delle Battaglie)				
A Masquerade		2.	489	Orleans Gallery
CESARI, Giuseppe				
Susanna and the Elders		2.	489	Orleans Gallery
CHAMPAGNE, Philippe de				
A Male Portrait		2.	66	Duke of Sutherland
The Stoning of Stephen		3.	300	Duke of Hamilton
Robert Arnaud d'Andilly		3.	459	Earl Spencer
Adoration of Shepherds		4.	87	Marquis of Hertford
Cardinal Mazarin		4.	263	Duc D'Aumale

	VOL. & PAGE	OWNER
La Mère Catherine Arnauld	4. 263	Duc D'Aumale
Portrait of Colbert	4. 335	Duke of Bedford
The Annunciation	4. 461	M'Lellan Gallery

CHANTREY, Sir Francis, R.A.

Statue of Canning	3. 230	Liverpool Town Hall
Bust of Canning	4. 428	Rev. Mr. Staniforth
Bust of Playfair	4. 434	Mr. Playfair
Bust of Canning	3. 352	Duke of Devonshire

CIGNANI, Carlo

A Picture	2. 39	Bridgewater House
St. Anthony and Infant Christ	2. 65	Duke of Sutherland
Christ Appearing to Magdalen	2. 489	Orleans Gallery
Joseph and Potiphar's Wife	3. 351	Duke of Devonshire
A Charity	4. 390	Lord Heytesbury
Madonna and Child	4. 395	Lord Methuen
Prometheus and Eagle	4. 520	Earl of Hardwicke

CIGOLI, Il (Lodovico Cardi)

John the Baptist, Young	2. 310	Mr. Wombwell
The Annunciation	3. 157	Marquis of Lansdowne
Adoration of the Kings	3. 172	Colt Hoare
St. Francis	4. 423	Earl of Burlington

CIVERCHIO, Vincenzio

Virgin and Child and 4 Saints	3. 200	Lord Northwick

CIVETTA (Herri de Bles)

A Pietà	2. 237	Lord Ward
Adoration of the Shepherds	2. 237	Lord Ward
Adam and Eve	2. 239	Marquis of Breadalbane
Christ on the Mount of Olives	3. 235	Liverpool R.I.

CLAUDE, Lorraine

Landscape, Lighthouse, and Fisherman, 1644	1. 339	National Gallery
St. Ursula and the Virgin	1. 339	,,
Embarkation of Queen of Sheba	1. 340	,,
Sinon Before Priam	1. 340	,,
Narcissus in Solitude	1. 340	,,
Hagar and Ishmael	1. 341	,,
Goatherd with his Flock	1. 341	,,
Death of Procris	1. 341	,,
Marriage of Isaac and Rebecca	1. 341	,,
Cephalus and Procris	1. 341	,,

		VOL. & PAGE		OWNER
CLAUDE, Lorraine—*continued*				
Sea coast, Europa and Bull		2.	23	Buckingham Palace
Morning No. 101 Liber		2.	37	Bridgewater House
Landscape, Girls Dancing „ 142 „		2.	37	„
Moses and Burning Bush „ 161 „		2.	37	„
Landscape, Demosthenes		2.	38	„
Landscape, a Trumpet Blower		2.	63	Duke of Sutherland
Shepherd playing Pipe		2.	78	S. Rogers
Landscape		2.	85	Earl De Grey
Landscape		2.	85	Earl De Grey
Landscape, Two Bridges		2.	87	Earl of Yarborough
Flight into Egypt (*copy*)		2.	114	H. T. Hope
Landscape, Rural Repast		2.	132	H. A. J. Munro
Landscape, Philip baptizing Eunuch		2.	133	H. A. J. Munro
Landscape		2.	155	Marquis of Hertford
Morning Landscape, 1651		2.	171	Marquis of Westminster
Evening Landscape		2.	171	„
Evening Landscape, small		2.	171	„
Morning Landscape, 1661		2.	171	„
Sermon on the Mount		2.	171	„
Adoration of Golden Calf		2.	171	„
Two Shepherds Dancing		2.	171	„
Bridge, Shepherd, and Shepherdess		2.	177	T. Baring
Laban Jacob, Rachael and Leah		2.	177	„
Sea coast, Sunshine		2.	177	„
Landscape, Shepherd Piping		2.	177	„
Setting Sun, Shepherd Piping		2.	177	„
Æneas Shooting Stag		2.	177	„
Landscape, Morning Light		2.	195	R. S. Holford
Landscape, Evening Light		2.	195	„
Several Drawings		2.	205	„
A Wood with Towers of a Castle		2.	224	Richard Ford
Small Landscape with Riposo		2.	243	H. Danby Seymour
Israelites and Golden Calf		2.	260	James Morrison
Europa		2.	261	James Morrison
Small Sea piece		2.	277	Duke of Wellington
Shepherd and Two Girls		2.	279	Earl of Carlisle
Large Landscape		2.	286	Duke of Bedford
Landscape, Roman Forum		2.	293	Wynn Ellis
A Seaport		2.	293	„
Mount Helicon, Swans		2.	294	„
Ferryboat, Man Milking Goat		2.	294	„
Goatherd and Flock		2.	294	„
Landscape, Morning		2.	330	C. S. Bale

	VOL. & PAGE		OWNER
Avenue of Trees	2.	330	C. S. Bale
A Seaport	2.	365	Hampton Court
Landscape, Man Conversing, Goats	2	420	Henry Labouchere
View of Spezzia	2.	420	Henry Labouchere
A Dark Ford	2.	430	Windsor Castle
A Seaport with Trees	2.	430	,,
A Harbour	2.	434	,,
Large Landscape	2.	434	,,
Large Landscape	2.	434	,,
A Seaport	2.	492	Orleans Gallery
The Enchanted Castle	3.	27	Lord Overstone
Picture engraved by Woollett	3.	33	Petworth
Buildings on Seashore	3.	35	Petworth
Landing of Æneas	3.	140	Earl of Radnor
Sunset, Fall of Roman Empire	3.	140	Earl of Radnor
Seaport in Morning Light	3.	161	Marquis of Lansdowne
Small Landscape	3.	170	Earl of Suffolk
Small Landscape, Evening	3.	170	Earl of Suffolk
Lake Nemi, engraved by Vivares	3.	172	Colt Hoare
Fishermen Drawing Net	3.	180	J. P. Miles
Temple of Apollo, Sacrificing an Ox	3.	180	,,
Æneas Landing in Italy, 1675	3.	181	,,
Temple, Morning Light	3.	183	,,
A Harbour	3.	185	,,
Landscape and Bridge with a Riposo	3.	198	Lord Northwick
Sunset on the Sea	3.	198	,,
Shepherd and 3 Cows	3.	198	,,
Shepherd Playing a Flute	3.	198	,,
A Seaport	3.	198	,,
Apollo and Female	3.	198	,,
A Landscape	3.	288	M'Lellan Gallery
Shepherd and Two Shepherdesses	3.	288	M'Lellan Gallery
A Seaport	3.	292	Sir A. Campbell
Landing of the Queen of Sheba	3.	310	Earl of Hopetown
A Landscape	3.	313	Duke of Buccleuch
Landscape, Sunny Lighting	3.	313	Duke of Buccleuch
A Picture	3.	314	Earl of Wemyss
A Picture	3.	315	Duke of Cleveland
Ruins of Temple, Shepherd	3.	334	Meynell Ingram
Landscape, Red Sky	3.	339	Earl Fitzwilliam
Seaport, Mercury and Argus	3.	347	Duke of Devonshire
Tobit and the Angel	3.	385	Earl of Shrewsbury
Tower on the Tiber	3.	393	Lord Scarsdale
Small Landscape, Red Sun	3.	396	Duke of Rutland
Flight into Egypt	3.	396	,,

CLAUDE, Lorraine—*continued*	VOL. & PAGE		OWNER
Water with a Boat	3.	397	Duke of Rutland
Herd of Cattle and Tree	3.	397	,,
Sunset at Sea, 2 Figures	3.	398	,,
Long narrow Landscape	3.	405	Marquis of Exeter
Long narrow Landscape	3.	405	Marquis of Exeter
Apollo and Marsyas	3.	419	Earl of Leicester
Landscape, Claude Drawing, 1675	3.	420	,,
Small Landscape	3.	421	,,
A Port, 1652, Man Drawing	3.	421	,,
Apollo and Admetus	3.	421	,,
Temple of Sibyl at Tivoli	3.	421	,,
Sun rising behind Cloud	3.	421	,,
Tall Tree and Bridge	3.	421	,,
Erminia and the Shepherds	3.	421	,,
A Riposo, a long narrow Landscape	3.	422	,,
Castle of St. Angelo	3.	465	Duke of Bedford
Sunset in beautiful Country	3.	484	Marquis of Bute
Seaport, Sun in Mist	3.	484	Marquis of Bute
Trees and Single Figure	4.	67	Earl of Yarborough
A large Landscape	4.	68	,,
A Ruin, Hagar and Ishmael	4.	69	,,
One of a Series of nine	4.	92	Marquis of Westminster
Europa and the Bull	4.	109	J. Morrison
Adoration of the Golden Calf	4.	111	J. Morrison
The Enchanted Castle	4.	140	Lord Overstone
Seaport with Vessels	4.	163	Abraham Robarts
Shepherds, and Goats, and Cows	4.	179	Rev. Mr. Townshend
Bridge and Water	4.	183	William Marshall
Morning, Bridge in Front	4.	270	Earl of Jersey
Evening, Trees, and Temple	4.	271	Earl of Jersey
Lake with Trees	4.	280	Sir C. Eardley
Castle of St. Angelo	4.	332	Duke of Bedford
Set of Landscapes	4.	344	Countess of Warwick
Landscape, cool reddish Sky	4.	350	Vernon Harcourt
Sunrise, Dawn of Roman Empire	4.	358	Lord Folkestone
Sunset, Decline of Roman Empire	4.	359	Lord Folkestone
Large Landscape	4.	363	General Buckley
Hill and Castle, Skiff on Water	4.	366	Earl of Normanton
Seaport, St. Ursula	4.	368	,,
Tree and Buildings	4.	369	,,
Piece of Water, Oval	4.	390	Lord Heytesbury
Piece of Water, Oval	4.	390	Lord Heytesbury
St. John in the Desert	4.	398	Lord Methuen
Repose in Egypt, upright	4.	421	Earl of Burlington

	VOL. & PAGE	OWNER
Mercury and Argus	4. 422	Earl of Burlington
Three Columns, Shepherd, blowing Bagpipe	4. 422	,,
Apollo and the Muses, No. 126 Liber	4. 423	,,
Cows driven through Water	4. 427	Rev. T. Staniforth
Philip and the Eunuch	4. 435	Duke of Buccleuch
Sea view, Sunshine	4. 436	Duke of Buccleuch
Sea view, Sunshine	4. 438	Earl of Wemyss
Christ and Disciples of Emmaus	4. 452	W. Stirling
Harbour by Sunset	4. 471	Duke of Northumberland
Trees, 3 Figures, and a Boy	4. 483	Matthew Anderson
Cattle near Water	4. 492	Lord Feversham
Herd of Cattle driven	4. 493	Lord Feversham
Sea coast at Sunrise	4. 505	Earl of Yarborough
Wooded Landscape with Water	4. 509	Duke of Newcastle
Three Cows and Trees	4. 510	Duke of Newcastle
Landscape, Shepherd, and Shepherdess	4. 514	Duke of Portland

CLOUET, Jean (see Janet)

Francis I	2. 236	Lord Ward
Leonora, Sister of Charles V	2. 363	Hampton Court
A young Girl	3. 204	Lord Northwick
Margaret de Valois	3. 236	Liverpool R.I.
Leonora, Sister of Charles V	4. 263	Duc D'Aumale

CLOVIO, Don Giulio

St. Anna and Virgin and Child	2. 63	Duke of Sutherland

COELLO, Alonso Sancheo

An Infant of Spain	4. 96	T. Baring

COIGNET, Leon

The Abduction, 1828	4. 86	Marquis of Hertford

COLA, de Amatricio

Virgin enthroned and Saints, 1522	4. 448	Lord Kinnaird

COLLINS, William, R.A.

Happy as a King	1. 379	Marlborough House
Prawn Fishers	1. 379	Marlborough House
Landscape, Cart before House	2. 189	T. Baring
Hilly Country, Group with Child	2. 189	,,
Two Fishing Lads, Tide coming in	2. 189	,,
Large Picture, Many Figures	2. 258	G. Young
Hallsands, Devonshire	2. 300	J. Sheepshanks
Sorrento, Bay of Naples	2. 302	J. Sheepshanks

	VOL. & PAGE		OWNER
COLLINS, William, R.A.—*continued*			
The Stray Kitten	2.	307	J. Sheepshanks
Fishermen on Seashore	2.	350	E. Bicknell
Two small Pictures	2.	461	Mr. Green
Sea coast with Grey Horse	3.	221	Howard Galton
Poor Children on Seashore	3.	242	John Naylor
Children playing by Palings	3.	352	Duke of Devonshire
A Sale of Fish	3.	466	Duke of Bedford
A Small Landscape	4.	176	Rev. C. H. Townshend
Three Children by some Water	4.	184	W. Marshall
Three Children afraid of Beggar	4.	184	,,
A Picture	4.	184	,,
A Picture	4.	184	,,
Fisherman's Farewell	4.	302	J. Morrison
Sale of Fish upon the Shore	4.	331	Duke of Bedford
Morning Landscape and Figures	4.	402	Edwin Bullock
View of a Seashore	4.	417	Samuel Ashton
CONEGLIANO, Cima da			
Virgin and Child, St. Peter and John	2.	265	Sir C. Eastlake
Virgin and Child, Angels and Saints	2.	314	Earl Brownlow
St. Catherine	3.	201	Lord Northwick
Virgin and Child	3.	201	Lord Northwick
Virgin and Child	3.	281	Mr. Dennistoun
Virgin and Child, Joseph, St. Catherine	3.	287	M'Lellan Gallery
St. Sebastian	4.	114	Sir C. Eastlake
St. Mark	4.	115	Sir C. Eastlake
Virgin and Child, 2 Female Saints	4.	460	M'Lellan Gallery
CONSTABLE, John, R.A.			
The Valley Farm	1.	385	Marlborough House
The Cornfield	1.	385	Marlborough House
Landscape, Large Trees	2.	257	George Young
Salisbury Cathedral	2.	301	J. Sheepshanks
Hampstead Heath	2.	302	,,
Boat building near Flatford	2.	303	,,
Richly Wooded Landscape	4.	302	J. Morrison
A Large Landscape	4.	403	Mr. Birch
Landscape	4.	403	Mr. Birch
A Picture	4.	403	Edwin Bullock
Landscape, Rainbow, Salisbury	4.	416	Samuel Ashton
COOKE, E. W., R.A.			
Dutch Boats in a Calm	1.	386	Marlborough House
View of a Harbour	2.	190	T. Baring

	VOL. & PAGE	OWNER
Lobster Pots	2. 303	J. Sheepshanks
Shanklin, Isle of Wight	2. 302	,,
Brighton Sands	2. 305	,,
Mont St. Michel	2. 305	,,
Mending the Bait Net	2. 307	,,
Mont St. Michel	3. 166	Marquis of Lansdowne
A Fresh Breeze	4. 416	Samuel Ashton

COOPER, Samuel

A Miniature	4. 512	Duke of Portland

COOPER, T. S., R.A.

Scene in Cumberland	1. 383	Marlborough House
Cattle with Farmer	1. 383	Marlborough House
Cows in Evening Light	3. 211	Lord Northwick
Cattle in the Highlands	3. 242	J. Naylor
Cow standing and two Sheep (*drawing*)	4. 415	Mr. Cooke
Flock of Sheep, twisted Horns, 1843	4. 416	Samuel Ashton
Three Cows	4. 417	Samuel Ashton
Cow grazing and two Sheep	4. 418	J. Chapman
Cattle at foot of Tree with Creswick	4. 419	J. Chapman

COPE, C. W., R.A.

The Black Prince receiving the Garter	1. 428	Palace of Westminster
Henry V and Gascoigne	1. 428	Palace of Westminster
A Cup of Cold Water	2. 142	H. A. J. Munro
Palpitation	2. 303	J. Sheepshanks
Il Pensieroso	2. 303	,,
Girl with fair Hair reading	2. 304	,,
Help thy Father in his age	2. 305	,,
L'Allegro	2. 305	,,
Girls going to Church with Grandmother	3. 165	Marquis of Lansdowne

COQUES, Gonzales

Family group in Garden	1. 404	Sir R. Peel
Mynheer Verhelst, etc.	2. 11	Buckingham Palace
Man in black Dress	2. 41	Bridgewater House
Three Gentlemen and Two Ladies at Table	2. 71	Duke of Sutherland
A rich Family piece	2. 125	H. T. Hope
An Architect and his Wife	2. 153	Marquis of Lansdowne
La Leçon de Musique	2. 158	Marquis of Hertford
Man at Piano, Wife and Child	2. 421	H. Labouchere
Dutch Family in a Room	3. 126	Duke of Marlborough
A Family with Guitar and Dog	3. 207	Lord Northwick

	VOL. & PAGE	OWNER
COQUES, Gonzales—*continued*		
Man, Woman and Girl, Youth with Guitar	3. 207	Lord Northwick
A Man and his Wife	3. 221	Howard Galton
Lady in blue playing Lute	4. 161	Abraham Robarts
Charles I and Henrietta Maria	4. 179	Rev. Mr. Townshend
Family group of six Persons	4. 295	J. Walter
A Family in open Air	4. 412	Smith Barry
CORREGGIO		
Vierge au Panier	1. 316 & 329	National Gallery
Ecce Homo	1. 316 & 326	„
Education of Cupid	1. 316 & 327	„
Christ on the Mount of Olives	1. 330	„
Vierge au Panier (*copy*)	2. 30	Bridgewater House
Packhorse and Ass, two Drivers	2. 62	Duke of Sutherland
St. Peter, Margaret, Magdalen, etc.	2. 99	Lord Ashburton
Several Heads (*copies*)	2. 178	T. Baring
Coronation of Virgin, Two Fragments	2. 233	Lord Ward
The Magdalen	2. 234	Lord Ward
Christ on the Mount of Olives	2. 275	Duke of Wellington
Virgin Kissing the Child	2. 278	Earl of Carlisle
St. John as a Boy in the Desert	2. 278	Earl of Carlisle
Man in Armour	2. 364	Hampton Court
John the Baptist with Cross	2. 468	Charles I
John the Baptist sitting with Cross	2. 468	„
Education of Cupid	2. 468	„
Sleeping Venus, Cupid and Satyr	2. 468	„
Punishment of Marsyas	2. 468	„
Triumph of Virtue over Vice	2. 468	„
Shepherds Dancing, and Vine	2. 469	„
Marriage of St. Catherine	2. 469	„
Mary Magdalen	2. 469	„
Virgin and Child and St. John	2. 482	„
Virgin and white Rabbit	2. 482	„
St. Catherine	2. 482	,
Lucretia stabbing Herself	2. 482	„
St. Cupid asleep	2. 483	„
St. Cecilia and two Brothers	2. 483	„
Virgin and Child	2. 489	Orleans Gallery
Packhorse and Ass	2. 489	„
Heads for Parma Cupola	2. 489	„
Heads for Parma Cupola	2. 490	„
Caesar Borgia	2. 490	„
A Portrait, " Le Roagian "	2. 490	„

	VOL. & PAGE	OWNER
Christ and Magdalen	2. 490	Orleans Gallery
Education of Cupid	2. 490	,,
A Holy Family	2. 490	,,
Danae	2. 490	,,
Virgin and Child and St. Joseph	3. 43	Petworth
St. Francis in Ecstasy	3. 184	J. P. Miles
St. John the Baptist	3. 184	J. P. Miles
Christ on the Mount of Olives	3. 189	Mr. Harford
Virgin contemplating the Child	3. 189	,,
St. George (copy)	3. 189	,,
Two Children in elegant Dress	3. 322	Earl of Carlisle
Holy Family, small	3. 395	Duke of Rutland
Magdalen (copy)	3. 483	Marquis of Bute
A Female Saint	4. 184	W. Marshall
An Allegory	4. 328	Sir T. Sebright
Ecce Homo	4. 345	Earl Cowper
Venus disarming Love	4. 359	Lord Folkestone
Virgin and Child and St. John	4. 365	Earl of Normanton
Vierge au Panier (copy)	4. 369	Earl of Normanton
Fall of Phaeton	4. 399	Lord Methuen
An Angel in the Cupola at Parma	4. 399	Lord Methuen
St. Catherine blessed by Christ	4. 503	Earl of Yarborough

CORTONA, Pietro da

A Picture	2. 39	Bridgewater House
Landscape with a Stream	2. 92	Devonshire House
Hagar in the Desert	2. 170	Duke of Westminster
The Flight of Jacob	2. 490	Orleans Gallery
Rape of the Sabines	3. 126	Duke of Marlborough
A Picture	3. 142	Earl of Radnor
Adoration of the Shepherds	3. 299	Duke of Hamilton
Christ and the Magdalen	3. 299	,,
Eleazar with Rachel	3. 299	,,
Joseph's Dream	4. 359	Lord Folkestone
Marriage of St. Catherine	4. 368	Earl of Normanton
The Virgin in Glory	4. 396	Lord Methuen

COSTA, Lorenzo

Adam and Eve	2. 279	Earl of Carlisle
Abraham and Isaac	2. 279	Earl of Carlisle
The Annunciation	4. 182	G. C. Legh

COTIGNOLA, Girolamo da

Altar Piece, The Almighty, etc.	3. 379	W. Davenport Bromley

	VOL. & PAGE		OWNER
COX, David			
Drawings	4.	403	Edwin Bullock
Drawings	4.	404	J. Gillott
COXCIE, Michael			
A Picture	2.	482	Charles I
CRAESBECKE, Joseph Van			
A Picture	2.	42	Bridgewater House
A Woman Making Pancakes	4.	208	Mr. Henderson
CRANACH, Lucas			
A Male Portrait, 1557	2.	260	W. A. Mackinnon
A Stag Hunt	2.	420	H. Labouchere
Portrait of Luther	2.	469	Charles I
Adam and Eve	2.	469	,,
Hans von Griffindorp	2.	469	,,
Cupid Stung, 1537	3.	210	Lord Northwick
Elector George of Saxony	3.	219	Lord Craven
A Female Portrait, 1534	3.	235	Liverpool R. I.
Judith with the head of Holofernes	3.	298	Duke of Hamilton
A Female Portrait	3.	388	Earl of Shrewsbury
Luther	3.	407	Marquis of Exeter
Suffer Little Children	4.	97	T. Baring
Elector of Saxony, Frederick the Wise	4.	97	,,
Elector of Saxony, John the Constant	4.	97	,,
The Entombment	4.	153	William Gladstone
CRAYER, Casper de			
Virgin and Child	2.	136	H. A. J. Munro
Six Females Dancing	3.	207	Lord Northwick
His Own Portrait	3.	448	Fitzwilliam Museum
An Assumption	4.	393	Lord Arundel
Don Ferdinando	4.	449	W. Stirling
CREDI, Lorenzo di			
Coronation of the Virgin	2.	76	S. Rogers
Virgin and Child	3.	53	Oxford University
Virgin and Child and St. John (*copy*)	3.	196	Lord Northwick
Virgin and Child	3.	196	,,
St. George	3.	196	,,
Virgin and Child Enthroned, etc.	4.	73	Alexander Barker
Virgin Kneeling and Adoring the Child	4.	73	,,
Virgin and Child Blessing St. John	4.	73	,,
Virgin and Joseph Kneeling before the Child	4.	73	,,
A Female Head	4.	117	C. S. Bale

	VOL. & PAGE	OWNER
Coronation of Virgin	4. 147	Lord Overstone
Virgin and Child and Angels	4. 399	Lord Methuen

CRESPI, Giuseppe
| Italian Peasant Girl | 2. 180 | T. Baring |

CRESWICK, Thomas, R.A.
The Way to Church	1. 387	Marlborough House
Canal with Trees and Village	2. 190	T. Baring
Landscape with lofty Trees	2. 258	George Young
A picture	2. 353	E. Bicknell
Landscape, 1847	3. 242	John Naylor
Girl crossing the Brook	4. 370	Earl of Normanton
Upright Landscape, Woman and Child	4. 415	Samuel Ashton
Landscape and Watermill	4. 419	J. Chapman
Cattle at foot of Tree, with Cooper	4. 419	J. Chapman

CRISTOPH
| St. Peter and St. Dorothea | 4. 228 | Prince Consort |

CRIVELLI, Carlo
A Pieta in the form of a Lunette	2. 127	Alexander Barker
The Magdalen	2. 127	,,
St. Catherine	2. 127	,,
St. Lucy	2. 127	,,
Virgin and Child, and six Saints	2. 234	Lord Ward
Virgin and Child, and Saints	2. 235	,,
A Pietà	2. 235	,,
The Annunciation, 1486	2. 419	H. Labouchere
Virgin and Child enthroned, etc.	4. 93	Marquis of Westminster
Virgin holding Child on Parapet	4. 95	T. Baring
The Ascension, with three sleeping Guards	4. 95	T. Baring

CROME, John
Landscape by Moonlight	2. 299	J. Sheepshank
Avenue of trees, Man and Dog	3. 438	Mr. Sherrington
Dark Wood, Countryman and Dog	3. 438	,,
Landscape and Cottage	3. 438	,,
Landscape and large Willow Trees	3. 438	,,
Five other pictures	3. 438	,,

CULMBACH, Hans Von
| A Young Man | 4. 227 | Prince Consort |

CUYP, Albert
| Landscape, Cows and Shepherdess | 1. 357 | National Gallery |

	VOL. & PAGE		OWNER
CUYP, Albert—*continued*			
Group of Cows	1.	408	Sir R. Peel
Horseman and Cattle	1.	408	,,
Old Castle with Tower	1.	408	,,
Horseman standing by grey Horse	2.	19	Buckingham Palace
Grey and a brown Horse, and Negro	2.	19	,,
Shepherd and Child in Landscape	2.	20	,,
Three Cows in a Meadow	2.	20	,,
Three Cows lying down	2.	20	,,
Gentleman and Lady riding	2.	20	,,
Two Cavalry Soldiers	2.	20	,,
Large Transport Ship	2.	20	,,
Ducks in the Water	2.	21	,,
View on the Maas, near Dort	2.	48	Bridgewater House
Woman Milking a Cow	2.	48	,,
Shepherd playing the Flute	2.	48	,,
Castle of Koningsvelt	2.	48	,,
Lady and Gentleman on Horseback	2.	48	,,
Frozen River and Skaters	2.	86	Earl of Yarborough
River, two Huntsmen on Horseback	2.	110	Lord Ashburton
Rocky Landscape, Herdsmen, etc.	2.	110	,,
Two Boys and three Cows	2.	110	,,
Man in black velvet Dress	2.	110	,,
Five Cows in a Meadow	2.	122	H. T. Hope
Ruin on Frozen River, grey Horse	2.	129	Baron Rothschild
Two Cows, with Buildings	2.	138	H. A. J. Munro
Cart laden with Sacks	2.	138	H. A. J. Munro
Horsemen	2.	160	Marquis of Hertford
Horsemen	2.	160	Marquis of Hertford
River, near the Walls of a Town	2.	167	Marquis of Westminster
River, group of Cows on Bank	2.	167	,,
Four Sheep and a Goat	2.	167	,,
Tents, Officer and two Horsemen	2.	186	T. Baring
River Maas with Vessels	2.	187	T. Baring
Dort, with Ships in the Scheldt	2.	202	R. S. Holford
A Watering Place	2.	228	Hon. E. Phipps
Large picture with Cattle	2.	237	Lord Ward
Several others	2.	237	Lord Ward
Eighteen Fishermen cutting holes in the Ice	2.	247	Joseph Neeld
Stable with Cows	2.	247	Joseph Neeld
Man on grey Horse, etc.	2.	255	F. Heusch
Shepherdess, Man on Ass, etc.	2.	261	J. Morrison
Town, two Horsemen and Shepherds	2.	279	Earl of Carlisle
A Sea piece, Vessel in foreground	2.	279	,,

	VOL. & PAGE	OWNER
Horsemen	2. 279	Earl of Carlisle
Horsemen	2. 279	,,
Cows and Horsemen	2. 279	,,
Herdsman and two Cows, grey Horse	2. 279	,,
A picture	2. 283	Sir A. Rothschild
Brown Horse in Stable	2. 285	Duke of Bedford
Horsemen with an Ox (*decorated*)	2. 285	,,
Horsemen with an Ox (*decorated*)	2. 285	,,
River, Boy asleep with Flocks	2. 285	,,
River Maas frozen, with Fishermen	2. 285	,,
Gentleman and two Sons	2. 289	R. Sanderson
Boy on Bank of the Maas, two Cows	2. 290	Charles Bredel
A Dutch Canal	2. 292	Charles Bredel
Dort, four Cows in foreground	2. 296	Wynn Ellis
Dort, numerous Ships	2. 316	Earl Brownlow
Fortress, Horseman, and Boys begging	2. 316	Earl Brownlow
Landscape	2. 336	Frederick Perkins
Group of Cows near a Canal	2. 344	Dulwich Gallery
Two Shepherds reposing	2. 344	,,
Canal and group of Cattle	2. 344	,,
Landscape with Animals	2. 344	,,
Man in red Mantle on grey Horse	2. 452	Richard Forster
Ruins of Castle, and Horseman	3. 28	Lord Ashburnham
Near Nimeguen, Shepherd Boy	3. 40	Petworth
Two Horsemen	3. 41	,,
Two Horses and two Men	3. 42	,,
Stream with Village Ferry	3. 42	,,
Cows grazing by Water	3. 43	,,
Sea piece	3. 159	Marquis of Lansdowne
Sea piece	3. 159	,,
On the Maas, Dort	3. 159	,,
Cow being milked	3. 163	,,
Male portrait, whole length	3. 208	Lord Northwick
Boy holding three Horses	3. 208	,,
Three Horsemen, one drinking	3. 208	,,
Gentleman pointing to Fleet	3. 208	,,
David and Abigail	3. 208	,,
Landscape, Three Horsemen	3. 208	,,
Moonlight Landscape, Cows	3. 208	,,
Two Horsemen, Grey and Brown Horse	3. 220	Howard Galton
Man with Horse and Dog	3. 221	Howard Galton
Landscape, Man watering Horse	3. 224	Mr. Martin
Landscape, Herdsman and Woman	3. 265	Earl of Lonsdale
A Landscape	3. 273	Edinburgh R.I.

CUYP, Albert—*continued*

	VOL. & PAGE		OWNER
Christ's Entry into Jerusalem	3.	286	M'Lellan Gallery
Grey Horse watered by Boy	3.	292	Sir A. Campbell
A kind of Riding School	3.	309	Earl of Hopetown
Six Cows in a Landscape	3.	310	Earl of Hopetown
A Picture	3.	314	Captain Stirling
Large Mountainous Landscape	3.	392	Lord Scarsdale
Four Cows reposing	3.	397	Duke of Rutland
Dort, Morning Light	3.	441	Mr. Tomline
Five Cows near some Water	3.	441	Mr. Tomline
A Cattle piece	3.	462	Glendon Hall
His own Portrait	3.	465	Duke of Bedford
Sleeping Boy and Sheep	3.	466	Duke of Bedford
River near Tower, Grey Horse	3.	479	Marquis of Bute
Three Cows lying, Horse standing	3.	480	„
Five Cows in Water	3.	480	„
Orpheus with Animals	3.	480	„
Frozen Stream, Ruin of Tower	4.	68	Earl of Yarborough
On the Maas by Dortrecht	4.	89	Marquis of Hertford
Cow and Shepherd, Flock of Sheep	4.	110	J. Morrison
Shepherdess in red Petticoat	4.	138	Lord Overstone
River Maas, Barge with Soldiers	4.	159	A. Robarts
Dort, Six Windmills	4.	159	„
Five Cows in the Maas	4.	163	„
Cows near the river Maas, Four standing	4.	163	„
Girl with Shepherd's Crook	4.	200	J. Tulloch
River Maas, three Cows, etc.	4.	209	Mr. Henderson
Landscape and Cattle, Evening	4.	210	„
Young Lady in black Dress	4.	213	„
Two Horsemen before a House	4.	235	Earl of Harrington
The Companion	4.	236	Earl of Harrington
On the Rhine, two Cows, etc.	4.	288	Edmund Foster
Landscape and two Horsemen	4.	318	Rev. Mr. Heath
On the Rhine with Nymwegen	4.	332	Duke of Bedford
His own Portrait	4.	336	„
Moonlight on piece of Water	4.	367	Earl of Normanton
Sportsman on his Knees, with Gun	4.	385	H. D. Seymour
Two Cows, one black	4.	404	J. Gillott
Philip baptizing the Eunuch	4.	441	Sir H. Campbell
Boy holding grey Horse	4.	455	Earl of Dunmore
Boy with Hat and Feathers	4.	455	Earl of Dunmore
Three Girls and several Sheep	4.	479	J. Anderson
Three Girls playing with Lamb	4.	480	Matthew Anderson
View on the Maas near Dort	4.	521	Earl of Hardwicke

	VOL. & PAGE	OWNER
DANBY, F., A.R.A.		
Destruction of Pharaoh's Host	2. 72	Duke of Sutherland
The Upas Tree	4. 177	Rev. Mr. Townshend
DAVID		
Napoleon, life size	3. 298	Duke of Hamilton
Belisarius, blind	3. 386	Earl of Shrewsbury
DE BLES, Henri (Civetta)		
Flight into Egypt	2. 461	Mr. Green
Virgin and Child enthroned	3. 140	Earl of Radnor
Mount Calvary	4. 230	Prince Consort
Adoration of the Kings	4. 230	,,
Deposition from the Cross	4. 230	,,
Virgin with Rose and Child	4. 316	Rev. Mr. Heath
DE BRAY, Jacob		
Anthony and Cleopatra	2. 356	Hampton Court
DE BRUYN, Bartholomew		
Two Saints in a Niche	2. 463	Rev. Mr. Russell
A Crucifixion	3. 314	Captain Stirling
Burgomaster of Cologne	3. 342	W. V. Wentworth
St. Jerome, altar-piece	3. 457	Earl Spencer
DE BYERS		
A Dutch Canal, 1758	4. 201	J. Tulloch
DECAMPS		
Arabian Horsemen, 1837	4. 85	Marquis of Hertford
DECKER, F.		
Landscape	1. 357	National Gallery
A Picture	2. 52	Bridgewater House
Landscape figures, by A. Van Ostade	2. 70	Duke of Sutherland
Landscape and Waterfall	2. 247	Joseph Neeld
Landscape with a Bridge	3. 223	Howard Galton
A Landscape	3. 265	Earl of Lonsdale
Old House surrounded by Trees	3. 337	Charles Wynn
Large Landscape, Watermill	4. 148	Earl of Caledon
Landscape, Buildings and Trees	4. 347	Vernon Harcourt

	VOL. & PAGE		OWNER
DE HEEM, Cornelius			
Grapes and Apricots	2.	52	Bridgewater House
DE HEEM, Jan David			
Flower piece	2.	228	Hon. E. Phipps
Flower piece	2.	228	Hon. E. Phipps
A Wreath of Fruit	2.	248	Joseph Neeld
Small Fruit piece	3.	221	Howard Galton
Small Fruit piece	3.	221	Howard Galton
Fruit piece	3.	388	Earl of Shrewsbury
A Breakfast Table with Fruits	3.	434	Earl of Orford
Fruit piece, Grapes, etc.	4.	148	Earl of Caledon
Fruit Tankard and Flowers, 1645	4.	357	Lord Folkestone
A Breakfast and large Bowl	4.	482	Matthew Anderson
A Flower piece	4.	482	Matthew Anderson
DE HEERE, Lucas			
Queen Elizabeth	2.	361	Hampton Court
Lord Darnley and Brother	2.	363	Hampton Court
Mary I	2.	421	H. Labouchere
A young Girl	4.	186	W. Russell
Mary Stuart	4.	357	Lord Folkestone
DE HEUSCH, Jacob			
Landscape, figures by Lingelbach	3.	222	Howard Galton
Landscape	3.	388	Earl of Shrewsbury
Landscape	3.	388	Earl of Shrewsbury
Landscape with Rocks	4.	363	General Buckley
Landscape, figures by Poelemberg	4.	365	Earl of Normanton
Landscape, figures by Poelemberg	4.	365	Earl of Normanton
Landscape	4.	425	Earl of Burlington
Rocky Landscape, with Poelemberg	4.	481	Matthew Anderson
DE HOOGE, Peter			
Woman and Child in Vineyard, 1658	1.	403	Sir R. Peel
Two Gentlemen and a Lady at Table	1.	403	Sir R. Peel
Three Gentlemen and Lady at Cards, 1658	2.	10	Buckingham Palace
A Woman Spinning at a Door	2.	11	,,
A Lady at the Harpsicord	2.	11	,,
A Mother making a Bed, etc.	2.	71	Duke of Sutherland
Woman with a Dish of roasted Apples	2.	105	Lord Ashburton
Two Gentlemen and two Ladies pouring out wine	2.	119	H. T. Hope

	VOL. & PAGE	OWNER
Two Men at Table, Woman drinking	2. 130	Baron L. Rothschild
Woman nursing Child	2. 227	Hon. E. Phipps
A Concert	2. 227	Hon. E. Phipps
Man and Woman looking at Dog	3. 222	Howard Galton
Man disputing with Landlady, 1658	3. 477	Marquis of Bute
A Woman peeling Apples	4. 87	Marquis of Hertford
A Man sitting at a Meal	4. 99	T. Baring
Back Court of House, Man and Pipe	4. 130	Lord Overstone
Dutch Garden and Flowers, Ninepins	4. 294	Mr. Walter
Courtyard of Wine House, etc.	4. 323	Lord Enfield
Woman holding Bread, Child praying	4. 342	Humphrey Mildmay

DE KEYSER, Nicaise

Old Man engaged in Study	4. 178	Rev. Mr. Townshend

DE KONINGH, Philip

Landscape	1. 411	Sir R. Peel
Landscape, distant	2. 166	Marquis of Westminster
Landscape, distant	2. 187	T. Baring
A Landscape	3. 283	Glasgow College
Thickly wooded Country, with A. Vandevelde	3. 388	Earl of Shrewsbury
Landscape, distant	3. 436	Earl of Orford
Landscape, distant	4. 92	Marquis of Westminster
Sandhill, Figures and Cattle	4. 211	Mr. Henderson
Distant view over flat Country	4. 482	Matthew Anderson

DE LAAR, Pieter (Bamboccio)

Stately Roman Ruins	4. 268	Duke of Northumberland

DE LA HAYE (Robert Tournière)

Lady and Gentleman playing Cards	3. 485	Marquis of Bute

DE LA HIRE, Laurent

Belisarius and Woman	4. 282	Sir C. Eardley

DELAROCHE, Paul

Charles I in Guard Room	2. 54	Bridgewater House
Lord Strafford and Laud	2. 66	Duke of Sutherland
Artist's Wife kissing Child	2. 192	T. Baring
Woman with Child asleep	4. 85	Marquis of Hertford

	VOL. & PAGE	OWNER
DELORME		
Interior of a Church	3. 209	Lord Northwick
Interior of a Church—Candlelight	3. 212	Earl of Warwick
Architectural piece	4. 511	Duke of Newcastle
DE LOUTHERBOURG, P., R.A.		
Storm and Avalanche in Alps	3. 38	Petworth
DENNER, Balthasar		
Man in furred Cap	2. 310	Mr. Wombwell
Youth	2. 364	Hampton Court
Age	2. 364	Hampton Court
A Man and his Wife	3. 388	Earl of Shrewsbury
An old Man	4. 170	Lord Wensleydale
An old Woman	4. 170	Lord Wensleydale
Portrait of Handel	4. 341	Knole
An old Woman, 1726	4. 391	Joseph Everett
DENNING, S. P.		
Six of Mr. Bicknell's Children	2. 352	E. Bicknell
DE PAPE, A.		
A Woman peeling Apples	3. 477	Marquis of Bute
DE RING, Pieter		
A piece of Still Life	3. 388	Earl of Shrewsbury
DESIDERIO		
An Architectural piece	2. 270	Miss Rogers
DE VLIEGER, Simon		
Coast of Scheveningen	2. 50	Bridgewater House
A Sea Coast	2. 228	Hon. E. Phipps
A Sea piece	2. 238	Lord Ward
A large Picture	2. 312	Earl of Listowel
A large Picture	2. 312	Earl of Listowel
A Thunderstorm at Sea	3. 40	Petworth
An agitated Sea	3. 225	Mr. Martin
A Storm at Sea	3. 226	Mr. Martin
A Sea piece	3. 293	Sir A. Campbell
Sea, near a Port	3. 449	Fitzwilliam Museum
A calm Sea	3. 449	Fitzwilliam Museum

	VOL. & PAGE		OWNER
View on River Maas	4.	165	A. Robarts
Rough Sea with Vessels	4.	202	J. Tulloch
An agitated Sea	4.	458	M'Lellan Gallery
A Storm at Sea	4.	459	M'Lellan Gallery

DE VOS, Cornelius

Portrait of a Lady	3.	297	Duke of Hamilton
A Female Portrait	3.	299	Duke of Hamilton
A Man in white Collar	3.	448	Fitzwilliam Museum

DE VOYS, Ary

A Boy with a Book	2.	44	Bridgewater House
A Man with a Pipe	2.	279	Earl of Carlisle
A Youth by a Windowsill	4.	318	Rev. Mr. Heath
Young Man looking upwards	4.	481	Matthew Anderson

DE VRIES

Landscape with a Village	3.	223	Howard Galton
A Landscape	3.	428	Sir J. Boileau
A Landscape	4.	458	M'Lellan Gallery

DE WINT, Peter

Harvest time, Drawing	2.	352	E. Bicknell

DE WITT, Emanuel

Interior of Dutch Church	2.	52	Bridgewater House
Interior of Gothic Church	2.	140	H. A. J. Munro
Architectural Subject	2.	188	T. Baring
Architectural Subject	2.	188	T. Baring
Interior of a Church	2.	228	Hon. E. Phipps
The Exchange at Antwerp	2.	248	Mr. Neeld
Interior of a Church	3.	388	Earl of Shrewsbury
Interior of a Church	4.	482	Matthew Anderson

DIETRICH

Wandering Musician	1.	358	National Gallery
Healing the lame Man	2.	310	Mr. Wombwell
A Picture	4.	68	Earl of Yarborough
A Picture	4.	68	Earl of Yarborough

DOBSON, William

Sir B. Gerbier, Sir C. Cotterell, etc.	1.	394	Duke of Northumberland
The Poet Cleveland	2.	53	Bridgewater House
A Family Picture	2.	95	Devonshire House

	VOL. & PAGE		OWNER
DOBSON, William—*continued*			
Himself and his Wife	2.	410	Hampton Court
A Portrait	3.	142	Earl of Radnor
Beheading of St. John	3.	154	Earl of Pembroke
A portrait in Armour	3.	214	Earl of Warwick
Charles II	3.	219	Earl of Craven
Portrait of Milton	3.	221	Howard Galton
Duke of Buccleuch	3.	313	Duke of Buccleuch
Duchess of Buccleuch	3.	313	Duke of Buccleuch
A Male Portrait	3.	431	A. Fountaine
An Officer with a Pistol	4.	149	Earl of Caledon
Earl of Albemarle and Page	4.	338	Knole
His own Portrait, hand on skull	4.	341	Knole
A Male Portrait	4.	344	Countess of Warwick
DOLCE, Carlo			
Head of Christ and Flowers	2.	92	Devonshire House
Virgin and Child	2.	151	Marquis of Lansdowne
Daughter of Herodias and Head	2.	171	Marquis of Westminster
Virgin praying, in Blue	2.	176	T. Baring
Virgin praying, in Blue	2.	232	Lord Ward
Virgin praying, in Blue	2.	310	Mr. Wombwell
St. Veronica	2.	347	Dulwich Gallery
Mater Dolorosa	2.	347	Dulwich Gallery
Magdalen	2.	434	Windsor Castle
Daughter of Herodias	2.	434	Windsor Castle
The Nativity	3.	15	Earl Cowper
Christ taking Cross from Joseph	3.	16	,,
Dolce's Wife	3.	16	,,
Virgin and Child and Saints	3.	20	Earl of Darnley
Adoration of the Kings	3.	122	Duke of Marlborough
Virgin with Crown of Stars	3.	124	Duke of Marlborough
His own Portrait	3.	140	Earl of Radnor
Daughter of Herodias and Head	3.	172	Colt Hoare
Virgin, Blue over Head	3.	184	J. P. Miles
Christ and Woman of Samaria	3.	190	Mr. Harford
Ecce Homo	3.	193	,,
Virgin and Profile	3.	193	,,
St. John the Evangelist	3.	197	Lord Northwick
Head of Female Saint	3.	393	Lord Scarsdale
St. Francis	3.	396	Duke of Rutland
Virgin and Child	3.	398	Duke of Rutland
Christ blessing Bread	3.	405	Marquis of Exeter
The Nativity	3.	405	Marquis of Exeter
Magdalen with Death's Head	3.	441	Mr. Tomline

	VOL. & PAGE		OWNER
Marriage of St. Catherine	3.	456	Earl Spencer
Head of Magdalen	3.	462	Glendon Hall
Virgin with a Torch	4.	140	Lord Overstone
Virgin holding standing Child	4.	181	Rev. Mr. Townshend
St. Anthony adoring Child	4.	240	R. P. Nichols
His own Portrait	4.	357	Lord Folkestone
Christ crowned with Thorns	4.	359	Lord Folkestone
Madonna in profile	4.	387	Lord Heytesbury
Christ blessing the Elements	4.	395	Lord Methuen
Magdalen washing Feet of Christ	4.	395	,,
Guardian Angel and Boy	4.	396	,,
Male Saint with Palm Branch	4.	427	Rev. Mr. Staniforth
A Christ	4.	491	Archdeacon of Durham
Martyrdom of St. Andrew	4.	493	Lord Feversham
Aged St. Mary Egyptiaca	4.	503	Earl of Yarborough
St. Cecilia	4.	513	Duke of Portland

DOMENICHINO

	VOL. & PAGE		OWNER
Erminia and the Shepherds	1.	336	National Gallery
Landscape, Tobit and Angel	1.	337	,,
St. George and the Dragon	1.	337	,,
Martyrdom of St. Stephen	1.	337	,,
Christ bearing his Cross	2.	35	Bridgewater House
Ecstasy of St. Francis	2.	35	,,
Head of Female Saint	2.	35	,,
Landscape, Story of Calisto	2.	35	,,
Landscape, 2 Lovers watched	2.	35	,,
Landscape, Fisherman and Women Washing	2.	36	,,
St. Catherine	2.	64	Duke of Sutherland
Landscape, Tobit	2.	78	S. Rogers
Landscape, Marsyas	2.	78	,,
Birdcatchers in Landscape	2.	78	,,
A Picture	2.	78	,,
Susannah and the Elders	2.	91	Devonshire House
Youthful Female Figure	2.	91	Devonshire House
Moses and burning Bush	2.	101	Lord Ashburton
The Repentant Magdalen	2.	130	Baron L. Rothschild
Landscape, Tobit and Angel	2.	135	H. A. J. Munro
St. Cecilia with a Violin	2.	152	Marquis of Lansdowne
The Sibyl	2.	155	Marquis of Hertford
Landscape, David and Abigail	2.	170	Marquis of Westminster
Infant Christ with a Nail	2.	179	T. Baring
Three Angels, Musical Instruments	2.	236	Lord Ward

DOMENICHINO—*continued*	VOL. & PAGE		OWNER
Horseman with Owl on Staff	2.	267	Miss Rogers
Landscape, Judgment of Paris	2.	270	Miss Rogers
Landscape with pyramids, etc.	2.	293	Wynn Ellis
Landscape, Finding of Moses	2.	420	Hon. H. Labouchere
St. Catherine	2.	433	Windsor Castle
St. Agnes, full length	2.	434	Windsor Castle
Christ bearing his Cross	2.	490	Orleans Gallery
Landscape, 2 Lovers	2.	490	,,
Vision of St. Francis	2.	490	,,
St. John the Evangelist	2.	490	,,
St. Jerome	2.	490	,,
Landscape with Sea Coast	2.	490	,,
A Sibyl	2.	490	,,
Landscape, Abraham and Isaac	2.	490	,,
A Cupid	3.	15	Earl Cowper
Landscape with still Water	3.	158	Marquis of Lansdowne
Landscape, Abraham and Isaac	3.	162	Marquis of Lansdowne
Widow of Cosmo II	3.	170	Earl of Suffolk
St. Cecilia	3.	171	Earl of Suffolk
Portrait of a Prelate	3.	172	Colt Hoare
Youths and sleeping Nymph	3.	180	J. P. Miles
St. John Evangelist and 2 Angels	3.	182	J. P. Miles
Cupid	3.	239	Liverpool R.I.
Martyrdom of St. Andrew	3.	273	Edinburgh R.I.
Wooded Landscape, Figure Bathing	3.	273	Edinburgh R.I.
Landscape with St. Jerome	3.	290	M'Lellan Gallery
St. John the Baptist reproving Herod	3.	302	Duke of Hamilton
St. John Evangelist looking up	3.	324	Earl of Carlisle
A Boy in a Landscape	3.	385	Earl of Shrewsbury
A Landscape	3.	393	Lord Scarsdale
Landscape, Sacrifice of Isaac	3.	420	Earl of Leicester
Martyrdom of St. Stephen	4.	65	Earl of Yarborough
The Sibyl	4.	80	Marquis of Hertford
Landscape with Grand Towers	4.	132	Lord Overstone
Cardinal Barberini	4.	152	Lady Waldegrave
Small Landscape, Boat on Stream	4.	157	St. John Mildmay
A Male Portrait	4.	272	Earl of Jersey
The Shame of Calisto	4.	319	Lord Enfield
Landscape, Diana and Nymphs	4.	324	Lord Enfield
A Sibyl	4.	338	Knole
Landscape, with Tobit and Angel	4.	366	Earl of Normanton
Landscape, St. John preaching	4.	390	Lord Heytesbury
St. Catherine	4.	398	Lord Methuen
Hilly Landscape and Waterfall	4.	484	G. Burdon

	VOL. & PAGE	OWNER
Adam and Eve with dead Abel	4. 493	Lord Feversham
Landscape, Naked Fisherman	4. 494	Lord Feversham
Landscape, Baptism of Christ	4. 504	Earl of Yarborough
A Cardinal seated	4. 509	Duke of Newcastle

DOMENICI, Francesco

His own Portrait, 1530	4. 175	Edward Cheney
His own Portrait, 1530	4. 186	Wm. Russell

DOSSI, Giovanni Battista

A Holy Family	2. 359	Hampton Court

DOSSI, Dosso

Duke Alfonso of Ferrara	2. 196	R. S. Holford
Virgin and Child playing with a Cock	2. 469	Charles I
Virgin and Child and St. Joseph	3. 199	Lord Northwick
The Circumcision	3. 239	Liverpool R.I.
Adoration of Shepherds	4. 456	Earl of Dunmore
Pianto, riso, ira, 2 Women, etc.	4. 469	Duke of Northumberland

DOW, Gerard

The Artist	1. 317, 355	National Gallery
Old Woman and Girl with Hare	1. 400	Sir. R. Peel
Girl at window scouring Pan	2. 6	Buckingham Palace
Girl chopping Onions	2. 6	,,
Grocer's Wife weighing Raisins	2. 6	,,
Old Woman watering Flower	2. 6	,,
An Old Man	2. 6	,,
Himself at Twenty-two	2. 43	Bridgewater House
Young Man with Violin	2. 43	Bridgewater House
Hermit praying before a Crucifix	2. 103	Lord Ashburton
Old Man in Cellar, Girl with Wine	2. 104	Lord Ashburton
Girl and Boy and Hare	2. 116	Henry Thomas Hope
Man with lighted Candle and Woman	2. 117	Henry Thomas Hope
Child attracted by a Rattle	2. 168	Marquis of Westminster
A Painter in his Room	2. 183	T. Baring
A Philosopher with a Globe	2. 262	J. Morrison
A Dentist	2. 295	Wynn Ellis
Woman selling herring to a Man	2. 308	Mr. Wombwell
A Grocer's Shop	2. 329	Mr. Oppenheim
The Violin Player	2. 500	Orleans Gallery
Old Woman by Lamplight	2. 500	,,
Woman on a Balcony	2. 500	,,
Two Girls by Lamplight	2. 500	,,

I

	VOL. & PAGE		OWNER
DOW, Gerard—*continued*			
A Wood scene with Robbers	3.	171	Lord Arundel
Doctor looking at a Bottle	3.	184	J. P. Miles
The Village Lawyer	3.	263	Earl of Lonsdale
A Female Portrait	3.	263	Earl of Lonsdale
Girl with a Pail, Man with a Trap	3.	395	Duke of Rutland
Schoolmaster and 4 Scholars	3.	448	Fitzwilliam Museum
Young Man holding a Picture	3.	448	Fitzwilliam Museum
Old Man, with white beard, in a Chair	3.	476	Marquis of Bute
Man looking at a laughing Girl	4.	98	T. Baring
Sage writing in his Study	4.	108	J. Morrison
Blind Tobias and Dog	4.	392	Lord Arundel
DROGSLODT			
Peasants in a Scuffle	4.	357	Lord Folkestone
DUBBELS			
A Sea Piece	2.	285	Duke of Bedford
DUCCIO di Buoninsegna			
The Crucifixion	4.	166	W. Davenport Bromley
A Saint with 2 Scrolls	4.	166	W. Davenport Bromley
DUCHATEL			
Numerous party of Peasants	3.	222	Howard Galton
DUJARDIN, Karl			
Cattle in a Meadow	1.	407	Sir R. Peel
Shepherdess with Dog, etc.	1.	407	Sir R. Peel
Shepherd seated, Ox and Ass	2.	17	Buckingham Palace
Cow lying down, Calf standing	2.	17	,,
Brown and white Cow	2.	18	,,
Lad loading Ass with Dung	2.	18	,,
Country People at a Ford	2.	47	Bridgewater House
Watermill in Hilly Country	2.	109	Lord Ashburton
Italian Scene, Artist drawing	2.	109	Lord Ashburton
Hunting party on Horseback, 1664	2.	121	H. T. Hope
Brown Cow lying down, etc.	2.	121	H. T. Hope
Horse and Cow, Man and Woman	2.	138	H. A. J. Munro
Le Menage, 1654	2.	186	T. Baring
Two Horsemen halting	2.	202	R. S. Holford
Gray Horse drinking, etc., 1660	2.	254	F. Heusch
Swineherd and 13 Pigs	2.	254	F. Heusch
Figures and Animals near Vase	2.	261	J. Morrison
A Picture	2.	284	Duke of Bedford

	VOL. & PAGE	OWNER
A Boy milking a Sheep, etc.	2. 309	Mr. Wombwell
A Picture	2. 329	Mr. Oppenheim
A Cow	2. 331	C. S. Bale
Herdswoman crossing a Ford	2. 452	Richard Forster
Woman Spinning	3. 134	J. Morrison
Shoeing a Horse	3. 134	J. Morrison
Brown Horse and 2 Falconers	3. 161	Marquis of Lansdowne
Man with Pack Horse and Woman	3. 208	Lord Northwick
Two Horsemen halting at a Tavern	3. 272	Edinburgh R.I.
A Smith at his Forge	3. 275	Edinburgh R.I.
Goat being Milked, etc.	3. 294	Sir Archibald Campbell
Landscape and Cattle, Arch of Bridge	3. 336	Charles Wynn
Young Man leading Mule, 1653	3. 479	Marquis of Bute
Landscape, Angel, Tobit and Fish	3. 479	Marquis of Bute
Interior of a Court	4. 89	Marquis of Hertford
Group of Children, etc.	4. 89	„
A Young Man	4. 89	„
A Cow and some Sheep, etc.	4. 102	R. S. Holford
Stem of a Tree, Ox and Sheep	4. 149	Earl of Caledon
Rocky Country, Man in Red Sleeves	4. 155	St. John Mildmay
William of Orange on Horseback	4. 183	G. Cornwall Legh
Shepherd and Shepherdess, Naked Boy, etc.	4. 291	J. Sanders
Three Boys bathing near Arches	4. 294	J. Walter
Brown Cow and Grey Horse	4. 307	J. Morrison
Farrier's Shop, Piebald Horse	4. 309	J. Morrison
Shepherdess and Child, Dog	4. 318	Rev. Mr. Heath
Ruins, Sheep being Milked	4. 318	Rev. Mr. Heath
Boy in Red Mantle with Fiddle	4. 320	Lord Enfield
Male Portrait, black Dress	4. 479	J. Anderson

DUNCAN, F.

The Waefu' Heart	2. 300	J. Sheepshanks

DUNCAN, Thomas

Pretender in a Cave	3. 282	Mr. Hill
Pretender, Entry into Edinburgh	3. 282	Mr. Hill

DÜRER, Albert

A Child weeping. (In Chalk)	2. 80	S. Rogers
Adoration of the Shepherds	2. 237	Lord Ward
A Pietà	2. 237	Lord Ward
Two Madonnas. (Pen and Ink)	2. 331	C. S. Bale
Virgin and Child, 1512	2. 334	Mr. Hall
A Young Man, 1506	2. 361	Hampton Court

	VOL. & PAGE		OWNER
DÜRER, Albert—*continued*			
Christ taking leave of His Mother	2.	463	Rev. Mr. Russell
His own Portrait (young)	2.	469	Charles I
Portrait of his Father	2.	469	,,
Man without a Beard	2.	469	,,
Adoration of the Kings	2.	500	Orleans Gallery
A Man with a Letter	2.	500	Orleans Gallery
Maximilian I, Red Dress	3.	210	Lord Northwick
His own Portrait, 1507	3.	298	Duke of Hamilton
A Male Portrait	3.	301	Duke of Hamilton
A Crucifixion	3.	333	Meynell Ingram
Man in broad brimmed Hat	3.	398	Duke of Rutland
A Last Supper	3.	400	Duke of Rutland
The Nativity	3.	407	Marquis of Exeter
Male Portrait with White Beard, 1514	4.	62	National Gallery
Portrait of his Father, 1497	4.	267	Duke of Northumberland
Civetta, etc.	4.	355	Lord Folkestone
The Annunciation	4.	356	Lord Folkestone
Adoration of the Shepherds	4.	394	Lord Methuen
Altar-piece, Nativity, etc.	4.	455	Earl of Dunmore
DUSART, Cornelius			
A Picture	2.	52	Bridgewater House
Peasant Family round Hearth	2.	185	T. Baring
Houses and Trees	2.	292	Charles Bredel
Figures before old Building	2.	343	Dulwich Gallery
Peasant family under Porch	4.	138	Lord Overstone
Ninepin players drinking	4.	161	A. Robarts
Hand Organ Player, and Peasant	4.	164	A. Robarts
DYCE, W., R.A.			
Baptism of Ethelbert	1.	427	House of Lords
A Female Head	4.	153	W. E. Gladstone
DYCKMANS, Joseph Laurens			
Grandmother at her Wheel	2.	191	T. Baring

	VOL. & PAGE	OWNER

EASTLAKE, Sir Charles, P.R.A.

A Female Head	1. 373	Marlborough House
Flight of Carrara	1. 373	,,
Christ Weeping over Jerusalem	1. 373	,,
Pilgrims in sight of Rome	2. 248	George Vivian
Peasant Woman and Snake	2. 302	J. Sheepshanks
Contadina and Children	2. 307	J. Sheepshanks
Peasant Family on their Way	2. 350	E. Bicknell
Eight Studies of Views	3. 7	W. Fuller Maitland
Pilgrims in sight of Rome	3. 166	Marquis of Lansdowne
A Picture	3. 166	Marquis of Lansdowne
The Erechtheum, etc.	3. 211	Lord Northwick
Christ Weeping over Jerusalem	3. 241	John Naylor
Pilgrims in sight of Rome	3. 466	Duke of Bedford
Two Sisters	4. 184	W. Marshall
Flight of Carrara	4. 301	James Morrison
Pilgrims in sight of Rome	4. 332	Duke of Bedford
Ruth Sleeping at feet of Boaz	4. 402	Edwin Bullock
Girl with a Dove, Irene	4. 418	John Chapman

ECKHOUT, Gerbrant Van den

Soldiers at Play	2. 70	Duke of Sutherland
St. John and Peter healing lame Man	2. 246	Mr. Neeld
A Corps de Garde	3. 35	Petworth
Adoration of the Kings	3. 207	Lord Northwick
A Male Portrait	3. 221	Howard Galton
A Picture	3. 225	Mr. Martin
St. Peter and John, and Lame Man	3. 265	Earl of Lonsdale
Haman carried in Triumph, 1665	3. 475	Marquis of Bute
Merrymaking in Guard-house	3. 475	Marquis of Bute

EDDIS, E. U.

Gipsy Woman	4. 144	Lord Overstone
Naomi, Ruth, and Orpah	4. 145	Lord Overstone

EGG, Augustus L., R.A.

The Diable Boiteux	1. 378	Marlborough House
Henrietta Maria	4. 416	Samuel Ashton

	VOL. & PAGE	OWNER
EL GRECO (Domenico Theotocopuli)		
A Male Portrait	2. 420	H. Labouchere
ELMORE, A., R.A.		
Origin of Guelfs and Ghibellines	4. 416	S. Ashton
Hotspur and the Fop	4. 416	S. Ashton
ELSASSER		
Ruggiero Chapel at Palermo	3. 176	Mr. Vivian
ELSHEIMER, Adam		
A Repose	2. 94	Devonshire House
Tobit and the Angel	2. 229	Hon. E. Phipps
Two Pictures	2. 482	Charles I
A Landscape	3. 400	Duke of Rutland
Cupid and Psyche	3. 449	Fitzwilliam Museum
A Venus	3. 450	Cambridge University
Jacob returning to Canaan	3. 482	Marquis of Bute
St. Paul dropping Snake	4. 394	Lord Methuen
Death of Procris	4. 396	Lord Methuen
St. Peter delivered from Prison	4. 444	Lord Elgin
EMPOLI, Jacopo da		
A Female Portrait	3. 436	Earl of Orford
ESPINOSA, Jacinto Geronimo		
Madonna with Infant Saviour	2. 259	G. A. Hoskins
ESPINOSA, Hyacinth Hieronymus de		
Francisco Vives de Faura	4. 382	Kingston Lacy
ESSEX, W.		
J. Flaxman, R.A., Enamel	4. 112	J. Morrison
ETTY, W., R.A.		
Two Females with Swans	1. 373	Marlborough House
Youth at the Prow, etc.	1. 373	Marlborough House
A Bacchanalian Festival	2. 73	Duke of Sutherland
Nude Female on Sea shore	2. 141	H. A. J. Munro
Cupid interceding for Psyche	2. 189	T. Baring
A Knight and a Maiden	2. 298	Wynn Ellis
Cupid sheltering Psyche	2. 307	J. Sheepshanks
One of Mr. Bicknell's Children	2. 350	E. Bicknell
Venus and Cupid	2. 353	E. Bicknell
Cleopatra sailing in a Vessel	2. 423	H. Labouchere

	VOL. & PAGE		OWNER
The Prodigal Son	3.	165	Marquis of Lansdowne
Judith killing Holofernes	3.	271	Royal Scottish Academy
Judith, servant waiting	3.	271	,,
Judith putting Head in Basket	3.	271	,,
Woman interceding for Vanquished	3.	271	,,
Benaiah slaying Lion-Men of Moab	3.	271	,,
A Sleeping Child	4.	369	Earl of Normanton
Several Pictures	4.	403	Edwin Bullock
Head of a young Girl	4.	403	Mr. Birch
Rape of Proserpine	4.	403	Joseph Gillott
The Three Graces	4.	403	,,
A Girl Bathing	4.	403	,,
Venus Anadyomene	4.	403	,,

EVERDINGEN, Albert Van

A Scene in Norway	2.	205	R. S. Holford
Norwegian Scene	2.	312	Earl of Listowel
Agitated Sea, Vessel on Shore	4.	165	Abraham Robarts
House and Trees, Water rushing	4.	292	Joseph Sanders

	VOL. & PAGE		OWNER

FABRIANO, Gentile da

Figures on Ships	2.	418	·H. Labouchere
Coronation of the Virgin	4.	397	Lord Methuen

FABRITIUS, Carel

A Male Portrait	2.	237	Lord Ward

FARINATO, Paolo

Daughter of Herodias and Head	2.	284	Duke of Bedford
Marriage at Cana	4.	277	Sir C. Eardley
Virgin and Child and four Saints	4.	410	Smith Barry

FERG, Franz de Paula

A Charletan Preaching	3.	303	Duke of Hamilton
Landscape, 2 Horses in Cart	4.	209	Mr. Henderson
Landscape	4.	354	Lord Folkestone
Landscape	4.	354	Lord Folkestone

FERRARA, School of

Adoration of the Kings	4.	411	Smith Barry

FERRARA, Mazzolino da

A Holy Family	1.	325	National Gallery
Holy Family with St. Francis	1.	325	National Gallery
Christ shown to the People	3.	199	Lord Northwick
A Warrior on Horseback	2.	365	Hampton Court

FERRARA, Scarsellino da

Entry of Christ into Jerusalem	3.	185	J. P. Miles

FERRARI, Gaudenzio

Virgin and three Angels Worshipping	2.	196	R. S. Holford
Holy Family	2.	244	Mr. Neeld
Virgin holding the Child	3.	200	Lord Northwick
Virgin and Joseph, adoring the Child	3.	294	Sir Archibald Campbell
Virgin and Child and St. Peter	4.	452	W. Stirling

FERRI, Ciro

Virgin and Child	2.	65	Duke of Sutherland
Triumph of Bacchus	2.	413	Hampton Court
A Picture	3.	393	Lord Scarsdale
A Picture	3.	403	Marquis of Exeter

	VOL. & PAGE		OWNER
FETI, Domenico			
David with Head of Goliath	2.	359	Hampton Court
Six Pictures	2.	482	Charles I
A Female Spinning	2.	490	Orleans Gallery
Family of Five Persons	3.	22	Earl of Darnley
Portrait of a Man	3.	322	Earl of Carlisle
Jacob's Dream	3.	383	Earl of Shrewsbury
Virgin and Child under a Tree	3.	483	Marquis of Bute
Blind leading the Blind	4.	470	Duke of Northumberland
Three Beggar Boys on Step	4.	485	George Burdon
Parable of the Vineyard	4.	503	Earl of Yarborough
FICHEL			
A Family Concert	4.	417	S. Ashton
FIELDING, Copley			
Burlington Quay, Drawing	2.	351	E. Bicknell
Riveaulx Abbey „	2.	351	„
Landscape, Light Shower „	2.	351	„
View in Westmoreland	3.	39	Petworth
Stormy Sea, Vessel in Danger, Drawing	4.	112	J. Morrison
FIESOLE			
Salome Dancing	2.	76	S. Rogers
Beheading of St. John	2.	76	S. Rogers
The Last Judgment	2.	231	Lord Ward
Virgin and Child Enthroned	2.	231	Lord Ward
A Sermon on the Mount	2.	417	H. Labouchere
Entombment of the Virgin	3.	2	W. Fuller Maitland
Virgin borne to Heaven	3.	3	W. Fuller Maitland
A Miracles, 4 Figures	3.	196	Lord Northwick
Virgin and Child and Pope Gregory	3.	281	Mr. Dennistoun
The Risen Christ and 2 Guards	3.	281	Mr. Dennistoun
Death of the Virgin	4.	397	Lord Methuen
FIORENTINO, Rosso			
Virgin and Child, etc.	3.	382	Earl of Shrewsbury
Adoration of Kings	4.	71	Alexander Barker
FIORE, Jacobello del			
St. Louis and St. Jerome	2.	127	Alexander Barker
St. James, St. George, etc., 4 Panels	3.	377	Davenport Bromley
FLATMAN			
Miniatures	4.	512	Duke of Portland

	VOL. & PAGE		OWNER

FLAXMAN (Sculptor)

Archangel Michael piercing Satan	3.	37	Petworth
A Shepherd Boy	3.	37	Petworth

FLEMISH SCHOOL

St. Jerome at a Desk	4.	285	Rev. J. F. Russell
An Old Woman	4.	317	Rev. Mr. Heath

FLEURY, Robert

Old Man weighing Gold	2.	192	T. Baring

FLINCK, Govaert

Joseph Interpreting Dreams	2.	283	Duke of Bedford
An Aged Rabbi	4.	290	Joseph Sanders

FLORENTINE SCHOOL

Angel of the Annunciation	2.	330	C. S. Bale

FLORIS, Frank

An Allegorical Subject	3.	287	M'Lellan Gallery
St. Catherine and St. Margaret	4.	459	M'Lellan Gallery

FONTANA, Lavinia

St. Cecilia and St. Sebastian	4.	399	Lord Methuen
Two Girls in a Boat, etc.	4.	452	W. Stirling

FONTANA, Prospero

Adoration of the Shepherds	2.	236	Lord Ward
A Holy Family	3.	483	Marquis of Bute

FORD, Thomas

Girl standing at Toilet Table, 1848	4.	293	Joseph Sanders

FRANCESCHINI, Marc Antonio

Magdalen Reading	3.	21	Earl of Darnley
Repentant Magdalen	3.	248	Blundell Weld
A Picture	3.	403	Marquis of Exeter
Birth of Adonis	4.	291	Joseph Sanders
St. Theresa and Angels	4.	497	W. Drury Lowe
A Charity	4.	521	Earl of Hardwicke

FRANCIA, Francesco

Virgin Enthroned	1.	316	National Gallery
A Pietà	1.	316	National Gallery
St. Francis receiving Stigmata	2.	135	H. A. J. Munro

	VOL. & PAGE		OWNER
FRANCIA, Francesco—*continued*			
Virgin and Child and St. Joseph	2.	235	Lord Ward
Virgin holding the Child on a Parapet	2.	334	Sir Frankland Lewis
Baptism of Christ	2.	365	Hampton Court
Baptism of Christ	2.	419	H. Labouchere
Holy Family with SS. Peter and Paul	2.	490	Orleans Gallery
The Annunciation	3.	199	Lord Northwick
Bartholomew Bianchini	3.	199	Lord Northwick
Lucretia Stabbing Herself	4.	94	T. Baring
Virgin and Child Enthroned (Apple)	4.	94	T. Baring
Baptism of Christ	4.	104	H. Labouchere
Female Saint in a Landscape	4.	182	G. Cornwall Legh
A Man in Youthful Years	4.	239	R. P. Nichols
Raphael's Portrait, after Raphael	4.	344	Countess of Warwick
Virgin holding Sleeping Child	4.	446	Lord Kinnaird
Virgin and Child	4.	456	Earl of Dunmore
FRANCIA, Giacomo			
Virgin and Child and Bird	2.	235	Lord Ward
Virgin and Child in Benediction	3.	199	Lord Northwick
Virgin and Child holding a Bird	3.	199	Lord Northwick
Virgin and Child, St. Francis, and St. Catherine	3.	294	Sir Archibald Campbell
A Holy Family	4.	182	G. Cornwall Legh
FRANCIA, Giulio			
Holy Family	4.	182	G. Cornwall Legh
FRANCIABIGIO			
Man pointing to a Manuscript	2.	243	Henry Danby Seymour
Parable of the Vineyard	3.	5	W. Fuller Maitland
Parable of the Vineyard	3.	5	W. Fuller Maitland
FRANCK, Franz			
Still Life, Pictures, etc.	2.	433	Windsor Castle
Pharaoh in Red Sea	3.	123	Duke of Marlborough
FRANCO, Bathista			
Baptism of Christ	4.	510	Duke of Newcastle
FREDI, Bartolo di			
Adoration of the Kings	2.	462	Rev. John Fuller Russell
Two Saints	3.	196	Lord Northwick
FRITH, W. P., R.A.			
Scene from " The Good-Natured Man "	2.	302	J. Sheepshanks

	VOL. & PAGE	OWNER
FROST, W. E., R.A.		
A Mirthful Girl	2. 351	E. Bicknell
The Sirens	2. 351	E. Bicknell
FRUITIERS, L.		
Woman near Cradle, 3 Children	2. 268	Miss Rogers
FURINI, Francesco		
A Picture	2. 311	Earl of Listowel
Head of St. Sebastian	3. 270	Edinburgh R.I.
Head of a Poetess	3. 270	Edinburgh R.I.
Sigismunda and the Heart of Tancred	4. 510	Duke of Newcastle
FYT, Jan		
A Picture	2. 42	Bridgewater House
Dogs with Dead Game	2. 165	Marquis of Westminster
Hawk pouncing on a Duck	2. 165	Marquis of Westminster
Dogs hunting Wild Fowl	3. 35	Petworth
A Wild Boar Hunt	3. 333	Meynell Ingram
Dogs and Game	3. 392	Lord Scarsdale
Large Hunting Piece	3. 430	Andrew Fountaine
A Large Boar Hunt	4. 485	Lord Ravensworth

	VOL. & PAGE	OWNER
GADDI, Taddeo		
Two Heads	1. 318	National Gallery
Coronation of the Virgin	2. 463	Rev. John Fuller Russell
Small altar-piece, Crucifixion	3. 2	W. Fuller Maitland
Adoration of the Kings	3. 281	Mr. Dennistoun
The Visitation	3. 281	Mr. Dennistoun
The Virgin enthroned	3. 377	W. Davenport Bromley
GAETANO, Scipio		
A Male Portrait	4. 261	Duc D'Aumale
An old Man of Jewish appearance	4. 261	Duc D'Aumale
GAINSBOROUGH, Thomas, R.A.		
The Watering Place	1. 368	Marlborough House
The Market Cart	1. 368	,,
Watering Place, small	1. 368	,,
Peasant Children	1. 368	,,
Cows in a Meadow	2. 53	Bridgewater House
A young Girl, half length	2. 72	Duke of Sutherland
Two Pictures	2. 75	S. Rogers
Portrait in a Landscape	2. 161	Marquis of Hertford
The Blue Boy	2. 173	Marquis of Westminster
The Cottage Door	2. 173	,,
Fishermen on Shore	2. 173	,,
House and Trees, Children on Steps	2. 189	T. Baring
Girl and Pigs	2. 280	Earl of Carlisle
Family before a Cottage	2. 298	Wynn Ellis
Mrs. Sheridan and Mrs. Tickell	2. 348	Dulwich Gallery
Fisher, the Composer	2. 369	Hampton Court
Miss McGill	3. 26	Earl of Darnley
A Female Portrait	3. 26	Earl of Darnley
Member of the Norfolk Family	3. 31	Duke of Norfolk
Member of the Norfolk Family	3. 31	Duke of Norfolk
Landscape, Shepherd and Shepherdess	3. 39	Petworth
Landscape, Cows, Sheep, and Goats	3. 39	Petworth
John, Duke of Bedford	3. 130	Duke of Marlborough
Herd of Cattle in Landscape	3. 158	Marquis of Lansdowne
Peasants going to Market	3. 173	Colt Hoare
The Market Cart	3. 210	Lord Northwick
Duke of Montague	3. 313	Duke of Buccleuch

	VOL. & PAGE	OWNER
GAINSBOROUGH, Thomas, R.A.—*continued*		
Duchess of Montague	3. 313	Duke of Buccleuch
Landscape, Cattle by some Water	3. 398	Duke of Rutland
Party of Country People near House	3. 399	,,
Herd of Cattle in a Landscape	3. 399	,,
Lady Chatham	3. 443	Mr. Tomline
Lady in white, seated with a Dog	4. 91	Marquis of Hertford
Lord Gage	4. 282	Sir Culling Eardley
Mountainous Landscape, Washerwomen	4. 290	Joseph Sanders
1st Duke of Bedford	4. 331	Duke of Bedford
Landscape, with Cattle	4. 331	,,
Landscape, with Cattle	4. 331	,,
Lord George Germain	4. 338	Knole
Countess Spencer	4. 348	Vernon Harcourt
Anne, Countess of Radnor	4. 354	Lord Folkestone
Hon. W. H. Bouverie	4. 362	,,
Hon. Edward Bouverie	4. 362	,,
William Pitt, young	4. 372	Earl of Normanton
Mother of Lord Normanton	4. 373	,,
William Pitt, in black chalk	4. 373	,,
A Picture	4. 374	Sir W. Knighton
Earl of Burlington, and Dog	4. 426	Earl of Burlington
Hon. Mrs. Graham	4. 434	Robert Graham
Mrs. Siddons, aged twenty-five	4. 435	Mrs. Mair
Duke of Montague	4. 436	Duke of Buccleuch
Duchess of Montague	4. 436	Duke of Buccleuch
Man in brownish Dress	4. 445	Lord Kinnaird
Lady as a Shepherdess	4. 477	W. W. Bardon
A Landscape	4. 484	Matthew Anderson
Several Portraits	4. 496	Earl of Harrington
A Beggar Child	4. 509	Duke of Newcastle
A Landscape	4. 511	Duke of Newcastle
GAMBARA, Lattanzio		
Several Frescoes	4. 232	Prince Consort
GANDINI, Giorgio		
Virgin and Child and 2 Angels	2. 293	Wynn Ellis
GARBO, Raffaelino del		
Virgin and Child, etc.	3. 3	W. Fuller Maitland
Virgin and Child and 2 Angels	3. 382	Earl of Shrewsbury
GAROFALO, Benvenuto		
A Holy Family	1. 316	National Gallery
Christ adored by St. Francis	1. 316	,,

	VOL. & PAGE		OWNER
St. Augustine and St. Catherine	1.	325	National Gallery
A Holy Family	1.	325	”
Marriage of St. Catherine	2.	63	Duke of Sutherland
St. John the Baptist	2.	176	T. Baring
Virgin and Child crowned by Angels	2.	195	R. S. Holford
Virgin and Child and 6 Saints	2.	244	Joseph Neeld
Holy Family in Landscape	2.	268	Miss Rogers
Virgin and Child and 2 Angels	2.	270	”
Holy Family, Elizabeth and John	2.	270	”
Virgin and Child, Anna and Joseph	2.	434	Windsor Castle
Virgin and Child, Joseph and St. John	2.	471	Charles I
Transfiguration (after Raphael)	2.	490	Orleans Gallery
A Holy Family	2.	490	”
A Holy Family and St. Catherine	2.	490	”
Martyrdom of St. Stephen	3.	199	Lord Northwick
Virgin and Child and Joseph	3.	199	Lord Northwick
Christ and Money Changers	3.	269	Edinburgh, R.I.
St. Augustin, School Copy	3.	288	M'Lellan Gallery
St. Catherine in ecstasy	3.	289	M'Lellan Gallery
Virgin and Child and Baptist	3.	294	Sir A. Campbell
Adoration of the Kings	3.	383	Earl of Shrewsbury
A Riposo	3.	482	Marquis of Bute
The Circumcision	4.	66	Earl of Yarborough
St. Christopher	4.	103	Henry Danby Seymour
The Circumcision	4.	104	H. Labouchere
John the Baptist and Lamb	4.	268	Duke of Northumberland
Judith with the Head of Holofernes	4.	339	Knole
Christ healing a Man	4.	466	Duke of Northumberland
Judith adorning Herself	4.	467	Duke of Northumberland

GARRARD, Mark

Three Female Portraits	3.	171	Earl of Suffolk
Queen Elizabeth (old)	3.	407	Marquis of Exeter
William Lord Burleigh	3.	408	”
Robert Earl of Essex	3.	408	”
Several Portraits	3.	464	Duke of Bedford
Queen Elizabeth (middle age)	4.	269	Duke of Northumberland

GARZI, Luigi

Landscape with a Riposo	3.	240	Liverpool R.I.

GAUERMANN of Vienna

Stag attacked by Wolves, 1834	2.	306	J. Sheepshanks
A Family of Wild Boars	2.	306	J. Sheepshanks

	VOL. & PAGE		OWNER

GELDER, Arnold de
Head of a Rabbi   3.   240   Liverpool R.I.

GENNAR, Benedetto
St. John Evangelist Reading   2.   491   Orleans Gallery
St. Jerome Translating the Bible   3.   239   Liverpool R. I.
Count Palliotti   3.   385   Earl of Shrewsbury

GENTILESCHI, Artemisia (Orazio Lomi)
Her own Portrait   2.   357   Hampton Court
Joseph and Potiphar's Wife   2.   359   Hampton Court
A Man with a Cat   2.   491   Orleans Gallery

GERARD
Emperor Alexander   2.   277   Duke of Wellington
King of France   2.   277   „
King of Prussia   2.   277   „

GERMAN SCHOOL
Altar-piece, Christ and Virgin   4.   190   A. J. B. Hope
David and Bathsheba   4.   461   M'Lellan Gallery

GESSI
A Picture   2.   39   Bridgewater House

GHENT, Justus Van
Gothic Church and Funeral of a Bishop   2.   263   Sir C. Eastlake

GHIRLANDAJO, Domenico
Altar-piece, Virgin and Child, etc.   2.   126   Alexander Barker
St. Dominic under Tree   3.   4   W. Fuller Maitland
A Youth   3.   53   Oxford University
A Picture   3.   314   Capt. Stirling
Virgin and Child, etc.   3.   423   Earl of Leicester
Virgin supporting leg of Child   4.   115   Sir C. Eastlake
Maria Tornabuoni   4.   497   W. Drury Lowe
A Young Man   4.   498   W. Drury Lowe

GHIRLANDAJO, Ridolfo
Virgin and Child and St. John   4.   398   Lord Methuen

GHISOLFI
Ruins and Broken Sculpture   3.   273   Edinburgh R.I.
Ruins and Broken Sculpture   3.   273   Edinburgh R.I.

	VOL. & PAGE		OWNER
GIBSON, John, R.A. (sculptor)			
Mars and Cupid	3.	367	Duke of Devonshire
Young Girl and Huntsman	4.	71	Earl of Yarborough
GIORDANO, Luca			
A Picture	2.	39	Bridgewater House
A Picture	2.	93	Devonshire House
Christ and Money Changers	2.	491	Orleans Gallery
Pool of Bethesda	2.	491	Orleans Gallery
Adoration of Shepherds	3.	22	Earl of Darnley
Death of Seneca	3.	131	Duke of Marlborough
Dionysius as a Schoolmaster	3.	240	Liverpool R.I.
Christ at the Pool of Bethesda	3.	254	Blundell Weld
Christ and the Money Changers	3.	254	,,
A Large Picture	3.	254	,,
A Large Picture	3.	254	,,
Acis and Galatea	3.	345	Duke of Devonshire
A Picture	3.	393	Lord Scarsdale
A Picture	3.	403	Marquis of Exeter
Venus and Cupid	4.	268	Duke of Northumberland
Shepherd and Shepherdess	4.	268	Duke of Northumberland
Christ Teaching in the Temple	4.	277	Sir C. Eardley
A series of Pictures	4.	374	Lady Featherstonhaugh
Philip II and Plan of the Escurial	4.	386	Lord Heytesbury
Leda and the Swan and Cupids	4.	521	Earl of Hardwicke
GIORGIONE			
Martyrdom of St. Peter	1.	334	National Gallery
Judgment of Paris	1.	416	Earl of Malmesbury
Horseman in a Landscape	2.	59	Duke of Sutherland
A Young Knight	2.	77	S. Rogers
Adoration of the Shepherds	2.	82	Lord Elcho
Energetic Man	2.	90	Devonshire House
A Girl and Lover	2.	100	Lord Ashburton
A Man	2.	100	Lord Ashburton
Holy Family in a Landscape	2.	133	H. A. J. Munro
Virgin and Child and St. John	2.	133	,,
Man with a Dagger	2.	133	,,
Daughter of Herodias and Head	2.	179	T. Baring
Daughter of Herodias and Head	2.	196	R. S. Holford
A Man and Woman	2.	197	R. S. Holford
Female with Wreath of Myrtle	2.	227	Hon. E. Phipps
St. George	2.	244	Joseph Neeld
A Knight and his Lady Love	2.	267	Miss Rogers
Youth taking off Warrior's Armour	2.	278	Earl of Carlisle

	VOL. & PAGE		OWNER
GIORGIONE—*continued*			
A Male Portrait	2.	293	Wynn Ellis
St. William	2.	355	Hampton Court
A Warrior	2.	357	,,
A Holy Family	2.	359	,,
A Gentleman and Lady	2.	410	,,
Virgin and Child and Saints	2.	471	Charles I
Virgin and Child and St. Joseph	2.	471	,,
Diana and Actaeon	2.	471	,,
Shepherd without a Beard	2.	471	,,
Man in a Black Cap	2.	471	,,
Executioner with the Baptist's Head	2.	483	,,
His own Portrait	2.	483	,,
His own Portrait with 2 statues	2.	483	,,
Adoration of the Shepherds	2.	483	,,
A Family, 10 Figures	2.	483	,,
A Woman holding her Apron	2.	483	,,
Four Persons Singing	2.	483	,,
His own Portrait, with Mistress	2.	483	,,
Thirteen Portraits	2.	483	,,
A Holy Family	2.	491	Orleans Gallery
Gaston de Foix	2.	491	,,
Milo of Crotona torn by Lions	2.	491	,,
Portrait of Pordenone	2.	491	,,
Portrait of Pico di Mirandola	2.	491	,,
Adoration of the Shepherds	2.	491	,,
Cupid complaining to Venus	2.	491	,,
Martyrdom of St. Peter	2.	491	,,
Caesar and the Head of Pompey	3.	19	Earl of Darnley
Milo torn by Lions	3.	19	Earl of Darnley
Shepherd in Sheepskin, etc.	3.	162	Marquis of Lansdowne
Woman taken in Adultery	3.	202	Lord Northwick
Venus and Cupid	3.	202	Lord Northwick
Ceres	3.	265	Earl of Lonsdale
Small Portrait of a Man	3.	270	Edinburgh R.I.
A Youth and a Maiden	3.	274	Edinburgh R.I.
Virgin and Child, St. John, etc.	3.	289	M'Lellan Gallery
Hippomenes and Atalanta, etc.	3.	303	Duke of Hamilton
Two Female Heads	3.	325	Earl of Carlisle
A Male Portrait	3.	345	Duke of Devonshire
A Man	3.	383	Earl of Shrewsbury
Adoration of Shepherds	3.	446	Fitzwilliam Museum
Virgin Enthroned and Child	4.	59	National Gallery
St. George (small full length)	4.	59	National Gallery
Virgin on Ground and Child, etc.	4.	290	Joseph Sanders

	VOL. & PAGE		OWNER
A Pretty Woman	4.	324	Lord Enfield
Christ Bearing His Cross	4.	326	Sir T. Sebright
Man in Armour holding a Spear	4.	329	Sir T. Sebright
Violante daughter of Palma Vecchio	4.	361	Lord Folkestone
Judgment of Solomon	4.	377	Kingston Lacy
Portrait of Scanderbeg	4.	394	Lord Methuen
Small Landscape, 2 Figures	4.	432	J. Gibson Craig
A Man	4.	441	Earl of Wemyss
Virgin and Child, Enthroned	4.	460	M'Lellan Gallery
Man seated in Gay Dress	4.	501	Earl of Yarborough

GIOTTO

St. Paul, and St. John, 2 Fragments	2.	76	S. Rogers
The Last Supper	2.	230	Lord Ward
Three Women with John the Baptist	3.	231	Liverpool R.I.
Daughter of Herodias receiving Head	3.	232	Liverpool R.I.
Virgin Enthroned (School of)	3.	253	Blundell Weld
Coronation of Virgin	3.	371	W. Davenport Bromley
Death of the Virgin	3.	374	W. Davenport Bromley
Marriage of the Virgin (School of)	4.	285	Rev. Mr. Russell
Frescoes from Church at Assisi	4.	299	Higford Burr
Small Altar-piece with Wings	4.	397	Lord Methuen
Half of a Diptych	4.	465	Duke of Northumberland

GIOVANNI, di San Giovanni

A Picture	3.	393	Lord Scarsdale
Virgin and Child and St. John	4.	398	Lord Methuen

GIOVANE, Palma (see Palma)

The Magdalen	2.	368	Hampton Court
Allegorical Subject	3.	303	Duke of Hamilton

GIROLAMO, da Carpi

A Riposo and 2 Angels	2.	178	T. Baring

GIROLAMO, dai Libri

Crucifixion (on vellum)	2.	224	Richard Ford
Altar-piece, Virgin and Child under a Tree	3.	296	Duke of Hamilton
Virgin and Child	4.	59	National Gallery

GIROLAMO, da Santa Croce

Virgin and Child and St. John	3.	201	Lord Northwick
Resurrection of Christ	3.	201	Lord Northwick
Resurrection of Christ	3.	238	Liverpool R.I.

	VOL. & PAGE	OWNER
GLAUBER, Johann (called Polydor)		
Landscape	3. 252	Blundell Weld
GOODALL, Fredk., R.A.		
Village Festival	1. 379	Marlborough House
The Tired Soldier	1. 379	Marlborough House
A Sick Room	3. 165	Marquis of Lansdowne
The Harvest Waggon (drawing, 1853)	4. 414	Mr. Cooke
Erection of the Maypole (drawing, 1853)	4. 414	Mr. Cooke
GORDON, Sir John Watson		
Sir Walter Scott	4. 453	William Stirling
GORZIUS, Gualdorp		
A Female Portrait, 1685	3. 177	Mr. Vivian
Earl of Essex	3. 210	Lord Northwick
GOTT (sculptor)		
Greyhound and 2 Dogs	3. 223	Howard Galton
Greyhound and 2 Boys	3. 367	Duke of Devonshire
GOYA		
4 Sketches of Boys Playing	4. 449	William Stirling
GOZZOLI, Benozzo		
Adoration of the Kings	2. 125	Alex. Barker
Virgin Adoring Child	2. 231	Lord Ward
Virgin Enthroned with Child	2. 267	Miss Rogers
The Annunciation	3. 53	Oxford University
Altar-piece, Virgin Enthroned	4. 53	National Gallery
Virgin and Child Enthroned	4. 117	C. S. Bale
Frescoes from S. Geminiano	4. 299	Higford Burr
GRAET, Bernard		
Family in the Open Air	2. 11	Buckingham Palace
GRANACCI, Francesco		
Virgin Enthroned with Child	3. 4	W. Fuller Maitland
The Annunciation	4. 399	Lord Methuen
GRANET		
Franciscans in Church	2. 24	Buckingham Palace
Franciscans in Church	3. 351	Duke of Devonshire

GREUZE

	VOL. & PAGE		OWNER
Mother with 3 Children	2.	24	Buckingham Palace
Girl in Cap seated on a Chair	2.	24	,,
Little Girl (circle)	2.	24	,,
Little Girl	2.	87	Earl of Yarborough
Girl by Bed looking at Watch	2.	130	Baron Lionel de Rothschild
Girl in Sorrow leaning on Hand	2.	130	Baron Lionel de Rothschild
A Young Girl	2.	152	Marquis of Lansdowne
Le Miroir Cassé	2.	156	Marquis of Hertford
Young Girl with a Dove	2.	157	,,
A Picture	2.	157	,,
A Boy	2.	182	T. Baring
Girl with a Dove	2.	199	R. S. Holford
A Young Girl	2.	199	R. S. Holford
Father Reading Prayers aloud	2.	249	Mr. Mills
A Girl and Boy	2.	249	,,
A Child	2.	249	,,
A Boy	2.	249	,,
Girl pulling the Petals of Flower	2.	261	J. Morrison
The Nursery (8 children)	2.	281	Sir A. Rothschild
Young Girl Looking Up	2.	282	Sir A. Rothschild
Two Children from Lord Coventry	2.	295	Wynn Ellis
Two Children from Count Morny	2.	295	Wynn Ellis
Two Pictures (oval)	2.	310	Mr. Wombwell
A Young Boy	2.	310	Mr. Wombwell
Girl with a Lap Dog	2.	453	Richard Forster
Girl watching a Cat and Ball	3.	163	Marquis of Lansdowne
Guitar Player Tuning	3.	223	Howard Galton
Interior: Woman Nursing a Child	3.	272	Edinburgh R.I.
Young Girl with a Letter	4.	69	Earl of Yarborough
Girl Kneeling before a Statue of Cupid	4.	84	Marquess of Hertford
A Young Girl	4.	84	,,
A Young Girl	4.	84	,,
A Young Girl	4.	84	,,
A Young Girl	4.	84	,,
Head of a Young Girl	4.	104	H. Labouchere
Girl Plucking Petals from Flowers	4.	112	J. Morrison
Girl in Red Corsage with Bird	4.	146	Lord Overstone
Girl hugging small Spaniel	4.	163	A. Robarts
Golden-haired Boy in White	4.	196	Mr. Field
Head of Father, Blessing, etc.	4.	312	J. Morrison
Four Pictures of Young Girls	4.	369	Earl of Normanton
A Sleeping Girl	4.	379	Kingston Lacy
Girl Lamenting the Death of a Canary	4.	430	Lord Murray
Schoolboy Closing a Book	4.	430	,,

	VOL. & PAGE		OWNER
GREUZE—*continued*			
Girl holding Flowers	4.	430	Lord Murray
A Young Girl	4.	430	,,
Girl Caressing a Lamb	4.	476	W. W. Bardon
GRIEFF			
Two Hunting Pieces	3.	41	Petworth
GRIFFIER, Jan			
A Picture	2.	122	Henry Thomas Hope
A Picture	3.	476	Marquis of Bute
Landscape	4.	514	Duke of Portland
GRIMALDI, Francesco (called Il Bolognese)			
Large Landscape	2.	180	T. Baring
Landscape	3.	310	Earl of Hopetoun
Landscape and Figures by A. Carracci	4.	350	Vernon Harcourt
Landscape, Naked Fisherman	4.	494	Lord Feversham
GRIMANI, Francesco			
Landscape	3.	251	Blundell Weld
Landscape, 2 Fishermen	3.	251	Blundell Weld
Large Landscape	3.	421	Earl of Leicester
GRIMMER, Abel			
Interior of a Saloon, Couple Dancing, 1608	4.	321	Lord Enfield
GRUNEWALD, Mathæus			
Altar-piece, Virgin and Child, etc.	3.	435	Earl of Orford
Virgin and Child in Glory	4.	230	Prince Consort
Miracle of the Crucifix	4.	461	M'Lellan Gallery
GUARDI, Francesco			
Views of Venice	3.	313	Duke of Buccleuch
View in Venice	4.	171	Edward Cheney
View in Venice	4.	171	Edward Cheney
A Marine Piece	4.	208	Mr. Henderson
4 Small Views of Venice	4.	210	,,
Ruins and Water	4.	210	,,
The Dogana and Salute	4.	211	,,
Church of St. Giorgio Maggiore	4.	211	,,
St. Mark's Cathedral	4.	211	,,
Church of S. Francesca della Vigna	4.	212	,,

	VOL. & PAGE	OWNER
View in Venice	4. 373	Earl of Normanton
View in Venice	4. 373	Earl of Normanton
Views in Venice	4. 436	Duke of Buccleuch
Church of S. Giorgio Maggiore	4. 460	M'Lellan Gallery

GUDIN

A Ship in a Storm	2. 66	Duke of Sutherland

GUERCINO

Christ Lamented by 3 Angels	1. 338	National Gallery
St. Sebastian Bound	1. 394	Duke of Northumberland
David and Abigail	2. 36	Bridgewater House
David and Abigail. (Drawing)	2. 36	„
The Cenci	2. 36	„
St. Paul borne by Angels	2. 65	Duke of Sutherland
St. Gregory and Dove, etc.	2. 65	„
David with Sword and Head	2. 65	„
Small Landscape	2. 65	„
The Annunciation	2. 87	Earl of Yarborough
Susanna and the Elders	2. 92	Devonshire House
St. Sebastian mourned by Angels	2. 101	Lord Ashburton
The Prodigal Son	2. 152	Marquis of Lansdowne
Virgin and Child and 2 Angels	2. 180	T. Baring
Portrait of a Cardinal	2. 236	Lord Ward
A Riposo	2. 245	Joseph Neeld
Head of Hagar	2. 260	G. A. Hoskins
Christ lamented by 2 Angels	2. 268	Miss Rogers
Landscape near St. Peter's	2. 269	Miss Rogers
Woman taken in Adultery	2. 347	Dulwich Gallery
His own Portrait	2. 357	Hampton Court
Faith	2. 369	Hampton Court
Woman of Samaria	2. 433	Windsor Castle
The Painter in his Studio	2. 433	„
A Sibyl	2. 434	„
A Picture	2. 482	Charles I
David and Abigail	2. 491	Orleans Gallery
Presentation in the Temple	2. 491	„
Head of the Virgin	2. 491	„
St. Jerome	2. 491	„
Return of the Prodigal Son	3. 15	Earl Cowper
A Sibyl	3. 21	Earl of Darnley
His own Portrait	3. 21	Earl of Darnley
Tidings brought to a queenly figure	3. 41	Petworth
The Virgin and Child	3. 172	Colt Hoare
The Good Shepherd	3. 172	Colt Hoare

M

	VOL. & PAGE	OWNER
GUERCINO—*continued*		
Evening Landscape	3. 177	Mr. Vivian
Morning Landscape	3. 177	Mr. Vivian
Youth with Hat and Feather	3. 190	Mr. Harford
Diana, a Head	3. 190	Mr. Harford
Angel giving Honeycomb, etc.	3. 200	Lord Northwick
Jacob Blessing Ephraim	3. 200	,,
St. Jerome, etc.	3. 200	,,
St. John the Baptist	3. 200	,,
The Magdalen (*copy*)	3. 239	Liverpool R.I.
Virgin and Child and St. John	3. 269	Edinburgh R.I.
St. Joseph with the Child	3. 294	Sir A. Campbell
Tancred and Erminia	3. 325	Earl of Carlisle
A Sibyl	3. 336	Charles Wynn
The Penitent Magdalen	3. 384	Earl of Shrewsbury
John the Baptist	3. 384	,,
The Entombment	3. 385	,,
Portrait of Himself	3. 385	,,
Israelites celebrating triumph of David	3. 393	Lord Scarsdale
Jacob receiving Joseph's Coat	3. 405	Marquis of Exeter
St. Luke painting the Virgin	3. 456	Earl Spencer
Assumption of the Virgin	3. 483	Marquis of Bute
The Annunciation	4. 66	Earl of Yarborough
St. Sebastian Reclining	4. 148	Earl of Caledon
Christ and the Woman of Samaria	4. 158	A. Robarts
St. Sebastian Pierced	4. 308	J. Morrison
Virgin with Child on her Lap	4. 326	Sir T. Sebright
Samson	4. 333	Duke of Bedford
His own Portrait	4. 336	Duke of Bedford
The Magdalen Seated	4. 389	Lord Heytesbury
Christ and the Woman of Samaria	4. 396	Lord Methuen
Infant Christ bearing Cross	4. 398	Lord Methuen
Dying Tancred lamented by Herminia	4. 410	Smith Barry
Lot and his Daughters	4. 426	Rev. T. Staniforth
Esther before Ahasuerus	4. 470	Duke of Northumberland
St. Peter Repentant	4. 497	W. Drury Lowe
Painting, Woman with Palette	4. 504	Earl of Yarborough
GUIDO, Reni		
Magdalen	1. 316, 337	National Gallery
Lot and his Daughters	1. 317, 338	,,
Susanna and the Elders	1. 317, 338	,,
Coronation of the Virgin	1. 337	,,
Perseus and Andromeda	1. 338	,,
Venus adored by the Hours	1. 338	,,

	VOL. & PAGE		OWNER
Aurora (*copy*)	1.	394	Duke of Northumberland
Infant Christ Sleeping	2.	36	Bridgewater House
Archangel Michael	2.	36	Bridgewater House
Mary Magdalen	2.	64	Duke of Sutherland
The Circumcision	2.	64	,,
Hippomenes and Atalanta	2.	64	,,
A Christ	2.	78	S. Rogers
Salome receiving the Head of the Baptist	2.	87	Earl of Yarborough
Perseus and Andromeda	2.	91	Devonshire House
Head of Christ	2.	101	Lord Ashburton
Triumph of Heavenly over Earthly Love	2.	113	H. T. Hope
Europa and the Bull	2.	135	H. A. J. Munro
Cleopatra, Full Length	2.	135	,,
St. Sebastian	2.	135	,,
Fortune	2.	170	Marquis of Westminster
The Nativity	2.	170	Marquis of Westminster
Ecce Homo	2.	180	T. Baring
St. James the Elder	2.	198	R. S. Holford
Virgin and Child and St. John	2.	198	R. S. Holford
St. Michael combating Satan	2.	227	Hon. E. Phipps
Death of Abel	2.	236	Lord Ward
St. Sebastian	2.	236	Lord Ward
Mater Dolorosa	2.	244	Joseph Neeld
Virgin holding Doves	2.	283	Duke of Bedford
St. Sebastian	2.	346	Dulwich Gallery
Judith with the Head of Holofernes	2.	360	Hampton Court
Cleopatra and the Asp	2.	434	Windsor Castle
Hercules and Cacus	2.	476	Charles I
Venus attired by the Graces	2.	476	,,
Judith cutting off the Head of Holofernes	2.	476	,,
Mary Magdalen	2.	476	,,
Infant Christ Sleeping	2.	494	Orleans Gallery
Mary Magdalen	2.	494	,,
Beheading John the Baptist	2.	494	,,
St. Bonaventura	2.	494	,,
Ecce Homo	2.	494	,,
A Sibyl	2.	494	,,
Triumph of Heavenly Love	2.	495	,,
Mary Magdalen	2.	495	,,
Martyrdom of St. Apollonia	2.	495	,,
Susanna and the Elders	2.	495	,,
Mater Dolorosa	2.	495	,,
David and Abigail	2.	495	,,
St. Sebastian	2.	495	,,

GUIDO, Reni—*continued*

	VOL. & PAGE	OWNER
A Sibyl	3. 15	Earl Cowper
Liberality and Modesty	3. 21	Earl of Darnley
Daughter of Herodias, and Head	3. 21	,,
Head of St. Francis	3. 21	,,
Head of repentant Magdalen	3. 21	,,
Magdalen	3. 140	Earl of Radnor
Adoration of the Shepherds	3. 170	Earl of Suffolk
St. Francis (a Sketch)	3. 172	Colt Hoare
Cleopatra	3. 184	J. P. Miles
Assumption of the Virgin	3. 190	Mr. Harford
The Crucifixion	3. 190	,,
Ecce Homo	3. 190	,,
St. Veronica	3. 192	,,
St. Matthew with Angel	3. 200	Lord Northwick
Virgin and sleeping Child	3. 200	Lord Northwick
St. Francis kneeling in Prayer	3. 264	Earl of Lonsdale
Ecce Homo	3. 275	Edinburgh R.I.
A Picture	3. 314	Captain Sterling
John the Baptist (whole length)	3. 332	Meynell Ingram
St Margaret with the Dragon	3. 333	Meynell Ingram
Cupid Sleeping	3. 340	Earl Fitzwilliam
Magdalen and 2 Angels	3. 384	Earl of Shrewsbury
Boy presenting the Head of the Baptist	3. 384	,,
A Bishop	3. 384	,,
Bacchus standing by Ariadne	3. 393	Lord Scarsdale
Boy with a Pigeon	3. 405	Marquis of Exeter
Joseph and Potiphar's Wife	3. 420	Earl of Leicester
Cupid in Car drawn by Doves	3. 422	Earl of Leicester
Venus and Cupid (whole length)	3. 430	A. Fountaine
Ecce Homo	4. 61	National Gallery
David holding the Head of Goliath	4. 67	Earl of Yarborough
Daughter of Herodias, and Head	4. 68	Earl of Yarborough
Sleeping Christ and Virgin	4. 136	Lord Overstone
A Sibyl, pointing	4. 142	Lord Overstone
St. Matthew reading	4. 150	Earl of Caledon
Triumph of Silenus	4. 152	Earl of Caledon
Fortuna	4. 170	Lord Wensleydale
The penitent Magdalen	4. 239	R. P. Nichols
St. Lucy (half length)	4. 240	R. P. Nichols
La Madonna della Pace	4. 262	Duc D'Aumale
Virgin seated with Infant	4. 271	Earl of Jersey
Magdalen looking upwards	4. 324	Lord Enfield
St. Jerome with Crucifix	4. 326	Sir T. Sebright
Virgin and Child	4. 344	Countess of Warwick

	VOL. & PAGE		OWNER
Saint with Infant Christ	4.	344	Countess of Warwick
The Magdalen	4.	358	Lord Folkestone
Jupiter and Europa	4.	359	Lord Folkestone
Flora, Hand on Pedestal	4.	367	Earl of Normanton
David and Abigail	4.	492	Lord Feversham
A Charity	4.	493	,,
St. Catherine with a Palm	4.	493	,,
Bacchus and Ariadne	4.	493	,,
Infant Christ Sleeping	4.	503	Earl of Yarborough
Mater Dolorosa	4.	505	Earl of Yarborough
Artemisia	4.	510	Duke of Newcastle

GUTTIERREZ, Juan Simon

St. Francis in Ecstasy	3.	240	Liverpool R.I.

GYSELS, Peter

Landscape, 1682	2.	122	H. T. Hope
Peacock, Swan, Heron, etc.	2.	124	H. T. Hope
Dead Game	4.	268	Duke of Northumberland
Swan, Roe, Hare, etc.	4.	309	J. Morrison

	VOL. & PAGE	OWNER
HACKAERT, Jan		
Hunting Party pursuing a Stag	1. 411	Sir R. Peel
Beech Wood near The Hague	2. 71	Duke of Sutherland
Lofty Trees near Water, with Adrian Van de Velde	2. 153	Marquis of Lansdowne
Stag pursued by Hounds	2. 255	Mr. Heusch
Mountainous Landscape and River	3. 481	Marquis of Bute
Woods at The Hague	4. 134	Lord Overstone
Large Landscape	4. 342	Humphrey Mildmay
A Wood, 1665	4. 481	Matthew Anderson
A composition with cattle by Van de Velde	4. 504	Earl of Yarborough
HACKAERT, Philip		
Landscape with Cattle, 1799	4. 451	W. Stirling
Landscape with Cattle, 1799	4. 451	W. Stirling
HAGHE, Louis		
Monks giving Drink to Pilgrims (drawing)	4. 415	Mr. Cooke
Interior of Hôtel de Ville (drawing)	4. 416	S. Ashton
HALS, Frank		
A Man holding a Glove	2. 4	Buckingham Palace
A Man	2. 94	Devonshire House
Male Portrait in Profile	2. 227	Hon. E. Phipps
A Portrait	2. 243	H. Danby Seymour
Young Musicians	2. 246	Joseph Neeld
Man in a broad Hat	3. 36	Petworth
A Dutch General in yellow Uniform	3. 262	Earl of Lonsdale
A Young Man	4. 214	Mrs. Andrew James
His own Portrait	4. 335	Duke of Bedford
Old Man (circular)	4. 354	Lord Folkestone
A Woman (circular)	4. 354	Lord Folkestone
An old Woman	4. 512	Duke of Portland
HARLOW, G. H.		
Trial of Queen Catherine	4. 311	J. Morrison

	VOL. & PAGE	OWNER
HART, Solomon, R.A.		
The Synagogue	1. 374	Marlborough House
Administration of the Sacrament	2. 142	H. A. J. Munro
HAYTER, Sir George		
Trial of Lord W. Russell	4. 332	Duke of Bedford
HEERE, Lucas de		
Eleanor Brandon, 1550	3. 342	W. V. Wentworth
HEMSKERK, Martin		
The Last Judgment	2. 358	Hampton Court
HERBERT, J. R., R.A.		
Sir Thomas More and Daughter	1. 374	Marlborough House
Lear disinheriting Cordelia	1. 428	Palace of Westminster
Marini Falieri as Doge	4. 414	Mr. Cooke
Baptism of King Ethelred	4. 416	S. Ashton
Lear banishing Cordelia	4. 419	J. Chapman
HERRARA, Francesco de		
St. Francis with the Stigmata	2. 259	G. A. Hoskins
Joseph and Infant Christ	4. 476	W. W. Bardon
HERRERA el Viego		
Legend of S. Bonaventura	2. 458	Earl of Clarendon
HILDEBRANDT, Edward		
Grey Horse reflected in Water, 1848	4. 178	Rev. Mr. Townshend
HILLIARD, Nicholas		
Miniatures	4. 512	Duke of Portland
HILTON, William, R.A.		
Sir Calepine delivering Serena	1. 372	Marlborough House
Abraham's servant and Rebecca	1. 372	„
Editha and Body of Harold	1. 372	„
Triumph of Galatea	2. 350	E. Bicknell
Diana and Nymphs Bathing	4. 91	Marquis of Hertford
Una and Comus	4. 301	J. Morrison
Penelope recognizing Ulysses	4. 303	J. Morrison
HOARE, W., R.A.		
Earl of Chesterfield (crayon)	4. 495	Earl of Harrington

	VOL. & PAGE	OWNER
HOBBEMA, Minderhout		
Richly wooded Landscape	1. 410	Sir R. Peel
A Water Mill	1. 410	,,
Ruins of a Castle	1. 410	,,
The Avenue	1. 410	,,
Watermill and Farmhouses	2. 21	Buckingham Palace
Road and many Figures	2. 21	Buckingham Palace
A Village among Trees	2. 49	Bridgewater House
Watermill, 1657	2. 50	Bridgewater House
Village lying amongst Trees	2. 111	Lord Ashburton
Houses, Figures on a Road	2. 122	H. T. Hope
Watermill and House and Water	2. 160	Marquis of Hertford
Wooded Village, Horseman, etc.	2. 166	Marquis of Westminster
Road over a Common	2. 166	Marquis of Westminster
Trees, Water, with a Boat	2. 187	T. Baring
Road through a Wood	2. 202	R. S. Holford
Landscape, Massive Oaks, etc.	2. 225	Richard Ford
Landscape, 1663	2. 251	Lord Hatherton
Landscape, 1665	2 255	Mr. Heusch
Cottage and Trees	2. 255	Mr. Heusch
Wide Stream, Boat, 2 Men	2. 290	Charles Bredel
Landscape, Gleams of Sunshine	2. 297	Wynn Ellis
A Watermill	2. 297	Wynn Ellis
Landscape	2. 336	Frederic Perkins
A Watermill	3. 35	Petworth
Landscape and Three Figures	3. 35	,,
A Dark Wood	3. 41	,,
Landscape	3. 134	J. Morrison
Landscape, 2 pointed Steeples	3. 159	Marquis of Lansdowne
Village in Trees, Bridge	3. 161	,,
Village in Sunshine, Water	3. 161	,,
Landscape with much Wood	3. 191	Mr. Harford
A wooded Landscape	3. 272	Edinburgh R.I.
A wooded Landscape, Boat and 3 Men	3. 274	Edinburgh R.I.
Landscape, light Cornfield	3. 287	M'Lellan Gallery
Houses and Trees near piece of Water	3. 288	,,
Cottage and Country People	3. 290	,,
Trees and Houses near piece of Water	3. 301	Duke of Hamilton
Houses among stiff Trees	3. 336	Chas. Wynn
A Landscape	3. 407	Marquis of Exeter
Village, Road with Trees	3. 481	Marquis of Bute
A Watermill, Footbridge	3. 481	Marquis of Bute
Village in Sunshine, etc.	4. 89	Marquis of Hertford
Landscape and Trees, Village at back	4. 139	Lord Overstone
A Mill, Gentleman and Lady	4. 141	Lord Overstone

N

HOBBEMA, Minderhout—*continued*

	VOL. & PAGE		OWNER
Haarlem Sluish at Amsterdam	4.	156	H. St. John Mildmay
Village, two Beggars	4.	161	A. Robarts
Landscape and Trees	4.	182	G. C. Legh
A Wood, Man on a grey Horse	4.	194	G. Field
Water, Woman dragging a Cow	4.	296	J. Walter
Cottage, Woman and 2 Men	4.	307	J. Morrison
Cottages, 4 Oxen and a Shepherd	4.	322	Lord Enfield
A Picture	4.	374	Sir W. Knighton
Houses and Church, etc.	4.	392	Lord Arundel
A Picture	4.	404	Joseph Gillott
Village, dark piece of Water	4.	422	Earl of Burlington
Villages on broad Plain	4	423	,,
Group of Trees, Figures	4.	424	,,
Piece of Water, Cow and Goat	4.	440	Earl of Wemyss
Watermill and Village	4.	455	Earl of Dunmore
Landscape	4.	458	M'Lellan Gallery
Large Landscape	4.	459	M'Lellan Gallery
Large Landscape, Rain Clouds	4.	492	Lord Feversham

HOGARTH, William

	VOL. & PAGE		OWNER
Marriage à la Mode, 6 Pictures	1.	363	Marlborough House
His own Portrait, 1745	1.	364	Marlborough House
Harlot's Progress, upsetting Table	2.	140	H. A. J. Munro
Harlot's Progress, Workhouse	2.	140	H. A. J. Munro
Distressed Poet	2.	172	Marquis of Westminster
Boy holding a Plan	2.	172	Marquis of Westminster
Two Pictures	2.	188	T. Baring
An old Woman	2.	229	Hon. E. Phipps
Gates of Calais	2.	249	Earl of Charlemont
Gamblers' last Stake	2.	249	Earl of Charlemont
Covent Garden Market	2.	284	Duke of Bedford
Four Election Scenes	2.	321	Sir J. Soane
Eight pictures, Rake's Progress	2.	321	Sir J. Soane
Music Master directing Pupils	3.	35	Petworth
The " Cognoscenti "	3.	38	,,
A Punch drinking party	3.	38	,,
A young Woman	3.	160	Marquis of Lansdowne
A Female Portrait	3.	185	J. P. Miles
The Shrimp Girl	3.	186	J. P. Miles
Dice Players	3.	210	Lord Northwick
Garrick as Richard III	3.	316	Lord Feversham
Family of the Earl of Rockingham	3.	339	Earl Fitzwilliam
Family Group	3.	431	A. Fountaine

	VOL. & PAGE	OWNER
Female Portrait	4. 103	H. D. Seymour
The Punch Club	4. 303	J. Morrison
His own Portrait	4. 335	Duke of Bedford
Three Girls and a Boy, Cat, etc.	4. 369	Earl of Normanton
Lady in Profile	4. 433	Gibson Craig
Harlot's Progress, Tea Table	4. 438	Earl of Wemyss

HOGUET
Landscape with Windmill	4. 177	Rev. Mr. Townshend

HOLBEIN, Hans
A Male Portrait (School)	1. 317	National Gallery
A Portrait	1. 349	National Gallery
Archbishop Warham	1. 429	Lambeth Palace
Man in light Hat and golden Fleece	2. 73	Duke of Sutherland
Duke of Norfolk	2. 86	Duke of Norfolk
Middle-aged Man in furred Robe	2. 93	Devonshire House
Head with Hands	2. 112	Lord Ashburton
Duke of Saxony	2. 199	R. S. Holford
Two other Portraits	2. 199	R. S. Holford
A Male Portrait	2. 237	Lord Ward
Henry VIII	2. 241	H. D. Seymour
A plump Child	2. 242	H. D. Seymour
Female with many Jewels, 1536	2. 245	Joseph Neeld
A Male Portrait, 1547	2. 245	Joseph Neeld
Henry VIII and Barber Surgeons	2. 328	Barbers' Hall
Edward VI on Throne	2. 328	Bridewell
Male Portrait in a rich Dress	2. 331	C. S. Bale
A Female Portrait	2. 332	C. S. Bale
Lady Vaux	2. 361	Hampton Court
The Battle of Pavia	2. 362	„
Henry VIII's Jester	2. 362	„
Henry VIII (youthful)	2. 362	„
A Man and a Woman	2. 362	„
Sir Henry Guildford, 1527	2. 362	„
Erasmus	2. 363	„
Frobenius	2. 363	„
His own Portrait	2. 364	„
Erasmus	2. 364	„
Henry VIII and Family	2. 366	„
Henry VIII embarking at Dover	2. 366	„
Drawing of a Female Saint	2. 420	H. Labouchere
Thomas, Duke of Norfolk	2. 430	Windsor Castle
Sir Henry Guildford	2. 430	„

HOLBEIN, Hans—*continued*

	VOL. & PAGE		OWNER
Young Man with a Cap	2.	430	Windsor Castle
Dr. Stokesby, Bishop of London	2.	431	,,
Man opening Letter, 1532	2.	431	,,
Edward VI	2.	431	,,
Henry VIII	2.	432	,,
A Merchant in Cap	2.	471	Charles I
Gentleman, pointed Beard	2.	471	,,
Gentleman in black Cap	2.	471	,,
Erasmus	2.	471	,,
Frobenius the Printer	2.	471	,,
Henry VIII	2.	471	,,
Henry VIII (circle)	2.	471	,,
Two Children of Duke of Brandon	2.	471	,,
Sir Thomas More	2.	471	,,
Queen Elizabeth when young	2.	472	,,
Henry VIII and Queen, etc.	2.	472	,,
Virgin, Christ, etc.	2.	483	,,
Portrait of Gysett	2.	500	Orleans Gallery
A Portrait	2.	500	Orleans Gallery
Young Man in furred Coat	3.	6	W. Fuller Maitland
Young Man in brown Dress	3.	6	W. Fuller Maitland
A Reformer in furred Cap	3.	23	Earl of Darnley
Christine, Daughter of Christian II	3.	29	Duke of Norfolk
Duke and Duchess of Norfolk	3.	30	,,
Duke of Norfolk (Staffs of Office)	3.	30	,,
Duke of Norfolk (Staffs of Office)	3.	31	,,
Female with Ring on Finger	3.	33	Petworth
Edward VI under Canopy, 1547	3.	36	,,
Henry VIII (whole-length)	3.	41	,,
Man with Falcon on Wrist	3.	41	,,
Man with a Letter	3.	41	,,
A Male Head	3.	123	Duke of Marlborough
Erasmus	3.	138	Earl of Radnor
Peter Ægydius	3.	139	,,
The Ambassadors	3.	139	,,
Luther	3.	139	,,
Anthony Denny	3.	139	,,
Œcolampadius	3.	140	,,
Edward VI	3.	140	,,
Father of Sir Thos. More	3.	152	Earl of Pembroke
William First, Earl of Pembroke	3.	152	,,
Edward VI, with Flower	3.	152	,,
Lord Cromwell (drawing)	3.	152	,,
Catherine Howard	3.	170	Earl of Suffolk

	VOL. & PAGE	OWNER
Undraped Figure, Bow and Arrow	3. 185	J. P. Miles
Fisher, Bishop of Rochester	3. 210	Lord Northwick
Henry VIII	3. 215	Earl of Warwick
Man in attitude of Prayer	3. 225	Mr. Martin
The Prodigal Son	3. 236	Liverpool R.I.
Sir Thomas More	3. 252	Blundell Weld
A Female Portrait	3. 264	Earl of Lonsdale
Sir Nicholas Carew	3. 313	Duke of Buccleuch
Duke of Norfolk	3. 323	Earl of Carlisle
Henry VIII	3. 323	Earl of Carlisle
A Male Portrait	3. 334	Meynell Ingram
Sir T. More and Family	3. 334	C. Wynn
Œcolampadius	3. 342	W. V. Wentworth
Henry VIII	3. 346	Duke of Devonshire
Head of an old Man	3. 347	,,
The Wheel of Fortune	3. 351	,,
Portrait of a Man	3. 388	Earl of Shrewsbury
Several Portraits	3. 394	Lord Berners
Henry VIII (full-length)	3. 398	Duke of Rutland
Henry VIII (half-length)	3. 407	Marquis of Exeter
Edward VI	3. 407	Marquis of Exeter
Anne Boleyn	3. 428	Sir J. Boileau
Woman with folded Hands	3. 443	George Tomline
A small Circle, 1527	3. 443	George Tomline
Henry VIII	3. 456	Earl Spencer
Henry VIII, Pss. Mary and Sommers	3. 456	Earl Spencer
Catherine Parr	3. 462	Glendon Hall
Several Portraits	3. 464	Duke of Bedford
James, King of Scotland, etc.	3. 482	Marquis of Bute
Henry VIII	3. 482	Marquis of Bute
Edward VI as Infant	4. 67	Earl of Yarborough
Henry VIII	4. 67	Earl of Yarborough
Man with long Hair and Hat	4. 77	A. Barker
Johann Herbster	4. 97	T. Baring
Queen Mary when young	4. 119	C. S. Bale
Edward VI as a Child	4. 269	Duke of Northumberland
Protector, Duke of Somerset	4. 269	Duke of Northumberland
Sir Thomas Gresham	4. 272	Earl of Jersey
John Russell	4. 331	Duke of Bedford
Henry VIII	4. 339	Knole
Sir Anthony Denny	4. 355	Lord Folkestone
Calvin	4. 356	,,
Œcolampadius	4. 356	,,
Beza	4. 356	,,
Erasmus	4. 356	,,

	VOL. & PAGE	OWNER
HOLBEIN, Hans—*continued*		
Peter Ægydius	4. 357	Lord Folkestone
The Ambassadors	4. 359	„
Male Portrait, called Luther	4. 360	„
Lady Carey	4. 361	„
Lady Jane Grey	4. 364	Earl of Normanton
Sir Nicholas Carew	4. 435	Duke of Buccleuch
Female with Pink	4. 461	M'Lellan Gallery
Lord Cromwell	4. 464	Lord Douglas
Sir Thomas More	4. 464	Lord Douglas
Henry VIII	4. 498	W. Drury Lowe
Man in black Dress and Cap	4. 509	Duke of Newcastle
Male Portrait with Cap and Baton	4. 511	Duke of Newcastle
Man in black Dress, and Palm	4. 515	Duke of Portland
Nicolas Kratzer	4. 516	Lord Galway
Henry VIII standing	4. 517	Lord Galway
HONDEKOETER, Melchior		
Barn-door Family	1. 358	National Gallery
Cocks and Hens, etc., and Dog	2. 23	Buckingham Palace
Dead Hare, etc.	2. 23	Buckingham Palace
Two Swans and Peacocks	2. 124	H. T. Hope
Fruit Pieces	2. 124	H. T. Hope
Family of Cocks and Hens	2. 258	George Young
Birds	2. 360	Hampton Court
Hawk, etc.	2. 422	H. Labouchere
Turkey-cock, etc.	2. 422	H. Labouchere
Poultry	3. 290	M'Lellan Gallery
Poultry	3. 334	Meynell Ingram
Turkey-cock and Chickens	3. 423	Earl of Leicester
Large Poultry Piece	3. 428	Joseph Muskett
Cock, Peacock, and other Birds	4. 91	Marquis of Hertford
Fowls	4. 192	H. T. Hope
Fowls	4. 192	H. T. Hope
Family of Fowls and Peacock	4. 206	Mr. Henderson
Turkey-cock and Fowls	4. 264	Duc D'Aumale
Fowls	4. 352	Vernon Harcourt
White Hen in open Air	4. 385	H. D. Seymour
Fowls	4. 403	E. Bullock
Hen and four Chickens	4. 440	Earl of Wemyss
Poultry	4. 459	M'Lellan Gallery
White Peacock, Pheasant, etc.	4. 508	Sir John Nelthorpe
Geese, Ducks, etc.	4. 508	Sir John Nelthorpe
Waterfowls	4. 512	Duke of Portland

	VOL. & PAGE		OWNER
Family of Hen and Chickens	4.	512	Duke of Portland
Poultry	4.	515	„
Poultry	4.	515	„

HONTHORST, Gerard

Christ before Caiaphas	2.	70	Duke of Sutherland
Queen of Bohemia (full-length)	2.	358	Hampton Court
Villiers, Duke of Buckingham	2.	360	Hampton Court
Queen of Bohemia	2.	455	Earl of Clarendon
Eight Pictures	2.	482	Charles I
Prince Rupert	3.	154	Earl of Pembroke
Christ before Pilate	3.	206	Lord Northwick
Queen of Bohemia	3.	219	Earl of Craven
King of Bohemia	3.	219	„
Charles I	3.	219	„
Prince Rupert	3.	219	„
Gerard Honthorst	3.	219	„
Circe and Nymphs, and Swine	3.	252	Blundell Weld
Peter released from Prison	3.	294	Sir A. Campbell
Finding of Moses	3.	319	Earl of Carlisle
A Concert	3.	326	Earl of Carlisle
A Mother and two Sons	3.	364	Duke of Devonshire
An Ecce Homo	3.	387	Earl of Shrewsbury
Christ at Emmaus	4.	262	Duc D'Aumale
Christ on Mount of Olives	4.	412	Smith Barry
Christ mocked	4.	412	„
Christ before Pilate (candlelight)	4.	413	„
Peter delivered from Prison	4.	413	„
Christ mocked	4.	471	Duke of Northumberland
Adoration of Shepherds	4.	516	Duke of Portland

HOOGSTRAETEN, Van

A Picture	2.	52	Bridgewater House

HOOK, J. C., R.A.

Musicians on a Gondola	3.	211	Lord Northwick

HOPPNER, John, R.A.

Venus and Adonis	3.	37	Petworth
Lady Palmerston	4.	346	Earl Cowper

HORSLEY, J. C., R.A.

The Pride of the Village	1.	374	Marlborough House
Power of Religion	1.	427	House of Lords
The Rival Performers	2.	300	J. Sheepshanks

		VOL. & PAGE		OWNER
HOSKINS, John				
Miniatures		3.	408	Marquis of Exeter
Miniatures		4.	512	Duke of Portland
HOUBRAKEN, Arnold				
The Shame of Calisto		4.	200	James Tulloch
HOWARD, Henry, R.A.				
A Wood of old Beeches		3.	38	Petworth
HUCHTENBURG, Jan				
A Picture		2.	52	Bridgewater House
Landscape, Horses and Horsemen		4.	209	Mr. Henderson
Combat between Orientals		4.	478	J. Anderson
HUNT, William				
Two Fruit Pieces	(Drawing)	2.	352	E. Bicknell
A Girl	„	2.	352	„
A Blackamoor	„	2.	352	„
A young Girl seated	„	4.	415	Mr. Cooke
A Kitchen	„	4.	415	S. Ashton
HURLSTONE				
Cupid		3.	165	Marquis of Lansdowne
HUYSMAN, Cornelius				
A Picture		2.	42	Bridgewater House
Poetic Landscape		3.	271	Edinburgh R.I.
Landscape		4.	330	Sir T. Sebright
Landscape		4.	330	Sir T. Sebright

	VOL. & PAGE		OWNER
IL GOBBO, dai Frutti			
Fruit piece	3.	385	Earl of Shrewsbury
Fruit piece	3.	385	Earl of Shrewsbury
IMOLA, Innocenzo da			
Virgin and Child, after Raphael	2.	293	Wynn Ellis
Birth of Christ	2.	491	Orleans Gallery
St. Paul and Nicholas and Blaise	3.	199	Lord Northwick
Virgin and Child and St. John	3.	199	Lord Northwick
Altar-piece, Virgin kneeling	3.	376	Davenport Bromley
Altar-piece, Marriage of the Virgin	4.	149	Earl of Caledon
Virgin and Child and St. John, etc.	4.	364	Earl of Normanton
Virgin and Child, Joseph, and John	4.	454	Earl of Dunmore
Virgin and Child, St. Ursula, etc.	4.	503	Earl of Yarborough
INGANNATI, Pietro degli			
Virgin and Sleeping Child	2.	82	Lord Elcho
Marriage of St. Catherine	3.	237	Liverpool R.I.
Child on the Lap of the Virgin	4.	115	Sir C. Eastlake
IRIARTE			
Landscape and Figures	2.	259	G. A. Hoskins
ISABY			
Crowd of Children going to School	4.	214	Mrs. Andrew James
ITALIAN SCHOOL			
Adoration of Kings	4.	221	Prince Consort
IVAN de las Roclas			
A Monk	4.	450	W. Stirling

	VOL. & PAGE	OWNER
JACKSON, John, R.A.		
Flaxman	2. 152	Marquis of Lansdowne
Flaxman	2. 335	Lady Dover
JANET (François Clouet)		
Series of Portraits from the Lenoir Gallery	2. 73	Duke of Sutherland
Mary Stuart, Queen of Scots	2. 363	Hampton Court
Francis II as a Child	2. 363	Hampton Court
Henry II of France	2. 437	Windsor Castle
Eight Pictures	2. 482	Charles I
François, Duc d'Alençon, 1572	3. 25	Earl of Darnley
Eighty-eight Portraits in red Chalk	3. 321	Earl of Carlisle
Catherine de Medici	3. 322	Earl of Carlisle
Jean d'Albret of Navarre	3. 428	Sir J. Boileau
Francis II of France	3. 457	Earl Spencer
A Female Portrait	3. 457	Earl Spencer
A Lord Hertford in Cap and Feather	4. 83	Marquis of Hertford
Queen of Charles IX	4. 263	Duc d'Aumale
Henry II of France and his Son	4. 263	„
Jeanne d'Albret, Limoges Enamel	4. 263	„
JANSEN, Cornelius		
Charles I and Court in Green Park	2. 4	Buckingham Palace
Portrait of a Man	2. 246	Joseph Neeld
Frederick, King of Bohemia	2. 364	Hampton Court
George, Duke of Buckingham	2. 456	Earl of Clarendon
A Female Portrait, 1657	2. 464	Rev. Mr. Russell
Portraits	3. 142	Earl of Radnor
Charles I	3. 170	Earl of Suffolk
Lord Aylesbury	3. 170	Earl of Suffolk
A young Girl	3. 310	Earl of Hopetown
Charles I, when young	3. 346	Duke of Devonshire
Henry Prince of Wales	3. 392	Lord Scarsdale
Lady Dorothy Nevill	3. 408	Marquis of Exeter
A Man	3. 462	Glendon Hall
A Woman	3. 462	Glendon Hall
His own Portrait	4. 356	Lord Folkestone
Mr. Taylor, Master of Revels	4. 361	Lord Folkestone
Male Portrait holding Glove	4. 412	Smith Barry
Queen of Bohemia	4. 495	Earl of Harrington

	VOL. & PAGE	OWNER
KALF, William		
A Fruit piece	2. 413	Hampton Court
KATWICK		
Small Landscape	4. 361	Lord Folkestone
KAUFFMANN, Angelica		
Religion and the Virtues	1. 358	National Gallery
Duchess of Brunswick	2. 368	Hampton Court
Three from Abelard and Eloisa	3. 407	Marquis of Exeter
Fame and Tomb of Shakespeare	3. 407	,,
Eleven other Pictures	3. 407	,,
Thirteen Pictures	4. 282	Sir C. Eardley
Coriolanus	4. 325	Lord Enfield
Several other Pictures	4. 325	Lord Enfield
KESSELS (Belgian Sculptor)		
A Discobolus	3. 366	Duke of Devonshire
KESSLER		
A Male Portrait, 1624	3. 40	Petworth
KIRNER, Johann		
Roman Revolution, 1848	4. 177	Rev. Mr. Townshend
KLOMP		
Cattle piece	3. 450	Cambridge University
Cattle piece	3. 450	Cambridge University
KNELLER, Sir Godfrey		
Seven Beauties of Court of William III	2. 355	Hampton Court
Peter the Great, 1698	2. 356	,,
Louis XIV (a drawing)	2. 368	,,
Duchess of Marlborough	3. 122	Duke of Marlborough
Shakespeare	3. 339	Earl Fitzwilliam
Gentleman in flowing Wig	3. 364	Duke of Devonshire
Family Portraits	3. 408	Marquis of Exeter
Sir John Robinson	3. 476	Marquis of Bute

	VOL. & PAGE	OWNER
KNELLER, Sir Godfrey—*continued*		
His own Portrait	4. 335	Duke of Bedford
Alexander Pope	4. 348	Vernon Harcourt
A Woman with a Child	4. 379	Kingston Lacy
Duchess of Marlborough	4. 433	Gibson Craig
Two Portraits	4. 463	Lord Douglas
A Portrait	4. 464	,,
A Portrait	4. 464	,,
John, Duke of Marlborough	4. 495	Earl of Harrington
KNUPFER		
George, Duke of Buckingham and brother, after Vandyck	2. 360	Hampton Court
KOEKKOEK, B. C.		
The Rhine at Coblentz	2. 192	T. Baring
A Winter Landscape	2. 192	T. Baring
A Winter Landscape	2. 329	Mr. Oppenheim
Daylight Landscape	4. 165	A. Robarts
KOEKKOEK, H.		
A Storm, Stranded Boat, 1842	4. 368	Earl of Normanton
KOEKKOEK, J. H.		
An agitated Sea, 1835	4. 521	Earl of Hardwicke
An agitated Sea, Sailing Boats, 1841	4. 522	,,
An agitated Sea, Sailing Boats, 1841	4. 522	,,
KONINCK, Solomon		
Young Man reading, 1630	2. 42	Bridgewater House
A Rabbi in a Chair	3. 345	Duke of Devonshire
Daniel and Nebuchadnezzar	3. 391	Lord Scarsdale
Nathan and David	4. 358	Lord Folkestone
KRUG, L.		
The Nativity	3. 236	Liverpool R.I.
KUPETSKY, Johann		
His own Portrait	4. 335	Duke of Bedford

	VOL. & PAGE	OWNER
LAAR, Pieter de		
Boys	2. 501	Orleans Gallery
LAGUERRE, Louis		
Large Pictures	3. 403	Marquis of Exeter
LAHIRE		
Landscape with a Riposo	3. 222	Howard Galton
LAIRESSE, Gerard		
Death of Cleopatra	2. 119	H. T. Hope
Jupiter and Antiope	3. 186	J. P. Miles
The Disgrace of Haman	3. 387	Earl of Shrewsbury
Coronation of Solomon	4. 482	Matthew Anderson
Death of Ananias	4. 495	Earl of Harrington
LANCE, George		
A Fruit piece	1. 388	Marlborough House
Fruit in Golden Vessel	4. 144	Lord Overstone
LANCRET		
The Four Ages	1. 346	National Gallery
A Picture	2. 93	Devonshire House
A Family Picture	3. 428	Sir J. Boileau
Ladies and Cavaliers, etc.	4. 84	Marquis of Hertford
LANDSEER, Charles, R.A.		
Clarissa Harlowe	1. 378	Marlborough House
Girl surprised with a Letter	2. 190	T. Baring
The Hermit	2. 306	J. Sheepshanks
Maria and her Dog	2. 306	J. Sheepshanks
LANDSEER, Sir Edwin, R.A.		
High Life	1. 382	Marlborough House
Low Life	1. 382	,,
Highland Music	1. 382	,,
King Charles' Spaniels	1. 382	,,
The Dying Stag (Mountain Torrent)	1. 382	,,
Miss Peel	1. 414	Sir R. Peel

	VOL. & PAGE		OWNER
LANDSEER, Sir Edwin, R.A.—*continued*			
Master Ponsonby on grey Horse	2.	84	Lord de Mauley
Travelled Monkey	2.	190	T. Baring
A Dog and a Cat	2.	229	Lord Ward
Larder invaded	2.	258	Sir C. Coote
Highlander and Family	2.	274	Duke of Wellington
Van Amberg and Animals	2.	277	Duke of Wellington
Roebuck and Rough Hounds	2.	300	J. Sheepshanks
Highland Breakfast	2.	300	,,
Highland Drovers	2.	300	,,
Angler's Guard	2.	301	,,
Dog and the Shadow	2.	302	,,
Four Dogs and Huntsman	2.	302	,,
The Eagle's Nest	2.	305	,,
Jack in Office	2.	306	,,
Shepherd's Chief Mourner	2.	306	,,
Tethered Rams	2.	306	,,
Highland Shepherd's Home	2.	307	,,
Crossing the Bridge	3.	164	Marquis of Lansdowne
Dog and dead Wild Fowl	3.	242	John Naylor
Bolton Abbey	3.	351	Duke of Devonshire
Chevy Chase	3.	466	Duke of Bedford
Brown Dog, Ptarmigan, etc.	4.	185	Wm. Russell
A Dead Lion	4.	189	Wm. Russell
Deerstalkers	4.	266	Duke of Northumberland
Stag Hunt (Chevy Chase)	4.	332	Duke of Bedford
Stags in Woburn Park	4.	332	Duke of Bedford
Heads of 2 Greyhounds (drawing)	4.	415	Mr. Cooke
Black Dog (Keeper)	4.	418	J. Chapman
A Dog looking up	4.	418	,,
Three Dogs watching a Ferret	4.	418	,,
LANFRANCO			
Ecstasy of St. Francis	2.	36	Bridgewater House
Head of a Saint	2.	355	Hampton Court
Head of St. Peter	2.	358	,,
Head of Judas	2.	358	,,
The Annunciation	2.	491	Orleans Gallery
Belisarius	3.	190	Mr. Harford
Christ walking on the Sea	3.	405	Marquis of Exeter
His own Portrait	4.	335	Duke of Bedford
LARGILLIÈRE			
A Male Portrait	4.	263	Duc d'Aumale
A Man with powdered Wig	4.	508	Sir J. Nelthorpe

	VOL. & PAGE		OWNER
LAURI, Philipo			
A Picture	2.	39	Bridgewater House
A Picture	2.	93	Devonshire House
St. Joseph and Infant Christ	2.	227	Hon. E. Phipps
Jacob fleeing from Laban	2.	357	Hampton Court
Acis and Galatea	3.	198	Lord Northwick
A Picture	3.	403	Marquis of Exeter
LAWRENCE, Sir Thomas, P.R.A.			
J. J. Angerstein	1.	380	Marlborough House
Kemble, as Hamlet	1.	380	,,
Mrs. Siddons	1.	381	,,
Miss Peel	1.	414	Sir R. Peel
Duchess of Sutherland	2.	72	Duke of Sutherland
Lord Clanwilliam	2.	72	Duke of Sutherland
Lord Lansdowne	2.	153	Marquis of Lansdowne
A Male Figure	2.	189	T. Baring
Lady Calcott	2.	266	Miss Rogers
Rt. Hon. William Pitt	2.	337	Miss Wilbraham
William Linley	2.	348	Dulwich Gallery
Mrs. Siddons	2.	351	E. Bicknell
M. von Gentz	2.	413	Hampton Court
Two Children of the Labouchere family	2.	422	H. Labouchere
Duke of Wellington	2.	424	Windsor Castle
Blücher	2.	424	,,
Platoff	2.	424	,,
Prince Schwartzenburg	2.	424	,,
Archduke Charles	2.	424	,,
Emperor Francis	2.	425	,,
King of Prussia	2.	425	,,
Emperor of Russia	2.	425	,,
Prince Hardenberg	2.	425	,,
Cardinal Gonsalvi	2.	425	,,
Count Nesselrode	2.	425	,,
Pope Pius VII	2.	425	,,
George IV	2.	425	,,
Duke of York	2.	425	,,
Duke of Cambridge	2.	425	,,
Lord Castlereagh	2.	425	,,
Lord Liverpool	2.	425	,,
Prince Metternich	2.	425	,,
Count Cape d' Istria	2.	425	,,
General Tchernicheff	2.	425	,,
William von Humboldt	2.	425	,,

	VOL. & PAGE		OWNER
LAWRENCE, Sir Thomas, P.R.A.—*continued*			
Canning	2.	425	Windsor Castle
Earl Bathurst	2.	425	,,
General Ouvaroff	2.	425	,,
M. von Gentz	2.	425	,,
Duchess of Norfolk	3.	31	Duke of Norfolk
Lady Lansdowne	3.	166	Marquis of Lansdowne
A Male Portrait	3.	169	Earl of Suffolk
Mrs. Harford	3.	191	Mr. Harford
Cardinal Gonsalvi	3.	193	,,
Mr. Harford	3.	193	,,
Duke of Devonshire	3.	325	Earl of Carlisle
Earl Fitzwilliam	3.	339	Earl Fitzwilliam
Portraits	3.	408	Marquis of Exeter
Lady Westmoreland	3.	411	Earl of Westmoreland
A Female Portrait	3.	466	Duke of Bedford
Duke of Northumberland	4.	266	Duke of Northumberland
George IV	4.	338	Knole
Lord Normanton	4.	369	Earl of Normanton
Lady Normanton	4.	373	Earl of Normanton
Portrait	4.	374	Sir W. Knighton
Miss Ridley	4.	379	Kingston Lacy
Portrait	4.	379	Kingston Lacy
Sir Sidney Smith	4.	478	J. Anderson
Lord Hardwicke	4.	518	Earl of Hardwicke
LE BRUN, Charles			
Horatius Cocles and Bridge	2.	348	Dulwich Gallery
Murder of the Innocents	2.	348	Dulwich Gallery
Murder of the Innocents	2.	491	Orleans Gallery
Hercules killing Horses	2.	491	Orleans Gallery
Carrying off Bride of Pirithous	3.	25	Earl of Darnley
A Visitation	4.	493	Lord Feversham
Perseus and Andromeda	4.	506	Sir J. Nelthorpe
LE DUC, Jan			
Room with Family and Dog	3.	221	Howard Galton
Party Playing Cards	3.	273	Edinburgh R.I.
A Tavern, Soldier with Glass	3.	290	M'Lellan Gallery
Party of Officers and Ladies	3.	478	Marquis of Bute
LEE, F. R., R.A.			
Scene on Lincolnshire Coast	1.	386	Marlborough House
Landscape, Drove of Cattle	2.	190	T. Baring

	VOL. & PAGE		OWNER
A Picture	2.	353	E. Bicknell
Avenue, 3 Horses	4.	183	Wm. Marshall
Two Sportsmen, Hare, and Pheasants	4.	419	J. Chapman

LEERMAN, Peter
A Concert	2.	253	F. Heusch

LELIENBERG
Dead Game, 1657	3.	326	Earl of Carlisle

LELY, Sir Peter
Series of the Beauties of Charles II's Court	2.	360	Hampton Court
Prince Rupert	2.	430	Windsor Castle
Henry Lord Cornbury	2.	454	Earl of Clarendon
Diana, Lady Newport	2.	455	,,
First Earl of Clarendon	2.	457	,,
Dorothea, Countess of Sunderland	3.	24	Earl of Darnley
Eleventh Earl of Northumberland	3.	33	Petworth
Children of Charles I	3.	37	,,
A Lady	3.	43	,,
A Lady	3.	43	,,
Lady Morton and Mrs. Killigrew	3.	128	Duke of Marlborough
A Lady, full length	3.	134	Lord Dillon
A Lady, full length	3.	134	Lord Dillon
Viscount Brouncker	3.	227	Lord Lyttelton
One of the beauties of Charles II	3.	297	Duke of Hamilton
Lucy Walters	3.	313	Duke of Buccleuch
James, Duke of York	3.	323	Earl of Carlisle
Jocelyn, Earl of Northumberland	3.	323	,,
Duchess of Richmond	3.	323	,,
Ladies Anne and Arabella Wentworth	3.	338	Earl Fitzwilliam
Two Children	3.	338	,,
Duke of Gloucester	3.	340	,,
Prince Rupert	3.	340	,,
A Female Portrait	3.	342	W. V. Wentworth
Rape of Europa	3.	348	Duke of Devonshire
Duke of Gloucester	3.	378	W. Davenport Bromley
A Man and his Wife	3.	400	Duke of Rutland
Susanna and the Elders	3.	406	Marquis of Exeter
Portraits	3.	408	Marquis of Exeter
Children of Earl of Leicester	3.	460	Duke of Buccleuch
Charles II, seated	4.	234	Earl of Harrington
Charles I and Duke of York	4.	266	Duke of Northumberlan(
Duke of Cleveland	4.	339	Knole

	VOL. & PAGE	OWNER
LELY, Sir Peter—*continued*		
His own Portrait	4. 361	Lord Folkestone
Sir Ralph Bankes	4. 380	Kingston Lacy
Mr. Stafford	4. 380	,,
Lady Middleton	4. 380	,,
Mr. Gilly	4. 380	,,
Lady Jenkinson	4. 380	,,
Miss Bankes	4. 380	,,
A Woman holding Drapery	4. 439	Earl of Wemyss
Nell Gwyn	4. 463	Lord Douglas
Four Pictures	4. 463	,,
Five Pictures	4. 463	,,
A Male Portrait in Armour	4. 495	Earl of Harrington
Other Pictures	4. 495	Earl of Harrington
LE NAIN		
Seven Boys, 4 playing Cards	2. 23	Buckingham Palace
Children listening to Piper	2. 66	Duke of Sutherland
Children in a Landscape	2. 245	Joseph Neeld
Old Woman, Man and Boy	2. 280	Earl of Carlisle
Two Lads and a Girl playing Music	2. 291	Charles Bredel
Old Woman and 7 Children	3. 35	Petworth
A Family	3. 205	Lord Northwick
Intoxicated Woman on Ass	3. 262	Earl of Lonsdale
Children dancing to the whistling of a Boy	3. 263	,,
Boy riding on a Goat	3. 264	,,
A Boy with Sheep	3. 291	M'Lellan Gallery
Man, Boy, and Woman	3. 399	Duke of Rutland
The Artist's own Studio	3. 484	Marquis of Bute
French Peasant Family	4. 148	Earl of Caledon
Woman and 3 Children	4. 149	Earl of Caledon
Poor Family taking a Meal	4. 318	Rev. Mr. Heath
Four Men playing Dice	4. 455	Earl of Dunmore
LENS, Bernard		
Miniatures	4. 512	Duke of Portland
LESLIE, C. R., R.A.		
Sancho Panza and Duchess	1. 378	Marlborough House
Uncle Toby	1. 378	Marlborough House
Roger de Coverley	2. 153	Marquis of Lansdowne
Duchess and Sancho Panza	2. 268	Miss Rogers
Queen Victoria kneeling	2. 299	J. Sheepshanks
Uncle Toby and Widow Wadman	2. 299	,,

	VOL. & PAGE		OWNER
Scene from " Taming of the Shrew "	2.	300	J. Sheepshanks
Who can this be?	2.	301	,,
Who can this be from?	2.	301	,,
" Merry Wives of Windsor "	2.	301	,,
Catherine of Aragon and Ladies	2.	301	,,
Girl looking at Jewelry	2.	302	,,
Florizel and Perdita	2.	304	,,
Autolycus	2.	304	,,
Le Bourgeois Gentilhomme	2.	305	,,
Les Femmes Savantes	2.	305	,,
Le Malade Imaginaire	2.	305	,,
A Girl at a Window	2.	349	E. Bicknell
Gulliver and the Brobdingnags	3.	37	Petworth
Sancho Panza and Duchess	3.	37	Petworth
Sir Roger de Coverley	3.	165	Marquis of Lansdowne
Party of Ladies and Gentlemen	3.	241	John Naylor
Lady Jane Grey refusing Crown	4.	332	Duke of Bedford
Christ with Martha and Mary	4.	403	Mr. Birch
A Picture	4.	403	E. Bullock

LESUEUR, Eustache

Queen of Sheba and Solomon	2.	93	Devonshire House
Alexander and his Physician	2.	492	Orleans Gallery
Death of Germanicus	3.	186	J. P. Miles
A Crucifixion	3.	385	Earl of Shrewsbury
Magdalen anointing Feet of Christ	3.	406	Marquis of Exeter
The Annunciation	4.	369	Earl of Normanton
Pope Clement blessing St. Dionysius	4.	395	Lord Methuen
A Holy Family	4.	410	Smith Barry

LEYDEN, Lucas van

Maximilian I (drawing)	2.	80	S. Rogers
The Crucifixion	2.	86	Duke of Norfolk
St. Mark and St. John	2.	269	Miss Rogers
Three Pictures, St. Sebastian	2.	472	Charles I
St. Jerome	2.	472	,,
Joseph brought before the Judge	2.	472	,,
A Dying Man	2.	472	,,
Chess Player	2.	472	,,
Virgin and Child with Rosary	3.	6	W. Fuller Maitland
Young Man in Brown	3.	6	W. Fuller Maitland
Calvin	3.	23	Earl of Darnley
A Female Portrait	3.	33	Petworth
Men and Women at Cards	3.	152	Earl of Pembroke
A young Knight and St. Hubert	3.	236	Liverpool R.I.

	VOL. & PAGE	OWNER
LINNELL, John		
The Windmill	1. 387	Marlborough House
Landscape and Woodcutters	1. 387	Marlborough House
Pictures	4. 403	Edwin Bullock
A Landscape	4. 404	Joseph Gillott
Landscape and Cattle, Cow being milked	4. 418	J. Chapman
LIPPI, Filippo		
Child caressing Virgin	2. 231	Lord Ward
Adoration of the Kings	3. 3	W. Fuller Maitland
St. Peter and John at Beautiful Gate	3. 3	W. Fuller Maitland
Procession of Virgins	3. 53	Oxford University
A Youth, " Antolinez "	3. 196	Lord Northwick
Virgin adoring Child	3. 253	Blundel Weld
Adoration of the Kings	3. 304	Duke of Hamilton
A Picture	3. 314	W. Stirling
Cupid and Psyche (long picture)	3. 374	Davenport Bromley
Jupiter and Calisto	3. 428	Sir J. Boileau
St. Bernard of Clairvaux, etc.	4. 54	National Gallery
Six Saints enthroned	4. 71	Alexander Barker
Adoration of the Kings (School of)	4. 190	A. J. B. Hope
The Annunciation	4. 398	Lord Methuen
An Angel	4. 398	,,
The Magdalen	4. 398	,,
LIPPI, Filippino		
Virgin with Child on arm	2. 231	Lord Ward
A Crucifixion	2. 231	,,
Virgin and Child, two Saints	2. 231	,,
Virgin and Child	2. 335	Beriah Botfield
A Young Female	2. 242	H. D. Seymour
Birth of the Virgin	3. 233	Liverpool R.I.
A Saint in red dress	3. 434	Earl of Orford
LOMBARD, Lambert		
Virgin and Child	3. 123	Duke of Marlborough
Virgin and Child, St. Anna, etc.	3. 251	Blundel Weld
Holy Family	3. 390	M. A. Whyte
LONGHI, Luca		
Holy Family	2. 84	Lord de Mauley
St. Catherine	4. 182	G. Cornwall Legh
Virgin and Child enthroned	4. 261	Duc D'Aumale

	VOL. & PAGE		OWNER
LONGHI, Pietro			
A Party in a Room	4.	171	E. Cheney
LOOTEN, P.			
Landscape	2.	360	Hampton Court
LORENZETTI, Ambrogio			
Martyrdom of St. Catherine	2.	233	Lord Ward
Five Pictures of Saints and Christ	3.	377	Davenport Bromley
Figures of S. Croce	4.	299	Higford Burr
LORENZO di S. Severino			
Virgin and Child enthroned	4.	55	National Gallery
LOTHENER, Stephen			
St. Catherine, St. Matthew, etc.	4.	223	Prince Consort
LOTTO, Lorenzo			
Virgin and Child and four Saints	2.	33	Bridgewater House
Portrait of a Sculptor	2.	356	Hampton Court
Virgin and Child and four Saints	2.	492	Orleans Gallery
A Male Portrait, 1537	3.	341	W. V. Wentworth
A Male Portrait (called Giorgione)	3.	345	Duke of Devonshire
LUCATELLI			
Large Landscape	3.	203	Lord Northwick
Two Landscapes	3.	421	Earl of Leicester
LUIGI d'Assisi (called L'Ingegno)			
Virgin and Child enthroned	2.	232	Lord Ward
LUINI, Bernardino			
A Female, called Da Vinci	2.	30	Bridgewater House
Virgin and Child	2.	99	Lord Ashburton
Virgin and Infant Child on her lap	2.	178	T. Baring
A Picture	2.	482	Charles I
The Magdalen (half length)	3.	159	Marquis of Lansdowne
A Female Head	3.	200	Lord Northwick
Boy with a Toy	3.	300	Duke of Hamilton
Marriage of St. Catherine	3.	314	Captain Stirling
Virgin caressing Child, etc.	3.	422	Earl of Leicester
Virgin looking at Child	4.	79	Marquis of Hertford
Virgin and Child, etc.	4.	181	G. C. Legh
Virgin and Joseph adoring Child	4.	261	Duc D'Aumale
St. Catherine (School of)	4.	279	Sir C. Eardley

	VOL. & PAGE		OWNER
A Picture	4.	374	Sir W. Knighton
Baptism of Christ	4.	387	Lord Heytesbury
Modesty and Vanity	4.	397	Lord Methuen
St. Catherine	4.	491	A Durham Collector

LUTI, Cavaliere Benedetto

A Picture	3.	403	Marquis of Exeter
A Picture	3.	393	Lord Scarsdale

	VOL. & PAGE		OWNER
MAAS, Dirk			
Battle of the Boyne	3.	40	Petworth
MAAS, Nicholas			
The Cradle	I.	355	National Gallery
A Dutch Ménage	I.	355	,,
The Idle Servant Maid	I.	355	,,
Girl coming down a Staircase	2.	6	Buckingham Palace
Girl threading a Needle	2.	42	Bridgewater House
Mother with two Children, etc.	2.	70	Duke of Sutherland
Girl peeling Apples	2.	70	Duke of Sutherland
Woman with three Children	2.	137	H. A. J. Munro
Woman asleep by a Cradle	2.	183	T. Baring
A Picture	2.	239	Marquis of Breadalbane
Girl seated making Lace	2.	292	Charles Bradel
The Listener—Girl and Jug	2.	421	H. Labouchere
A Lacemaker at Work	2.	421	H. Labouchere
An Old Man on a Chair	3.	35	Petworth
Child in Cradle, Sister near	3.	163	Marquis of Lansdowne
Two Women conversing	3.	207	Lord Northwick
Mother with a Child on her Lap	3.	221	Howard Galton
Woman seated by a Cradle	3.	290	M'Lellan Gallery
Old Woman seated with a Bible	4.	162	A. Robarts
Old Woman in an Armchair	4.	297	J. Walter
Boy and Girl playing Cards	4.	344	Countess of Warwick
A Cook preparing Fish	4.	482	Matthew Anderson
A Student in his Library	4.	495	Earl of Harrington
MABUSE, (Jean Gossaert)			
Children of Henry VII	2.	364	Hampton Court
James IV of Scotland and his brother	2.	366	,,
St. George with Queen of James IV	2.	366	,,
Adam and Eve	2.	368	,,
Crucifixion (with the donors)	2.	460	Mr. Green
A Male Portrait	2.	460	Mr. Green
Children of Henry VII	2.	472	Charles I
Adam and Eve	2.	472	Charles I
Adoration of the Kings (called Dürer)	2.	500	Orleans Gallery
Three Children of Henry VII	3.	152	Earl of Pembroke

	VOL. & PAGE		OWNER
MABUSE—*continued*			
Virgin and Child enthroned, etc.	3.	249	Blundel Weld
St. George and the Donor	3.	289	M'Lellan Gallery
Adoration of the Kings	3.	303	Duke of Hamilton
Adoration of the Kings	3.	320	Earl of Carlisle
St. Ursula entering Vessel	3.	348	Duke of Devonshire
Virgin and Child enthroned	4.	98	T. Baring
Virgin and Child on a Throne	4.	98	T. Baring
Mass of Pope Gregory	4.	104	H. Labouchere
An Ecclesiastic	4.	227	Prince Consort
A Girl writing	4.	230	„
Madonna and Child in a Landscape	4.	230	„
Virgin and Joseph adoring the Child	4.	316	Rev. Mr. Heath
Children of Henry VII	4.	358	Lord Folkestone
Virgin and Child	4.	379	Kingston Lacy
Children of Henry VII (*copy*)	4.	395	Lord Methuen
Virgin and Child	4.	483	Matthew Anderson
Story of Count of Toulouse	4.	507	Sir J. Nethorpe
M'CULLOCH			
Mountains and Sunny Plain	4.	433	Gibson Craig
MACLISE, Daniel, R.A.			
Malvolio	1.	373	Marlborough House
Play Scene in "Hamlet"	1.	373	Marlborough House
Justice	1.	427	House of Lords
Chivalry	1.	427	House of Lords
Robin Hood and his Band	4.	403	Mr. Birch
Banquet after Masquerade	4.	403	Mr. Birch
Sleeping Princess and her Court	4.	403	J. Gillott
The Hand Kiss	4.	415	Mr. Cooke
Departure of Moses	4.	419	J. Chapman
Return of Moses from the Fair	4.	419	J. Chapman
MANFREDI, Bartholomew			
A Picture	2.	482	Charles I
MANS, F. H.			
Winter Landscape, 1669	3.	241	Liverpool R.I.
A Dutch Canal, 1675	4.	361	Lord Folkestone
MANTEGNA, Andrea			
Christ on the Mount of Olives	2.	178	T. Baring
A large Chalice (Drawing)	2.	204	R. S. Holford

	VOL. & PAGE		OWNER
Triumph of Scipio	2.	248	George Vivian
Triumphs of Julius Cæsar (9 pictures)	2.	410	Hampton Court
Three Maries at the Sepulchre	2.	419	H. Labouchere
Triumphs of Julius Cæsar	2.	472	Charles I
Virgin and Child and St. John, etc.	2.	472	,,
Death of the Virgin	2	473	,,
Woman taken in Adultery	2.	473	,,
Mucius Scævola, etc.	2.	473	,,
Judith putting Head in a Bag	3.	151	Earl of Pembroke
Dead Christ on the Lap of the Virgin	3.	234	Liverpool R.I.
Gentleman and his Wife	3.	298	Duke of Hamilton
Summer	3.	304	,,
Autumn	3.	304	,,
Virgin and Child enthroned	4.	57	National Gallery
Virgin with Child in Lap	4.	113	Sir C. Eastlake

MANZUOLI, di San Triano

The Annunciation	2.	113	H. T. Hope

MARATTI, Carlo

A Cardinal	I.	324	National Gallery
Virgin teaching the Child to read	2.	65	Duke of Sutherland
St. Chiara and the Infant Christ	2.	227	Hon. E. Phipps
Virgin and St. Francis	2.	357	Hampton Court
Triumph of Galatea	2.	492	Orleans Gallery
Virgin on a Globe, and Angels	3.	125	Duke of Marlborough
Flight into Egypt	3.	172	Colt Hoare
The Painter and the three Graces	3.	172	Colt Hoare
A Holy Family	3.	186	J. P. Miles
A Cardinal	3.	198	Lord Northwick
A Picture	3.	403	Marquis of Exeter
Judith giving the Head to a Maid	3.	422	Earl of Leicester
Cupid on a Car	3.	422	Earl of Leicester
Holy Family	3.	484	Marquis of Bute
Virgin holding the Child	4.	291	J. Sanders
Holy Family	4.	356	Lord Folkestone
Child and Virgin with a Book	4.	366	Earl of Normanton
Virgin and Child	4.	441	Earl of Wemyss
Cardinal Antonio Barberino	4.	471	Duke of Northumberland
The Virgin in Glory	4.	494	Lord Feversham
Cardinal Bentivoglio	4.	495	Earl of Harrington

MAROCHETTI, Baron

Duke of Wellington	3.	283	Glasgow College

	VOL. & PAGE	OWNER
MARTIN, John		
Belshazzar's Feast	3. 242	J. Naylor
Joshua with his Host	3. 242	,,
Flight into Egypt	3. 242	,,
MASACCIO		
A Male Portrait	3. 196	Lord Northwick
9 Monks, chiaroscuro	3. 314	Captain Stirling
MASTELLETTA, Il (Giov. Andrea Donducci)		
A Sketch	2. 490	Orleans Gallery
MASTER of the Lieversberg Passion		
Presentation in the Temple	4. 224	Prince Consort
MASTER of the Death of the Virgin		
Virgin nursing the Child	3. 6	W. Fuller Maitland
Virgin under Canopy, and the Child	3. 250	Blundell Weld
Descent from the Cross	4. 386	Lord Heytesbury
MATSYS, Quentin		
A frightful old Woman	2. 243	H. D. Seymour
The Misers	2. 432	Windsor Castle
Virgin and Child enthroned, etc.	2. 432	Windsor Castle
Virgin on the Grass, Child on Cushion	2. 460	Mr. Green
A Male Portrait, 1531	3. 206	Lord Northwick
The Misers (*old copy*)	3. 227	Lord Lyttelton
The Misers (*old copy*)	3. 300	Duke of Hamilton
Virgin and Child enthroned	4. 76	A. Barker
Christ and John as Children	4. 145	Lord Overstone
Virgin and Child	4. 285	Rev. Fuller Russell
Head of the sorrowing Virgin	4. 314	Rev. Mr. Heath
The Misers (*old copy*)	4. 427	Rev. T. Staniforth
The Misers (*old copy*)	4. 438	Earl of Wemyss
A Male Portrait	4. 495	Earl of Harrington
MATSYS, Jan		
Two Men and 2 Women playing Cards	3. 35	Petworth
Virgin kissing the Child	3. 392	Lord Scarsdale
MATTEIS, Paolo de		
Salmacis	2. 492	Orleans Gallery
MATTEO, da Siena		
Virgin and Child, St. John and Angel	3. 233	Liverpool R.I.

	VOL. & PAGE		OWNER

MAZZOLINO di Ferrara

The Circumcision	2.	30	Bridgewater House
Adoration of the Shepherds	2.	196	R. S. Holford
A Warrior on Horseback	2.	365	Hampton Court
Christ teaching in the Temple	4.	95	T. Baring
Adoration of the Kings	4.	339	Knole
Christ and the Money-changers	4.	469	Duke of Northumberland

MAZZUOLA, Girolamo

Scourging of Christ	3.	176	Mr. Vivian
Virgin borne by Angels	3.	185	J. P. Miles

MAZZUOLI, Filippo

A Portrait	2.	434	Windsor Castle

MEISSONIER

Painter looking over a Portfolio	2.	192	T. Baring

MEMLING, Hans

Man in red Dress, 1462	2.	78	S. Rogers
Old Woman kneeling, etc.	2.	269	Miss Rogers
A Pietà	2.	459	Mr. Green
Virgin and Child	4.	225	Prince Consort
The Crucifixion (Diptych)	4.	285	Rev. J. F. Russell
Dead Christ, Virgin, etc.	4.	313	Rev. Mr. Heath
St. Christopher and the Infant Christ	4.	423	Earl of Burlington
St. Sebastian	4.	440	Earl of Wemyss

MEMMI, Simone, or MARTINI

A Crucifixion	3.	53	Oxford University
A Pietà	3.	53	Oxford University
St. Catherine	3.	373	W. Davenport Bromley
Figures from Sienna Palace	4.	299	Higford Burr

MENGS, Raphael

Antony and Cleopatra	3.	172	Colt Hoare
Virgin and Child enthroned	3.	185	J. P. Miles

MESSINA, Antonello da

Head of Christ	2.	90	Devonshire House
Christ blessing, with Apostles	2.	269	Miss Rogers
Young Man in red Dress	3.	302	Duke of Hamilton

	VOL. & PAGE	OWNER
MESSYS, Jan		
Virgin and standing Child	4. 234	Earl of Harrington
METZU, Gabriel		
Woman singing, Man with Violin	1. 401	Sir R. Peel
Woman at Harpsichord	1. 401	Sir R. Peel
Female Fruit Dealer selling Grapes	2. 7	Buckingham Palace
Gentleman near Harpsichord	2. 7	"
His own Portrait at Bow Window	2. 7	"
Girl drinking Champagne	2. 7	"
Corset Bleu (repetition)	2. 7	"
A Cook before a Door	2. 8	"
Woman selling Herrings	2. 43	Bridgewater House
Lady caressing a Spaniel	2. 43	"
Horseman halting, and Lady with Wine	2. 43	"
Girl in Scarlet, drawing from a bust	2. 104	Lord Ashburton
Old Woman at a Window reading	2. 104	Lord Ashburton
Lady in crimson Bodice, etc.	2. 116	H. T. Hope
Gentleman writing a Letter	2. 116	"
Lady at a Window reading a Letter	2. 116	"
Lady in Blue holding a Miniature	2. 116	"
Le Chasseur endormi	2. 159	Marquis of Hertford
The Intruder, 2 Ladies and Gentleman	2. 183	T. Baring
Le Corset Bleu, etc.	2. 246	Joseph Neeld
Girl playing with a Dog	2. 252	Henry Bevan
Man tickling a sleeping Woman	2. 295	Wynn Ellis
Two Figures	2. 329	Mr. Oppenheim
A Woman weighing Gold	2. 422	H. Labouchere
Gentleman courting a Lady	3. 448	Fitzwilliam Museum
Old Woman feeding a Spaniel	3. 476	Marquis of Bute
Fishmonger and Girl	4. 87	Marquis of Hertford
Single Figure of a Girl	4. 87	Marquis of Hertford
Woman holding up a Fish to a Lady	4. 317	Rev. Mr. Heath
Apothecary at a Window	4. 427	Rev. T. Staniforth
MIEL, Jan		
Italians before Door of a house	2. 18	Buckingham Palace
Priest distributing Alms	2. 71	Duke of Sutherland
Two Herdsmen and Herdswoman	2. 286	Duke of Bedford
Landscape and Figures	3. 270	Edinburgh R.I.
Peasant Party in the open Air	3. 336	Charles Wynn
A Picture	3. 434	Earl of Orford
Family of beggars among Ruins	4. 339	Knole
MIERIS, Franz van		
Woman at a Window, and green Parrot	1. 401	Sir R. Peel

	VOL. & PAGE		OWNER
Boy blowing Bubbles, 1663	2.	8	Buckingham Palace
Man Smoking, giving Wine to Girl	2.	8	Buckingham Palace
His own Portrait, aged 45	2.	44	Bridgewater House
Lady in red Bodice tying Cap	2.	44	,,
A Picture	2.	52	,,
Gentleman in brown Cap, etc., 1660	2.	117	H. T. Hope
Gentleman, Lady and Negro Boy	2.	117	H. T. Hope
A Woman reading Music	2.	183	T. Baring
Pedestrian with Flask	2.	200	R. S. Holford
His own Portrait, 1667	2.	252	F. Heusch
Frank Wouters	2.	252	,,
Woman selling Poultry	2.	253	,,
Man seated, Girl pouring Wine, 1659	2.	289	C. Bredel
The Alchymist	2.	501	Orleans Gallery
A Bacchanalian Scene	2.	501	,,
Lady eating Oysters	2.	501	,,
A Sleeping Woman	2.	501	,,
Mother reprimanding her Daughter	3.	476	Marquis of Bute
Painter holding a Palette, 1667	4.	297	J. Walter
The Water Doctor	4.	476	W. W. Bardon

MIERIS, William van

A Female with Poultry	1.	402	Sir R. Peel
Three Pictures	2.	9	Buckingham Palace
Woman with a Violin Player	2.	44	Bridgewater House
Two Girls	2.	118	H. T. Hope
Man giving Grapes to a Woman	2.	118	,,
David and Bathsheba, 1708	2.	118	,,
Four Pictures	2.	118	,,
An old Woman and a Girl	2.	183	T. Baring
Ragged Lad with a Raree Show	2.	252	F. Heusch
Cook Maid at a Window with Salmon	2.	253	F. Heusch
Bacchus and Ariadne	2.	295	Wynn Ellis
Angelica and Medora	3.	337	Charles Wynn
Woman selling Chestnuts at a Window	4.	138	Lord Overstone
Woman selling Vegetables, etc.	4.	162	A. Robarts
Death of Cleopatra, 1688	4.	442	Sir H. Campbell

MIGNARD, Pierre

Portrait of Descartes	3.	323	Earl of Carlisle
Julie d'Angennes	3.	459	Earl Spencer

MIGNON, Abraham

Fruit, Flowers, etc.	3.	388	Earl of Shrewsbury
Flower Piece	3.	482	Marquis of Bute
Fruit Piece	4.	298	J. Walter

R

	VOL. & PAGE	OWNER
MILANI, Giulio Cesare		
Portrait of a Child	2. 364	Hampton Court
MILET, François		
Alps and Glaciers, Storm	2. 310	Mr. Wombwell
Hilly Landscape	3. 170	Earl of Suffolk
Landscape, Youth and Girl	3. 248	Blundell Weld
Landscape, three Shepherds	3. 350	Duke of Devonshire
Landscape, Figures by S. Bourdon	4. 482	Matthew Anderson
MIREVELT, Michael		
A Picture	2. 52	Bridgewater House
Old Man holding a Shell	2. 433	Windsor Castle
Six Pictures	2. 482	Charles I
A Picture	3. 142	Earl of Radnor
Collection of Portraits	3. 219	Earl of Craven
A Male Portrait	3. 221	Howard Galton
A Picture	3. 314	Capt. Stirling
Maurice, Prince of Orange	3. 333	Meynell Ingram
A Portrait	3. 465	Duke of Bedford
A Male Portrait	4. 148	Earl of Caledon
A Female Portrait	4. 148	Earl of Caledon
Prince Henry of Orange	4. 266	Duke of Northumberland
His own Portrait	4. 335	Duke of Bedford
A Prince of Orange	4. 354	Lord Folkestone
A Prince of Orange	4. 355	,,
Sir Peter Young, aged 79	4. 361	,,
MOCETTO, Girolamo		
Incredulity of St. Thomas	3. 201	Lord Northwick
MOLA, Pietro Francesco		
A Riposo	1. 338	National Gallery
Landscape with Leda	1. 338	,,
St. John preaching	1. 338	,,
A Picture	2. 39	Bridgewater House
St. John preaching	2. 65	Duke of Sutherland
Long Landscape, Figures and Trees	2. 83	Lord Elcho
A smaller Landscape	2. 83	Lord Elcho
Two Pictures	2. 86	Duke of Norfolk
A Picture	2. 93	Devonshire House
Landscape, Girls bathing	2. 245	Joseph Neeld
Hagar in the Desert	2. 268	Miss Rogers
Portrait of a Boy	2. 285	Duke of Bedford
A Picture	2. 311	Earl of Listowel
Rape of Proserpine	2. 347	Dulwich Gallery

	VOL. & PAGE		OWNER
Preaching of John the Baptist	2.	492	Orleans Gallery
Archimedes	2.	492	,,
Landscape, Flight into Egypt	2.	492	,,
Poetical Landscape	3.	122	Duke of Marlborough
A Riposo	3.	158	Marquis of Lansdowne
Landscape, Virgin and Child, etc.	3.	158	Marquis of Lansdowne
Landscape, Hagar and Ishmael	3.	169	Earl of Suffolk
David and Goliah	3.	172	Colt Hoare
Flight into Egypt	3.	222	Howard Galton
Preaching of St. John	3.	226	Mr. Martin
Landscape, Monk in white	3.	226	Mr. Martin
Landscape with St. Jerome	3.	310	Earl of Hopetoun
Landscape with a Hermit	3.	332	Meynell Ingram
David Rizzio playing Violoncello	3.	422	Earl of Leicester
Landscape, Hagar and Ishmael	4.	186	Wm. Russell
A Landscape	4.	358	Lord Folkestone
St. Bruno in a Landscape	4.	471	Duke of Northumberland
St. Bruno in ecstasy	4.	484	Matthew Anderson

MOLANEZO

Virgin and Child, etc.	2.	473	Charles I

MOLENAER, Cornelis

Hunting Party, painted with C. Matsys	3.	252	Blundell Weld

MOLENAER, Jan Mienze

Peasant Woman and Boy	2.	10	Buckingham Palace
A Picture	2.	52	Bridgewater House
Man and Woman in Conversation	3.	224	Howard Galton
A Tailor's Shop	3.	387	Earl of Shrewsbury
Winter Landscape, Windmill	4.	193	G. Field
Winter Landscape, Men and Animals	4.	209	Mr. Henderson

MOMMERS, Hendrik

Landscape	3.	222	Howard Galton
Landscape	3.	222	Howard Galton
Hunting Party on a Hill	4.	439	Earl of Wemyss

MOMPER, Judocus de

A Picture	2.	95	Devonshire House
Girl sleeping and an old Woman	2.	458	Earl of Clarendon
Landscape, Figures by Breughel	3.	349	Duke of Devonshire
Landscape, Figures by Breughel	3.	392	Lord Scarsdale
Landscape	4.	269	Duke of Northumberland
Landscape	4.	354	Lord Folkestone
Landscape, Conversion of St. Paul	4.	458	M'Lellan Gallery

	VOL. & PAGE	OWNER
MONTAGNA, Bartolommeo		
A Male Portrait	2. 336	V. Fitzgerald
A Procession to Calvary	3. 201	Lord Northwick
MOOR, Karel de		
A Mother and two Children	2. 105	Lord Ashburton
MORALES, Luis de		
Christ bearing the Cross	2. 181	T. Baring
Head of Christ crowned with Thorns	2. 248	George Vivian
Christ at the Column	2. 259	G. A. Hoskins
Christ bearing the Cross	2. 259	G. A. Hoskins
Christ bound to a Pillar	4. 381	Kingston Lacy
Child in the Lap of the Virgin	4. 385	H. D. Seymour
Virgin lamenting over the body of Christ	4. 449	W. Stirling
MORANDA, Rodrigo de		
Courtiers shooting	4. 482	Matthew Anderson
MORE, Sir Antonio		
A Woman	2. 87	Earl of Yarborough
Earl of Essex	2. 87	Earl of Yarborough
Sir F. Walsingham	2. 199	R. S. Holford
Sir Thomas Gresham	2. 246	Joseph Neeld
A Portrait	2. 246	Joseph Neeld
His own Portrait	2. 327	Society of Antiquaries
Philip II	2. 362	Hampton Court
Emperor Charles V in armour	2. 432	Windsor Castle
Duke of Alba	2. 432	Windsor Castle
Philip II	2. 473	Charles I
Grandmother of the Duke of Savoy	2. 473	,,
Grandfather of the Duke of Savoy	2. 473	,,
Portrait of a Child	2. 473	,,
Mary I	2. 473	,,
His own Portrait	2. 501	Orleans Gallery
Dr. Butts	3. 6	W. Fuller Maitland
Mrs. Butts	3. 6	W. Fuller Maitland
Sir Philip Sidney's Mother, 1553	3. 41	Petworth
Sir Henry Sidney, 1553	3. 41	Petworth
A Male Portrait, 1568	3. 134	Lord Dillon
Philip II	3. 134	Lord Dillon
Lady of Honour to Mary I	3. 171	Earl of Suffolk
Third Wife of Philip II	3. 206	Lord Northwick
Mary I	3. 323	Earl of Carlisle
Isabella, Queen of Philip II	3. 378	W. Davenport Bromley

	VOL. & PAGE		OWNER
Edward VI and Princess Elizabeth	3.	429	A. Fountaine
Philip II	3.	429	A. Fountaine
A Man with Gloves	3.	443	Mr. Tomline
His own Portrait	3.	457	Earl Spencer
Philip II	3.	457	„
Head of a Lady	3.	457	„
Jane Seymour	3.	464	Duke of Bedford
Philip II	3.	464	„
Mary I	3.	464	„
Another Portrait	3.	464	„
Earl of Essex	4.	64	Earl of Yarborough
Mary I	4.	65	Earl of Yarborough
Mary I	4.	336	Duke of Bedford
Mary and Philip, 2 pictures	4.	337	Duke of Bedford
A Female Portrait	4.	338	Knole

MORETTO, Il (Allessandro Bonvicino)

Virgin enthroned, Canopy	3.	293	Sir A. Campbell
Old bald Man and Maltese Cross	4.	175	E Cheney
Bartolommeo Capello, 1546	4.	498	W. Drury Lowe

MORETTO of Brescia

Aged Smith with a Hammer	4.	444	Lord Elgin
St. Bartholomew	4.	491	Archdeacon of Durham
A Saint	4.	491	Archdeacon of Durham

MOREELSE, Paul

A Female Portrait	3.	387	Earl of Shrewsbury

MORGENSTERN, Christian

A Plain with Water, Alps, 1847	4.	177	Rev. Mr. Townshend

MORLAND, George

Horse coming out of Water	4.	370	Earl of Normanton

MORONI, Giovanni Battista

A Jesuit in a Chair	2.	60	Duke of Sutherland
A Venetian Nobleman	2.	369	Hampton Court
An Ecclesiastic with a Beard	2.	419	H. Labouchere
A Man looking round	3.	15	Earl Cowper
A Man	3.	216	Earl of Warwick
A Male Portrait, 1561	3.	302	Duke of Hamilton
A Picture	3.	314	Capt. Stirling
A Man about to write	4.	69	Earl of Yarborough
A General in Armour	4.	95	T. Baring
A Portrait	4.	104	H. Labouchere

	VOL. & PAGE		OWNER

MOSTAERT, Jean

A Picture	2.	182	T. Baring
Virgin pressing Child to her lips	2.	225	R. Ford
Sophonisba	2.	365	Hampton Court
A Holy Family	2.	458	Earl of Clarendon
Adoration of the Kings	3.	206	Lord Northwick
Virgin and Child	3.	237	Liverpool R.I.
Magdalen and the Pot of Ointment	3.	251	Blundell Weld
A Riposo, Virgin nursing the Child	3.	253	Blundell Weld
A Pietà	4.	230	Prince Consort
The Entombment	4.	316	Rev. Mr. Heath
A Male Portrait	4.	358	Lord Folkestone
Virgin in purple Mantle, and Child	4.	509	Duke of Newcastle

MOUCHERON, Frederic

Landscape	1.	411	Sir R. Peel
A Waterfall	2.	501	Orleans Gallery
Landscape, Figures by Lingelbach	3.	221	Howard Galton
Landscape, Figures by A. Van de Velde	3.	222	Howard Galton
Landscape	3.	240	Liverpool R.I.
Landscape	4.	211	Mr. Henderson
Landscape, lofty Pillar, painted with A. Van de Velde	4.	291	J. Sanders
Landscape	4.	297	J. Walter
Landscape	4.	422	Earl of Burlington
Landscape	4.	458	M'Lellan Gallery

MOYA, Pedro de

Girl with Birds and Vegetables	2.	224	R. Ford
A jovial Party	3.	385	Earl of Shrewsbury
A Priest	4.	241	R. P. Nichols
Virgin and Child and St. Joseph	4.	481	Matthew Anderson

MULLER, W. J.

A Picture	2.	353	E. Bicknell
Several Landscapes	3.	211	Lord Northwick
Girl with sick Lamb, etc.	4.	176	Rev. C. H. Townshend
Pictures	4.	403	E. Bullock
Pictures	4.	404	J. Gillott
Figures praying in a Desert	4.	404	Mr. Sharpe
Landscape	4.	404	Mr. Sharpe
Salisbury Cathedral	4.	416	S. Ashton

MULREADY, W., R.A.

Fair Time	1.	377	Marlborough House
The Ford	1.	377	,,

	VOL. & PAGE	OWNER
The last in	1. 377	Marlborough House
Haymaking	2. 189	T. Baring
Two Figures on a Rock	2. 189	T. Baring
Kensington Gravel Pits	2. 302	J. Sheepshanks
Kensington Gravel Pits	2. 302	,,
Seven Ages of Man	2. 302	,,
The Fight interrupted	2. 303	,,
Loan of a Bite, 1836	2. 303	,,
Lad with Cherry, 1840	2. 303	,,
Open your Mouth, etc.	2. 303	,,
Brothers and Sisters, Pinch of the Ear, 1873	2. 303	,,
Choosing Wedding Gown	2. 303	,,
Mr. Sheepshanks seated by fireplace	2. 304	,,
The Sonnet	2. 304	,,
A Sailing Match	2. 304	,,
A Toy Seller	2. 304	,,
The Butt. Shooting a Cherry	2. 304	,,
Cottages	2. 307	,,
Boy giving Alms	4. 100	T. Baring
Girls bathing	4. 100	,,
Companion	4. 100	,,
Wooded Landscape	4. 178	Rev. Mr. Townshend
The travelling Druggist	4. 417	J. Chapman

MURANI, PELLEGRINO +

Virgin and Child on a Throne	2. 62	Duke of Sutherland

MURILLO

The Holy Family	1. 316, 347	National Gallery
Infant St. John	1. 316, 348	National Gallery
Lazarus and the Rich Man	2. 40	Bridgewater House
The Prodigal Son	2. 67	Duke of Sutherland
Abraham with three Angels	2. 68	,,
St. Anthony of Padua and the Child	2. 68	,,
Saint caressing the Child	2. 68	,,
Adoration of Shepherds, etc.	2. 68	,,
A Priest	2. 68	,,
Virgin and Child and St. Joseph	2. 68	,,
St. Peter	2. 87	Earl of Yarborough
St. Thomas of Villa Nueva as a child	2. 101	Lord Ashburton
Madonna in Glory	2. 101	,,
Virgin and Child on Clouds	2. 101	,,
Christ looking upward	2. 102	,,
Miracle of the Loaves and Fishes	2. 136	H. A. J. Munro
St. Peter in Prison	2. 136	,,

MURILLO—*continued*	VOL. & PAGE		OWNER
Infant Christ and St. Anthony	2.	136	H. A. J. Munro
Virgin surrounded by Angels	2.	152	Marquis of Lansdowne
St. Thomas de Villa Nueva	2.	156	Marquis of Hertford
Virgin in Glory and 4 Saints	2.	156	,,
The Annunciation	2.	156	,,
Ascension of the Virgin	2.	156	,,
Laban searching for Idols	2.	172	Marquis of Westminster
Don Andrea di Andrada	2.	180	T. Baring
A Riposo	2.	181	,,
Shepherd Boy crowned with Ivy	2.	181	,,
Virgin upon a Crescent	2.	181	,,
The Ascension	2.	181	,,
A Carpenter's Shop	2.	181	,,
The Virgin praying	2.	199	R. S. Holford
Head of the Virgin	2.	199	,,
A Girl	2.	199	,,
Two Monks under a Tree	2.	223	R. Ford
Virgin nursing Infant	2.	224	,,
The Crucifixion (drawing)	2.	224	,,
St. John and Lamb, etc. (drawing)	2.	224	,,
Infant Christ sleeping	2.	259	G. A. Hoskins
St. Thomas and Infant Christ	2.	259	G. A. Hoskins
Infant Christ and St. Anthony	2.	267	Miss Rogers
A Picture	2.	283	Sir A. Rothschild
Virgin holding the Child in her Lap	2.	283	Duke of Bedford
Virgin in Glory, etc.	2.	289	R. Sanderson
St. Joseph and Child	2.	294	Wynn Ellis
The Annunciation	2.	295	,,
Two Shepherd Girls	2.	295	,,
The Sposalizio	2.	311	Earl of Listowel
Birth of the Baptist	2.	311	,,
Virgin and Child and Saints	2.	312	,,
Virgin in Glory, etc.	2.	345	Dulwich Gallery
Jacob and Rachael	2.	345	,,
Crucifixion of St. Peter	2.	346	,,
Girl holding some Roses, etc.	2.	346	,,
Boy begging another for Cakes	2.	346	,,
Boy eating a Cake	2.	346	,,
Christ bearing His Cross	2.	346	,,
A Sketch	2.	458	Earl of Clarendon
St. Veronica	3.	27	Lord Overstone
Virgin and Child	3.	27	Lord Overstone
Monks discoursing	3.	43	Petworth
Two Figures in a Landscape	3.	141	Earl of Radnor

	VOL. & PAGE		OWNER
An Ecclesiastic	3.	160	Marquis of Lansdowne
Ascension of the Virgin (sketch)	3.	170	Earl of Suffolk
Coronation of the Virgin (sketch)	3.	170	Earl of Suffolk
Joseph relating his Dream	3.	171	Lord Arundel
An old Woman	3.	172	Colt Hoare
Martyrdom of St. Andrew	3.	179	J. P. Miles
Holy Family	3.	179	,,
Virgin and sleeping Child	3.	184	,,
St. John the Evangelist	3.	184	,,
Jacob and drinking Troughs	3.	204	Lord Northwick
A Boy laughing, pointing at Spectator	3.	214	Earl of Warwick
Two Beggar Boys and Pigeon	3.	263	Earl of Lonsdale
A Boy *faisant la chasse*	3.	265	Earl of Lonsdale
Shepherd Boy singing	3.	270	Edinburgh R.I.
Christ as the Good Shepherd	3.	283	Glasgow College
Sleeping Child contemplated by Virgin	3.	286	M'Lellan Gallery
St. John Baptist as a Child	3.	301	Duke of Hamilton
Belisarius	3.	346	Duke of Devonshire
Virgin gazing on the sleeping Child	3.	351	Duke of Devonshire
St. Theresa praying	3.	385	Earl of Shrewsbury
Preaching of John the Baptist	3.	385	Earl of Shrewsbury
Virgin and Child and St. Rosalia	3.	398	Duke of Rutland
Adoration of the Kings	3.	398	,,
Virgin and Child and St. John	3.	402	,,
Diogenes and Cup	3.	406	Marquis of Exeter
Christ bearing His Cross	3.	435	Earl of Orford
Christ at the Pool of Bethesda	3.	440	Mr. Tomline
St. Augustine in ecstasy	3.	441	,,
St. Joseph and the flowering Wand	3.	442	,,
A Spanish Boy	3.	462	Glendon Hall
Angels flying	3.	465	Duke of Bedford
A Monk kneeling	4.	63	Lord Elcho
The Annunciation	4.	81	Marquis of Hertford
Marriage of the Virgin	4.	81	,,
Virgin in Glory	4.	82	,,
Virgin holding the Child	4.	82	,,
Virgin and Child	4.	82	,,
Adoration of the Shepherds	4.	82	,,
The Holy Family	4.	82	,,
St. Joseph sold by his Brethren	4.	83	,,
Virgin in Glory	4.	140	Lord Overstone
Virgin holding the Child in her Lap	4.	141	,,
Virgin in Glory	4.	144	,,
Head of Christ crowned with Thorns	4.	144	,,
Virgin in Glory with Infant	4.	145	,,

S

	VOL. & PAGE	OWNER
MURILLO—*continued*		
Virgin showing the sleeping Child	4. 146	Lord Overstone
Virgin in Glory	4. 150	Earl of Caledon
A Man in an Oval	4. 151	,,
Lady in a rich Dress	4. 151	,,
A laughing Boy	4. 164	A. Robarts
His own Portrait in black Dress	4. 183	W. Marshall
Head of Christ	4. 192	A. J. Beresford Hope
Immaculate Conception	4. 240	R. P. Nichols
St. Joseph and Infant Christ	4. 262	Duc D'Aumale
Assumption of the Virgin	4. 275	Sir C. Eardley
Flight into Egypt	4. 276	Sir C. Eardley
Assumption of the Virgin	4. 287	Edmund Foster
Virgin and Infant asleep, and Joseph	4. 288	Edmund Foster
Repose in Egypt	4. 320	Lord Enfield
St. Joseph with Lily and Infant Christ	4. 324	Lord Enfield
Assumption of the Virgin	4. 328	Sir T. Sebright
Large Picture with Angels	4. 333	Duke of Bedford
His own Portrait	4. 336	Duke of Bedford
Boy with Fruit and Lizard	4. 349	Vernon Harcourt
Two Beggars in a Landscape	4. 350	Vernon Harcourt
Ruth and Naomi	4. 358	Lord Folkestone
Moses striking the Rock (sketch)	4. 365	Earl of Normanton
Four Angels (life-size)	4. 367	,,
Slave with a Basket of Flowers	4. 367	,,
Infant Christ sleeping on a white Cloth	4. 369	,,
A Picture	4. 374	Sir W. Knighton
Angel, on Stone, with Cardinal's Hat	4. 381	Kingston Lacy
St. Augustine seated, with Pen	4. 382	,,
Two Beggar Boys, Grapes and Melon	4. 382	,,
St. Rosa in a white Dress	4. 382	,,
St. John and Lamb	4. 388	Lord Heytesbury
"Las Gallegas," 2 Girls at a Window	4. 388	,,
Virgin showing the Infant to Joseph	4. 390	,,
Assumption of the Virgin	4. 420	Jacob Fletcher
Joseph giving the Child to the Virgin	4. 427	Rev. T. Staniforth
The Good Shepherd	4. 438	Earl of Wemyss
Virgin looking down on the Child	4. 449	W. Stirling
Baptism of Christ	4. 475	W. W. Bardon
John the Baptist and 3 Pharisees	4. 477	J. Anderson
Two Beggar Boys eating Grapes	4. 508	Sir J. Nelthorpe
Virgin on the Crescent	4. 511	Duke of Portland
MUZIANO, Girolamo		
Raising of Lazarus	2. 492	Orleans Gallery

	VOL. & PAGE		OWNER
MYTENS, Daniel			
Earl of Arundel, Lady and Children	2.	86	Duke of Norfolk
A Picture	2.	95	Devonshire House
James, 1st Marquis of Hamilton	2.	355	Hampton Court
Lord Zouch	2.	362	,,
Scene of a Play with Charles I	2.	365	,,
A Duke of Brunswick	2.	367	,,
Don Gusman	2.	368	,,
11 Pictures	2.	482	Charles I
Female Portrait with Guitar	3.	222	Howard Galton
Two portraits	3.	297	Duke of Hamilton
Marquis of Hamilton	3.	311	Earl of Hopetown
First Earl of Portland	4.	331	Duke of Bedford
Charles I and Queen and Negro	4.	454	Earl of Dunmore
Charles I and Queen and Geoffrey Hudson	4.	516	Lord Galway
MYTENS, Isaac			
Charles I, Queen and Child	2.	4	Buckingham Palace

	VOL. & PAGE		OWNER
NAAS, Peter (? NEEFS)			
Interior of a Church	2.	298	Wynn Ellis
NASH, Joseph			
Interior of Audley End, 1849	2.	352	E. Bicknell
NASMYTH, Alexander			
A College	1.	387	Marlborough House
A Wood with a Stream	1.	387	Marlborough House
Landscape, Oak and Water	4.	303	J. Morrison
NASMYTH, Patrick			
Landscape with Houses	2.	190	T. Baring
Landscape, Oak in foreground	2.	190	T. Baring
A Picture	2.	353	E. Bicknell
Windsor Castle, 1830	3.	211	Lord Northwick
A Wood Scene	3.	211	Lord Northwick
Extensive Landscape	4.	290	J. Sanders
A Landscape	4.	368	Earl of Normanton
Windsor Castle, 1826	4.	484	Matthew Anderson
NASON, Peter			
Old Lady, half length	3.	224	Howard Galton
NAVARETE, Juan Fernandez (El Mudo)			
Spanish Lady in Mantilla	3.	159	Marquis of Lansdowne
His own Portrait	4.	450	W. Stirling
NEEFS, Peter			
Interior of a Church	2.	269	Miss Rogers
Interior of a Church	2.	269	Miss Rogers
Interior of Antwerp Cathedral, 1652	2.	329	Mr. Oppenheim
Four Pictures	2.	435	Windsor Castle
An Architectural Piece	2.	501	Orleans Gallery
An Architectural Piece, figures by Teniers	2.	501	Orleans Gallery
Interior of a Church	3.	6	W. Fuller Maitland
Interior of a Church	3.	122	Duke of Marlborough
St. Peter in Prison	3.	216	Earl of Warwick

	VOL. & PAGE		OWNER
NEEFS, Peter—*continued*			
St. Peter delivered from Prison	3.	216	Earl of Warwick
Interior of a Church	3.	274	Edinburgh R.I.
A Picture	3.	482	Marquis of Bute
Interior, Antwerp Cathedral	4.	147	Lord Overstone
Interior of a Church	4.	150	Earl of Caledon
Interior of a Church	4.	280	Sir C. Eardley
Interior of a Church	4.	280	Sir C. Eardley
Interior of a Church by day	4.	425	Earl of Burlington
Interior of a Church by candlelight	4.	425	Earl of Burlington
Interior of a Church by candlelight	4.	440	Earl of Wemyss
Interior of a Church by candlelight	4.	514	Duke of Portland
Interior of a Church	4.	522	Earl of Hardwicke
Interior of a Church	4.	522	Earl of Hardwicke
NELLI, Plautilla			
Madonna di Casa Colonna	3.	382	Earl of Shrewsbury
NERONI, Bartolommeo (Il Maestro Riccio)			
Adoration of the Shepherds	2.	233	Lord Ward
NETHERLANDS SCHOOL			
Magdalen and the Pot of Ointment	2.	128	A. Barker
Virgin and Child and St. Catherine	2.	128	A. Barker
Mass of St. Gregory	3.	205	Lord Northwick
The Crucifixion	3.	205	Lord Northwick
Three Kings on three Hills	3.	251	Blundell Weld
Woman with a close-fitting Cap	3.	253	Blundell Weld
Virgin and Child in a Garden	4.	228	Prince Consort
The Entombment	4.	262	Duc D'Aumale
The Stem of Jesse	4.	279	Sir C. Eardley
Charles V as a Boy	4.	478	J. Anderson
Adoration of the Shepherds	4.	491	Archdeacon of Durham
NETSCHER, Caspar			
Girl being taught to read	1.	402	Sir R. Peel
Two Boys blowing Bubbles, 1670	1.	402	,,
Girl in velvet Jacket, 1665	1.	402	,,
William III	2.	8	Buckingham Palace
Duchess of Mazarin, etc.	2.	44	Bridgewater House
Boy blowing Bubbles	2.	104	Lord Ashburton
Lady in White with a Parrot	2.	117	H. T. Hope
Portrait with a Page	2.	130	Baron L. Rothschild
A Mother and Child	2.	183	T. Baring
Young Lady and an old Woman	2.	183	T. Baring

	VOL. & PAGE	OWNER
Little Girl with a Dog	2. 247	Joseph Neeld
Vertumnus and Pomona	2. 247	,,
Sarah giving Hagar to Abraham	2. 247	,,
Figures in a Room	2. 277	Duke of Wellington
Boy caressing a Spaniel	2. 421	H. Labouchere
Portrait of Himself	2. 501	Orleans Gallery
Gipsies	2. 501	,,
Hagar and Ishmael	2. 501	,,
A sleeping Woman	2. 501	,,
Judgment of Paris	2. 501	,,
The Schoolmistress	2. 501	,,
The Birdcage	2. 501	,,
A stout Lady	3. 224	Howard Galton
A noble Boy	3. 271	Edinburgh R.I.
A Lady	3. 288	M'Lellan Gallery
Girl in Crimson making Lace	4. 87	Marquis of Hertford
The Shame of Calisto	4. 202	J. Tulloch
A Female Portrait, 1680	4. 358	Lord Folkestone
William III when Prince of Orange	4. 372	Earl of Normanton
A Female Portrait	4. 427	Rev. T. Staniforth
A Lady, 1671	4. 459	M'Lellan Gallery
William III, full length	4. 512	Duke of Portland

NETSCHER, Constantine

Anne Hyde, Countess of Clarendon	4. 237	Earl of Harrington
Duchess de Chevreux	4. 237	,,
Girl in Hat with Roses	4. 239	,,
Three Children	4. 482	Matthew Anderson

NEUREUTHER

Das Wold Fräulein (drawing)	4. 178	Rev. Mr. Townshend

NEWTON, Gilbert Stuart, R.A.

Yorick and Grisette	1. 378	Marlborough House
A Girl at a Window	1. 378	Marlborough House
Jessica taking leave of Shylock	2. 423	H. Labouchere
Scene from " Beggar's Opera "	3. 165	Marquis of Lansdowne
Mother turning from Olivia	3. 165	Marquis of Lansdowne
Scene from " Gil Blas "	3. 352	Duke of Devonshire

NICCOLA di Ancona

Virgin adoring the Child	2. 128	A. Barker

NICCOLO di Pietro

Frescoes from Pisa	4. 299	Higford Burr

	VOL. & PAGE		OWNER
NICCOLO del Abate			
Rape of Proserpine	2.	62	Duke of Sutherland
NOGARI, Giuseppe			
His Wife	2.	224	Richard Ford
A Woman	3.	248	Blundell Weld
A Man	3.	248	Blundell Weld
NOLLEKENS, J. R.A. (Sculptor)			
William, Duke of Devonshire	3.	352	Duke of Devonshire
Lord George Cavendish	3.	352	,,
Frances, Duke of Bedford	3.	352	,,
Charles James Fox	3.	352	,,
Death of Germanicus	3.	418	Earl of Leicester
William Pitt	4.	71	Earl of Yarborough
C. J. Fox	4.	71	,,
Venus and Cupid	4.	71	,,
NORTHCOTE, James, R.A.			
Murder of Princes in the Tower	3.	38	Petworth
A Picture	4.	374	Sir W. Knighton

T

	VOL. & PAGE		OWNER
ORIZONTE—*continued*			
Landscape	3.	248	Blundell Weld
Landscape	3.	293	Sir A. Campbell
Landscape	3.	293	,,
Landscape, figures by Lauri	3.	294	,,
Landscape	3.	336	Charles Wynn
Two Landscapes	3.	421	Earl of Leicester
ORRENTE, Pedro			
St. John and Lamb	2.	259	G. A. Hoskins
Moses before Burning Bush	4.	383	Kingston Lacy
David killing the Lion	4.	383	Kingston Lacy
OSTADE, Adrian van			
An Alchymist, 1661	1.	404	Sir R. Peel
Woman with Child on her arm, etc.	2.	13	Buckingham Palace
Child playing with a Doll, etc., 1668	2.	13	,,
A Country Woman, 1668	2.	13	,,
Peasants Singing and Playing, 1656	2.	13	,,
Five Peasants and a Woman, etc.	2.	13	,,
Five Peasants playing Cards	2.	14	,,
Three Peasants smoking, 1667	2.	14	,,
Dutchman and Wife in a Bower	2.	14	,,
Two Men playing Backgammon, 1644	2.	45	Bridgewater House
Man and Woman in a Doorway, 1667	2.	45	,,
Lawyer reading a Paper, 1671	2.	45	,,
Peasants before Alehouse, 1676	2.	46	,,
Man drinking, 1677	2.	46	,,
Peasants in an Alehouse	2.	46	,,
Man and Wife at a Table, 1661	2.	106	Lord Ashburton
Three Boors at a Table, 1661	2.	106	,,
Ten Figures at a Farmhouse, 1663	2.	106	,,
Mother and Child at a Door, 1667	2.	107	,,
Father and Mother at a Fireside	2.	107	,,
Village with Road, 1676	2.	107	,,
Bagpiper and large Party, 1657	2.	119	H. T. Hope
Woman at a Doorway	2.	119	,,
Family in a Courtyard	2.	119	,,
Old Woman drinking	2.	138	H. A. J. Munro
Interior and Figures	2.	159	Marquis of Hertford
Four Peasants playing Cards	2.	185	T. Baring
A travelling Musician	2.	185	T. Baring
Man and Wife, Child with a Dog, 1661	2.	200	R. S. Holford
Five Men and a Woman at Table	2.	200	,,
A Large Drawing	2.	204	,,
A Smaller Drawing	2.	204	,,

	VOL. & PAGE		OWNER
Three Peasants at Cards	2.	240	Lord Colborne
A Village Festival, 1659	2.	253	F. Heusch
Three Peasants at Cards, 1674	2.	253	,,
Two Men and Women with a News-			
paper	2.	254	,,
Lawyer in Velvet Cap, reading	2.	262	J. Morrison
Boors drinking, and playing Ninepins	2.	274	Duke of Wellington
Country People dancing to Fiddle, 1660	2.	282	Sir A. Rothschild
Five Peasants at Cards	2.	290	C. Bredel
A Peasant drinking	2.	295	Wynn Ellis
Four Peasants at a Fireplace	2.	296	Wynn Ellis
Eight Boors in a Room	2.	330	C. S. Bale
Two pretty Landscapes	2.	331	C. S. Bale
A Party in a House	2.	336	Hayward Hawkins
Three Boors, one playing Fiddle, 1652	2.	343	Dulwich Gallery
Country People in a Tavern, 1674	2.	451	Richard Forster
An Interior	3.	134	J. Morrison
Concert of four Persons	3.	207	Lord Northwick
Two old Women drinking	3.	263	Earl of Lonsdale
Two couples dancing, 1656	3.	264	,,
Nine Figures in an Inn, 1654	3.	264	,,
Interior of Peasant's House	3.	303	Duke of Hamilton
A Peasant wedding	3.	339	Earl Fitzwilliam
Old couple in a Bower	3.	396	Duke of Rutland
Peasants dancing, 1675	3.	440	Mr. Tomline
Lawyer reading a Paper, 1671	3.	478	Marquis of Bute
Schoolmaster and Boy	3.	478	,,
Two Boors playing Backgammon	3.	478	,,
Five Peasants round Table, etc.	4.	88	Marquis of Hertford
Peasant cleaning Fish	4.	88	Marquis of Hertford
Uproar at Card Table	4.	99	T. Baring
Lawyer reading a Letter, 1671	4.	107	J. Morrison
Lawyer reading	4.	117	C. S. Bale
Still Life, Fish, etc.	4.	143	Lord Overstone
Lawyer reading Papers	4.	163	A. Robarts
Old Woman in Blue with her Spindle	4.	163	,,
Man with Jug at a Door	4.	163	,,
Three Peasants, one asleep	4.	180	Rev. Mr. Townshend
Peasants playing Ninepipes, 1655	4.	193	G. Field
Peasant lighting Pipe, 1673	4.	193	G. Field
Hilarious Peasant	4.	209	Mr. Henderson
A Party in an interior	4.	295	J. Walter
Adoration of Shepherds, 1669	4.	296	J. Walter
Woman and Child and six Peasants, 1669	4.	311	J. Morrison
Ninepin Players, 1665	4.	480	Matthew Anderson

	VOL. & PAGE		OWNER
OSTADE, Isaac van			
Man on a grey Horse, and Dogs	1.	405	Sir R. Peel
Winter scene, grey Horse, and Sledge	1.	405	Rir R. Peel
Travellers halting	2.	14	Buckingham Palace
Family before a House Door	2.	14	Buckingham Palace
Travellers at an Alehouse	2.	107	Lord Ashburton
A Village Scene	2.	129	Baron L. Rothschild
Winter Evening on the Ice	2.	153	Marquis of Lansdowne
Winter on Canal, Sledges	2.	185	T. Baring
Travellers halting, Bagpiper	2.	201	R. S. Holford
Three Men and two Horses	2.	247	Joseph Neeld
A Picture	2.	262	J. Morrison
Party before a Tavern	2.	284	Duke of Bedford
Village, numerous Figures	2.	289	R. Sanderson
Frozen Canal, grey Horse	2.	296	Wynn Ellis
Village, Figures dancing	2.	296	Wynn Ellis
Ninepin Players	2.	335	George Field
Party before a Tavern Door	3.	27	Lord Overstone
Peasants in Village, two Pigs	3.	176	Mr. Vivian
Landscape and a grey Horse	3.	300	Duke of Hamilton
Peasants before a Door	3.	388	Earl of Shrewsbury
Town, Figures, and a grey Horse	4.	88	Marquis of Hertford
Man on a grey Horse, halting	4.	107	J. Morrison
A Country Inn, Man on a grey Horse	4.	131	Lord Overstone
Peasant on Horseback, etc.	4.	139	Lord Overstone
House with lofty Steps, etc.	4.	164	A. Robarts
Man leaning out of a Door	4.	295	J. Walter
Peasants passing a Ford	4.	297	J. Walter
Village and Figures	4.	342	Humphrey Mildmay
A Picture	4.	374	Sir W. Knighton
Horses and Carriage, etc., at an Inn	4.	391	J. Everett
Large Landscape	4.	404	J. Gillott
Man with a grey Horse, Stump of a Tree	4.	453	W. Stirling
OSTENDORFER, Michael			
Pardon through Faith, etc.	3.	252	Blundell Weld

	VOL. & PAGE	OWNER
PACCHIAROTTO, Jacopo		
Virgin offering her breast to the Child	4. 54	National Gallery
Virgin and Child and Cross	4. 167	W. Davenport Bromley
Virgin and Child and other Figures	4. 182	G. Cornwall Legh
PADOVANINO, Il (Alessandro Varotari)		
A Picture	3. 483	Marquis of Bute
Ecce Homo	4. 452	W. Stirling
Jephthah's Daughter	2. 61	Duke of Sutherland
Rinaldo and Armida	2. 492	Orleans Gallery
PAGANI, Vincenzo		
The Annunciation	3. 379	W. Davenport Bromley
PALAMEDES		
A Male Portrait (full length)	3. 347	Duke of Devonshire
Soldiers in an Interior	4. 149	Earl of Caledon
Courtyard with a Trumpeter	4. 180	Rev. Mr. Townshend
Party of seven Persons	4. 478	John Anderson
Interior with Figures	4. 502	Earl of Yarborough
Interior with Figures	4. 502	Earl of Yarborough
PALMA, Giovane		
The Last Supper	2. 474	Charles I
Virtue and Vice, etc.	2. 474	,,
Venus with a Mirror, and Cupid	2. 474	,,
The Entombment	3. 293	Sir A. Campbell
The Entombment	4. 271	Earl of Jersey
Executioner and Pope Sixtus	4. 393	Lord Arundel
A Last Supper	4. 413	Smith Barry
Virgin enthroned	4. 460	M'Lellan Gallery
PALMA, Vecchio		
A Doge on a red Seat	2. 33	Bridgewater House
Holy Family	2. 33	,,
Holy Family	2. 33	,,
Virgin and Child and St. John	2. 134	H. A. J. Munro
Virgin and Child and St. Catherine	2. 134	H. A. J. Munro
Virgin and Child and Saints	2. 197	R. S. Holford

	VOL. & PAGE	OWNER
PALMA, Vecchio—*continued*		
Diana and Actæon	2. 358	Hampton Court
Adoration of Shepherds	2. 358	,,
A Holy Family	2. 360	,,
Virgin and Child	2. 369	,,
Virgin and Child and St. John	2. 473	Charles I
The Resurrection	2. 473	,,
Conversion of St. Paul	2. 473	,,
David with the Head of Goliah	2. 473	,,
Virgin and Child and St. Sebastian	2. 473	,,
Virgin and Child and Elizabeth	2. 483	,,
Virgin and Child and Angels	2. 483	,,
Christ and the Woman of Samaria	2. 483	,,
Woman with bare Breast	2. 483	,,
A Holy Family	2. 492	Orleans Gallery
A Doge	2. 492	,,
St. Catherine	2. 492	,,
Salome and the Head of the Baptist	2. 492	,,
A Female	2. 492	,,
Venus and Cupid	2. 492	,,
Youth with a Guitar, and 2 Females	3. 202	Lord Northwick
Virgin and Child, St. John, etc.	3. 202	Lord Northwick
Adoration of Shepherds	3. 269	Edinburgh R.I.
Virgin and Child and St. John	3. 293	Sir A. Campbell
A Doge in an Armchair	3. 309	Lord Hopetoun
Virgin and Child with a Globe	3. 339	Earl Fitzwilliam
Birth of Adonis	3. 383	Earl of Shrewsbury
Death of Adonis	3. 383	,,
Venus and Cupid	3. 447	Fitzwilliam Museum
Christ on Virgin's lap and St. Joseph	4. 115	Sir C. Eastlake
Nude Youth kneeling, and Girl	4. 167	W. Davenport Bromley
Marriage of St. Catherine	4. 278	Sir C. Eardley
Virgin with the Child in her lap, etc.	4. 521	Earl of Hardwick
PALMEZZANO, Marco da Forli		
Virgin enthroned, etc.	3. 373	W. Davenport Bromley
John Baptist drinking	4. 95	T. Baring
Judith	4. 223	Prince Consort
PALOMINO		
A Franciscan	2. 259	G. A. Hoskins
PANNINI		
Ruins	1. 325	National Gallery
Interior of a Picture Gallery	2. 30	Bridgewater House

	VOL. & PAGE		OWNER
Interior of St. Peter's and Procession	2.	30	Bridgewater House
Interior, Marriage of Cana	2.	63	Duke of Sutherland
Interior of St. Peter's	2.	245	Joseph Neeld
Interior of S. Paolo	2.	336	Haywood Hawkins
Baths of Titus	3.	313	Duke of Buccleuch
Ruins of Rome	3.	313	Duke of Buccleuch
The Forum	3.	324	Earl of Carlisle
The Colosseum	3.	324	Earl of Carlisle
The Colosseum	3.	443	Mr. Tomline
Pyramid of Cestius	3.	443	Mr. Tomline
Interior of Pantheon	4.	368	Earl of Normanton
Architectural Piece	4.	421	Jacob Fletcher
Roman Ruins	4.	433	Gibson Craig
Baths of Titus	4.	436	Duke of Buccleuch
Roman Ruins	4.	436	Duke of Buccleuch
Interior of St. Peter's	4.	518	Lord Galway

PANTOJA, de la Cruz, Juan

A Prince (whole length)	3.	25	Earl of Darnley
A Princess (whole length)	3.	25	Earl of Darnley
Margaret of Austria, Wife of Philip III	4.	449	W. Stirling
A Princess	4.	450	W. Stirling

PARCELLIS

Two Pictures	2.	482	Charles I

PAREJA, Juan de

Philip of Bourbon	4.	66	Earl of Yarborough
Isabella of Bourbon	4.	66	Earl of Yarborough

PARMIGIANINO, Il

Virgin and Child in Glory	1.	330	National Gallery
Cupid mending his Bow	2.	30	Bridgewater House
Virgin and Child, St. John, etc.	2.	30	Bridgewater House
Man in a furred Garment	2.	60	Duke of Sutherland
Holy Family and Saints	2.	62	,,
A Young Man in Crimson and Fur	2.	62	,,
Magdalen in the Desert	2.	91	Devonshire House
Angel teaching Christ to read	2.	133	H. A. J. Munro
Sketch for National Gallery picture	2.	170	Marquis of Westminster
A Holy Family	2.	178	T. Baring
St. Luke painting the Virgin	2.	224	Richard Ford
Adam (drawing)	2.	224	,,
Eve (drawing)	2.	224	,,

PARMIGIANINO, Il—*continued*

	VOL. & PAGE		OWNER
Virgin and Child, St. John and St. Catherine	2.	262	J. Morrison
The Nativity and St. John	2.	268	Miss Rogers
Lady with Orrery and Dog	2.	368	Hampton Court
A Man	2.	432	Windsor Castle
A Young Man	2.	433	,,
Male Portrait with a Book	2.	434	,,
Virgin and Child and St. Jerome	2.	474	Charles I
Christ and St. John embracing	2.	474	,,
St. Catherine and 2 Angels	2.	474	,,
Virgin and Child, St. John and Joseph	2.	474	,,
Virgin and Child and St. Catherine	2.	474	,,
Virgin and Child and a Globe	2.	474	,,
Virgin and Child, St. John and Joseph	2.	474	,,
Woman with naked arms	2.	474	,,
A Nobleman	2.	474	,,
Woman in profile, in red Dress	2.	474	,,
Learned Man in black Dress	2.	474	,,
Virgin and Child, 2 Saints	2.	483	,,
Virgin and Child and Catherine	2.	483	,,
Christ and St. John naked	2.	483	,,
Cupid making his Bow	2.	483	,,
Young Man in black, Hand on Sword	2.	483	,,
Two Pictures	2.	483	,,
Cupid bending his Bow	2.	492	Orleans Gallery
Holy Family	2.	492	,,
Virgin and Child and Gifts	2.	492	,,
Marriage of St. Catherine	2.	492	,,
Holy Family and St. Francis	3.	493	,,
St. John the Evangelist	3.	493	,,
Ceres	3.	151	Earl of Pembroke
A Count Sanvitale	3.	176	Mr. Vivian
St. John the Baptist	3.	184	J. P. Miles
Sketch for National Gallery.	3.	185	,,
Virgin borne by Angels	3.	185	,,
Marriage of St. Catherine	3.	189	Mr. Harford
Virgin and Child and Saints	3.	189	Mr. Harford
Venus and Graces bathing	3.	304	Duke of Hamilton
A Male Portrait	3.	350	Duke of Devonshire
Magdalen in a Cavern	3.	422	Earl of Leicester
Two Pictures	3.	483	Marquis of Bute
Virgin seated and Child, etc.	4.	107	J. Morrison
Heads of Children (in red chalk)	4.	117	C. S. Bale
Study of Trees (drawing)	4.	117	C. S. Bale

	VOL. & PAGE		OWNER
Virgin, seated on ground, and Child	4.	147	Lord Overstone
Ganymede carried off by an Eagle	4.	235	Earl of Harrington
Cupid borne aloft by Amorini	4.	305	J. Morrison
Male Portrait in a furred Coat	4.	323	Lord Enfield
St. John the Baptist	4.	329	Sir T. Sebright
Marriage of St. Catherine	4.	367	Earl of Normanton
Music and the Graces	4.	456	Earl of Dunmore
Infant Christ in a Cradle	4.	503	Earl of Yarborough

PAROCEL

A Battle Piece and Cross	2.	229	Hon. E. Phipps

PATENIER, Joachim

The Visitation	2.	461	Mr. Green
Legend of Canonized Bishop	3.	6	W. Fuller Maitland
A Riposo	3.	253	Blundell Weld
Marriage of the Virgin	3.	254	Blundell Weld
Adoration of the Kings	3.	287	M'Lellan Gallery
Virgin and Child in a Landscape	3.	289	M'Lellan Gallery
A Crucifixion	3.	314	Capt. Stirling
Christ on the Mount of Olives	4.	103	Lord Ward
Virgin and Child, with 2 female Saints	4.	153	W. Gladstone
Virgin giving Breast to Christ	4.	186	W. Russell
The Magdalen	4.	229	Prince Consort
St. Christopher	4.	229	„
St. John at Patmos	4.	229	„
The Crucifixion	4.	229	„
Virgin lamenting over Christ	4.	316	Rev. Mr. Heath
Christ taking leave of His Mother	4.	461	M'Lellan Gallery
Adoration of the Kings (School of)	4.	461	„
Virgin and Child	4.	461	„

PATER

Large Party in a Landscape	3.	286	M'Lellan Gallery
Ladies and Gentlemen resting	4.	84	Marquis of Hertford
Ladies and Gentlemen resting	4.	430	Lord Murray
A small Picture	4.	430	Lord Murray

PAYNE

Doges' Palace, Venice	4.	418	J. Chapman
Grand Canal	4.	418	J. Chapman

PEDRINI, Giovanni

A Female Saint	2.	84	Lord De Mauley
Christ as a Boy, with Globe	3.	348	Duke of Devonshire

U

	VOL. & PAGE		OWNER

PEDRINI, Giovanni—*continued*

Repentant Magdalen pointing to a Skull	3.	441	Mr. Tomline
Virgin and Child	4.	427	Rev. T. Staniforth
Mary Magdalen	1.	417	Lord Malmesbury

PENNI, Francesco (Il Fattore)

Female nursing two Children	2.	244	Joseph Neeld
Virgin stooping to the Child	3.	151	Earl of Pembroke

PENS, George

Erasmus, 1536	2.	430	Windsor Castle
A young Man with Gloves	2.	474	Charles I
Erasmus	2.	474	Charles I

PERUGINO, Pietro

Virgin and Child	1.	316	National Gallery
Virgin and Child and St. John	1.	323	National Gallery
3 large Compartments	2.	127	A. Barker
Virgin, Child standing	2.	195	R. S. Holford
A Crucifixion	2.	231	Lord Ward
Virgin with Child standing	2.	331	C. S. Bale
A Pietà, with St. John	2.	418	H. Labouchere
The Entombment	2.	493	Orleans Gallery
Virgin and Child	2.	493	"
Christ being worshipped	2.	493	"
Virgin and Child, Benediction	3.	159	Marquis of Lansdowne
Crucifixion (School of)	3.	375	W. Davenport Bromley
Virgin kneeling (altar-piece)	4.	55	National Gallery
Martyrdom of St. Sebastian	4.	299	Higford Burr
Virgin and Child, St. Jerome, etc.	4.	340	Knole
A Male Portrait	4.	345	Earl Cowper
Virgin seated, Child on her Lap	4.	439	Earl of Wemyss

PERUZZI, Balthazar

Adoration of the Kings (drawing)	1.	325	National Gallery
Adoration of the Kings	1.	326	National Gallery
Adoration of the Kings	2.	30	Bridgewater House
Adoration of the Kings	2.	493	Orleans Gallery
Birth of the Virgin	3.	151	Earl of Pembroke

PESARO, Simone da

A Picture	4.	492	Lord Feversham

	VOL. & PAGE	OWNER
PESELLI, Pesello		
Virgin and Child and St. John	2. 231	Lord Ward
Christ on the Cross	3. 375	W. Davenport Bromley
Virgin with Child held by an Angel	4. 167	W. Davenport Bromley
PESELLINO (Francesco di Pesello)		
Exhibition of a Relic in Florence	3. 233	Liverpool R.I.
PESNE, Antoine		
Frederick the Great	2. 368	Hampton Court
PETERS, Bonaventura		
An agitated Sea	3. 222	Howard Galton
PETITOT, (Miniature)		
Charles I	2. 97	Miss Burdett Coutts
Charles II	2. 97	„
James II	2. 97	„
Duchess of Orleans	2. 97	„
Young Pretender	2. 97	„
Miniatures	3. 408	Marquis of Exeter
Madame de Grignon	4. 213	Mr. Henderson
Queen of Louis XIV	4. 264	Duc D'Aumale
The Grand Condé	4. 264	Duc D'Aumale
Miniatures	4. 453	W. Stirling
Miniatures	4. 512	Duke of Portland
PHILLIPS, Thomas, R.A.		
Sir David Wilkie, R.A.	1. 381	Marlborough House
Venus detaining Adonis	2. 72	Duke of Sutherland
Mr. Green and his Lady	2. 461	Mr. Green
PICKERSGILL, H. W., R.A.		
Robert Vernon	1. 381	Marlborough House
The Syrian Maid	1. 381	Marlborough House
Alexander von Humboldt	4. 303	J. Morrison
PIER di Cosimo		
Bacchanalian Subject	4. 327	Sir T. Sebright
Bacchanalian Subject	4. 327	Sir T. Sebright
PIETRO della Francesca		
Isotta Rimini	4. 74	A. Barker
Heads from Arezzo frescoes	4. 299	Higford Burr
Youth with light Hair	4. 498	W. Drury Lowe

	VOL. & PAGE	OWNER
PIETRO della Vecchia		
Male Head (called S. Rosa)	3. 203	Lord Northwick
Male Head (called Giorgione)	3. 203	Lord Northwick
St. Roch, and the Plague stricken	3. 225	Mr. Martin
Soldiers at Cards	3. 265	Earl of Lonsdale
Soldiers at Cards	3. 265	Earl of Lonsdale
Four Fathers of the Church	3. 298	Duke of Hamilton
Three Lads playing Cards	4. 279	Sir C. Eardley
A Girl singing, and Man with a Guitar	4. 410	Smith Barry
Abner with Head of Goliah	4. 520	Earl of Hardwicke
PINTURICCIO, Bernardino		
Two small Pictures	2. 232	Lord Ward
Return of Ulysses	4. 74	A. Barker
Virgin and Child	4. 223	Prince Consort
Frescoes from Spello	4. 299	Higford Burr
Virgin with Child on Arm	4. 366	Earl of Normanton
Dismissal of Hagar	4. 396	Lord Methuen
PIOMBO, Sebastian del		
Raising of Lazarus	1. 315, 320	National Gallery
S. del Piombo and Cardinal	1. 333	”
A Female Saint	1. 333	”
Titian (circle), 1542	1. 417	Lord Malmesbury
The Entombment	2. 32	Bridgewater House
A Male Portrait	2. 150	Marquis of Lansdowne
Virgin and Child and St. John	2. 175	T. Baring
A Female Portrait	2. 175	T. Baring
A Male Portrait	2. 197	R. S. Holford
A Male Portrait	2. 239	Marquis of Breadalbane
Young Man with silver Vessel	2. 283	Duke of Bedford
Group of Portraits	2. 287	H. Labouchere
Old Man, Hand on Breast	2. 474	Charles I
Descent from the Cross	2. 493	Orleans Gallery
Raising of Lazarus	2. 493	Orleans Gallery
St. Sebastian	3. 140	Earl of Radnor
A Female Portrait (called Raphael)	3. 140	Earl of Radnor
A Monk with a Skull	3. 162	Marquis of Lansdowne
A Pietà with two Angels	3. 187	Mr. Harford
Holy Family	3. 188	”
Male Head	3. 188	”
Altar-piece, a Pietà, etc.	3. 206	Lord Northwick
Bacchus and Ariadne	3. 269	Edinburgh R.I.
Pope Clement VII seated	3. 303	Duke of Hamilton
The Transfiguration	3. 305	Duke of Hamilton

	VOL. & PAGE	OWNER
The Visitation, etc.	3. 376	W. Davenport Bromley
Pope Clement VII	4. 62	Lord Elcho
Amerigo Vespucci submitting Maps	4. 104	H. Labouchere
A Male Portrait	4. 343	Countess of Warwick
St. Sebastian bound	4. 358	Lord Folkestone
Francesco Albizzi	4. 397	Lord Methuen
Female Portrait with both Hands	4. 444	Earl of Elgin
Christ's entry into Jerusalem	4. 456	Earl of Dunmore
Andrea Doria in profile	4. 498	W. Drury Lowe
Descent from the Cross	4. 502	Earl of Yarborough
A Man in a Black Dress	4. 518	Earl of Hardwicke

PLASSAN

A Party of the time of Louis XIV	4. 417	S. Ashton

PLAZER, Johann George

2 Pictures	4. 298	J. Walter

POELENBURG, Cornelius

Campo Vaccino and Figures	2. 4	Buckingham Palace
A Picture	2. 95	Devonshire House
A Riposo	2. 242	H. D. Seymour
Cymon and Iphigenia	2. 283	Duke of Bedford
4 Pictures	2. 482	Charles I
Mountainous Landscape and Figures	2. 501	Orleans Gallery
Landscape, with Nymphs	2. 501	,,
Landscape, Ruins and Figures	2. 501	,,
Small Landscape	2. 501	,,
Small Landscape	2. 501	,,
A Picture	3. 310	Earl of Hopetoun
Nymphs bathing	3. 313	Duke of Buccleuch
A Charity, 6 Children and Angels	3. 332	Meynell Ingram
A Riposo	3. 347	Duke of Devonshire
Adoration of the Shepherds	3. 398	Duke of Rutland
St. Lawrence	3. 400	Duke of Rutland
Christ at Emmaus	3. 406	Marquess of Exeter
A Picture	3. 434	Earl of Orford
Four Pictures	3. 449	Fitzwilliam Museum
A Riposo	3. 476	Marquis of Bute
St. Peter	4. 209	Mr. Henderson
Baptism of Christ	4. 236	Earl of Harrington
A Riposo in a Landscape	4. 289	J. Sanders
Landscape, Figures bathing	4. 361	Lord Folkestone
Tobit and the Angel	4. 424	Earl of Burlington
Expulsion from Paradise	4. 458	M'Lellan Gallery
Landscape, Ruins and Nymphs	4. 509	Duke of Newcastle

	VOL. & PAGE	OWNER
POLIDORO da Caravaggio		
Seven fresco Paintings	2. 475	Charles I
Destruction of Pharaoh, Red Sea	3. 383	Earl of Shrewsbury
POLLAJUOLO, Antonio		
Lady with full Bust	2. 269	Miss Rogers
A youthful Portrait	2. 330	C. S. Bale
Female Portrait in profile	4. 167	W. Davenport Bromley
PONTORMO, Jacobo		
Young Man in a Black Hat	2. 176	T. Baring
Alessandro de Medici	2. 232	Lord Ward
A young Man with a Paper	4. 62	Lord Elcho
A young Woman	4. 62	Lord Elcho
Virgin and Child	4. 467	Duke of Northumberland
Birth of the Virgin	4. 467	Duke of Northumberland
Gaston de Medici	3. 302	Duke of Hamilton
Oval Portrait	4. 345	Earl Cowper
Virgin and Child and St. John	4. 398	Lord Methuen
His own Portrait	4. 398	Lord Methuen
POOLE, P. F., R.A.		
Convent of Nuns, time of Henry VIII	2. 142	H. A. J. Munro
A Girl surprised bathing	4. 417	S. Ashton
PORDENONE (Licinio Regillo)		
Woman taken in Adultery	2. 60	Duke of Sutherland
Man with Music Book, 1524	2. 314	Earl Brownlow
Man drinking, Flask in Hand	2. 314	,,
Man with Hands on Parapet	2. 314	,,
A Male Portrait	2. 355	Hampton Court
Portrait of a Knight	2. 356	,,
A Holy Family	2. 358	,,
Lady playing on the Spinet	2. 359	,,
Solomon sacrificing to Idols	2. 475	Charles I
Family Picture	2. 475	,,
His own Portrait, playing on the Lute	2. 475	,,
An intoxicated Satyr	2. 475	,,
Hercules killing Antaeus	2. 493	Orleans Gallery
Judith	2. 493	Orleans Gallery
Hercules and Achelous	3. 19	Earl of Darnley
Christ on the Mount of Olives	3. 269	Edinburgh R.I.
Virgin holding Child	3. 304	Duke of Hamilton
Two Men and two Women	3. 378	W. Davenport Bromley
Death of Peter Martyr	3. 383	Earl of Shrewsbury

	VOL. & PAGE		OWNER
Finding of Moses	3.	404	Marquis of Exeter
Adoration of the Kings	3.	404	Marquis of Exeter
Copy of Belvedere Apollo	4.	171	E. Cheney
Adoration of the Kings	4.	429	Edinburgh R.I.

PORTA, Giuseppe (Del Salviati)

The Annunciation	4.	68	Earl of Yarborough
Joseph and Potiphar's Wife	4.	454	Earl of Dunmore

POST

Two American Landscapes	3.	460	Duke of Buccleuch

POTTER, Paul

Four Cows, Sheep and Horse	1.	405	Sir R. Peel
Young Bull and 2 Cows	2.	14	Buckingham Palace
Two Huntsmen on Horseback	2.	14	,,
Two Pigs lying down	2.	15	,,
Stable Boy crying	2.	15	,,
Three Oxen in a Meadow	2.	46	Bridgewater House
Six Cows, a Bull, and 2 Sheep	2.	107	Lord Ashburton
Two Oxen butting each other	2.	107	Lord Ashburton
Young Bull near a Black Cow	2.	120	H. T. Hope
Man with a Grey Horse	2.	120	,,
Five Cows on a bare Hill	2.	120	,,
Five Cows, a Bull, and 5 Sheep	2.	167	Marquis of Westminster
Young brown Bull and 2 Sheep, 1647	2.	185	T. Baring
An Ass and 2 Goats, 1647	2.	201	R. S. Holford
A Chalk Drawing	2.	204	,,
A Chalk Drawing—Drove of Oxen	2.	204	,,
A Hunting Party, Lady and Falcon	2.	286	Duke of Bedford
Oxen, Cows, etc., in a Meadow, 1657	2.	286	Duke of Bedford
A Picture	2.	287	H. Labouchere
Grey Horse and Brown Horse	2.	289	R. Sanderson
A Stag Hunt	2.	296	Wynn Ellis
Cattle in a Meadow	2.	331	C. S. Bale
A Drawing	2.	334	Mr. Townley
Farm House and 5 Cows	2.	337	Duke of Somerset
Ox and Tree in Shade	2.	422	H. Labouchere
Two Cows and Ox in a Meadow, 1647	2.	453	J. Walter
Landscape	3.	134	J. Morrison
Three Cows in a Meadow, 1652	3.	184	J. P. Miles
Two Cattle Pieces	3.	313	Duke of Buccleuch
A Hunting Piece, 1613	3.	466	Duke of Bedford
Cow with yellow Spots	4.	293	J. Walter
Cows under Trees, 1652	4.	310	J. Morrison

	VOL. & PAGE		OWNER
POTTER, Paul—*continued*			
Landscape with Cattle	4.	332	Duke of Bedford
A Cow's Head, over life size	4.	385	Danby Seymour
Two brown Cows feeding	4.	391	Mr. Everett
POURBUS, Franz			
Two Portraits	3.	475	Marquis of Bute
POUSSIN, Gaspar			
A Land Storm	1.	342	National Gallery
A Storm—Dido and Æneas	1.	343	,,
Abraham and Isaac	1.	343	,,
A View of Aricia	1.	343	,,
Lake of Albano	1.	343	,,
Waterfall with snow-topped Hills	1.	343	,,
Landscape with two Figures	2.	23	Buckingham Palace
A violent Storm	2.	38	Bridgewater House
Environs of Tivoli	2.	38	,,
Landscape traversed by River	2.	38	,,
Richly wooded Valley	2.	38	,,
A Poetic Landscape	2.	63	Duke of Sutherland
A Landscape	2.	86	Earl of Yarborough
Buildings, with a loving Couple	2.	133	H. A. J. Munro
Tivoli, a narrow Picture	2.	155	Marquis of Hertford
A Landscape	2.	171	Marquis of Westminster
Tivoli	2.	171	Marquis of Westminster
Landscape with a Cave	2.	177	T. Baring
View of the Campagna	2.	195	R. S. Holford
Shepherd and Flock of Sheep	2.	195	,,
Landscape, two Figures	2.	195	,,
Landscape, Flock of Goats	2.	195	,,
Landscape with Waterfall	2.	233	Lord Ward
Large Landscape	2.	260	W. A. Mackinnon
Landscape	2.	262	J. Morrison
A Landscape	2.	267	Miss Rogers
An enclosed Scene	2.	268	,,
A dark Landscape	2.	270	,,
Three Landscapes	2.	280	Earl of Carlisle
A small Landscape	2.	285	Duke of Bedford
Apollo pursuing Daphne	2.	294	Wynn Ellis
Buildings in middle distance	2.	294	,,
A Storm, 2 Figures	2.	294	,,
A dark Landscape	2.	347	Dulwich Gallery
Poetic Landscape	2.	434	Windsor Castle
Poetic Landscape, Waterfall	2.	434	Windsor Castle

	VOL. & PAGE		OWNER
Man angling and a Woman	3.	36	Petworth
Disciples going to Emmaus	3.	134	J. Morrison
Small Landscape	3.	141	Earl of Radnor
Small Landscape	3.	141	Earl of Radnor
Small Landscape	3.	170	Earl of Suffolk
Small Landscape	3.	170	„
Temple of Sibyl, Tivoli	3.	170	„
A Landscape	3.	172	Colt Hoare
Large Landscape, Elijah and an Angel	3.	179	J. P. Miles
Tivoli	3.	185	„
Tivoli	3.	185	„
Landscape, Figures and Water	3.	185	„
Landscape with Fortress	3.	190	Mr. Harford
A Storm	3.	193	„
Landscape, 2 Monks	3.	193	„
Landscape and 2 Shepherds	3.	198	Lord Northwick
Landscape, Shepherd and Sheep	3.	198	„
Campagna of Rome	3.	198	„
Landscape, sleeping Figure	3.	198	„
Landscape, Shepherd and 2 Dogs	3.	225	Mr. Martin
Tivoli, Temple of Sibyl	3.	225	Mr. Martin
Landscape, a Man with an Ass	3.	260	Earl of Lonsdale
Large Landscape	3.	261	Earl of Lonsdale
Landscape	3.	269	Edinburgh R.I.
A Land Storm	3.	275	Edinburgh R.I.
Landscape and 2 figures	3.	290	M'Lellan Gallery
Thunderstorm, Bolt falling	3.	300	Duke of Hamilton
Landscape, Flock of Sheep	3.	301	Duke of Hamilton
Landscape	3.	334	Meynell Ingram
Long Landscape	3.	348	Duke of Devonshire
Four circular Pictures, Tivoli, etc.	3.	348	Duke of Devonshire
Landscape	3.	380	W. Davenport Bromley
Landscape	3.	380	W. Davenport Bromley
Christ going to Emmaus	3.	398	Duke of Rutland
Large Landscape	3.	398	„
Landscape	3.	400	„
Five Pictures	3.	421	Earl of Leicester
Large Landscape	3.	430	A. Fountaine
Small Landscape	3.	447	Fitzwilliam Museum
Small Landscape	3.	456	Earl Spencer
Landscape from Stowe	3.	462	Glendon Hall
Large Landscape	3.	465	Duke of Bedford
Large Landscape	3.	465	Duke of Bedford
Two Landscapes	3.	484	Marquis of Bute
Landscape, Town and Waterfall	4.	67	Earl of Yarborough

x

POUSSIN, Gasper—*continued*

	VOL. & PAGE		OWNER
Landscape, Castle, and 2 Figures	4.	70	Earl of Yarborough
Landscape	4.	70	,,
Landscape with Waterfall	4.	83	Marquis of Hertford
Large Tree, Shepherd and Sheep	4.	107	J. Morrison
Landscape, 2 Sportsmen	4.	153	Hoare Family
Cattle descending Hill	4.	153	Hoare Family
Landscape	4.	268	Duke of Northumberland
Landscape	4.	268	Duke of Northumberland
Extensive View, 3 Figures	4.	270	Earl of Jersey
The Campagna	4.	271	,,
Landscape	4.	272	,,
Landscape	4.	272	,,
Chain of Rocks, 2 Nymphs	4.	272	,,
Dark Landscape	4.	278	Sir C. Eardley
Dark Landscape, 4 Figures	4.	278	,,
Figures in a Boat	4.	283	,,
Landscape, Shepherd, and 4 Goats	4.	307	J. Morrison
Landscape, stately Building	4.	308	,,
Wooded Hill, 2 Persons	4.	311	,,
Landscape, 2 Men and an Animal	4.	327	Sir T. Sebright
Landscape, Hercules and Centaur	4.	327	Sir T. Sebright
Landscape, 2 Persons conversing	4.	332	Duke of Bedford
High Hills and Water	4.	332	,,
Chain of Hills, Sea View	4.	333	,,
Small Landscape	4.	346	Earl Cowper
Small Landscape	4.	346	Earl Cowper
Landscape, Figure reposing, etc.	4.	350	Vernon Harcourt
Dark Landscape	4.	355	Lord Folkestone
Falls at Tivoli	4.	355	Lord Folkestone
Landscape, Waterfall	4.	365	Earl of Normanton
A Picture	4.	374	Sir W. Knighton
A Landscape	4.	386	H. D. Seymour
Landscape with Hills	4.	389	Lord Heytesbury
Landscape, Waterfall	4.	393	Lord Arundel
Landscape, Waterfall	4.	393	Lord Arundel
Landscape, Waterfall	4.	411	Smith Barry
Circular Landscape	4.	412	,,
Landscape	4.	413	,,
Lofty Hill, 2 Figures and a Dog	4.	424	Earl of Burlington
Landscape, 2 Friars	4.	451	W. Stirling
Landscape, a Man reposing	4.	452	W. Stirling
Hilly Landscape, Figures bathing	4.	454	Earl of Dunmore
Upright Landscape	4.	455	,,
Landscape, stately Trees	4.	456	,,

	VOL. & PAGE		OWNER
A Landscape	4.	462	M'Lellan Gallery
A Landscape, 2 young Men	4.	462	M'Lellan Gallery
A Landscape, Shepherd and Flock	4.	481	Matthew Anderson
A Landscape	4.	485	Lord Ravensworth
Landscape, Water and 2 Figures	4.	497	W. Drury Lowe
Rocks and Caves and Waterfall	4.	503	Earl of Yarborough
Companion	4.	503	"
An Eminence with Trees	4.	504	"
Trees, and 2 Figures by Water	4.	504	"
Stately Buildings and Waterfall	4.	505	"
Trees, Figures under them	4.	505	"
Poetic Landscape	4.	510	Duke of Newcastle
Poetic Landscape	4.	510	"
Hill and Campagna	4.	510	"
Small Landscape	4.	513	Duke of Portland
Upright Landscape, 2 Figures	4.	514	"
Companion	4.	514	"
Light Landscape	4.	521	Earl of Hardwicke

POUSSIN, Nicholas

	VOL. & PAGE		OWNER
Dance of Fauns and Bacchantes	1.	344	National Gallery
A Bacchanal	1.	345	"
Sleeping Nymph and Satyr	1.	345	"
Cephalus and Aurora	1.	345	"
The Plague at Ashdod	1.	345	"
Perseus with Medusa's Head	1.	345	"
Landscape, Nymph and Satyrs	1.	346	"
Landscape, with Phocian bathing feet	1.	346	"
The Seven Sacraments (7 pictures)	2.	39	Bridgewater House
Moses striking the Rock	2.	39	Bridgewater House
A Holy Family	2.	66	Duke of Sutherland
Bacchante and Satyr	2.	66	Duke of Sutherland
Large Landscape	2.	78	S. Rogers
Small historical Picture	2.	78	"
Small historical Picture	2.	78	"
Tivoli	2.	87	Earl of Yarborough
Jehovah in Glory, etc.	2.	93	Devonshire House
Et in Arcadia ego	2.	93	"
Holy Family and Angels	2.	93	"
The Forum	2.	93	"
The Forum	2.	93	"
Venus and Adonis	2.	136	H. A. J. Munro
Architectural Subject	2.	136	H. A. J. Munro
Dance of the Seasons	2.	156	Marquis of Hertford
Virgin and Child and Angels	2.	172	Marquis of Westminster

		VOL. & PAGE	OWNER
POUSSIN, Nicholas—*continued*			
Jupiter and Callisto		2. 172	Marquis of Westminster
Preaching of St. John		2. 236	Lord Ward
Children of Bacchus drinking		2. 245	Mr. Neeld
Copy of Bellini's Picture		2. 266	Sir C. Eastlake
Bathsheba and an old Woman		2. 284	Duke of Bedford
Infant Moses and Pharaoh's Crown		2. 284	Duke of Bedford
Antiope and Jupiter		2. 313	Earl of Listowel
Assumption of Virgin		2. 347	Dulwich Gallery
Figures of Children		2. 347	,,
Triumph of David		2. 347	,,
Jupiter nursed by Goat		2. 347	,,
A Landscape		2. 348	,,
Nymphs and Satyrs		2. 365	Hampton Court
The Seven Sacraments (7 pictures)		2. 493	Orleans Gallery
Moses striking the Rock		2. 493	,,
Moses with the Crown of Pharaoh		2. 493	,,
St. Paul carried by Angels		2. 493	,,
Exposure of Moses		2. 493	,,
Birth of Bacchus		2. 493	,,
Du Quesnoy the Sculptor		3. 16	Earl Cowper
Nymph on shoulders of Satyr		3. 25	Earl of Darnley
Cupid kissing Nymph		3. 25	,,
Bacchanalian Children		3. 25	,,
Bacchanalian Fête		3. 134	J. Morrison
Departure of the Israelites		3. 141	Earl of Radnor
Worshipping the Golden Calf		3. 141	Earl of Radnor
Rape of the Sabines		3. 172	Colt Hoare
The Choice of Hercules		3. 172	Colt Hoare
The Plague at Athens		3. 180	J. P. Miles
Landscape, Man, Woman, and Grey Horse		3. 192	Mr. Harford
Apollo and Daphne		3. 204	Lord Northwick
Pan Kneeling before Nymph		3. 204	,,
Sleeping Satyrs and a Boy		3. 205	,,
Venus showing Armour to Æneas		3. 205	,,
Landscape, with Goatherd		3. 205	,,
Landscape, Arcadian Shepherds		3. 240	Liverpool R.I.
Old Man and sick Wife		3. 294	Sir A. Campbell
The Entombment		3. 300	Duke of Hamilton
Virgin and Child, St. John and Elizabeth		3. 332	Meynell Ingram
Holy Family, Angels and Flowers		3. 347	Duke of Devonshire
Rinaldo and Armida		3. 393	Lord Scarsdale
Baptism		3. 401	Duke of Rutland
Confirmation		3. 401	,,
Confession		3. 401	,,

	VOL. & PAGE	OWNER
The Last Supper	3. 401	Duke of Rutland
Marriage of the Virgin	3. 401	„
Extreme Unction	3. 401	„
Ordination, Christ and St. Peter	3. 401	„
Angels with Instruments of the Passion	3. 406	Marquis of Exeter
Assumption of Virgin	3. 406	Marquis of Exeter
A Storm	3. 419	Earl of Leicester
Thunderstorm, Lightning striking Tower	3. 420	„
A Landscape	3. 421	„
Mythological Subject	3. 430	A. Fountaine
Boys catching Birds	3. 462	Glendon Hall
Large Landscape	3. 484	Marquis of Bute
Large Landscape	3. 484	Marquis of Bute
Poetic Landscape	4. 68	Earl of Yarborough
Virgin and Child, St. John and Joseph	4. 69	Earl of Yarborough
A Landscape	4. 101	R. S. Holford
Landscape, Sarcophagus, Temple, etc.	4. 151	Earl of Caledon
Virgin and Child and Ruins	4. 152	Earl of Caledon
Murder of the Innocents	4. 263	Duc D'Aumale
Silenus sleeping, and Nymph	4. 271	Earl of Jersey
A Bacchanal, Nymph and Tambourine	4. 304	J. Morrison
Calm Lake, old Man and Paper	4. 321	Lord Enfield
Poetical Landscape	4. 333	Duke of Bedford
Moses striking the Rock	4. 349	Vernon Harcourt
Venus and Mars	4. 350	„
Rocky Hills and Buildings	4. 351	„
Landscape and Figures	4. 351	„
Landscape, circular Tower	4. 352	„
Adoration of the Golden Calf	4. 359	Lord Folkestone
Exodus of the Israelites	4. 359	Lord Folkestone
View of Ponte Molle	4. 390	Lord Heytesbury
Herminia on piebald Horse	4. 390	Lord Heytesbury
Orion meeting the rising Sun	4. 396	Lord Methuen
Landscape, Angler, and Figures	4. 413	Smith Barry
Buildings and lofty Hills	4. 413	Smith Barry
Baptism of Christ	4. 438	Earl of Wemyss
Finding of Moses	4. 452	W. Stirling
Orpheus and Eurydice bitten by the Asp	4. 454	Earl of Dunmore
Copy of Raphael's St. Peter	4. 471	Duke of Northumberland
Venus on Clouds kissing Cupid	4. 476	W. W. Bardon
Venus and the Loves at a Brazier	4. 476	„
Landscape, two Women conversing	4. 477	„
Copy of St. Andrew, after Domenichino	4. 483	Matthew Anderson
Rebecca and Eleazar at the Well	4. 485	Lord Ravensworth

	VOL. & PAGE	OWNER
POUSSIN, Nicholas—*continued*		
Poetical Landscape	4. 485	Lord Ravensworth
Poetical Landscape	4. 491	Mr. Fenderson
A Storm	4. 493	Lord Feversham
Rinaldo and Armida	4. 504	Earl of Yarborough
Sleeping Nymphs and 2 Satyrs	4. 505	Earl of Yarborough
Apostle baptizing Converts	4. 506	Sir J. Nelthorpe
PRETI, Mattia (Il Cavaliere Calabrese)		
Time unveiling Truth	3. 405	Marquis of Exeter
Adoration of the Kings	3. 423	Earl of Leicester
PREVITALI, Andrea		
Three Men and a Woman with Lute	4. 451	W. Stirling
PRIMATICCIO, Francesco		
Nymphs with Branches	2. 26	Bridgewater House
Penelope and Ulysses	3. 322	Earl of Carlisle
Cardinal de Chatillon, 1548	4. 261	Duc D'Aumale
PROCACCINI, Camillo		
Holy Family	2. 245	Joseph Neeld
The Tribute Money	3. 192	Mr. Harford
Dead Christ, Magdalen and Angels	3. 273	Edinburgh R.I.
Virgin and Child, St. John and Joseph	3. 288	M'Lellan Gallery
PROCACCINI, Giulio Cesare		
Marriage of St. Catherine	3. 239	Liverpool R.I.
PROUT, Samuel		
Doges' Palace (drawing)	4. 112	J. Morrison
PYNAKER, Adam		
Rocky Coast and Pirates	2. 139	A. J. Munro
Arch of Bridge, Sun shining through it	2. 187	T. Baring
Landscape	2. 248	Joseph Neeld
Landscape	2. 286	Duke of Bedford
Waterfall, Mule on broken Bridge	2. 291	C. Bredel
A Landscape	2. 297	Wynn Ellis
A Landscape	3. 165	Marquis of Lansdowne
Herd of Cattle in a Storm	3. 223	Howard Galton
Shepherd Boy, Dog and Cow	3. 273	Edinburgh R.I.
A Landscape	3. 292	Sir A. Campbell
Small Landscape and Cattle	3. 396	Duke of Rutland

	VOL. & PAGE	OWNER
RAEBURN, Sir Henry, R.A.		
A Lady, half-length	4. 433	Gibson Craig
A Male Portrait	4. 433	Gibson Craig
Playfair the Metaphysician	4. 434	Mr. Playfair
Helen Stirling, girl seated	4. 453	W. Stirling
RAPHAEL		
St. Catherine	1. 316, 323	National Gallery
Vision of a Knight	1. 317, 323	„
Murder of the Innocents	1. 324	„
Julius II, Pope	1. 324	„
Seven Cartoons (*copies* by Thornhill)	1. 392	Royal Academy
School of Athens (*copy*)	1. 394	Duke of Northumberland
Assembly of the Gods (*copy*)	1. 394	„
Marriage of Cupid and Psyche (*copy*)	1. 394	„
Madonna with Fan Palm	2. 26	Bridgewater House
Virgin contemplating Child	2. 27	„
Virgin in Landscape, Hand on Child	2. 28	„
Virgin lifting Veil from sleeping Infant	2. 29	„
Christ on the Mount of Olives	2. 76	S. Rogers
Virgin with downcast Eyes, etc.	2. 76	„
Entombment (drawing)	2. 80	„
Madonna dei Candelabri	2. 132	H. A. J. Munro
Virgin raising Veil from Infant with St. John	2. 169	Marquis of Westminster
Holy Family (*copy*)	2. 176	T. Baring
The Crucifixion	2. 232	Lord Ward
The Three Graces	2. 233	„
Johanna of Arragon (*copy*)	2. 243	H. D. Seymour
Virgin and Child and St. John	2. 250	Lady Garvagh
The Pietà (drawing)	2. 330	C. S. Bale
St. Francis	2. 346	Dulwich Gallery
St. Anthony	2. 346	Dulwich Gallery
Seven Cartoons	2. 475	Charles I
Virgin and Child, Elizabeth and St. John	2. 475	„
Virgin and Child and St. John	2. 475	„
St. George and the Dragon	2. 475	„
Virgin, Christ and Priest	2. 475	„
Virgin and Child, Joseph and Lamb	2. 476	„
Young Man in red Hat with Medal on it	2. 476	„
His own Portrait, in black Cap	2. 483	„

Y

	VOL. & PAGE		OWNER
RAPHAEL—*continued*			
An Italian Duchess	2.	484	Charles I
Holy Family with the Palm	2.	493	Orleans Gallery
Virgin and Child	2.	493	„
Virgin with Child kissing St. John	2.	493	„
John the Baptist in the Wilderness	2.	494	„
Vision of Ezekiel	2.	494	„
Virgin with Child on her Knee	2.	494	„
Christ bearing Cross	2.	494	„
Virgin lifting Veil from sleeping Christ	2.	494	„
Virgin, Child on Pedestal	2.	494	„
A Pietà, Christ in the Lap of His Mother	2.	494	„
Christ on the Mount of Olives	2.	494	„
Pope Julius II	2.	494	„
Christ and Disciples on the Mount of Olives	3.	5	Fuller Maitland
Virgin on a Stone Bench and Child	3.	8	Earl Cowper
Virgin, Child on a Cushion	3.	9	Earl Cowper
A Male Portrait	3.	42	Petworth
Three Boys and a fourth in a Tub	3.	47	Oxford, Guise Collection
Murder of the Innocents (fragment)	3.	47	Oxford, Guise Collection
A Female Portrait	3.	125	Duke of Marlborough
Virgin enthroned and Child (Ansidei)	3.	127	Duke of Marlborough
John the Baptist preaching	3.	161	Marquis of Lansdowne
Head of an Apostle	3.	162	Marquis of Lansdowne
Christ bearing Cross	3.	183	J. P. Miles
Virgin lifting Veil from the Child	3.	183	„
Pope Julius II	3.	184	„
Lo Spasimo	3.	191	Mr. Harford
La Belle Jardinière (*copy*)	3.	193	Mr. Harford
Bartholomew Bianchini	3.	199	Lord Northwick
Joanna of Aragon	3.	213	Earl of Warwick
Madonna with the Pink	3.	253	Blundell Weld
Holy Family	3.	316	Rock
Virgin and Child	3.	339	Earl Fitzwilliam
Man in black, Hand on a Skull	3.	378	W. Davenport Bromley
A Pietà, Christ on Knees of the Virgin	3.	390	M. A. Whyte
La Belle Vierge (*copy*)	3.	404	Marquis of Exeter
Virgin at Sepulchre (*copy*)	3.	404	Marquis of Exeter
Leo IX and 2 Cardinals	3.	420	Earl of Leicester
Virgin standing with Book, etc.	3.	423	Earl of Leicester
La Fornarina	3.	443	Mr. Tomline
Murder of the Innocents (fragment)	3.	455	Earl Spencer
Holy Family (*copy*)	3.	455	Earl Spencer
Male Portrait, with Hands	4.	68	Earl of Yarborough

	VOL. & PAGE	OWNER
The Three Graces	4. 102	Lord Ward
La Belle Jardinière	4. 179	Rev. Mr. Townshend
Virgin and Child (?)	4. 182	G. Cornwall Legh
St. Jerome and Crucifix	4. 327	Sir T. Sebright
A Female Portrait	4. 360	Lord Folkestone
Virgin standing with Child	4. 376	Kingston Lacy
Holy Family	4. 388	Lord Heytesbury
Madonna dell Impannata	4. 397	Lord Methuen
Virgin and Child with a Pink	4. 466	Duke of Northumberland
Virgin ascending from Tomb	4. 499	Earl of Warwick
Virgin and Child and St. Anna	4. 502	Earl of Yarborough
Holy Family (copy)	4. 514	Duke of Portland

RAUCH (Sculptor)

Emperor Nicholas of Russia	3. 352	Duke of Devonshire
Empress of Russia	3. 352	Duke of Devonshire

RAVESTEYN, Jan Van

A Prince of Orange	4. 358	Lord Folkestone
Heinrich Spelman	4. 519	Earl of Hardwicke

RAZZI, Giovanni Antonio

Virgin and Child and St. John	2. 82	Lord Elcho
Christ with St. Sebastian and St. Roch	3. 300	Duke of Hamilton
A Picture	3. 314	Captain Stirling
Virgin with Child on a Parapet	4. 103	Lord Ward

REDGRAVE, Richard, R.A.

Country Cousins	1. 378	Marlborough House
Landscape with a Waterfall	2. 301	J. Sheepshanks
Ophelia seated on a Willow Tree	2. 305	"
Bolton Abbey	2. 306	"
Landscape with a Brick House	4. 419	J. Chapman

REGEMORTER

Jan Steen's Tavern Sign, 1828	3. 223	Howard Galton

REGILLO, Bernardino

Female Figure with a Book	4. 446	Lord Kinnaird

REMBRANDT

A Rabbi	1. 317, 354	National Gallery
His own Portrait	1. 317, 354	"
Woman taken in Adultery	1. 352	"
Adoration of the Shepherds	1. 353	"

REMBRANDT—*continued*

	VOL. & PAGE		OWNER
Descent from the Cross (sketch)	I.	353	National Gallery
A Woman wading	I.	354	,,
A Capuchin Friar	I.	354	,,
A Jew	I.	354	,,
Landscape, Tobit and the Angel	I.	355	,,
Man with falling Collar	I.	399	Sir R. Peel
Landscape and Cattle	I.	399	Sir R. Peel
A Shipbuilder and his Wife	2.	4	Buckingham Palace
Magdalen at the Sepulchre	2.	5	,,
His own Portrait, aged 36	2.	5	,,
Wife of Burgomaster Pancras	2.	5	,,
Woman at a Window, 1641	2.	5	,,
Adoration of the Kings	2.	5	,,
A Rabbi	2.	6	,,
His own Portrait	2.	42	Bridgewater House
A Female Portrait	2.	42	,,
Head of a Man	2.	42	,,
An old Woman and a Boy kneeling	2.	42	,,
Deliverance of United Provinces	2.	79	S. Rogers
His own Portrait (old)	2.	80	,,
Landscape, Horseman and a Man	2.	80	,,
A middle-aged Man	2.	103	Lord Ashburton
His own Portrait (old)	2.	103	,,
Lieven Van Coppenol	2.	103	,,
A Man	2.	103	,,
A Woman, 1641	2.	103	,,
Christ sleeping on a Ship, 1633	2.	115	H. T. Hope
Family Group	2.	115	,,
A Plain traversed by a River	2.	115	,,
Lucretia stabbing herself	2.	137	H. A. J. Munro
His own Portrait (old)	2.	137	H. A. J. Munro
Male Portrait in wide Ruff	2.	151	Marquis of Lansdowne
Female in white Cap and Ruff, 1642	2.	151	,,
His own Portrait (old)	2.	151	,,
Jan Pellicorne	2.	158	Marquis of Hertford
His own Portrait, 1643	2.	158	,,
Poetic Landscape	2.	158	,,
Small Male Portrait	2.	158	,,
The Rembrandt from Stowe	2.	158	,,
A Negro	2.	158	,,
The Visitation, 1640	2.	165	Marquis of Westminster
Young Man with a Falcon, 1643	2.	166	,,
N. Berghem, 1644	2.	166	,,
His Wife, 1644	2.	166	,,

	VOL. & PAGE	OWNER
Landscape with Figures	2. 166	Marquis of Westminster
Adoration of the Kings	2. 182	T. Baring
Man with Hand on Breast	2. 200	R. S. Holford
Old Woman in Armchair	2. 200	,,
Male Portrait in gold Chain	2. 200	,,
A Drawing	2. 204	,,
Landscape—a Drawing	2. 204	,,
St. John preaching	2. 237	Lord Ward
Male Portrait from Stowe	2. 237	Lord Ward
An old Man	2. 240	Lord Colborne
Potiphar's Wife complaining	2. 246	Joseph Neeld
His own Portrait (old)	2. 246	Joseph Neeld
Old Woman in black Dress, 1634	2. 264	Sir C. Eastlake
His own Portrait (young)	2. 280	Earl of Carlisle
Man with Pen and Paper in both hands	2. 280	Earl of Carlisle
A young Girl	2. 285	Duke of Bedford
A Man and his Wife, 1632	2. 295	Wynn Ellis
Lucretia with Dagger, 1666	2. 308	Mr. Wombwell
Angel announcing the Birth of Samson	2. 308	,,
Man with a Falcon	2. 308	,,
A Man	2. 313	Earl of Listowel
A Woman	2. 313	Earl of Listowel
Stately Man with hand on Bust of Homer	2. 315	Earl Brownlow
A Set of Drawings	2. 331	C. S. Bale
Burgomaster Six	2. 335	Lady Dover
A Rabbi	2. 336	James Gray
Catherine Hoogh	2. 336	E. Higginson
A Dutch Lady	2. 365	Hampton Court
Young Man, Turkish Costume, 1631	2. 430	Windsor Castle
His own Portrait, gold chain	2. 476	Charles I
Young Man in red Cap reading a Book	2. 476	,,
Old Woman with white Veil	2. 476	,,
A Dutchman	2. 501	Orleans Gallery
His Wife	2. 501	,,
A Burgomaster	2. 501	,,
Birth of Christ	2. 501	,,
The Mill	2. 502	,,
St. Francis	2. 502	,,
His own Portrait	2. 502	,,
Marshall Turenne	3. 16	Earl Cowper
Young Man taking cap from nail	3. 16	Earl Cowper
A Portrait	3. 27	Lord Overstone
Rainier Anslo and his Mother	3. 27	Earl of Ashburnham
Earl of Northumberland	3. 33	Petworth
A female Portrait	3. 41	Petworth

REMBRANDT—*continued*

	VOL. & PAGE		OWNER
His own Portrait (young)	3.	42	Petworth
Woman taken in Adultery	3.	126	Duke of Marlborough
Rembrandt's Daughter	3.	134	J. Morrison
The Mill	3.	157	Marquis of Lansdowne
Bridge with Sun on it	3.	164	,,
Village Church, Trees, and 3 Figures	3.	165	,,
Elijah and the Widow's Son	3.	172	Colt Hoare
Two Gipsies by Moonlight	3.	172	Colt Hoare
Tobit and the Angel	3.	207	Lord Northwick
A Male Portrait	3.	207	,,
A Man and a Woman	3.	207	,,
Belisarius with a Youth	3.	265	Earl of Lonsdale
A Wooded Landscape	3.	272	Edinburgh R.I.
A hilly Landscape	3.	274	Edinburgh R.I.
The Entombment	3.	283	Glasgow College
Prince Adolphus of Geldern	3.	308	Duke of Hamilton
A young Woman	3.	309	Duke of Hamilton
His Grandmother, 1636	3.	311	Earl of Hopetoun
A female Portrait	3.	314	Duke of Buccleuch
Christ at Emmaus	3.	332	Meynell Ingram
His own Portrait (old)	3.	333	Meynell Ingram
A Rabbi in a Chair	3.	346	Duke of Devonshire
Young Man	3.	398	Duke of Rutland
Small Portrait (? W. Tell)	3.	406	Marquis of Exeter
Rev. John Elison, 1634	3.	432	Rev. Mr. Colby
Mrs. Elison, 1634	3.	432	Rev. Mr. Colby
Officer in steel Cuirass, 1635	3.	448	Fitzwilliam Museum
The Circumcision, 1661	3.	459	Earl Spencer
Rembrandt's Mother	3.	459	Earl Spencer
The enraged Prisoner	3.	462	Glendon Hall
Head of old Man from Stowe	3.	462	Glendon Hall
His own Portrait when young	3.	465	Duke of Bedford
Old Rabbi with gold Chain	3.	465	Duke of Bedford
Old Man	4.	62	National Gallery
Old Woman in armchair	4.	66	Earl of Yarborough
The unjust Steward	4.	87	Marquis of Hertford
Young Man with hat and feathers	4.	87	,,
A Negro as huntsman	4.	87	,,
Large Landscape	4.	92	Marquis of Westminster
An aged Rabbi	4.	98	T. Baring
Small Landscape and Buildings	4.	98	T. Baring
Extensive Landscape	4.	131	Lord Overstone
Artist's Grandmother, 1660	4.	135	,,
Woman taken in Adultery	4.	147	,,

	VOL. & PAGE		OWNER
A Portrait	4.	148	Earl of Caledon
A young Man	4.	150	„
His own Portrait	4.	150	„
Man in Black, and broad hat, 1667	4.	281	Sir C. Eardley
Old Man with strange smile	4.	281	„
King and Priest with Books (School)	4.	283	„
A female Portrait	4.	304	J. Morrison
Joseph and the Chief Baker, etc.	4.	333	Duke of Bedford
An aged Rabbi	4.	334	„
His own Portrait, middle age	4.	335	„
Gerard Dow	4.	336	„
A Male Portrait	4.	354	Lord Folkestone
A Picture	4.	374	Sir W. Knighton
Landscape with grey Horse	4.	392	Lord Arundel
A female Portrait	4.	436	Duke of Buccleuch
Man with white Turban, 1661	4.	447	Lord Kinnaird
Rembrandt studying from a female Model	4.	459	M'Lellan Gallery
Lucretia with Dagger	4.	477	W. W. Bardon
A Male Portrait	4.	502	Earl of Yarborough
Man holding Roll of Paper	4.	510	Duke of Newcastle
His own Portrait (old)	4.	515	Duke of Portland

RESCHI, Pandolfo

A Battle Piece	3.	270	Edinburgh R.I.

REYNOLDS, Sir Joshua, P.R.A.

Lord Heathfield	1.	365	Marlborough House
Sir William Hamilton	1.	365	„
Adorning the Term of Hymen	1.	365	„
Infant Samuel	1.	365	„
Heads of Angels	1.	365	„
Banished Lord	1.	365	„
Holy Family	1.	366	„
Age of Innocence	1.	366	„
His own Portrait	1.	366	„
His own Portrait (young)	1.	413	Sir R. Peel
Admiral Keppel	1.	413	„
Samuel Johnson	1.	414	„
Girl feeding a Bird	1.	414	„
Mrs. Musters (called Mrs. Siddons)	1.	414	„
His own Portrait, spectacles	2.	24	Buckingham Palace
Death of Dido	2.	24	„
Cymon and Iphigenia	2.	24	„
Lord and Lady Clive and Hindoo Nurse	2.	53	Bridgewater House
Dr. Johnson	2.	72	Duke of Sutherland

		VOL. & PAGE		OWNER
REYNOLDS, Sir Joshua, P.R.A.—*continued*				
Strawberry Girl	2.	75		S. Rogers
Sleeping Girl	2.	75		,,
Girl with a Bird	2.	75		,,
Puck	2.	75		,,
Cupid and Psyche	2.	75		,,
Landscape	2.	75		,,
Lord Richard Cavendish	2.	96		Devonshire House
Georgiana, Duchess of Devonshire	2.	96		Devonshire House
Kitty Fisher	2.	140		H. A. J. Munro
Mrs. Robinson as Perdita	2.	140		,,
Mrs. Stanhope	2.	140		,,
Macklin as Lear	2.	140		,,
Laurence Sterne	2.	152		Marquis of Lansdowne
David Garrick	2.	152		,,
Kitty Fisher	2.	152		,,
Lady Bunbury	2.	152		,,
Lady Ilchester and 3 Children	2.	153		Marquis of Lansdowne
Nelly O'Brien	2.	160		Marquis of Hertford
A Girl with a Child	2.	161		Marquis of Hertford
Mrs. Siddons as Tragic Muse	2.	172		Marquis of Westminster
Little Girl	2.	188		T. Baring
A young Lady	2.	188		,,
Venus and Cupid	2.	188		,,
Girl and 2 Boys by Torchlight	2.	188		,,
Benjamin Booth	2.	225		Richard Ford
A Girl with a Lamb	2.	225		,,
St. Agnes	2.	225		,,
Girl and Man laughing	2.	229		Hon. E. Phipps
Mrs. Nesbitt and Dove	2.	229		,,
Mrs. Robinson, Perdita	2.	229		,,
Young Lady in straw Bonnet	2.	242		H. D. Seymour
Diana	2.	250		Col. Rawdon
Dr. Johnson	2.	263		J. Morrison
A Girl writing, in a Landscape	2.	268		Miss Rogers
Figure in Armour with a Baton	2.	268		Miss Rogers
A Lady	2.	298		Wynn Ellis
Lady Clarke as young Girl (Miss Hunter)	2.	311		Mr. Wombwell
Ugolino	2.	334		Knole
Master Bunbury	2.	335		Sir H. Bunbury
His own Portrait (spectacles)	2.	348		Dulwich Gallery
Mrs. Siddons as Tragic Muse	2.	348		,,
Infant Samuel	2.	348		,,
A Mother and sick Child	2.	348		,,
Death of Cardinal Beaufort	2.	348		,,

	VOL. & PAGE	OWNER
Duke of Cumberland	2. 424	Windsor Castle
Infant Samuel	3. 26	Earl of Darnley
Lady Frances Cole and a dog	3. 26	,,
Mrs. D. Monk	3. 26	,,
Countess of Clanwilliam	3. 26	,,
Virgin and Child	3. 33	Petworth
Woodward with a Mask	3. 33	,,
Death of Cardinal Beaufort	3. 37	,,
Macbeth	3. 37	,,
A Male Portrait	3. 39	,,
Prince Boothby	3. 40	,,
Lady with a Letter (Miss Darby)	3. 40	,,
Female Portrait in Turban	3. 41	,,
The Marquis of Granby	3. 41	,,
Marlborough Family	3. 130	Luke of Marlborough
Lady Charlotte Spencer	3. 130	,,
Lord Charles Spencer	3. 130	,,
Marquis of Tavistock	3. 130	,,
Other portraits	3. 130	,,
A Child in contemplation	3. 158	Marquis of Lansdowne
Peasant Girl, Hands crossed	3. 158	,,
Mrs. Billington (Sheridan) as St. Cecilia	3. 160	,,
A Greek Lady (Mrs. Baldwin)	3. 160	,,
Love nourished by Hope	3. 161	,,
Marquis of Lansdowne	3. 166	,,
Four Family Portraits	3. 171	Lord Arundel
A Picture	3. 177	Mr. Vivian
Lady resting on her Arm	3. 210	Lord Northwick
Infant Hercules	3. 210	Lord Northwick
A Schoolboy	3. 216	Earl of Warwick
Duke and Duchess of Hamilton	3. 220	Howard Galton
His own Portrait (young)	3. 221	,,
A Landscape	3. 223	,,
Dr. Hunter	3. 283	Glasgow College
Woman in School for Scandal (study)	3. 289	M'Lellan Gallery
Marchioness of Queensbury	3. 313	Duke of Buccleuch
Duchess of Buccleuch	3. 313	,,
Charles, Duke of Buccleuch	3. 313	,,
Omai	3. 323	Earl of Carlisle
Earl of Carlisle	3. 323	Earl of Carlisle
Marchioness of Hertford	3. 333	Meynell Ingram
Viscountess Irvine	3. 333	,,
Charles, Lord Irvine	3. 333	,,
A Shepherd Boy	3. 334	,,
Marquis of Rockingham	3. 338	Earl Fitzwilliam

z

	VOL. & PAGE		OWNER
REYNOLDS, Sir Joshua, P.R.A.—*continued*			
Countess Fitzwilliam	3.	339	Earl Fitzwilliam
Earl Fitzwilliam	3.	339	,,
Infant Hercules	3.	340	,,
Two Shepherds (Oxford window)	3.	340	,,
Shepherd Boy (Oxford window)	3.	340	,,
Georgiana Duchess of Devonshire	3.	352	Duke of Devonshire
Girl and Boy with a Dog	3.	397	Duke of Rutland
Lady, to the Knees (Lady Tyrconnel)	3.	399	,,
A young Man	3.	402	,,
8th Earl of Westmoreland	3.	411	Earl of Westmoreland
9th Earl of Westmoreland	3.	411	,,
Hon. Mr. Fane and Guardians	3.	411	,,
Marchioness Camden	3.	459	Earl Spencer
Other Family Portraits	3.	459	Earl Spencer
Duke of Bedford	3.	464	Duke of Bedford
Duchess of Bedford	3.	464	,,
Other Family Portraits	3.	464	,,
Lord Bute	3.	485	Marquis of Bute
Lady Bute	3.	485	,,
Lord Bute and Secretary	3.	485	,,
Sir Richard Worsley	4.	66	Earl of Yarborough
Mrs. Pelham feeding Chickens	4.	68	Earl of Yarborough
Nelly O'Brien	4.	91	Marquis of Hertford
The Strawberry Girl	4.	91	,,
Little Girl holding a Dog (Miss Bowles)	4.	91	,,
A Landscape	4.	100	T. Baring
Dr. Johnson	4.	106	J. Morrison
Three Ladies Waldegrave	4.	152	Lady Waldegrave
Their Brother	4.	152	,,
Duchess of Gloucester	4.	152	,,
Sir Robert Walpole	4.	152	,,
Una kneeling by the Lion	4.	188	W. Russell
Mrs. Abingdon as a Page (oval)	4.	210	Mr. Henderson
David Garrick	4.	233	General Fox
Female in profile	4.	233	General Fox
Hon. Francis Stanhope	4.	236	Earl of Harrington
Hon. Lincoln Stanhope	4.	236	,,
Hon. Leicester Stanhope	4.	236	,,
Lady Harrington and Children	4.	236	,,
Hon. Fitzroy Stanhope	4.	236	,,
1st Duchess of Northumberland	4.	266	Duke of Northumberland
Queen Charlotte	4.	266	Duke of Northumberland
Mrs. Child (oval)	4.	273	Earl of Jersey
Mr. Child	4.	273	Earl of Jersey

	VOL. & PAGE	OWNER
Lady Eardley	4. 281	Sir C. Eardley
Sir J. E. Wilmot	4. 281	,,
Lady Saye and Sele and Boy	4. 282	,,
His own Portrait, young	4. 292	J. Sanders
His own Portrait, young	4. 311	J. Morrison
Mr. Croft	4. 330	Sir T. Sebright
Mrs. Croft	4. 330	Sir T. Sebright
Marquis of Tavistock	4. 331	Duke of Bedford
Lady Caroline Russell	4. 331	,,
Several others	4. 331	,,
Marchioness of Tavistock	4. 333	,,
Marchioness of Tavistock (half length)	4. 334	,,
His own Portrait	4. 336	,,
Oliver Goldsmith	4. 336	,,
David Garrick	4. 336	,,
3rd Earl of Dorset	4. 338	Knole
Ugolino	4. 338	,,
Madame Baccelli	4. 339	,,
Robinetta	4. 340	,,
The Fortune Teller	4. 340	,,
Madame Schindlerin	4. 340	,,
Infant Samuel	4. 340	,,
Mrs. Abingdon	4. 340	,,
Oliver Goldsmith	4. 341	,,
David Garrick	4. 341	,,
Sacchini, Composer	4. 341	,,
Dr. Johnson	4. 341	,,
Sir J. Reynolds holding paper	4. 341	,,
Three Children of Lord Melbourne	4. 346	Earl Cowper
Girl warming herself	4. 346	Earl Cowper
Lady leaning on right Hand	4. 348	Vernon Harcourt
Schoolboy with large Book	4. 348	,,
The Harcourt Family	4. 348	,,
Infant Samuel kneeling	4. 349	,,
Granville, Marquis of Stafford	4. 349	,,
Mary, Countess of Harcourt	4. 349	,,
Simon, Earl Harcourt	4. 352	,,
Father of Earl Harcourt	4. 352	,,
Master Jacob Bouverie	4. 355	Lord Folkestone
Lady Tilney Long	4. 362	,,
Anne, Countess of Radnor	4. 362	,,
Adoration of Shepherds (sketch)	4. 364	Earl of Normanton
Virgin and Child, St. John and Joseph	4. 368	,,
Gipsy telling Girl's Fortune	4. 370	
Una kneeling, and Lioness	4. 370	

	VOL. & PAGE		OWNER
REYNOLDS, Sir Joshua, P.R.A.—*continued*			
Henry, Earl of Pembroke	4.	370	Earl of Normanton
David Garrick	4.	370	„
Justice	4.	370	„
Temperance	4.	370	„
Charity	4.	370	„
Faith	4.	370	„
Hope	4.	371	„
Prudence	4.	371	„
Fortitude	4.	371	„
Lady Hamilton	4.	371	„
Girl in white in Go-cart	4.	371	„
His own Portrait, young	4.	371	„
Girl hugging a white Kitten	4.	371	„
Two Sisters (Misses Horneck)	4.	371	„
Mrs. Inchbald	4.	371	„
Lady Pembroke	4.	371	„
Infant Samuel	4.	371	„
Miss Gwynn	4.	372	„
Girl standing with a Dog	4.	372	„
Nelson	4.	372	„
A Picture	4.	374	Sir W. Knighton
Mr. Woodley (?) Mrs.	4.	379	Kingston Lacy
A Lady	4.	392	Lord Arundel
Sir William Lowther	4.	422	Earl of Burlington
Duchess of Buccleuch and child	4.	436	Duke of Buccleuch
Marquis of Dalkeith	4.	436	„
Other Pictures	4.	436	„
The banished Lord	4.	448	Lord Kinnaird
Young Hannibal	4.	455	Earl of Dunmore
Earl of Dunmore	4.	456	Earl of Dunmore
Miss Linley	4.	462	M'Lellan Gallery
Margaret, Duchess of Douglas	4.	463	Lord Douglas
Lady of Rev. George Hudspath	4.	479	J. Anderson
Sir George Young	4.	479	J. Anderson
Jane, Lady Harrington	4.	495	Earl of Harrington
Lady Fleming	4.	495	„
His own Portrait (young)	4.	496	„
Earl of Harrington	4.	496	„
Marquis of Tichfield	4.	512	Duke of Portland
Lord Richard Cavendish	4.	514	„
Charity	4.	515	„
Hope	4.	515	„
Allegorical Figure	4.	515	„
Allegorical Figure	4.	515	„

	VOL. & PAGE	OWNER
Angel on Clouds	4. 515	Duke of Portland
3rd Duke of Portland	4. 515	Duke of Portland
Marquis of Rockingham	4. 522	Earl of Hardwicke
Lord Hardwicke pointing	4. 523	Earl of Hardwicke

RHENISH SCHOOL

Virgin and Child and Joseph	3. 205	Lord Northwick
Virgin and Child and Joseph	4. 224	Prince Consort
Holy Family	4. 225	Prince Consort
Adoration of the Kings	4. 317	Rev. Mr. Heath

RIBALTA, Francisco de

Christ bearing Cross, 1612	2. 223	R. Ford
Christ bearing Cross, 1612	2. 259	G. A. Hoskins
Virgin holding Child before her	4. 381	Kingston Lacy

RIBALTA, Juan de

St. John and the Lamb	2. 259	G. A. Hoskins

RIBERA, Guiseppe

Christ at Emmaus	2. 66	Duke of Sutherland
Diogenes	2. 170	Marquis of Westminster
Virgin and Child and St. Anna	2. 180	T. Baring
Several Pictures of Saints	2. 236	Lord Ward
Christ as the Good Shepherd	2. 241	Lord Colborne
St. Catherine	4. 64	Earl of Yarborough
St. Simon and St. James-the-Less	4. 481	Matthew Anderson
St. Peter looking up	4. 508	Sir J. Nelthorpe

RICCI, Marco

A Picture	2. 93	Devonshire House
A Picture	2. 311	Earl of Listowel
Marriage of Bacchus and Ariadne	3. 248	Blundell Weld
Adoration of the Kings	3. 384	Earl of Shrewsbury

RICCI, Sebastian

A Picture	2. 93	Devonshire House
Magdalen washing Feet of Christ	2. 357	Hampton Court
Healing the lame Man	2. 357	„
Woman taken in Adultery	2. 357	„
Two others	2. 357	„
A Picture	3. 403	Marquis of Exeter

RICHARDSON, Jonathan

Alex. Pope and Dog Bounce	3. 227	Lord Lyttelton

RIGAUD, Hyacinth

Louis XV, whole length	3. 434	Earl of Orford
Louis XV, whole length in Robes	4. 263	Duc D'Aumale

	VOL. & PAGE		OWNER
ROBBIA, Luca della (Potter)			
Madonna and Child with Lily (bas-relief)	2.	263	J. Morrison
A Statue of Charity	4.	103	H. D. Seymour
Virgin and Child (relief)	4.	112	J. Morrison
ROBERT, Leopold			
Neapolitan Woman with a Boy, after an Earthquake	4.	263	Duc D'Aumale
ROBERTS, David, R.A.			
Cathedral of Bruges	1.	387	Marlborough House
Choir of St. Paul's, Antwerp	1.	387	Marlborough House
Buildings on the Darra, Granada	2.	300	J. Sheepshanks
Crypt of Roslyn Chapel	2.	301	J. Sheepshanks
A Street in Cairo, 1846	2.	349	E. Bicknell
Temple at Baalbec	2.	350	,,
Interior of Church at Xeres	2.	351	,,
Drawings of Baalbec, etc.	2.	352	,,
Interior of St. Gomar, Lierre	2.	353	,,
Melrose Abbey	2.	353	,,
Temple on the Nile	2.	354	,,
The Alhambra (drawing)	2.	354	,,
Donaldson's Hospital	4.	434	Mr. Playfair
ROELAS, Ivan de las			
Portrait of a Monk	4.	450	W. Stirling
Meeting of Christ and St. John, etc.	2.	259	G. A. Hoskins
ROMANELLI, Francesco			
A Picture	2.	93	Devonshire House
A female Figure	3.	180	J. P. Miles
The flight of Clelia	3.	240	Liverpool R.I.
Rape of Proserpine	3.	248	Blundell Weld
Death of Adonis	3.	248	Blundell Weld
ROMANINO, Girolamo			
Woman taken in Adultery	3.	202	Lord Northwick
Christ bearing his Cross	4.	484	George Burdon
ROMANO, Giulio			
A Charity	1.	324	National Gallery
Juno and infant Hercules	2.	29	Bridgewater House
St. John in Wilderness	2.	55	Bridgewater House
Virgin holding Infant	2.	132	H. A. J. Munro
St. Luke painting the Virgin	2.	169	Marquis of Westminster
Battle of Constantine	2.	355	Hampton Court
Jupiter and Europa	2.	356	Hampton Court

	VOL. & PAGE	OWNER
An ancient Sacrifice	2. 360	Hampton Court
Burning of Rome	2. 414	Hampton Court
The Deluge	2. 476	Charles I
The Birth of Christ	2. 476	,,
St. Jerome	2. 476	,,
Jupiter, Juno and Minerva	2. 476	,,
Birth of Hercules	2. 476	,,
Cupid and 4 others on a Bench	2. 476	,,
Mermaid suckling Children	2. 477	,,
A Sacrifice to Jupiter	2. 477	,,
Child suckled by a Goat	2. 477	,,
Meleager and Atalanta	2. 477	,,
Triumph of Vespasian, etc.	2. 477	,,
Julius Cæsar at the Senate	2. 477	,,
Eleven Roman Emperors	2. 477	,,
Rome burning	2. 477	,,
An Italian Prelate	2. 477	,,
A Man in Black Dress	2. 477	,,
His own Portrait	2. 477	,,
Europa	2. 484	,,
A Centaur and wild Boar	2. 484	,,
Landscape, Birth of a Child	2. 484	,,
A Dead Emperor on funeral Pile	2. 484	,,
An Emperor on Horseback	2. 484	,,
An Emperor on Horseback	2. 484	,,
St. Paul driven out of the City	2. 484	,,
Adam and Eve washing their Clothes	2. 484	,,
Juno tearing Hercules from Breast	2. 495	Orleans Gallery
Rape of the Sabines	2. 495	,,
Women reconciling Sabines and Romans	2. 495	,,
Coriolanus won over by his Mother	2. 495	,,
Continence of Scipio	2. 495	,,
Scipio rewarding his Soldiers	2. 495	,,
Scipio besieging New Carthage	2. 495	,,
Birth of Hercules	2. 495	,,
Birth of Jupiter	2. 495	,,
The Corybantes raising a Noise, etc.	3. 198	Lord Northwick
Procession of Men and Animals	3. 237	Liverpool R.I.
Battle of Constantine	3. 272	Edinburgh R.I.
Head of Julius II	3. 383	Earl of Shrewsbury
Virgin holding Child	4. 94	T. Baring
A Female Portrait	4. 261	Duc D'Aumale
Bramante, Architect	4. 293	J. Sanders
Holy Family	4. 319	Lord Enfield
Marriage of St. Catherine	4. 390	Lord Heytesbury

	VOL. & PAGE		OWNER
ROMANO, Giulio—*continued*			
A triumphal Procession	4.	439	Earl of Wemyss
Virgin and Child and St. John	4.	456	Earl of Dunmòre
Conversion of St. Paul	4.	456	Earl of Dunmore
Giuliano de Medici	4.	466	Duke of Northumberland
Holy Family (*copy*)	4.	466	Duke of Northumberland
ROMEYN, William			
Landscape and white Cow	2.	71	Duke of Sutherland
Cattle piece	2.	344	Dulwich Gallery
Cattle piece	2.	344	Dulwich Gallery
Mountainous Landscape, Cattle	4.	155	St. John Mildmay
ROMNEY, George			
Lady Hamilton	1.	369	Marlborough House
Lady Hamilton as Cassandra	4.	104	H. Labouchere
Young Man leaning on Hand	4.	290	J. Sanders
Lady Hamilton	4.	372	Earl of Normanton
Mrs. Bankes (whole length)	4.	380	Kingston Lacy
RONDANI, Francesco Maria			
Marriage of St. Catherine	4.	94	T. Baring
ROSA, Salvator			
A Landscape	1.	317	National Gallery
Landscape, Mercury and Woodman	1.	344	National Gallery
Rocky Country (Les Augures)	2.	38	Bridgewater House
Jacob and his Flocks	2.	39	Bridgewater House
Jason pouring the soporific charm on Dragon	2.	84	Lord De Mauley
Poetical Composition	2.	85	Earl De Grey
Dark Landscape and Robbers	2.	86	Earl of Yarborough
St. Jerome	2.	87	Earl of Yarborough
Jacob's Dream	2.	92	Devonshire House
Sea with High Rocks, etc.	2.	113	H. T. Hope
Apollo and the Sybil	2.	155	Marquis of Hertford
Democritus	2.	170	Marquis of Westminster
Diogenes throwing away the Cup	2.	170	,,
Three Maries at Sepulchre	2.	171	
St. John preaching	2.	180	T. Baring
Sea Coast with Soldiers	2.	180	T. Baring
Landscape and high Mountains	2.	198	R. S. Holford
Landscape, Rocks in Foreground	2.	236	Lord Ward
Figures with Rocks	2.	236	Lord Ward
A Sea Coast	2.	245	Mr. Neeld
Rocky Landscape	2.	285	Duke of Bedford
Rocky Landscape	2.	285	Duke of Bedford

	VOL. & PAGE		OWNER
Mountains on Seashore	2.	294	Wynn Ellis
An Attack by Robbers	2.	294	Wynn Ellis
Landscape, Monks fishing	2.	347	Dulwich Gallery
Soldiers at Play	2.	347	Dulwich Gallery
Robbers (oval)	2.	420	H. Labouchere
Landscape (oval)	2.	420	H. Labouchere
Sea Coast and Fishermen	3.	15	Earl Cowper
Landscape with Horsemen	3.	15	,,
Landscape and Banditti	3.	15	,,
Landscape and Banditti	3.	15	,,
Pythagoras teaching the Fishes	3.	22	Earl of Darnley
Death of Regulus	3.	22	,,
Jason pouring the Sleeping Charm over the Dragon	3.	22	,,
Birth of Orion	3.	22	,,
A Sea Coast	3.	141	Earl of Radnor
A Small Waterfall	3.	151	Earl of Pembroke
His own Portrait	3.	157	Marquis of Lansdowne
Young Woman with Book and Pen	3.	157	Marquis of Lansdowne
Landscape and Banditti	3.	180	J. P. Miles
Large Landscape	3.	191	Mr. Harford
Large Landscape	3.	191	,,
Landscape, Man on Rock	3.	191	,,
Landscape, a Cave	3.	191	,,
A Seashore Scene	3.	191	,,
L'umana fragilità	3.	203	Lord Northwick
Sea Coast with Rocks, etc.	3.	204	,,
Soldiers upon Rocks	3.	204	,,
Soldiers at Dice	3.	204	,,
Two Robbers under large Trees	3.	212	Earl of Warwick
Democritus	3.	213	,,
Old Man and Hermit	3.	216	,,
Angel and Tobit	3.	225	Mr. Martin
An Enchantress	3.	247	Blundell Weld
Landscape with Soldiers	3.	261	Earl of Lonsdale
St. Jerome	3.	265	Earl of Lonsdale
Wild Scene with Robbers	3.	274	Edinburgh R.I.
Laomedon, Neptune and Apollo	3.	283	Glasgow College
A Hero, animated action	3.	298	Duke of Hamilton
A careful Landscape	3.	313	Duke of Buccleuch
Man with white Dove	3.	325	Earl of Carlisle
Jason and Dragon	3.	338	Earl Fitzwilliam
Rocky Sea Coast	3.	339	Earl Fitzwilliam
David cutting off Head of Goliath	3.	350	Duke of Devonshire
Jacob wrestling with the Angel	3.	350	Duke of Devonshire

A A

	VOL. & PAGE	OWNER
ROSA, Salvator—*continued*		
A Knight and a Woman	3. 351	Duke of Devonshire
A Rocky Landscape	3. 421	Earl of Leicester
Belisarius	3. 439	Lord Charles Townshend
Wild Rocky Country	3. 442	Mr. Tomline
St. Jerome	4. 65	Earl of Yarborough
Castle and Robbers	4. 67	Earl of Yarborough
Tobit and the Angel	4. 142	Lord Overstone
The Sea God Glaucus, etc.	4. 148	Earl of Caledon
Sea Coast, rocky Shore	4. 149	,,
Knight bound to a Tree	4. 149	,,
Small Landscape, Water, and Figures	4. 182	G. C. Legh
Sea Coast in Calabria, Boats, etc.	4. 199	J. Tulloch
Horsemen fighting	4. 238	Earl of Harrington
Horsemen fighting	4. 238	Earl of Harrington
Daniel in Lions' Den	4. 262	Duc D'Aumale
Daniel in Lions' Den, Deliverance, etc.	4. 262	,,
Landscape and St. Jerome	4. 262	,,
A Monk praying	4. 262	,,
Rocky Landscape with Banditti	4. 268	Duke of Northumberland
Tobit and the Angel	4. 270	Earl of Jersey.
Seashore, Apollo and Sibyl	4. 270	,,
Jonah ejected by Whale	4. 272	,,
Poetic Landscape	4. 273	,,
Poetic Landscape	4. 273	,,
Landscape, Trees, Man fishing	4. 292	J. Sanders
Landscape, Warriors, one on a Horse	4. 327	Sir T. Sebright
Landscape, Rock, 3 Figures, 1 kneeling	4. 328	,,
Male Head with a kind of Cloth	4. 329	,,
Diogenes	4. 334	Duke of Bedford
Seaports with Vessels	4. 354	Lord Folkestone
An Impetuous Fight	4. 364	Earl of Normanton
Landscape, Three Men on a Rock	4. 368	Earl of Normanton
Mr. Altham as a Hermit	4. 378	Kingston Lacy
A Man	4. 390	Lord Heytesbury
Landscape, Trees and Banditti	4. 393	Lord Arundel
Landscape, Trees and Banditti	4. 393	Lord Arundel
Two rich Landscapes	4. 398	Lord Methuen
Angel announcing birth of Samson	4. 409	Smith Barry
Raising of Lazarus	4. 409	,,
Landscape with Rocks upon Water	4. 413	,,
Landscape with Rocks upon Water	4. 413	,,
Poetic Landscape	4. 437	Duke of Buccleuch
Rock with Trees, 4 Figures	4. 440	Earl of Wemyss
Warrior in Armour	4. 444	Earl of Elgin

	VOL. & PAGE	OWNER
Landscape, Hagar and Ishmael	4. 457	Earl of Dunmore
Landscape with Waterfall	4. 460	M'Lellan Gallery
Upright Landscape, Soldiers on Rock	4. 460	M'Lellan Gallery
Landscape with Tree and 3 Soldiers	4. 482	Matthew Anderson
Landscape, dark Lake and Figures	4. 484	Matthew Anderson
Landscape	4. 491	Mr. Fenderson
Small Landscape	4. 494	Lord Feversham
Small Landscape	4. 494	Lord Feversham
A Combat of Horsemen	4. 502	Earl of Yarborough
Landscape with large Cave	4. 503	,,
Landscape with Hermit	4. 504	,,
Landscape with Water, 3 Soldiers	4. 521	Earl of Hardwicke

ROSA, da Tivoli (Philip Roos)

A Stag hunt	3. 241	Liverpool R.I.
Cattle and old Castle	4. 201	J. Tulloch

ROSS, Sir William, R.A.

A Lady (*miniature*)	2. 97	Miss Burdett Coutts

ROSELLI, Cosimo

Christ on the Cross	3. 4	W. Fuller Maitland
Virgin and Child enthroned	3. 372	W. Davenport Bromley

ROSSO, Fiorentino

Woman taken in Adultery	2. 495	Orleans Gallery
Sebastian del Piombo	4. 467	Duke of Northumberland

ROTHENHAMMER, Johann

Holy Family, painted with Seghers	2. 69	Duke of Sutherland
Several Pictures	2. 94	Devonshire House
Two Pictures	2. 482	Charles I
Paul at Lystra	3. 210	Lord Northwick
A Bacchanal	3. 287	M'Lellan Gallery
Descent from the Cross	4. 356	Lord Folkestone
Christ on the Mount of Olives	4. 507	Sir John Nelthorpe

ROTHMANN

Bay of Aulis	4. 176	Rev. Mr. Townshend

RÖTING

Sir Culling Eardley	4. 281	Sir C. Eardley

ROUTBOUT

Landscape, Windmill and Water	3. 221	Howard Galton

RUBENS, Sir Peter Paul

	VOL. & PAGE	OWNER
The Brazen Serpent	1. 316, 349	National Gallery
Judgement of Paris	1. 317, 349	„
Large Landscape	1. 317	„
The Blessings of Peace	1. 317, 349	„
St. Bavin relieving the Poor	1. 350	„
Rape of the Sabines	1. 350	„
Ceiling at Whitehall (sketch)	1. 351	„
Château de Stein	1. 351	„
Small Landscape, Evening	1. 351	„
A Holy Family	1. 351	„
The Chapeau de Paille	1. 398	Sir R. Peel
Bacchanalian Scene	1. 399	„
A young Woman (drawing)	1. 414	„
A Boy (drawing)	1. 415	„
Lady in black and red (drawing)	1. 415	„
The Crucifixion (drawing)	1. 415	„
Beheading a Saint (drawing)	1. 415	„
Descent of Holy Ghost (drawing)	1. 415	„
A Lion Hunt (drawing)	1. 415	„
Assumption of the Virgin	2. 2	Buckingham Palace
Pythagoras and Pupils	2. 2	„
Pan and Syrinx	2. 2	„
Head of the Bishop of Antwerp	2. 3	„
Man with a Falcon	2. 3	„
St. George and the Dragon	2. 3	„
Prairie de Lacken	2. 3	„
Oldenborneveldt and Son	2. 3	„
Marriage of St. Catherine	2. 68	Duke of Sutherland
Virgin and Child in Landscape	2. 68	„
Coronation of Mary de Medici	2. 69	„
Triumph of Julius Caesar	2. 79	S. Rogers
Terrors of War	2. 79	„
Moonlight Scene	2. 79	„
Catherine Brandt	2. 86	Duke of Norfolk
A Wolf Hunt	2. 102	Lord Ashburton
Rape of the Sabines	2. 102	„
Reconciliation of the Sabines	2. 102	„
Diana and Nymphs and Stag	2. 102	„
Shipwreck of Æneas	2. 114	H. T. Hope
St. Sebastian	2. 136	H. A. J. Munro
Virgin and sleeping Child	2. 136	„
Meeting of Jacob and Esau	2. 136	„
Female Portrait (half length)	2. 136	„
Christ giving Keys to St. Peter	2. 157	Marquis of Hertford

	VOL. & PAGE	OWNER
A Holy Family, etc.	2. 157	Marquis of Hertford
A Portrait	2. 157	Marquis of Hertford
Gathering of Manna	2. 163	Marquis of Westminster
Procession of Saints	2. 163	,,
The Four Evangelists	2. 163	,,
Abraham and Melchizedeck	2. 163	,,
Pausias and Glycera	2. 164	,,
Ixion embracing the Cloud	2. 164	,,
Sarah sending away Hagar	2. 164	,,
A Hilly Landscape	2. 164	,,
Diana departing for Chase	2. 182	T. Baring
Abraham and Melchizedeck (sketch)	2. 182	T. Baring
Descent from Cross, etc. (sketch)	2. 199	R. S. Holford
Assumption of Virgin, etc. (sketch)	2. 200	R. S. Holford
Two spirited Sketches	2. 227	Hon. E. Phipps
Landscape with Rainbow	2. 239	Marquis of Breadalbane
A Man seated (half length)	2. 246	Joseph Neeld
Four Evangelists (sketch)	2. 261	J. Morrison
Charles V and Deputation	2. 261	,,
Legend of St. Mark	2. 263	,,
Triumph of Constantine	2. 270	Miss Rogers
Wooded Landscape, Shepherd, etc.	2. 278	Earl of Carlisle
Portrait of a Warrior	2. 281	Sir A. Rothschild
Christ upon the Globe, and Saints	2. 292	C. Bredel
Helena Forman	2. 295	Wynn Ellis
Infant Christ and St. John	2. 308	Mr. Wombwell
Achilles among the Daughters of Lycomedes, etc.	2. 314	Earl Brownlow
Landscape, Shepherd with Flute	2. 342	Dulwich Gallery
Magdalen clasping Hands	2. 342	Dulwich Gallery
Nymphs and Satyrs	2. 365	Hampton Court
Magdalen anointing the Feet of Christ	2. 433	Windsor Castle
Helena Forman	2. 435	,,
St. Martin dividing Cloak with a Beggar	2. 435	,,
Virgin and Child and Saints	2. 435	,,
Philip IV of Spain, horseback	2. 435	,,
His own Portrait	2. 435	,,
A Winter Landscape	2. 436	,,
Archduke Albert of Austria	2. 436	,,
Landscape	2. 436	,,
Family of Sir B. Gerbier	2. 437	,,
Male Portrait with large Ruff	2. 437	,,
Virgin with Child on her Lap	2. 451	Richard Forster
Blessings of Peace	2. 477	Charles I
Daniel in Lion's Den	2. 477	Charles I

	VOL. & PAGE	OWNER
RUBENS, Sir Peter Paul—*continued*		
St. George	2. 477	Charles I
Brother of Duke of Mantua	2. 477	,,
His own Portrait	2. 478	,,
Apotheosis of James I (sketch)	2. 478	,,
The Resurrection	2. 484	,,
Rape of the Sabines	2. 484	,,
Rape of the Sabines	2. 484	,,
Naked Figures	2. 484	,,
A Roman Charity	2. 484	,,
A Ruin with five Turks	2. 484	,,
Vandyck in Dutch Costume	2. 484	,,
Three Nymphs and Five Satyrs (Dead Game by Snyders)	2. 484	,,
Judgment of Paris	2. 502	Orleans Gallery
Rape of Ganymede	2. 502	,,
Venus returning from Chase	2. 502	,,
Scipio giving back his Bride	2. 502	,,
Queen Tomyris and Head of Cyrus	2. 502	,,
Fortunes of Philopœmen	2. 502	,,
St. George (View of Richmond)	2. 502	,,
Marriage of Constantine	2. 502	,,
Cross appearing to Constantine	2. 502	,,
Constantine with Standard of the Cross	2. 502	,,
Battle of Constantine	2. 502	,,
Death of Maximilian	2. 502	,,
Triumph of Constantine	2. 502	,,
Entry of Constantine into Rome	2. 502	,,
Constantine and Roman Senate	2. 502	,,
Constantine and Crispus	2. 502	,,
Founding of Constantinople	2. 502	,,
Constantine adoring Cross	2. 502	,,
Constantine being baptized	2. 502	,,
Queen Tomyris and Head of Cyrus	3. 23	Earl of Darnley
Children blowing Bubbles	3. 23	,,
A Lion Hunt	3. 23	,,
Triumph of Henry IV	3. 23	,,
Jupiter, Venus and Cupid	3. 24	,,
Wild Boar Hunt	3. 24	,,
Two Prelates Kneeling	3. 40	Petworth
Two Prelates Kneeling	3. 40	Petworth
Bacchanalian Festival	3. 123	Duke of Marlborough
Lot with Wife and Daughters	3. 124	,,
Return of Holy Family	3. 124	,,
A Roman Charity	3. 124	,,

	VOL. & PAGE	OWNER
Parocelsus	3. 124	Duke of Marlborough
Adoration of the Kings	3. 125	,,
A Holy Family	3. 125	,,
Suffer little Children, etc.	3. 125	,,
Virgin and Child	3. 126	,,
Catherine de Medici	3. 126	,,
Helena Forman	3. 126	,,
Andromeda	3. 129	,,
Rubens, Wife and Child	3. 129	,,
Virgin and Child on Throne	3. 129	,,
A Holy Family	3. 130	,,
Lot and his Daughters	3. 130	,,
Three Women gathering fruit	3. 131	,,
Venus, Cupid and Adonis	3. 131	,,
A Bacchanalian Procession	3. 131	,,
Rape of Proserpine	3. 133	,,
Holy Family	3. 134	J. Morrison
Landscape near the Escurial	3. 141	Earl of Radnor
Venus and her Nymphs	3. 141	Earl of Radnor
Assumption of Virgin	3. 152	Earl of Pembroke
Landscape with Sunset	3. 152	,,
Christ and St. John as Children	3. 153	,,
Descent from the Cross	3. 171	Lord Arundel
Hugo Grotius	3. 171	,,
Woman taken in Adultery	3. 181	J. P. Miles
Virgin and Child and Saints	3. 182	,,
Conversion of St. Paul	3. 186	,,
A Sposalizio	3. 206	Lord Northwick
Baptism of Philip	3. 206	Lord Northwick
Thos. Howard, Earl of Arundel	3. 213	Earl of Warwick
Marquis of Spinola	3. 213	,,
Ignatius Loyola	3. 214	,,
Virgin and Female Saints	4. 225	Mr. Martin
Figures and Fruit (with Snyders)	3. 227	Hon. R. Clive
The Crucifixion	3. 240	Liverpool R.I.
Virgin seated with Child, etc.	3. 261	Earl of Lonsdale
Head of Woman in Adultery (study)	3. 283	Glasgow College
Daniel in the Lion's Den	3. 296	Duke of Hamilton
Venus rising from Sea	3. 301	,,
Male and Female Centaurs	3. 301	,,
Count Olivarez	3. 308	,,
Christ triumphant	3. 308	,,
A Combat	3. 308	,,
Adoration of Shepherds	3. 310	Earl of Hopetoun
St. John and Lamb	3. 316	Rock

RUBENS, Sir Peter Paul—*continued*

	VOL. & PAGE		OWNER
Daughter of Herodias and Head	3.	319	Earl of Carlisle
Thomas Howard, Earl of Arundel	3.	323	Earl of Carlisle
Virgin and Child, St. John, etc.	3.	332	Meynell Ingram
A General with a Baton	3.	342	W. V. Wentworth
Romulus and Remus	3.	386	Earl of Shrewsbury
Landscape	3.	390	M. A. Whyte
Sketch of Holy Family	3.	396	Duke of Rutland
Virgin and Child crowning Catherine	3.	399	,,
Discovery of the child Erachthonius	3.	399	,,
Shepherd caressing seated Woman	3.	400	,,
Landscape	3.	400	,,
Return from Flight into Egypt	3.	419	Earl of Leicester
Prodigal Son in Stable	3.	429	A Fountaine
Fruit Piece (with Snyders)	3.	429	A Fountaine
Rainbow Landscape	3.	434	Earl of Orford
David presenting Thank Offering	3.	458	Earl Spencer
Don Ferdinand of the Netherlands	3.	458	Earl Spencer
Abel dead	3.	465	Duke of Bedford
Boy sitting on Kitchen Dresser	3.	475	Marquis of Bute
Adoration of Kings (sketch)	3.	475	,,
Arch at Antwerp in 1635	3.	475	,,
Triumph of Julius Cæsar	4.	62	National Gallery
Allegory of War	4.	62	National Gallery
Rainbow Landscape	4.	86	Marquis of Hertford
Old Man holding Glove	4.	86	,,
Battle between Constantine and Maxentius	4.	86	,,
Two Children	4.	92	Marquis of Westminster
Landscape, Cart, and 2 Horses	4.	98	T. Baring
A young Woman	4.	102	R. S. Holford
Elevation of the Cross	4.	102	R. S. Holford
St. Francesca de Paula	4.	106	J. Morrison
Four Evangelists	4.	109	,,
Emperor Charles V. enthroned	4.	111	,,
Fall of Phaeton (*copy*)	4.	152	Earl of Caledon
Virgin with Child, standing	4.	160	A. Robarts
Triumph of Saul	4.	180	Rev. Mr. Townshend
Conversion of St. Paul	4.	185	W. Russell
Apotheosis of a Hero, etc.	4.	200	J. Tulloch
Woman in Adultery (*copy*)	4.	235	Earl of Harrington
Ascension of Virgin	4.	240	R. P. Nichols
George Villiers, Duke of Buckingham	4.	272	Earl of Jersey
Triumphal Arch	4.	283	Sir C. Eardley
Virgin and Child on white Cushion	4.	305	J. Morrison

	VOL. & PAGE	OWNER
Christ bearing Cross	4. 324	Lord Enfield
Male Portrait, Hand on Staff, with Chain	4. 329	Sir T. Sebright
Abel dead	4. 333	Duke of Bedford
His own Portrait	4. 335	Duke of Bedford
Pope and Emperor worshipping	4. 346	Earl Cowper
La Charrette embourbée	4. 349	Vernon Harcourt
Landscape, Figures and Animals, painted with Van Uden	4. 350	Vernon Harcourt
A Male Portrait	4. 354	Lord Folkestone
Cupids occupied with Harvest	4. 355	,,
Diana and her Nymphs (sketch)	4. 356	,,
Portrait of his Son	4. 360	,,
A Woman	4. 361	,,
Duke of Alva on Horseback	4. 362	,,
Mary de Medici	4. 362	,,
Four Couples feasting	4. 365	Earl of Normanton
Lioness writhing in Death	4. 373	Earl of Normanton
A Picture	4. 374	Sir W. Knighton
Marchesa Brigitta Spinola	4. 375	Kingston Lacy
Princess Grimaldi	4. 375	Kingston Lacy
A Wolf Hunt	4. 395	Lord Methuen
Three Amorini occupied with Harvest	4. 411	Smith Barry
Six sketches from Life of Achilles	4. 411	Smith Barry
Landscape, 2 Sportsmen	4. 423	Earl of Burlington
Vertumnus and Pomona	4. 440	Earl of Wemys
Sketch for Whitehall Ceiling	4. 443	Sir H. Campbell
Man in black Dress and white Collar	4. 447	Lord Kinnaird
Philip IV of Spain	4. 449	W. Stirling
Catherine Brandt	4. 450	,,
An Emperor, Eagle and Wreath	4. 452	,,
Soldiers maltreating Peasants	4. 455	Earl of Dunmore
Christ and St. John as Children	4. 459	M'Lellan Gallery
St. Francis and Lamb	4. 480	Matthew Anderson
A Saint, Dog with Torch	4. 480	,,
Catherine Brandt	4. 483	,,
Young Woman in rich Dress	4. 498	W. Drury Lowe
A Girl smelling a Flower	4. 510	Duke of Newcastle
Woman with a Bunch of Grapes	4. 510	,,
A Jesuit preaching to Peasants	4. 510	,,
Garden of Love (copy)	4. 514	Duke of Portland
A Triton and Sea Nymphs	4. 515	Duke of Portland
Two old Men	4. 518	Earl of Hardwicke
Marchese Spinola	4. 519	,,
A Roman Charity	4. 522	,,

	VOL. & PAGE		OWNER
RUGENDAS			
Eight Battles from Campaigns in the Netherlands	2.	355	Hampton Court
RUMANINO, Girolamo			
A Picture	2.	482	Charles I
RUSSIAN SCHOOL			
Monastery of Solowetsk	4.	221	Prince Consort
Small Altar-piece	4.	451	W. Stirling
RUTHARTS, Karel			
Hunting Piece	4.	149	Earl of Caledon
Hunting Piece	4.	149	Earl of Caledon
RUTHHART			
A Bear hunt	3.	387	Earl of Shrewsbury
Two other Pictures	3.	388	Earl of Shrewsbury
A Bear hunt	4.	491	Earl of Harrington
RUYSCH, Rachel			
A Picture, 1687	2.	309	Mr. Wombwell
A Bunch of Flowers	3.	289	M'Lellan Gallery
Fruit Piece	3.	388	Earl of Shrewsbury
Flowers in dark Vessel	4.	421	Jacob Fletcher
RUYSDAEL, Jacob			
A Waterfall	1.	409	Sir R. Peel
Canal in Winter	1.	409	„
An Oak Wood	1.	409	„
Village and Windmill	2.	21	Buckingham Palace
Plain, near Haarlem	2.	49	Bridgewater House
Road to Village, figures by Wouvermans	2.	49	„
A Sluice with Bridge	2.	49	„
Stream by wooded Hill	2.	49	„
Stream through Forest	2.	49	„
A Castle and Waterfall	2.	49	„
Trees and Cattle, with A. van de Velde	2.	70	Duke of Sutherland
A Village	2.	110	Lord Ashburton
Landscape	2.	110	„
Landscape	2.	110	„
Landscape	2.	110	„
Landscape	2.	110	„
Stream between Hills	2.	122	H. T. Hope
Dark Forest and Sunbeam	2.	130	Baron L. Rothschild

	VOL. & PAGE	OWNER
Wood with Water, with A. van de Velde	2. 130	Baron L. Rothschild
A Canal, Sun in Clouds	2. 139	H. A. J. Munro
Sea piece with red Sail	2. 139	„
Sea piece, dark Water	2. 139	„
A Waterfall	2. 160	Marquis of Hertford
Agitated Water, 6 Vessels	2. 187	T. Baring
Cornfields	2. 187	„
Ruins and piece of Water	2. 187	„
Castle, Mill and Village	2. 202	R. S. Holford
Dark Wood, Water and 3 Cows	2. 225	Richard Ford
Landscape, Oaks and Cattle, with A. van de Velde	2. 228	Hon. E. Phipps
Winter Landscape, warm Sun	2. 228	Hon. E. Phipps
Winter Landscape	2. 237	Lord Ward
Sea Coast at Scheveningen	2. 247	Joseph Neeld
Landscape, Evening Sun	2. 255	F. Heusch
Wooden Bridge over Stream	2. 261	J. Morrison
Sea Coast at Scheveningen	2. 280	Earl of Carlisle
Several Lions	2. 285	Duke of Bedford
Rich Plain, Ruins of Castle	2. 288	R. Sanderson
A Grand Waterfall	2. 289	R. Sanderson
Landscape with Ruin	2. 289	C. Bredel
Winter Landscape and Windmills	2. 296	Wynn Ellis
Water and Ducks	2. 296	„
Watermill, Hills in background	2. 297	„
Ruins near Water	2. 297	„
Small dark Waterfall	2. 297	„
Stream with Oak Trees	2. 309	Mr. Wombwell
Four fine Oaks	2. 309	„
Strongly lighted Tree	2. 309	„
Landscape, Cows and Sheep with A. van de Velde	2. 316	Earl Brownlow
Waterfall	2. 329	Mr. Oppenheim
Dark Landscape	2. 336	Haywood Hawkins
Waterfalls	2. 344	Dulwich Gallery
Large dark Landscape	2. 422	H. Labouchere
View on the Y	2. 452	Richard Forster
A Waterfall	3. 35	Petworth
A Waterfall	3. 40	Petworth
Landscape and Oak Tree	3. 50	Oxford University
Heavy Storm at Sea	3. 158	Marquis of Lansdowne
Town on a Stream	3. 160	„
Hilly Landscape with Stream	3. 164	„
Poetic Landscape	3. 177	Mr. Vivian
Landscape with Waterfall, 1636	3. 209	Lord Northwick

	VOL. & PAGE	OWNER
RUYSDAEL, Jacob—*continued*		
Landscape with Waterfall	3. 225	Mr. Martin
Landscape, Figures angling	3. 273	Edinburgh R.I.
Landscape, watering Horses	3. 273	,,
Sea piece and Boats	3. 274	,,
Town of Katwyck	3. 287	M'Lellan Gallery
Landscape, Fishermen	3. 289	M'Lellan Gallery
A wooded Landscape	3. 313	Duke of Buccleuch
Canal, Houses and Trees	3. 336	Charles Wynn
Sea piece, Coast in distance	3. 397	Duke of Rutland
Sea piece, Coast in foreground	3. 397	Duke of Rutland
A Waterfall	3. 406	Marquis of Exeter
Sea piece, brown Sail	3. 430	A. Fountaine
Sea Coast, cloudy Sky	3. 430	,,
Flat Country, sunny Fields	3. 430	,,
A small Picture	3. 430	,,
Sea piece, raging Storm	3. 434	Earl of Orford
Rocky Country, Ruins and Sheep	3. 480	Marquis of Bute
Two Shepherds under Tree	3. 481	,,
Interior of Church, Amsterdam	3. 481	,,
Landscape and Waterfall	4. 90	Marquis of Hertford
Windmill and Water	4. 99	T. Baring
Plain before Haarlem	4. 99	,,
Landscape and Waterfall	4. 99	,,
Mill on rushing Stream	4. 111	J. Morrison
Road over rising ground	4. 133	Lord Overstone
Waterfall	4. 135	,,
Waterfall, Church, etc.	4. 141	,,
Wooded height, 2 Men and Sheep	4. 142	,,
Two Windmills on Canal	4. 146	,,
Coast of Scheveningen	4. 154	H. S. Mildmay
Sea Coast, Town of Muyden	4. 154	H. S. Mildmay
Waterfall, Shepherd and Flock	4. 159	A. Robarts
Watermill and Trees	4. 194	G. Field
Houses near Trees	4. 194	,,
Small Lake, Ruin, etc.	4. 195	,,
Town of Haarlem	4. 211	Mr. Henderson
Cottage, wreath of Smoke	4. 214	Mrs. James
Landscape, Water with Aquatic Flowers	4. 273	Earl of Jersey
Watermill, Man, and White Dog	4. 287	E. Foster
Waterfall and Mountains	4. 291	J. Sanders
Castle of the Counts of Bentheim	4. 296	J. Walter
Water with 2 Swans	4. 318	Rev. Mr. Heath
Waterfall and Trees	4. 323	Lord Enfield
Small Waterfall	4. 350	V. Harcourt

	VOL. & PAGE		OWNER
Moonlight Landscape	4.	355	Lord Folkestone
Man and Woman on Road	4.	368	Earl of Normanton
Watermill, Shepherd and Dog	4.	369	Earl of Normanton
A Picture	4.	374	Sir W. Knighton
A Waterfall	4.	386	H. D. Seymour
Landscape	4.	403	Edwin Bullock
Two Pictures	4.	404	J. Gillott
Eminence with Trees	4.	424	Earl of Burlington
Landscape	4.	425	,,
Landscape	4.	425	,,
Cottage and Trees	4.	425	,,
Extensive level Country	4.	425	,,
Wooded Landscape	4.	436	Duke of Buccleuch
Town of Haarlem	4.	437	Earl of Wemyss
Plain of Haarlem	4.	437	,,
Winter Landscape, House, etc.	4.	439	,,
Canal, Ruins and Boats	4.	440	,,
Forest Scene and Cascades	4.	441	Sir H. Campbell
Trees reflected in Water	4.	442	,,
The Cottage	4.	442	,,
Seated Figure conversing	4.	454	Earl of Dunmore
Rock between Trees	4.	454	Earl of Dunmore
Dark Wood, Sportsman and Dog	4.	476	W. W. Bardon
Sandhill, with Animals by Berghem	4.	483	Matthew Anderson
Waterfall and Hill	4.	504	Earl of Yarborough
A stormy Sea with Breakers	4.	509	Duke of Newcastle
Wooded Eminence, House, etc.	4.	509	Duke of Newcastle
Landscape, with grand Oaks	4.	513	Duke of Portland

RUYSDAEL, Solomon

	VOL. & PAGE		OWNER
Landscape, Cows in front	3.	220	Howard Galton
A Dutch Canal	3.	250	Blundell Weld
Landscape, Ferry on Canal	3.	252	Blundell Weld
Landscape	3.	304	Duke of Hamilton
Dutch Canal	4.	179	Rev. Mr. Townshend
A Dutch Village	4.	207	Mr. Henderson
Landscape	4.	486	Lord Ravenworth

RYCKAERT, David

	VOL. & PAGE		OWNER
A Party of Peasants	4.	439	Earl of Wemyss
A Party of Peasants, interior	4.	482	Matthew Anderson

RYSBRAECK *see also* **RUYSBRAECK**

	VOL. & PAGE		OWNER
A Picture	2.	95	Devonshire House
Landscape and Dolphin Fountain	4.	507	Sir J. Nelthorpe

	VOL. & PAGE	OWNER
SABBATINI, Andrea (Andrea da Salerno)		
Adoring the Cross	3. 435	Earl of Orford
Virgin and Child enthroned	3. 435	Earl of Orford
SABBATINI, Lorenzo		
Presentation in the Temple	2. 244	Mr. Neeld
SACCHI, Andrea		
Christ bearing the Cross	2. 76	S. Rogers
A Picture	2. 93	Devonshire House
St. Bruno	2. 170	Marquis of Westminster
Christ bearing the Cross	2. 495	Orleans Gallery
Adam lamenting the Death of Abel	2. 495	Orleans Gallery
A Picture	3. 403	Marquis of Exeter
A Pope with Moustache	4. 439	Earl of Wemyss
The dead Abel	4. 506	Earl of Yarborough
SACHTLEVEN, Cornelius		
Mother, Children and Goats	4. 268	Duke of Northumberland
Woman, Girl, Boy and Cow	4. 269	Duke of Northumberland
Ducks and Geese and Cows	4. 478	J. Anderson
SACHTLEVEN, Herrman		
Small Landscape	2. 122	H. T. Hope
View of a Ruin	2. 502	Orleans Gallery
View of a Ruin	2. 502	Orleans Gallery
ST. JEAN		
Large Flower Piece, 1846	4. 86	Marquis of Hertford
Fruit in a Dish	4. 86	Marquis of Hertford
SALAINO, Il		
St. Anne with the Virgin in her Lap	4. 481	Matthew Anderson
SALERNO, Andrea da		
St. Catherine	2. 29	Bridgewater House
St. Rosalie	2. 29	Bridgewater House
SALIMBENI, Ventura		
St. Catherine seated	4. 65	Earl of Yarborough

	VOL. & PAGE	OWNER
SALVIATI, Francesco		
Rape of the Sabines	2. 495	Orleans Gallery
SANO, di Pietro		
Baptism of Christ	2. 463	Rev. Mr. Russell
St. Peter restoring Tabitha	3. 4	W. Fuller Maitland
Virgin and Child, etc.	3. 53	Oxford University
Miracle of St. Clara	3. 428	Sir J. Boileau
Virgin and Child	4. 222	Prince Consort
A Picture	4. 234	General Fox
SANTA CROCE, Girolamo da		
A Male Portrait	3. 300	Duke of Hamilton
David playing the Harp	4. 239	R. P. Nichols
The Crucifixion	4. 412	Smith Barry
Virgin, Child lying on the Ground	4. 484	George Burdon
SANTI, Giovanni		
Boy in Profile	3. 281	Mr. Dennistoun
Adoration of the Kings	4. 330	Sir T. Sebright
SARACINO, Carlo (Carlo Veneziano)		
Death of the Virgin	2. 495	Orleans Gallery
Death of the Virgin	3. 324	Earl of Carlisle
SARTO, Andrea del		
Holy Family	1. 322	National Gallery
Virgin and Child and St. John	2. 63	Duke of Sutherland
Studies in Chalk for Frescoes	2. 80	S. Rogers
A Male Portrait	2. 84	Lord de Mauley
Dead Christ, Virgin, etc.	2. 132	H. A. J. Munro
Virgin seated on Ground, etc.	1. 155	Marquis of Hertford
Virgin seated, Child on Lap	2. 175	T. Baring
St. John the Baptist	2. 175	T. Baring
Virgin and Child and Veil	2. 195	R. S. Holford
Virgin and Child and St. John	2. 244	Joseph Neeld
A Carita	2. 251	Hon. Mr. Ashburnham
A Female Head, Chalk Drawing	2. 331	C. S. Bale
Virgin and Child and St. John	2. 432	Windsor Castle
A Holy Family	2. 434	Windsor Castle
Virgin and Child and St. John	2. 478	Charles I
Virgin and Child and Joseph	2. 478	,,
Man without a Beard	2. 478	,,
Leda with the Swan	2. 495	Orleans Gallery
Lucretia	2. 495	Orleans Gallery

	VOL. & PAGE		OWNER
His own Portrait	3.	11	Earl Cowper
A Woman in a red Dress	3.	11	„
Young Man in Black	3.	11	„
Joseph and his Brethren	3.	11	„
Legend of a Saint	3.	12	„
Legend of a Saint	3.	12	„
His own Portrait (oval)	3.	12	„
Two Pictures (copies)	3.	32	Petworth
A young Man	3.	160	Marquis of Lansdowne
Virgin and Child, SS. John and Ambrose	3.	172	Colt Hoare
Michael Angelo	3.	176	Mr. Vivian
Virgin and Child and St. John	3.	179	J. P. Miles
Female in a black dress	3.	197	Lord Northwick
Virgin and Child and St. John	3.	237	Liverpool R.I.
Virgin and Child and St. John	3.	237	Liverpool R.I.
A Holy Family	3.	248	Blundell Weld
Portrait of his Wife as Magdalen	3.	300	Duke of Hamilton
Meeting of Fathers of the Church	3.	314	Duke of Buccleuch
His Wife Lucretia Fede	3.	382	Earl of Shrewsbury
Michael Angelo	3.	443	Mr. Tomline
Virgin with Child on her Arm	3.	482	Marquis of Bute
Virgin holding the Child before her	4.	66	Earl of Yarborough
Young Man in a black dress	4.	329	Sir T. Sebright
Virgin and Child and St. John	4.	340	Knole
A Man	4.	396	Lord Methuen
Six Saints, 2 kneeling	4.	436	Duke of Buccleuch
The Holy Family	4.	444	Earl of Elgin
Man with Moustaches and Beard	4.	447	Lord Kinnaird
His own Portrait	4.	467	Duke of Northumberland
Virgin holding the Child	4.	497	Drury Lowe

SASSOFERRATO

	VOL. & PAGE		OWNER
The Madonna	2.	30	Bridgewater House
A Virgin and Child	2.	63	Duke of Sutherland
Madonna	2.	92	Devonshire House
A Holy Family	2.	132	H. A. J. Munro
Virgin looking upwards	2.	176	T. Baring
The Annunciation	2.	242	H. D. Seymour
A Holy Family	2.	277	Duke of Wellington
The Last Supper	2.	286	Duke of Bedford
Madonna praying	3.	20	Earl of Darnley
Virgin and sleeping Child	3.	261	Earl of Lonsdale
Madonna praying	3.	305	Duke of Hamilton
A Picture	3.	314	Captain Stirling

C C

	VOL. & PAGE		OWNER
SASSOFERRATO—*continued*			
Madonna	3.	350	Duke of Devonshire
Marriage of St. Catherine	3.	434	Earl of Orford
Virgin holding the Child, and Joseph	3.	484	Marquis of Bute
Virgin holding the Child asleep	3.	484	„
Virgin praying	3.	484	„
Marriage of St. Catherine	4.	80	Marquis of Hertford
Virgin and Child	4.	241	R. P. Nichols
Virgin and Child and Joseph	4.	262	Duc D'Aumale
Virgin and Child	4.	295	J. Walter
Copy of a Solario	4.	391	J. Everett
Virgin and sleeping Child	4.	392	Lord Arundel
Virgin and sleeping Child	4.	392	Lord Arundel
Virgin and sleeping Child	4.	446	Lord Kinnaird
Virgin praying	4.	481	Matthew Anderson
Virgin praying	4.	513	Duke of Portland
SAVARY, Roland			
A Picture	2.	95	Devonshire House
A Picture	2.	482	Charles I
Orpheus attracting Animals	3.	123	Duke of Marlborough
A Wood, Lady and Gentleman on			
Horseback	3.	448	Fitzwilliam Museum
A Picture	3.	476	Marquis of Bute
Landscape with Animals called Breughel	4.	269	Duke of Northumberland
Daniel in the Lions' Den	4.	426	Earl of Burlington
An Animal Piece	4.	512	Duke of Portland
SAVOLDO			
A Nun with violet and white Cloth	4.	145	Lord Overstone
SCARCELLINO, da Ferrara			
Christ at Emmaus	2.	496	Orleans Gallery
SCHADOW, Rudolph (Sculptor)			
Statue, Female spinning	3.	366	Duke of Devonshire
A Discobolus, 1821	4.	446	Lord Kinnaird
SCHAFNER, Martin (of Ulm)			
Two delicate Pictures, Religious Subjects	4.	104	H. Labouchere
Infant Christ learning to walk	4.	228	Prince Consort
Marriage of the Virgin, etc.	4.	317	Rev. Mr. Heath
Cornelius with Horn of Oil	4.	351	Vernon Harcourt

	VOL. & PAGE		OWNER

SCHALKEN, Godefroy

A Girl with a Candle	1.	394	Duke of Northumberland
Le Roi Detroussé	2.	8	Buckingham Palace
The Painter and his Family	2.	9	,,
Girl with a Candle	2.	9	,,
A Smoker by Candlelight	2.	117	H. T. Hope
A Male Portrait	2.	183	T. Baring
Cookmaid with a Candle	2.	291	C. Bredel
A Daylight Picture	2.	329	Mr. Oppenheim
La Fille Retrouvée	2.	502	Orleans Gallery
A Girl and a Boy (Daylight)	3.	400	Duke of Rutland
A Girl and a Boy (Candlelight)	·3.	400	Duke of Rutland
Girl by Candlelight	4.	88	Marquis of Hertford
Maidservant by Candlelight	4.	200	J. Tulloch
A Man	4.	519	Earl of Hardwicke
His Wife	4.	519	Earl of Hardwicke

SCHAÜFFELEIN, Hans

Man, white Beard and Watch	4.	267	Duke of Northumberland
Girl in black, and gold Chain	4.	432	Gibson Craig

SCHEFFER, Ary

Christ and three Maries	4.	416	Samuel Ashton
Four from " Faust " in one Frame	4.	417	Samuel Ashton

SCHELFHOUT

A Shore Scene	2.	191	T. Baring
Winter Landscape with Mill	4.	176	Rev. Mr. Townshend

SCHIAVONE, Andrea

Christ before Pilate	2.	33	Bridgewater House
Marriage of St. Catherine	2.	33	Bridgewater House
Dead Christ and Angels	2.	60	Duke of Sutherland
Expulsion from Paradise	2.	87	Earl of Yarborough
St. Jerome in the Desert	2.	90	Devonshire House
Cupid and Psyche	2.	135	H. A. J. Munro
Woman taken in Adultery	2.	244	Joseph Neeld
Several Figures entering a Boat	2.	267	Miss Rogers
The Nativity of the Virgin	2.	270	Miss Rogers
Four Landscapes	2.	355	Hampton Court
Tobit with the Angel	2.	357	Hampton Court
Two Pictures	2.	482	Charles I
Christ before Pilate	2.	496	Orleans Gallery
Dead Christ and Angels	2.	496	Orleans Gallery
A Flagellation	3.	19	Earl of Darnley

	VOL. & PAGE		OWNER
SCHIAVONE, Andrea—*continued*			
Country People in a Landscape	3.	166	Marquis of Lansdowne
Country People in a Landscape	3.	166	Marquis of Lansdowne
Venus and Cupid	3.	203	Lord Northwick
Virgin and Child	3.	281	Mr. Dennistoun
Ecce Homo and Pilate	3.	304	Duke of Hamilton
Marriage of St. Catherine	3.	404	Marquis of Exeter
Finding of Moses	3.	404	Marquis of Exeter
The new-born Jupiter	4.	63	Lord Elcho
Adam and Eve expelled	4.	68	Earl of Yarborough
Birth of the Virgin	4.	168	W. Davenport Bromley
7 small Pictures, Apollo, etc.	4.	171	E. Cheney
Exposure of Infant Moses	4.	171	„
Sacrifice of Isaac	4.	172	„
Judith	4.	172	„
David	4.	172	„
Landscape, Cupid shooting at Girls	4.	172	„
Judgment of Paris	4.	186	W. Russell
Christ and 5 Disciples	4.	292	J. Sanders
Daughter of Herodius, etc.	4.	460	M'Lellan Gallery
SCHIDONE, Bartolommeo			
Virgin teaching Christ to read	2.	30	Bridgewater House
The Entombment	2.	101	Lord Ashburton
The Holy Family	2.	135	H. A. J. Munro
The Virgin and Child	2.	152	Marquis of Lansdowne
A Riposo	2.	180	T. Baring
Virgin and Child and St. John	2.	245	Joseph Neeld
Holy Family	2.	284	Duke of Bedford
Holy Family	2.	420	H. Labouchere
Virgin and Child and St. John	2.	478	Charles I
The Transfiguration	3.	21	Earl of Darnley
Virgin and Child and Joseph	3.	151	Earl of Pembroke
Virgin and Child	3.	172	Colt Hoare
St. John and the Lamb	3.	172	„
An old Man	3.	172	„
St. John the Evangelist	3.	192	Mr. Harford
The Magdalen	3.	250	Blundell Weld
Assumption of the Virgin	3.	304	Duke of Hamilton
The Holy Family	3.	396	Duke of Rutland
Four Ladies of Parma Family	3.	405	Marquis of Exeter
Virgin and Child and Joseph	4.	64	Earl of Yarborough
Cupid seated on the Ground	4.	185	W. Russell
Virgin holding Child, etc.	4.	388	Lord Heytesbury
Cupid	4.	426	Earl of Burlington

	VOL. & PAGE		OWNER
John the Baptist sleeping	4.	444	Earl of Elgin
Holy Family and Joseph	4.	447	Lord Kinnaird
Boy placing a Wreath on a Skull	4.	470	Duke of Northumberland
Virgin and Child	4.	503	Earl of Yarborough

SCHLEICH, Edward

Scenery around Munich	4.	178	Rev. Mr. Townshend

SCHONGAUER, Martin

Pilate and the Jews	2.	459	Mr. Green
Virgin and Child	4.	225	Prince Consort
Crucifixion	4.	225	Prince Consort

SCHOREEL, Jan

Virgin and Child and St. Andrew and Archangel Michael, called Mabuse	2.	358	Hampton Court
Learned Man with Book	2.	478	Charles I
A Landscape	2.	478	Charles I
An old Woman	3.	6	W. Fuller Maitland
Presentation in the Temple	4.	267	Duke of Northumberland
Raising of Lazarus	4.	268	Duke of Northumberland

SCHOTEL, J. C.

A quiet Sea	2.	191	T. Baring
An agitated Sea with a Boat	2.	191	„
A Storm, 2 Boats	2.	191	„

SCHÜTZ, Christian George

Alpine Landscape	4.	201	J. Tulloch

SEGHERS, Daniel

Bouquet of Flowers	2.	345	Dulwich Gallery
A Flower Piece	2.	365	Hampton Court
Two Pictures	2.	482	Charles I

SEGHERS, Gerard (Pater)

Three Flower Pieces	3.	254	Blundell Weld

SEVERN

Esther (Prudence)	4.	343	Countess of Warwick
Eleanor (Resolution)	4.	343	„
Penelope (Patience)	3.	343	„
Another Virtue	3.	343	„

SEYFARTH, Louisa

Group of Women, etc. (Drawing)	2.	352	E. Bicknell

	VOL. & PAGE	OWNER
SIENESE SCHOOL		
St. Peter, St. Paul, etc.	3. 375	W. Davenport Bromley
SIGNORELLI, Luca		
Virgin and Child (circle)	2. 126	A. Barker
St. George and the Dragon	2. 126	„
St. Bernard, etc.	2. 126	„
Angel and Tobit	2. 126	„
Martyrdom of St. Catherine	2. 417	H. Labouchere
Circumcision of Christ	3. 299	Duke of Hamilton
A Picture	3. 314	Captain Stirling
A Picture	3. 314	W. Stirling
Two Frescoes	4. 73	A. Barker
Coriolanus and his Mother	4. 74	A. Barker
A Pietà	4. 451	W. Stirling
SIMPSON		
Duke of Wellington	4. 372	Earl of Normanton
SIRANI, Elisabetta		
A Picture	2. 39	Bridgewater House
The Magdalen	3. 265	Earl of Lonsdale
St. John	3. 270	Edinburgh R.I.
SLINGELANDT, Peter van		
A Family, Child praying	1. 402	Sir R. Peel
Mother with a Child at her Breast	2. 8	Buckingham Palace
Woman sewing, Child in Cradle	2. 8	Buckingham Palace
Man offering Partridges to a Cook	2. 44	Bridgewater House
Mother reproving smoking Girl	2. 184	T. Baring
A Kitchen Girl scouring Kettle	3. 476	Marquis of Bute
Maidservant Baking, etc.	4. 162	A. Robarts
SMITH, Colvin		
Sir Walter Scott, 1816	4. 173	E. Cheney
SNAYERS, Peter		
A Cavalry Skirmish	2. 343	Dulwich Gallery
The Fight of Forty	2. 358	Hampton Court
SNYDERS		
A Fox Hunt	1. 394	Duke of Northumberland
A Deer Hunt	1. 394	Duke of Northumberland
A Bear Hunt	2. 165	Marquis of Westminster
A Lion Hunt	2. 165	Marquis of Westminster

	VOL. & PAGE		OWNER
Two Heads of Dogs	2.	331	C. S. Bale
Two Cocks fighting	2.	422	H. Labouchere
A Stag Hunt	3.	24	Earl of Darnley
Landscape, Hare and Tortoise	3.	24	,,
Heads of Stags	3.	24	,,
Concert of Birds	3.	36	Petworth
Concert of Birds, Hawk pouncing	3.	36	Petworth
Game and Fruit, painted with Rubens	3.	227	Hon. R. Clive
Many Pictures	3.	265	Earl of Lonsdale
A Bear Hunt	3.	270	Edinburgh R.I.
A Wolf Hunt	3.	274	,,
A Bear Hunt (copy)	3.	276	,,
Pantry of Provisions, dead Stag	3.	283	Glasgow College
A Picture	3.	315	Lennox Castle
Dead Game and Fruit	3.	387	Earl of Shrewsbury
A Dog biting a Fox	3.	387	Earl of Shrewsbury
Dead Swan, Peacock, etc.	3.	392	Lord Scarsdale
Ducks pursued by a Hawk	3.	392	Lord Scarsdale
Large and small Parrots	3.	422	Earl of Leicester
Fruit Piece with Figures by Rubens	3.	429	A. Fountaine
His own Portrait, Wife and Child	3.	443	Mr. Tomline
Two Pictures	3.	449	Fitzwilliam Museum
Wild Boar Hunt	4.	267	Duke of Northumberland
Two blue earthen Vessels with Crabs	4.	278	Sir C. Eardley
Two Panthers	4.	327	Sir T. Sebright
Combat between Wolves and Dogs	4.	342	Humphrey Mildmay
Combat between Bears and Dogs	4.	342	Humphrey Mildmay
Dogs and dead Game	4.	348	Vernon Harcourt
A Horse torn by Wolves	4.	375	Kingston Lacy
A Bull fighting with Dogs	4.	375	Kingston Lacy
A Stag Hunt	4.	441	Earl of Wemyss
A Kitchen Subject	4.	441	,,
Lobster and Dish of Strawberries	4.	441	,,
A Wild Boar Hunt	4.	471	Duke of Northumberland
A Stag Hunt	4.	471	Duke of Northumberland
Poultry Market	4.	508	Duke of Newcastle
Fruit Market	4.	508	,,
Fish Market	4.	508	,,
A Market	4.	508	,,
A Lioness tearing a Boar	4.	511	,,
Two Lionesses following a Roe	4.	513	Duke of Portland
Four large Pictures	4.	514	,,
Wild Boar Hunt	4.	516	,,
Wild Boar Hunt	4.	516	,,
A Bull Fight	4.	516	,,

	VOL. & PAGE	OWNER
SOGLIANI, Giovanni Antonio		
Adoration of the Shepherds	2. 276	Duke of Wellington
The Virgin and Child	3. 196	Lord Northwick
The Virgin and Child	4. 167	W. Davenport Bromley
SOLARIO, Andrea		
A Female Figure in a blue Mantle	2. 62	Duke of Sutherland
The Virgin and Child	2. 196	R. S. Holford
A Holy Family	2. 233	Lord Ward
Daughter of Herodias with the Head	2. 496	Orleans Gallery
A Pietà	4. 448	Lord Kinnaird
SOLIMENE		
Virgin and Child and Angels	3. 240	Liverpool R.I.
SOMACHINO, Orazio		
A Picture	2. 482	Charles I
SPADA, Leonello		
A Male Portrait	2. 65	Duke of Sutherland
Christ with two Guards	4. 262	Duc D'Aumale
David with Head of Goliah	4. 395	Lord Methuen
SPAGNA, Lo		
The Virgin and Child	2. 82	Lord Elcho
The Virgin and Child	2. 176	T. Baring
Six small Pictures of Saints	2. 232	Lord Ward
St. Catherine	2. 232	Lord Ward
Two Portions of Predillas	2. 463	Rev. Mr. Russell
Virgin and Child, called Perugino	3. 159	Marquis of Lansdowne
Virgin and Child, called Francia	3. 197	Lord Northwick
Virgin holding the Child	3. 304	Duke of Hamilton
A Picture	3. 314	Captain Stirling
The Virgin enthroned, and Angels	3. 434	Earl of Orford
Virgin and Child on a lofty Throne	4. 56	National Gallery
Magdalen with the Box of Ointment	4. 411	Smith Barry
Magdalen and St. Catherine	4. 466	Duke of Northumberland
SPAGNOLETTO, Lo (see Ribera)		
Christ teaching in the Temple	2. 37	Bridgewater House
Lo Stregozzo	2. 276	Duke of Wellington
Christ disputing with the Doctors	2. 496	Orleans Gallery
Heraclitus	2. 496	,,
Democritus	2. 496	,,
Heraclitus	2. 496	,,

	VOL. & PAGE		OWNER
Democritus	2.	496	Orleans Gallery
Democritus	3.	23	Earl of Darnley
Heraclitus	3.	23	Earl of Darnley
A Picture	3.	171	Lord Arundel
St. Jerome and Angel blowing trumpet	3.	204	Lord Northwick
Martyrdom of St. Sebastian	3.	270	Edinburgh R.I.
Release of Peter from Prison	3.	270	Edinburgh R.I.
Archimedes	3.	385	Earl of Shrewsbury
His own Portrait	3.	385	Earl of Shrewsbury
The Flight into Egypt	3.	405	Marquis of Exeter
The Adoration of the Shepherds	3.	428	Sir J. Boileau
Christ as the Good Shepherd	4.	61	National Gallery
A Pietà	4.	393	Lord Arundel

SPANISH SCHOOL

	VOL. & PAGE		OWNER
Saint with 2 Monks walking on the Water	4.	153	William Gladstone
Christ as Ecce Homo	4.	477	W. W. Bardon
Christ bound to the Column	4.	482	Matthew Anderson

SPINELLO, of Arezzo (Aretino)

	VOL. & PAGE		OWNER
A Crucifixion	2.	264	Sir C. Eastlake
The Crucifixion	2.	463	Rev. Mr. Russell

STANFIELD, Clarkson, R.A.

	VOL. & PAGE		OWNER
The Giudecca, Venice	1.	386	Marlborough House
Entrance to Zuyder Zee	1.	386	Marlborough House
An agitated Sea	2.	257	George Young
A quiet Sea	2.	257	George Young
Palace at Avignon	2.	259	Sir C. Coote
A Market Boat on the Scheldt	2.	302	J. Sheepshanks
Beilstein on the Moselle	2.	350	E. Bicknell
Several Views of Venice	3.	166	Marquis of Lansdowne
View of Tivoli	3.	166	Marquis of Lansdowne
Storm on Coast of Calais	3.	242	John Naylor
Coast Scene with Boats	3.	443	Mr. Tomline
Rocky Italian Valley	4.	133	Lord Overstone
Sunny Court between Rocks, etc.	4.	134	Lord Overstone
Rocky Seacoast with Town	4.	178	Rev. Mr. Townshend
Agitated Sea with Pier	4.	206	Mr. Henderson
Italian Seacoast	4.	303	J. Morrison
Sea piece	4.	404	Joseph Gillott
Sea piece	4.	404	Joseph Gillott
View of a Port, 1846	4.	417	S. Ashton
A Fresh Breeze, 1848	4.	418	John Chapman

	VOL. & PAGE		OWNER
STANZIONI, Massimo			
Italian Peasant Woman	2.	65	Duke of Sutherland
A Mr. Bankes	4.	378	Kingston Lacy
STAP, J. W.			
Old Man reading and Boy warming			
Hands	4.	426	Earl of Burlington
STEEN, Jan			
Girl at Harpsichord, 1671	1.	403	Sir R. Peel
Girl putting on Stockings, 1663	2.	9	Buckingham Palace
Eleven Persons playing Cards	2.	10	,,
Country People eating and dancing	2.	10	,,
Twelfth Night	2.	10	,,
Country People before an Inn	2.	10	,,
Four Men and one Woman at Cards	2.	10	,,
Fishmonger offering Haddock	2.	44	Bridgewater House
A Schoolmaster cutting Pen	2.	45	Bridgewater House
An Alehouse, 13 Figures	2.	105	Lord Ashburton
Playing at Skittles	2.	105	Lord Ashburton
The Glutton, 1661	2.	118	H. T. Hope
A Christening	2.	118	,,
Large Party in Courtyard, 1663	2.	118	,,
The Painter smoking	2.	137	H. A. J. Munro
The Painter with his Family	2.	137	,,
Two Boors playing Cards	2.	137	,,
Fowl-yard and Pigeons	2.	137	,,
A Fight	2.	137	,,
The Fat Family	2.	137	,,
The Lean Family	2.	137	,,
The Christening	2.	138	,,
Mother asleep with Children	2.	138	,,
Doctor feeling the Pulse of a Lady	2.	138	,,
The Murder of the Innocents	2.	138	,,
A Wedding	2.	184	T. Baring
The Painter singing to his Lute	2.	184	,,
Doctor writing, with a Girl in Bed	2.	184	,,
Mischievous School Boys	2.	184	,,
A Girl at the Piano and Music Master	2.	227	Hon. E. Phipps
A Man, Woman and Child	2.	227	,,
Man and Wife weighing Gold	2.	228	,,
Man and Woman sleeping	2.	237	Lord Ward
Woman seated, in large Straw Hat	2.	247	Joseph Neeld
Sacrifice of Iphigenia	2.	250	Colonel Rawdon
Two Women listening to Music	2.	253	F. Heusch

	VOL. & PAGE	OWNER
Grace before Dinner	2. 262	J. Morrison
A Physician feeling Pulse of a girl	2. 273	Duke of Wellington
A Mother napping, drunk	2. 273	,,
Boors revelling	2. 273	,,
Boors revelling	2. 273	,,
Twelfth Night, Cat eating a Candle	2. 284	Duke of Bedford
An old Beau bowing to a Woman	2. 290	C. Bredel
A Party at Cards, Girl with Ace	2. 329	Mr. Oppenheim
Cakes baking	2. 336	W. Lambert
Examining a Piece of Linen	2. 433	Windsor Castle
Old Man holding a Girl's Apron	2. 451	Richard Forster
An Alchemist	3. 27	Lord Overstone
A Doctor feeling Girl's Pulse	3. 163	Marquis of Lansdowne
A Concert in the open Air	3. 207	Lord Northwick
A rich Composition	3. 207	Lord Northwick
The Wooing	3. 224	Howard Galton
The Painter eating Oysters	3. 262	Earl of Lonsdale
A sick Lady in Bed, Doctor, etc.	3. 274	Edinburgh R.I.
Children skating	3. 290	M'Lellan Gallery
Playing at Toccodille and Cards	3. 387	Earl of Shrewsbury
A Blind Beggar and 2 Figures	3. 392	Lord Scarsdale
A Poor Family saying Grace	3. 397	Duke of Rutland
Seven Persons, Girl with Wreath	3. 441	Mr. Tomline
A Cock Fight	3. 477	Marquess of Bute
Military Stragglers plundering	3. 477	,,
A Girl in white Silk	3. 477	,,
Ugly old Woman bringing Letter	3. 477	,,
Saying Grace	4. 108	J. Morrison
An Alchemist at a Stove, 1668	4. 137	Lord Overstone
A Dutch Proverb	4. 143	Lord Overstone
A Candlelight Scene	4. 155	H. St. John Mildmay
Officer with a Girl on his Knee	4. 161	A. Robarts
Marriage at Cana	4. 296	J. Walter
His own Portrait	4. 336	Duke of Bedford
Man and Wife in Bower of Vines	4. 391	J. Everett
Merrymaking	4. 418	J. Chapman
A Party in the open Air	4. 428	Rev. Mr. Staniforth
Peasants regaling at an Inn	4. 442	Sir H. Campbell
Gentleman giving Oyster to a Lady	4. 442	Sir H. Campbell
Christ visiting Sisters at Bethlehem	4. 452	W. Stirling
A Merry Party	4. 459	M'Lellan Gallery
Five Figures, 2 at a Meal	4. 477	W. W. Bardon
Three Men offering Presents to a Girl	4. 480	Matthew Anderson
Cincinnatus eating Turnips	4. 483	Matthew Anderson

	VOL. & PAGE		OWNER
STEENWYCK, Hendreck Van			
A Picture	2.	42	Bridgewater House
A Picture	2.	95	Devonshire House
A Prison	2.	433	Windsor Castle
Five Pictures	2.	482	Charles I
Interior of a Church, 1621	3.	38	Petworth
Interior of a Church	3.	250	Blundell Weld
A larger Ditto	3.	250	Blundell Weld
A Picture	3.	482	Marquis of Bute
Still Life	4.	148	Earl of Caledon
Interior of a Church	4.	150	Earl of Caledon
Interior of a Church, painted with Franck	4.	504	Earl of Yarborough
Interior of a Prison by Torchlight	4.	507	Sir J. Nelthorpe
St. Jerome and his Lion, 1624	4.	512	Duke of Portland
Deliverance of St. Peter	4.	513	Duke of Portland
STEINHAUSER, Madame (née Baumann)			
Polish Family in Exile	2.	152	Marquis of Lansdowne
STEINLE			
Madonna and Child and Saints	2.	54	Bridgewater House
STEVENS, Palamedes			
A Party in a Room	4.	268	Duke of Northumberland
STONE, Frank, A.R.A.			
Youths and Maidens	2.	153	Marquis of Lansdowne
STONE, Old			
Charles I and Duke of Gloucester (*copy*)	3.	322	Earl of Carlisle
STOOP, D.			
A Picture	2.	52	Bridgewater House
A Battle Piece, called Wouvermans	3.	422	Earl of Leicester
STORCK, Abraham			
Rotterdam	1.	358	National Gallery
A Sea Coast, with Pier	4.	208	Mr. Henderson
A Calm, with Pier	4.	290	J. Sanders
A large Sea piece	4.	404	J. Gillott
STOTHARD, Thomas, R.A.			
Nymphs binding Cupid	1.	368	Marlborough House
Groups of Bacchantes and Amorini	1.	368	,,
Nymphs bathing	1.	368	,,

	VOL. & PAGE	OWNER
The Vintage	1. 368	Marlborough House
A Battle Piece	1. 369	Marlborough House
A fond Couple on Seashore	2. 268	Miss Rogers
Three small spirited Pictures	2. 299	J. Sheepshanks
Shakespeare Characters	2. 306	"
John Gilpin	2. 306	"
Eight Shakespeare Pictures	2. 349	E. Bicknell
Prince Arthur and his Gaolers	2. 461	Mr. Green
The Pilgrimage to Canterbury	3. 185	J. P. Miles
Cleopatra and Mark Antony	3. 407	Marquis of Exeter
Orpheus and Eurydice	3. 407	"
Terrors of War	3. 407	"
Jacob's Dream	4. 134	Lord Overstone
Twelve Pictures of Pilgrim's Progress	4. 139	Lord Overstone
Seven Pictures	4. 186	W. Russell
Heloise	4. 214	Mrs. James
Girl and Fortune Teller	4. 214	"
Two small Pictures	4. 214	"
A Centaur Family	4. 239	Earl of Harrington

STREET, William

The Earl of Surrey	3. 30	Duke of Norfolk

STROZZI, Bernardo (Il Prete Genovese)

St. Lawrence	3. 131	Duke of Marlborough
A Picture	3. 393	Lord Scarsdale
A Magdalen	4. 290	J. Sanders
Christ in the Temple	4. 471	Duke of Northumberland

STUBBS, George, A.R.A.

Horses near Oak-trees	2. 174	Marquis of Westminster
Several Pictures	2. 458	Earl of Clarendon
A Brown Horse	3. 339	Earl Fitzwilliam
Two small Pictures	3. 455	Earl Spencer

SUBLEYRAS, Pierre

Pope Benedict XIV, 1740	2. 66	Duke of Sutherland
Fall of Simon the Sorcerer	3. 386	Earl of Shrewsbury

SUSTERMAN, Justus

Alessandro Farnese	3. 269	Edinburgh R.I.
Galileo	4. 397	Lord Metheun

SWABIAN SCHOOL

St. Anna and the Virgin	3. 251	Blundell Weld

SWANEVELDT, Hermann

	VOL. & PAGE	OWNER
Two Landscapes	2. 358	Hampton Court
Landscape and Cattle	2. 414	Hampton Court
Landscape	3. 36	Petworth
Four Landscapes	3. 171	Lord Arundel
A warm Landscape	3. 177	Mr. Vivian
Woman on a Donkey	3. 293	Sir A. Campbell
Landscape with Water	3. 309	Earl of Hopetoun
Flight into Egypt	3. 337	Charles Wynn
Two Landscapes	3. 449	Fitzwilliam Museum
A large Landscape	3. 481	Marquis of Bute

	VOL. & PAGE	OWNER
TACHONI, Francesco		
Virgin with Child on Lap, 1489	4. 59	National Gallery
TADDEO, di Bartolo		
Coronation of the Virgin	2. 462	Rev. Mr. Russell
Virgin and Child, Benediction	2. 462	Rev. Mr. Russell
Figures from Siena Chapel	4. 299	Higford Burr
TADDOLINI (Sculptor)		
Ganymede caressing Eagle	3. 367	Duke of Devonshire
TASSI, Agostino		
Landscape, like Claude	2. 177	T. Baring
Landscape, painted with Jan Miel	3. 222	Howard Galton
TAYLER, Frederick		
Lady and Gentleman with Falcons	4. 415	S. Ashton
TEMPESTA, A.		
A Picture	2. 311	Earl of Listowel
Two large Landscapes	3. 485	Marquis of Bute
TENERANI (Sculptor)		
Cupid drawing Thorn, etc.	3. 366	Duke of Devonshire
Bust of Pio Nono	3. 366	Duke of Devonshire
TENIERS, Old		
St. Anthony before a Cave	4. 438	Earl of Wemyss
TENIERS, David, Junior		
The Music Party	1. 356	National Gallery
Peasants drinking	1. 356	,,
The Money Changers	1. 356	,,
Old Peasant caressing Girl	1. 404	Sir R. Peel
A Magician and infernal Spirits	1. 404	,,
The Four Seasons (4 pictures)	1. 404	,,
Four Boors playing Cards	2. 11	Buckingham Palace
Boors dancing near Castle	2. 11	,,
Yard of Village Alehouse	2. 12	,,

TENIERS, David, Junr.—*continued*	VOL. & PAGE		OWNER
A Village Fête	2.	12	Buckingham Palace
A Village Fair	2.	12	,,
Thirty Persons dancing	2.	12	,,
Civic Guard getting under Arms	2.	12	,,
Old Cook peeling Turnips	2.	12	,,
Two Men conversing on Road	2.	12	,,
Four Fishermen on Seacoast	2.	13	,,
Teniers and two Ladies	2.	13	,,
Several Landscapes	2.	13	,,
Playing at Skittles	2.	41	Bridgewater House
Alchymist blowing a Fire	2.	41	,,
Peasants at play	2.	41	,,
Boors smoking	2.	41	,,
Peasant with a Basket, and a Woman	2.	41	,,
A Village Festival	2.	41	,,
A Peasants' Wedding	2.	41	,,
A Witch before a Cauldron	2.	69	Duke of Sutherland
A Group of Ducks	2.	69	Duke of Sutherland
The Seven Works of Mercy	2.	105	Lord Ashburton
Le Manchot	2.	106	,,
His own Portrait in Spanish Costume	2.	106	,,
Dancing at a Village Alehouse	2.	106	,,
Shepherds with Cows and Sheep	2.	106	,,
Four Soldiers smoking	2.	119	H. T. Hope
Two Soldiers playing Backgammon	2.	119	H. T. Hope
Four Cows in a Landscape	2.	129	Baron L. Rothschild
An old Man and Woman	2.	129	Baron L. Rothschild
Teniers and Wife with Gardener	2.	168	Marquis of Westminster
Family saying Grace	2.	169	,,
Peasants	2.	169	,,
Peasants	2.	169	,,
A Corps de Garde	2.	184	T. Baring
A Village Festival	2.	184	,,
Monkeys shaving Cats	2.	185	,,
A Harvest Scene	2.	185	,,
A Peasant Family	2.	185	,,
Peasant Fête in a Village	2.	201	R. S. Holford
Peasants dancing	2.	201	,,
Three Peasants talking	2.	201	,,
Peasants playing Ninepins	2.	201	,,
The Triumph of Galatea	2.	201	,,
The Artist and Father in Picture Gallery	2.	228	Hon. E. Phipps
Two Peasants, one smoking	2.	228	,,
Three Monkeys playing Cards	2.	228	,,

	VOL. & PAGE	OWNER
Christ crowned with Thorns	2. 237	Lord Ward
Woman with Cat on her Lap	2. 237	Lord Ward
Backgammon Players	2. 240	Lord Colborne
Peasant making love to a Cook	2. 240	„
Old Woman smelling a Pink	2. 240	„
Temptation of St. Anthony	2. 247	Joseph Neeld
A Picture	2. 252	Henry Bevan
The Market at Ghent	2. 254	F. Heusch
The Seven Works of Charity	2. 260	J. Morrison
The Guard-room	2. 261	„
A Dutch Merrymaking	2. 261	„
A Witch with Cerberus, etc.	2. 266	Miss Rogers
A Cave, Peasants praying before Cross	2. 267	Miss Rogers
A Peasant's Wedding, 1655	2. 274	Duke of Wellington
The Father of Teniers	2. 279	Earl of Carlisle
Peasant and Gipsy Woman, etc.	2. 280	Earl of Carlisle
Cook-maid cleaning a Kettle	2. 281	Sir A. Rothschild
Peasants playing la Morra	2. 283	Sir A. Rothschild
An old Woman with a Child	2. 285	Duke of Bedford
A Rural Feast	2. 285	Duke of Bedford
Dentist pulling out a Tooth	2. 290	C. Bredel
Two Figures dancing to Bagpipe	2. 290	C. Bredel
A Rustic Feast	2. 295	Wynn Ellis
Landscape with Peasant and 3 Women	2. 308	Mr. Wombwell
Sportsman and wild Duck	2. 316	Earl Brownlow
A Village Festival	2. 329	Mr. Oppenheim
Three Peasants (chalk drawing)	2. 331	C. S. Bale
A rich Drawing	2. 334	Mr. Hall
Card Players	2. 335	George Field
Interior of a Barn	2. 336	James Gray
Smoking Boors	2. 336	James Gray
A Man chopping Straw	2. 343	Dulwich
A small Picture	2. 422	H. Labouchere
A large Landscape	2. 431	Windsor Castle
The Alchymist	2. 502	Orleans Gallery
The Lute Player	2. 502	„
An old Man	2. 502	„
The Smokers	2. 503	„
Boors playing Backgammon	2. 503	„
The Newspaper	2. 503	„
The Smoking Room	2. 503	„
The Ale-house	2. 503	„
The Shepherd	2. 503	„
A Village Festival	3. 28	Lord Ashburnham
Archduke Leopold in a Picture Gallery	3. 36	Petworth

E E

	VOL. & PAGE	OWNER
TENIERS, David, Junr.—*continued*		
Giving Bread to the Hungry	3. 43	Petworth
Several small Pictures	3. 134	J. Morrison
Temptation of St. Anthony	3. 163	Marquis of Lansdowne
Man and Woman in a Landscape	3. 163	,,
A Building and a Bridge	3. 163	,,
The Painter playing the Violoncello	3. 163	,,
Woman coming over a Hill	3. 165	,,
An Alchemist	3. 207	Lord Northwick
Abraham and Melchisedek	3. 207	,,
Woman taken in Adultery	3. 208	,,
A Guard-room	3. 215	Earl of Warwick
Rustics dancing	3. 222	Howard Galton
St. Paul and St. Anthony	3. 225	Mr. Martin
An Alchemist	3. 251	Blundell Weld
A Rural Fête	3. 261	Earl of Lonsdale
Rustics Eating and Drinking	3. 262	,,
Large rural Merrymaking	3. 262	,,
Two Peasants at Cards	3. 263	,,
A Woman on Horseback	3. 274	Edinburgh R.I.
Peasants playing at Skittles	3. 275	Edinburgh R.I.
Peasants before a House	3. 288	M'Lellan Gallery
The Visitation	3. 289	,,
The Plundering of a Village	3. 289	,,
A Cow being milked	3. 290	,,
Peasants at Cards, a Woman in a Cellar	3. 293	Sir A. Campbell
Seashore and 2 Fishermen and Fish	3. 293	Sir A. Campbell
Stable, Woman milking a Cow	3. 302	Duke of Hamilton
Woman leading drunken Husband	3. 302	,,
View of his Country House	3. 303	,
A Moonlight Landscape	3. 309	,,
Landscape, Painter and Wife in a Boat	3. 309	Earl of Hopetoun
Temptation of St. Anthony	3. 311	Earl of Hopetoun
Two Landscapes	3. 314	Captain Stirling
Rocky Landscape and Peasants	3. 339	Earl Fitzwilliam
Temptation of St. Anthony	3. 347	Duke of Devonshire
Gold Changers	3. 350	Duke of Devonshire
Interior of Cattle Stable	3. 395	Duke of Rutland
The Quack Doctor	3. 396	,,
Two Men playing Cards	3. 396	,,
Four small Pictures	3. 396	,,
Dutch Proverbs	3. 397	,,
Five Storks in Water	3. 399	,,
Temptation of St. Anthony	3. 400	,,
Shepherd with Dog and Flock	3. 406	Marquis of Exeter

	VOL. & PAGE	OWNER
The Four Elements	3. 430	A. Fountaine
Three Peasants in a Courtyard	3. 430	A. Fountaine
Village Festival	3. 439	Lord C. Townshend
Courtyard of House, merrymaking	3. 441	Mr. Tomline
Eight small Pictures	3. 459	Earl Spencer
Preparations for a Rural Festival	3. 465	Duke of Bedford
Three Card Players	3. 478	Marquis of Bute
Stragglers plundering Farm-house	3. 478	,,
Figures amusing Themselves	3. 478	,,
Backgammon Players	4. 62	National Gallery
Mass performed in a Cave	4. 69	Earl of Yarborough
Cooking and feasting in a Ruin	4. 69	Earl of Yarborough
Two Pictures	4. 88	Marquis of Hertford
Peasants at a Village Tavern	4. 107	J. Morrison
St. Peter delivered from Prison	4. 111	,,
The Seven Works of Mercy	4. 112	,,
An Alchemist in Laboratory	4. 131	Lord Overstone
Young Man seated on a Table	4. 132	,,
Country People before their Homes	4. 139	,,
A dancing Couple	4. 139	,,
Young Woman seated with Glass of Wine	4. 143	,,
Landscape, Hills and Buildings	4. 149	Earl of Caledon
Maid peeling Onions	4. 150	Earl of Caledon
Six Peasants smoking	4. 160	A. Robarts
Shepherd, Bagpipes, and Cattle	4. 180	Rev. Mr. Townshend
Landscape and Figures	4. 182	G. C. Legh
Four Peasants, Two playing Cards	4. 192	G. Field
Three Peasants and a Dog	4. 192	G. Field
Three Peasants by a Fire	4. 199	J. Tulloch
Peasant with Glass and Jug	4. 209	Mr. Henderson
Nine Men playing Ninepins	4. 236	Earl of Harrington
Old and young Man playing Cards	4. 236	,,
Organman with Dog	4. 238	,,
Shepherd and Flock	4. 268	Duke of Northumberland
Archduke Leopold in a Picture Gallery	4. 277	Sir C. Eardley
Teniers painting an old Woman	4. 278	Sir C. Eardley
Two Peasants, one holding a Jug	4. 297	J. Walter
The Water Doctor	4. 306	J. Morrison
Interior of Stable, Cow, etc.	4. 308	J. Morrison
Poetical Landscape	4. 318	Rev. Mr. Heath
Interior, Village Alehouse	4. 322	Lord Enfield
His own Portrait	4. 335	Duke of Bedford
Dancing in Front of a House	4. 339	Knole
A Guard-room	4. 339	Knole
Interior of an Oil Mill	4. 346	Earl Cowper

	VOL. & PAGE		OWNER
TENIERS, David, Junr.—*continued*			
Return from the Chase	4.	354	Lord Folkestone
Peasants Merrymaking	4.	354	Lord Folkestone
Castle in Stormy Weather	4.	365	Earl of Normanton
Castle, Figures angling	4.	365	Earl of Normanton
A Picture	4.	374	Sir W. Knighton
Old Peasant caressing a Girl	4.	386	Lord Heytesbury
Interior of a Guard-house	4.	387	,,
Houses and Peasants	4.	388	,,
Seven People at Table	4.	388	,,
St. Anthony in a Cavern	4.	388	,,
Towers and a Bridge, 1646	4.	388	,,
A Cow being milked	4.	388	,,
Peasants fighting after Cards	4.	391	J. Everett
Large Landscape	4.	393	Lord Arundel
Young Peasant smoking	4.	419	J. Chapman
Two Peasants at Cards	4.	425	Earl of Burlington
Spring	4.	427	Rev. T. Staniforth
Summer	4.	427	,,
Autumn	4.	427	,,
Winter	4.	427	,,
Young Man smoking, etc.	4.	438	Earl of Wemyss
A Corps de Garde	4.	442	Sir H. Campbell
Temptation of St. Anthony	4.	442	Sir H. Campbell
Landscape, Man, Woman, and Child	4.	452	W. Stirling
Peasants turned into Frogs	4.	458	M'Lellan Gallery
The Surgeon	4.	458	M'Lellan Gallery
Woman eating Olives, etc.	4.	475	W. W. Bardon
Brandy Seller and a Woman	4.	478	J. Anderson
Five Persons by Moonlight	4.	478	,,
An Après Diner	4.	478	,,
A stout Man at a Meal	4.	478	,,
Man and Woman, open air	4.	481	Matthew Anderson
Large Rocky Landscape	4.	481	,,
Old Man and 2 Women	4.	483	,,
Landscape with Harvest	4.	484	,,
Two Peasants playing Cards	4.	495	Earl of Harrington
Three Fishermen on Seashore	4.	504	Earl of Yarborough
Two Shepherds, Cows, and Sheep	4.	504	Earl of Yarborough
Maid Servant sweeping	4.	510	Duke of Newcastle
Village and Figures, with Van Uden	4.	510	,,
Cow, Stable, Woman pouring Milk	4.	511	,,
Shepherd playing the Flute	4.	511	,,
Temptation of St. Anthony	4.	521	Earl of Hardwicke
Old Woman, with Bundle of Onions	4.	522	,,
Card Players in Front of a House	4.	522	,,

	VOL. & PAGE	OWNER
TERBURG, Gerard		
Girl in a Yellow Jacket, etc.	1. 400	Sir R. Peel
Girl in a White Satin Dress, etc.	2. 6	Buckingham Palace
Girl at a Table, and Gentleman	2. 7	Buckingham Palace
"Consul Paternel"	2. 43	Bridgewater House
Gentleman, and Lady in Satin	2. 71	Duke of Sutherland
Girl in a Yellow Jacket, holding a Lute	2. 104	Lord Ashburton
Military Man with Champagne	2. 115	H. T. Hope
Officer writing	2. 115	”
Lady in Crimson Jacket, with a Lute	2. 116	”
Girl in Blue and White Satin	2. 129	Baron L. Rothschild
Girl drinking a Glass of Wine	2. 137	H. A. J. Munro
Girl in Morning Dress drinking	2. 137	H. A. J. Munro
Young Girl reading	2. 159	Marquis of Hertford
Girl writing in Profile	2. 183	T. Baring
Girl drinking	2. 183	T. Baring
A Male Portrait	3. 177	Mr. Vivian
Soldier with a Pipe	3. 207	Lord Northwick
A Male Portrait	3. 207	Lord Northwick
Two Ladies with Music	3. 398	Duke of Rutland
Gentleman in his Library	3. 476	Marquis of Bute
Lady in Dressing Room	3. 476	Marquis of Bute
Girl pouring out of a Jug	4. 297	J. Walter
A Family Picture	4. 361	Lord Folkestone
Portrait of Cinq Mars	4. 450	W. Stirling
THEED, W., R.A. (Sculptor)		
The Prodigal Son	4. 71	Earl of Yarborough
THEODORICH, of Prague		
A Picture	3. 314	Captain Stirling
THOMSON, Rev. John of Duddingstone		
Castle of Turnberry	3. 271	Edinburgh R.I.
Four Landscapes	3. 314	Duke of Buccleuch
Castle of Dunbar	4. 433	Gibson Craig
A small Landscape	4. 433	Gibson Craig
Dark Sea and Rocks	4. 434	Mr. Playfair
THORBURN, Robert, A.R.A.		
Lady Melbourne	4. 345	Earl Cowper
THORNHILL, Sir James		
Seven Cartoons (after Raphael)	1. 392	Royal Academy

		VOL. & PAGE	OWNER
THORWALDSEN (Sculptor)			
Anacreon and Cupid	(relief)	3. 223	Howard Galton
Bacchus and Cupid	„	3. 223	„
Bacchante and Satyr	„	3. 223	„
Pan and Olympus	„	3. 223	„
Venus and Cupid kissing	„	3. 223	„
Venus	„	3. 223	„
Muse crowned	„	3. 223	„
Venus with the Apple		3. 366	Duke of Devonshire
Cardinal Gonsalvi		3. 366	„
6 Reliefs		3. 366	„
Mercury		3. 411	Earl of Westmoreland
TIARINI, Alessandro			
Assumption of the Virgin		3. 192	Mr. Harford
TIEPOLO			
A Saint enthroned, etc.		2. 235	Lord Ward
The Finding of Moses		3. 271	Edinburgh R.I.
Landing of Pharaoh's Daughter		3. 271	Edinburgh R.I.
Christ sleeping in the Storm		4. 172	E. Cheney
19 Sketches for Ceilings		4. 173	E. Cheney
Sacrifice of Iphigenia		4. 412	Smith Barry
The Companion		4. 412	Smith Barry
2 Pictures		4. 504	Earl of Yarborough
TILBORG, Egidius Van			
Party of country People		2. 312	Earl of Listowel
Soldiers playing Cards		3. 226	Mr. Martin
TILBURGH, Gillis Van			
A Peasant's Wedding		2. 42	Bridgewater House
TIMOTEO, della Vite			
Christ on the Mount of Olives		4. 182	G. C. Legh
TINTORETTO			
St. George and the Dragon		1. 333	National Gallery
The Entombment		2. 33	Bridgewater House
A Venetian Nobleman		2. 33	„
Man with large open book		2. 33	„
A Venetian Senator		2. 33	„
A Pope surrounded by Cardinals		2. 61	Duke of Sutherland
Musician and a Man on Horseback		2. 61	Duke of Sutherland

	VOL. & PAGE		OWNER
A Male Portrait	2.	61	Duke of Sutherland
A Male Portrait	2.	61	Duke of Sutherland
Sketch for Miracle of the Slave	2.	77	S. Rogers
His own Portrait	2.	83	Lord Elcho
Descent from the Cross	2.	87	Earl of Yarborough
Nude Female on a Couch, etc.	2.	134	H. A. J. Munro
Descent from the Cross	2.	134	,,
Woman taken in Adultery	2.	134	,,
Vertumnus and Pomona	2.	135	,,
A Procurator of St. Mark	2.	197	R. S. Holford
A Male Portrait	2.	197	R. S. Holford
A Procurator of St. Mark	2.	241	Lord Colborne
A Venetian Gentleman	2.	265	Sir C. Eastlake
Doge Francesca Donati	2.	314	Earl Brownlow
The Crucifixion	2.	331	C. S. Bale
A Nobleman	2.	355	Hampton Court
A Male Portrait	2.	358	,,
Expulsion of Heresy	2.	358	,,
Esther before Ahasuerus	2.	359	,,
The Muses	2.	359	,,
Virgin and Child	2.	414	,,
Holy Family with Saint	2.	433	Windsor Castle
Esther and Ahasuerus	2.	478	Charles I
Washing Disciples' feet	2.	478	,,
Marriage at Cana	2.	478	,,
Birth of Christ	2.	478	,,
A Male Portrait	2.	478	,,
A Male Portrait	2.	478	,,
A Venetian Nobleman	2.	478	,,
A Doge	2.	479	,,
Descent from the Cross	2.	496	Orleans Gallery
The Last Judgment	2.	496	,,
Presentation in Temple	2.	496	,,
A Man with a Book	2.	496	,,
A Man	2.	496	,,
Duke of Ferrara	2.	496	,,
Aretino	2.	496	,,
Titian	2.	496	,,
A Convocation	2.	496	,,
Hercules nursed by Juno	2.	496	,,
The Unbelieving Thomas	2.	496	,,
Leda with the Swan	2.	496	,,
Juno and Infant Hercules	3.	20	Earl of Darnley
Male Portrait	3.	33	Petworth
Sketch for Paradise	3.	176	Mr. Vivian

	VOL. & PAGE	OWNER
Apollo and the Muses	4. 379	Kingston Lacy
A Procurator of St. Mark's	4. 397	Lord Methuen
St. Catherine	4. 410	Smith Barry
Venetian Admiral	4. 412	Smith Barry
Man in Black Dress	4. 422	Earl of Burlington
Conversion of St. Paul	4. 448	W. Stirling
Admiral Capello	4. 454	Earl of Dunmore
Finding of Moses	4. 457	Earl of Dunmore
An Ecce Homo	4. 469	Duke of Northumberland
St. Augustine writing	4. 481	Matthew Anderson
A Male Portrait	4. 501	Earl of Yarborough
Man with left Hand on a Book	4. 513	Duke of Portland

TITIAN

	VOL. & PAGE	OWNER
Bacchus and Ariadne	1. 316, 331	National Gallery
Adoration of the Shepherds	1. 332	„
Rape of Ganymede	1. 332	„
Man teaching a Boy to sing	1. 332	„
Venus and Adonis	1. 333	„
The Conara Family	1. 393	Duke of Northumberland
Landscape, Cattle, etc.	2. 2	Buckingham Palace
The Three Ages of Life	2. 30	Bridgewater House
La Venus à la Coquille	2. 31	„
Diana and Actæon	2. 31	„
Fable of Calisto	2. 32	„
Pope Clement VII	2. 32	„
Mercury teaching Cupid to read	2. 60	Duke of Sutherland
A Cardinal	2. 60	„
An old Man	2. 60	„
— Christ appearing to the Magdalen	2. 76	S. Rogers
La Gloria di Tiziano	2. 77	S. Rogers
St. Sebastian	2. 83	Lord Elcho
Titian's Daughter	2. 85	Earl de Grey
Diana and Actæon (sketch)	2. 87	Earl of Yarborough
The Magdalen	2. 87	Earl of Yarborough
Daughter of Herodias and Head	2. 100	Lord Ashburton
Venus holding Mirror to Cupid	2. 100	Lord Ashburton
Temptation of Christ	2. 113	H. T. Hope
Virgin nursing the Child	2. 133	H. A. J. Munro
Venus	2. 133	H. A. J. Munro
A Male Portrait	2. 151	Marquis of Lansdowne
Tarquin and Lucretia	2. 155	Marquis of Hertford
Woman taken in Adultery	2. 169	Marquis of Westminster
A Landscape	2. 170	Marquis of Westminster
A Riposo	2. 197	R. S. Holford

TITIAN—*continued*

	VOL. & PAGE		OWNER
A Duke of Milan	2.	197	R. S. Holford
The Virgin and Child	2.	235	Lord Ward
A Venus	2.	244	Joseph Neeld
His own Portrait	2.	261	J. Morrison
Callonna Lady (*copy*)	2.	266	Miss Rogers
Man with a Falcon	2.	278	Earl of Carlisle
Mary Magdalen	2.	313	Earl Brownlow
Christ bearing His Cross	2.	313	,,
Emperor Otho	2.	313	,,
Andrea Navagero	2.	313	,,
Diana discharging an Arrow at Actæon	2.	313	,,
Death of Peter Martyr (sketch)	2.	331	C. S. Bale
A Male Portrait	2.	357	Hampton Court
A Portrait	2.	358	,,
Venus and Adonis	2.	358	,,
David and Goliath	2.	360	,,
Lucretia	2.	365	,,
Marquis del Guesto and Page	2.	414	,,
Landscape, Virgin and Child	2.	419	H. Labouchere
Virgin and Child and Donor	2.	479	Charles I
Virgin and Child, Angel and St. Mark	2.	479	,,
Virgin and Child and Joseph	2.	479	,,
Virgin and Child with Ox and Ass	2.	479	,,
Virgin and Child, St. John and Elizabeth	2.	479	,,
St. Sebastian	2.	479	,,
St. Margaret and Dragon	2.	479	,,
The Entombment	2.	479	,,
The Entombment, Christ foreshortened	2.	479	,,
Christ at Emmaus	2.	479	,,
Magdalen with clasped Hands	2.	479	,,
Pope presents Admiral to St. Peter	2.	479	,,
Salome with Head of John the Baptist	2.	480	,,
Venus del Pardo	2.	480	,,
Naked Woman on Couch, and Dog	2.	480	,,
Tarquin and Lucretia	2.	480	,,
Lucretia standing with red Veil	2.	480	,,
Lucretia with Dagger	2.	480	,,
A Musical Party	2.	480	,,
Three Heads in one Picture	2.	480	,,
Three Heads, one a Woman fainting	2.	480	,,
Twelve Roman Emperors	2.	480	,,
Emperor Charles V	2.	481	,,
Consort of Charles V	2.	481	,,
Marquis Vaugona addressing Soldiers	2.	481	,,

	VOL. & PAGE	OWNER
Marquis Guasto and Soldiers	2. 481	Charles I
Pope Alexander VI and Caesar Borgia	2. 481	,,
The Doge Gritti	2. 481	,,
Marchioness of Mantua	2. 481	,,
Titian and a Senator	2. 481	,,
Titian and his Mistress	2. 481	,,
An Italian Woman, etc.	2. 481	,,
Male Portrait in black	2. 481	,,
A naked Woman dressing herself	2. 481	,,
Virgin and Child, John and Catherine	2. 484	,,
Mary with Tobit and the Angel	2. 484	,,
Virgin and Child, John and Catherine	2. 484	,,
An Ecce Homo	2. 484	,,
Mary Magdalen	2. 484	,,
Mary Magdalen	2. 484	,,
Diana and Actæon	2. 484	,,
Diana and Cupid	2. 484	,,
A Naked Venus, Woman looking into a Chest	2. 484	,,
A Naked Venus with a Warrior	2. 484	,,
Titian and Aretin	2. 484	,,
His own Portrait	2. 484	,,
Man with bald Head	2. 484	,,
Charles V in Armour	2. 484	,,
The Three Stages of Life	2. 496	Orleans Gallery
Venus rising from the Sea	2. 497	,,
Diana and Actæon	2. 497	,,
Diana and Calisto	2. 497	,,
Pope Clement VII	2. 497	,,
His own Portrait	2. 497	,,
Education of Cupid	2. 497	,,
Charles V on Horseback	2. 497	,,
Jupiter carrying off Europa	2. 497	,,
Titian's Mistress	2. 497	,,
Emperor Vitellius	2. 497	,,
Emperor Vespasian	2. 497	,,
Venus admiring herself	2. 497	,,
Venus and Adonis	2. 497	,,
Princess Eboli as Venus	2. 497	,,
A Concert	2. 497	,,
Christ tempted	2. 497	,,
Diana pursuing Actæon	2. 497	,,
Titian's Daughter and Casket	2. 497	,,
Mary Magdalen	2. 497	,,
Virgin and Child, John and Joseph	2. 497	,,

TITIAN—*continued*

	VOL. & PAGE		OWNER
Christ appearing to the Magdalen	2.	497	Orleans Gallery
Perseus and Andromeda	2.	497	,,
A Portrait called L'Esclavone	2.	497	,,
A Female	2.	497	,,
Count Castiglione	2.	497	,,
A young Man	2.	497	,,
A Head	2.	497	,,
Three Children, one in Cradle	3.	12	Earl Cowper
Europa and the Bull	3.	18	Earl of Darnley
Venus and Adonis	3.	18	,,
A Christ	3.	19	,,
A Male Portrait	3.	19	,,
Ariosto	3.	19	,,
Danäe and Golden Shower	3.	19	,,
Venus, Cupid holding a Mirror	3.	19	,,
Titian and Francesco del Masaicio	3.	19	,,
A Woman in a Brown Dress	3.	33	Petworth
A Man with a Pen	3.	34	,,
Cardinal de Medici	3.	42	,,
St. Sebastian	3.	122	Duke of Marlborough
A Male Head	3.	123	,,
Pope Gregory and a Female Saint	3.	125	,,
Mars and Venus	3.	132	,,
Cupid and Psyche	3.	132	,,
Apollo and Daphne	3.	132	,,
Pluto and Proserpine	3.	132	,,
Hercules and Dejanira	3.	132	,,
Vulcan and Ceres	3.	132	,,
Bacchus and Ariadne	3.	132	,,
Jupiter and Juno	3.	132	,,
Neptune and Amphitrite	3.	132	,,
A Knight, whole length	3.	140	Earl of Radnor
Cæsar Borgia	3.	140	,,
A Male Portrait, with piece of Sculpture	3.	140	,,
Violante, Daughter of Palma Vecchio	3.	140	,,
Virgin and Child and St. John	3.	159	Marquis of Lansdowne
Infant Christ sleeping on the Cross	3.	171	Lord Arundel
John the Baptist in Wilderness	3.	172	Colt Hoare
A Count of Nassau	3.	177	Mr. Vivian
Venus and Adonis	3.	182	J. P. Miles
The Three Graces	3.	186	J. P. Miles
Pope Paul III	3.	203	Lord Northwick
A Woman	3.	203	Lord Northwick
Macchiavelli	3.	214	Earl of Warwick

	VOL. & PAGE	OWNER
Margaret of Parma	3. 215	Earl of Warwick
A Riposo (copy)	3. 238	Liverpool R.I.
Coronation of the Virgin	3. 238	Liverpool R.I.
A Male Portrait	3. 264	Earl of Lonsdale
A Spanish General	3. 265	Earl of Lonsdale
Landscape, noon	3. 269	Edinburgh R.I.
A Portrait	3. 269	„
The Virgin and Child	3. 272	„
St. Jerome in a Landscape	3. 292	Sir A. Campbell
Philip II, with Figure of Fame	3. 299	Duke of Hamilton
Three Sportsmen with Dogs	3. 310	Earl of Hopetoun
Duke of Palma as a Child	3. 313	Duke of Buccleuch
Duke of Alba in Armour	3. 313	Duke of Buccleuch
A Picture	3. 315	Duke of Cleveland
Butcher's Dog and 3 Cats	3. 322	Earl of Carlisle
Martin Bucer	3. 334	Meynall Ingram
A Holy Family	3. 339	Earl Fitzwilliam
Magdalen	3. 341	Earl Fitzwilliam
Philip II of Spain	3. 346	Duke of Devonshire
Rich poetical Landscape	3. 347	„
St. Jerome in a Landscape	3. 350	„
A Family Picture	3. 351	„
A Female Portrait	3. 420	Earl of Leicester
Emperor Charles V	3. 440	Mr. Tomline
Francis I	3. 441	„
Julius Cæsar	3. 443	„
Venus, called Princess of Eboli	3. 446	Fitzwilliam Museum
Titian with his Mistress	3. 456	Earl Spencer
A young Woman	3. 456	Earl Spencer
Christ appearing to the Magdalen	4. 59	National Gallery
The Tribute Money	4. 59	National Gallery
St. Sebastian	4. 63	Lord Elcho
Venus and Adonis	4. 63	Lord Elcho
The Repentant Magdalen	4. 65	Earl of Yarborough
Christ at Emmaus	4. 66	„
Actæon and Diana (sketch)	4. 66	„
Virgin and Child and Saints	4. 69	„
Charles V in Armour	4. 95	T. Baring
A Female (Catherine Cornaro)	4. 101	R. S. Holford
The Painter and his Mistress	4. 110	J. Morrison
Landscape, chain of Alps at Friuli	4. 117	C. S. Bale
The Last Supper (sketch)	4. 142	Lord Overstone
A Repose in Egypt	4. 171	E. Cheney
An aged Doge in his Robes	4. 172	„
A Venetian General in Armour	4. 172	„

	VOL. & PAGE	OWNER
TITIAN—*continued*		
Christ before Pilate	4. 173	E. Cheney
Philip II (young)	4. 181	Earl Stanhope
Peter drawing Net (School)	4. 192	A. J. B. Hope
Holy Family (School)	4. 240	R. P. Nichols
Jacob and Rachel	4. 273	Earl of Jersey
David anointed by Samuel	4. 273	Earl of Jersey
The Magdalen	4. 292	J. Sanders
Virgin with the Child in her Lap	4. 323	Lord Enfield
His own Portrait	4. 335	Duke of Bedford
Vesalius	4. 335	Duke of Bedford
St. Margaret (*copy*)	4. 350	Vernon Harcourt
Cæsar Borgia	4. 360	Lord Folkestone
A General	4. 360	„
A Sculptor	4. 361	„
Venus and Adonis	4. 366	Earl of Normanton
A Picture	4. 374	Sir W. Knighton
Marchese di Savorgnano	4. 378	Kingston Lacy
Venus with Jewelry	4. 378	Kingston Lacy
Peter Martyr (*copy*)	4. 409	Smith Barry
A large Dog	4. 411	Smith Barry
Virgin as Mater Dolorosa	4. 420	J. Fletcher
Duke of Parma as a Child	4. 436	Duke of Buccleuch
A female Portrait	4. 447	Lord Kinnaird
Adoration of the Shepherds	4. 455	Earl of Dunmore
Male Portrait in crimson	4. 456	Earl of Dunmore
Danae and golden Shower	4. 460	M'Lellan Gallery
Venus and Adonis	4. 468	Duke of Northumberland
An Admiral in Armour	4. 468	„
Member of Barbarego family	4. 468	„
Pope Paul III	4. 468	„
Virgin holding Child in lap	4. 484	G. Burdon
Madonna with the Rabbit (*copy*)	4. 493	Lord Feversham
Holy Family in Landscape	4. 493	„
Venus and Adonis kissing	4. 493	„
Cupid playing on the Lute	4. 502	Earl of Yarborough
Man in a Blue Dress	4. 509	Duke of Newcastle
Man leaning on left Hand	4. 515	Duke of Portland
TITIANO, Orazio		
Virgin adoring the Child	4. 468	Duke of Northumberland
TOBAR		
Portrait of Murillo	4. 450	W. Stirling
St. Joseph with Child	4. 461	M'Lellan Gallery

	VOL. & PAGE		OWNER
TOPHAM, F. W.			
A Mother and Child	4.	414	Mr. Cooke
A Mother stooping	4.	414	,,
Gipsy telling a Girl's Fortune	4.	414	,,
TORREGIANO, Pietro (Sculptor)			
Henry VII, 1509	4.	269	Duke of Northumberland
TREVISO, Girolamo da			
Virgin and Child enthroned	3.	202	Lord Northwick
TURA, Cosimo (Il Cosmè)			
St. Jerome	2.	234	Lord Ward
Virgin and Child on Throne	4.	116	Sir C. Eastlake
TURCHI, Alessandro (L'Orbetto)			
Christ and the Woman of Samaria	2.	61	Duke of Sutherland
Cupid visited by Psyche	2.	90	Devonshire House
Virgin and Child, Donor and Saint	2.	347	Dulwich Gallery
Joseph and Potiphar's Wife	2.	498	Orleans Gallery
Adam visited by Angels	2.	498	Orleans Gallery
A Pietà painted on stone	4.	385	H. D. Seymour
Psyche and sleeping Cupid	4.	453	Earl of Dunmore
TURNER, J. M. W., R.A.			
Lake Avernus with Sibyl	1.	385	Marlborough House
View of Venice	1.	385	,,
View of Venice	1.	385	,,
Prince of Orange at Torbay	1.	385	,,
A Sea Storm	2.	53	Bridgewater House
Wreck of the Minotaur	2.	87	Earl of Yarborough
Vintage of Mâçon	2.	87	Earl of Yarborough
Venus and Adonis	2.	140	H. A. J. Munro
Large Sea-piece	2.	141	,,
Venice	2.	141	,,
Several Pictures	2.	141	,,
Three large Drawings, one with Stags in foreground	2.	226	R. Ford
Plagues of Egypt	2.	257	George Young
Drawing with Swan's Nest (drawing)	2.	263	J. Morrison
A Storm	2.	268	Miss Rogers
Temple of Jupiter	2.	298	Wynn Ellis
Whalley Bridge	2.	298	Wynn Ellis
Vessels in Distress off Yarmouth	2.	300	J. Sheepshanks
Cowes with Royal Yacht Squadron	2.	301	J. Sheepshanks

	VOL. & PAGE		OWNER
TURNER, J. M. W., R.A.—*continued*			
Line Fishing off Hastings	2.	305	J. Sheepshanks
Venice	2.	305	,,
St. Michael's Mount	2.	305	,,
Waterfall with Rainbow (drawing)	2.	331	C. S. Bale
Port Ruysdael	2.	350	E. Bicknell
View in Venice	2.	350	,,
Palestrina	2.	350	,,
View of Venice	2.	351	,,
Lake of Lucerne (drawing)	2.	352	,,
The Righi, evening (drawing)	2.	352	,,
Ivy Bridge	2.	353	,,
Several Drawings	2.	416	Rev. Edward Coleridge
Echo and Narcissus	3.	37	Petworth
Landscape, Cows and Water	3.	37	,,
Agitated Sea with Ships	3.	37	,,
Tabley House, Cheshire	3.	37	,,
Thames at Windsor	3.	38	,,
Thames at Eton	3.	38	,,
Jessica, from the Merchant of Venice	3.	38	,,
Thames at Weybridge	3.	39	,,
Thames at Windsor	3.	39	,,
View of Venice	3.	241	John Naylor
A Harbour (Rotterdam)	3.	242	John Naylor
Vintage of Mâcon, 1803	4.	70	Earl of Yarborough
Wreck of the Minotaur	4.	70	Earl of Yarborough
Mountains round Lake, etc.	4.	113	J. Morrison
A large Lake Picture	4.	184	W. Marshall
Landscape, Trees, Ruins, etc.	4.	301	J. Morrison
Landscape, Shepherd and Shepherdess	4.	302	J. Morrison
Drawings	4.	374	Sir W. Knighton
Windsor Castle	4.	414	Mr. Cooke
Trees on a Piece of Water, drawing	4.	416	S. Ashton
Fishmarket on the Shore, drawing	4.	419	J. Chapman
Rape of Proserpine, drawing	4.	419	J. Chapman
TYSSENS, Peter			
Bacchus and Children, painted with			
Artois and Snyders	4.	206	Mr. Henderson

	VOL. & PAGE	OWNER
VAGA, Perino del		
Child on the Ground adored by the Virgin	2. 233	Lord Ward
Parnassus	2. 481	Charles I
Venus, Juno, and Minerva	2. 498	Orleans Gallery
A Knight	3. 304	Duke of Hamilton
Holy Family, Christ and St. John kissing	3. 325	Earl of Carlisle
Cardinal Pole	3. 455	Earl Spencer
VALENTIN, Moyse		
A Concert	2. 498	Orleans Gallery
Four Stages of Life	2. 498	,,
The Five Senses	2. 498	,,
Jacob and Joseph's Coat	3. 225	Mr. Martin
Soldiers in violent Quarrel	3. 264	Earl of Lonsdale
The Tribute Money	3. 264	Earl of Lonsdale
Incredulity of St. Thomas	3. 290	M'Lellan Gallery
The Prodigal Son	3. 294	Sir A. Campbell
VAN AELST, Evert, Peter and William		
Man with a Watch (Peter)	2. 413	Hampton Court
Two dead Fowls (William)	3. 291	M'Lellan Gallery
Dead Game (William)	3. 336	Charles Wynn
Dead Game (Evert)	3. 337	Charles Wynn
A Partridge, 1674 (William)	4. 206	Mr. Henderson
Peaches, Grapes, Nuts, etc. (William)	4. 206	Mr. Henderson
A Breakfast (Evert)	4. 269	Duke of Northumberland
Still Life (William)	4. 458	M'Lellan Gallery
VAN BASSAN		
State Dinner with Charles I	2. 361	Hampton Court
State Dinner with King of Bohemia	2. 361	Hampton Court
VAN BERGEN, Dirk		
A Cattle Piece	3. 208	Lord Northwick
Cattle in a Landscape	4. 325	Lord Enfield
VAN BOOM, A.		
Landscape with Ruins	3. 337	Charles Wynn

	VOL. & PAGE		OWNER
VAN CEULEN, Janson			
A Male Portrait	3.	171	Earl of Suffolk
De Witt and his Wife	3.	475	Marquis of Bute
An old Man	4.	440	Earl of Wemyss
A young Girl	4.	441	Earl of Wemyss
VAN CLEEF, Joas			
Himself and his Wife	2.	433	Windsor Castle
Himself and his Wife	2.	468	Charles I
A Male Portrait	3.	32	Petworth
A Male Portrait with Letter	3.	41	Petworth
His own Portrait	3.	456	Earl Spencer
A Man	3.	475	Marquis of Bute
VAN DE CAPELLA, Jan			
A Picture	2.	52	Bridgewater House
A quiet Sea, Sunshine	2.	140	H. A. J. Munro
Agitated Sea and Vessels	2.	152	Marquis of Lansdowne
Quiet Sea with Boats	2.	188	T. Baring
A Sea Piece	2.	248	Joseph Neeld
A Sea Piece, Pier, etc.	2.	283	Duke of Bedford
A Sea Piece	2.	285	Duke of Bedford
A quiet Sea and Vessels	2.	297	Wynn Ellis
Evening Sun on a quiet Sea	2.	297	Wynn Ellis
Agitated Sea, Boat lowering Sail	3.	164	Marquis of Lansdowne
A Sea Piece	3.	209	Lord Northwick
Quiet Sea, Coast in foreground	4.	137	Lord Overstone
A calm Sea, Boats and Man-of-War	4.	157	St. John Mildmay
Quiet Water, Ships foreshortened	4.	162	A. Robarts
A Winter Landscape, Canal, 1653	4.	207	Mr. Henderson
Calm Sea with Boats	4.	212	Mr. Henderson
A Stream with both Banks seen	4.	368	Earl of Normanton
A calm Sea, Boats with Men	4.	424	Earl of Burlington
VAN DELEN, Dirk			
Interior of a Church	2.	123	H. T. Hope
Rubens' House at Antwerp	2.	228	Hon. E. Phipps
A Party at a Meal	3.	221	Howard Galton
Interior of Jesuit Church	3.	224	Howard Galton
An Architectural Piece	3.	269	Edinburgh R.I.
Interior of a Church	3.	336	Charles Wynn
Architectural piece, a Man kneeling	3.	351	Duke of Devonshire
A Church, with Van Herp	4.	149	Earl of Caledon
Interior of a Church	4.	458	M'Lellan Gallery
Architectural, Figures by Teniers	4.	484	Matthew Anderson

	VOL. & PAGE		OWNER
VAN DER DOES, Simon			
A Cattle Piece	2.	312	Earl of Listowel
Joachim rejected by Priests	3.	205	Lord Northwick
Sheep and Goats	3.	222	Howard Galton
VAN DER GOES, Hugo			
Virgin and Child	3.	5	W. Fuller Maitland
Virgin and Child, Angel and Fruit	3.	253	Blundell Weld
A Picture	3.	314	Captain Stirling
Virgin standing and Child, etc.	3.	386	Earl of Shrewsbury
Virgin and Child under Canopy	4.	315	Rev. Mr. Heath
VAN DER HELST, Bartholomew			
Eight Persons in a Landscape	2.	115	H. T. Hope
A Male Portrait	2.	227	Hon. E. Phipps
A Dutch Family	4.	70	Earl of Yarborough
Girl in blue Frock	4.	391	Joseph Everett
VAN DER HEYDEN, Jan			
Street in Cologne, fig. by V. de Velde	1.	413	Sir R. Peel
House by a Canal, fig. by V. de Velde	2.	22	Buckingham Palace
Dutch Town and Figures, fig. by V. de Velde	2.	23	Buckingham Palace
Dutch Town, Canal, and Bridge, fig. by V. de Velde	2.	52	Bridgewater House
A Market Place, fig. by V. de Velde	2.	111	Lord Ashburton
Street with Church, fig. by V. de Velde	2.	123	H. T. Hope
Village Church on Hill, fig. by V. de Velde	2.	123	H. T. Hope
Buildings	2.	131	Baron L. Rothschild
Buildings, fig. by V. de Velde	2.	160	Marquis of Hertford
Buildings, fig. by V. de Velde	2.	160	Marquis of Hertford
Gothic Church, fig. by V. de Velde	2.	188	T. Baring
Château and Brick Wall, fig. by V. de Velde	2.	256	Mr. Heusch
Broad Street in Cologne, fig. by E. van der Neer	2.	256	Mr. Heusch
Buildings, with Landscape	2.	262	J. Morrison
View of Veght near Maassen	2.	274	Duke of Wellington
Buildings, fig. by V. de Velde	2.	298	Wynn Ellis
Street with Canal	3.	163	Marquis of Lansdowne
A Town Gate, fig. by V. de Velde	3.	163	Marquis of Lansdowne
An Architectural Piece, fig. by V. de Velde	3.	170	Earl of Suffolk
An Architectural Piece	3.	209	Lord Northwick
A Wood with Stags	3.	275	Edinburgh R.I.
A large Church	3.	395	Duke of Rutland
Houses on Canal	3.	396	Duke of Rutland

	VOL. & PAGE		OWNER
VAN DER HEYDEN, Jan—*continued*			
Market Place with Church, fig. by V. de Velde	3.	482	Marquis of Bute
Landscape with Fortifications, fig. by V. de Velde	3.	482	Marquis of Bute
Village on rising Ground with V. de Velde	4.	110	J. Morrison
Town, Gate in centre, fig. by E. van der Neer	4.	149	Earl of Caledon
Town, Canal in foreground with V. de Velde	4.	160	A. Robarts
Cross in front of a Wall with V. de Velde	4.	196	G. Field
Summer-house and a Wall	4.	210	Mr. Henderson
Town in middle distance with V. de Velde	4.	297	J. Walter
Buildings and blue Hills	4.	297	J. Walter
A signed Picture	4.	342	Humphrey Mildmay
House among Trees, Shepherd, with V. de Velde	4.	385	H. D. Seymour
Canal, Woman washing, and White Cow, two Men Walking	4.	439	Earl of Wemyss
VAN DER HOECK, Robert			
Combat of Horsemen	3.	336	Charles Wynn
VAN DER HOOG			
Interior of a Church, 1651	2.	267	Miss Rogers
VAN DER MEER, Jan			
Sheep in a Landscape	2.	309	Mr. Wombwell
Evening Landscape	2.	501	Orleans Gallery
A Ram, Sheep, and Cow	4.	211	Mr. Henderson
Shepherdess with Sheep and Child	4.	268	Duke of Northumberland
VAN DER MEER, de Delf			
An old Woman	4.	482	Matthew Anderson
VAN DER MEERE, Gerhart			
Virgin and Child	4.	226	Prince Consort
The Virgin enthroned	4.	315	Rev. Mr. Heath
Virgin looking down at Child	4.	315	Rev. Mr. Heath
VAN DER MEULEN, Anton Franz			
View of Versailles, with Louis XIV	2.	19	Buckingham Palace
Horsemen fighting, with Louis XIV	2.	19	„
A Camp, Siege in Background	2.	19	„
Louis XIV and Suite	2.	19	„
Building of Versailles	2.	19	„
A Picture	2.	95	Devonshire House
Louis XIV and a large Retinue	2.	225	R. Ford

	VOL. & PAGE		OWNER
Travellers attacked by Robbers	3.	39	Petworth
Four Pictures, one with Louis XIV	3.	40	,,
Scene from Life of Louis XIV	3.	42	,,
Scene from Life of Louis XIV	3.	42	,,
Battle Piece	3.	226	Mr. Martin
Battle Piece	3.	226	Mr. Martin
Louis XIV in State Carriage	3.	272	Edinburgh R.I.
A Picture	3.	476	Marquis of Bute
A Siege	4.	515	Duke of Portland

VAN DER NEER, Adrian

Landscape, Moonlight	3.	398	Duke of Rutland

VAN DER NEER, Arnold

A Dutch Canal	2.	228	Hon. E. Phipps

VAN DER NEER, Artus

Landscape, Evening Sun	1.	357	National Gallery
An Evening Landscape	2.	21	Buckingham Palace
A Winter Landscape	2.	139	H. A. J. Munro
A Picture	2.	160	Marquis of Hertford
Landscape by Moonlight	2.	240	Lord Colborne
Evening Landscape with Water	2.	248	Joseph Neeld
A Winter Piece	2.	252	Henry Bevan
A Moonlight	2.	268	Miss Rogers
A Fire Effect	2.	268	Miss Rogers
Frozen Piece of Water	2.	291	C. Bredel
A Winter Landscape	2.	336	James Gray
A small Sunset	3.	127	Duke of Marlborough
Large Landscape	3.	127	Duke of Marlborough
A Moonlight Piece	3.	209	Lord Northwick
Landscape by Daylight	3.	209	Lord Northwick
Moonlight, 2 Men	3.	248	Blundell Weld
A Winter Landscape	3.	290	M'Lellan Gallery
Large Moonlight Piece	3.	298	Duke of Hamilton
Landscape by Moonlight	3.	388	Earl of Shrewsbury
Landscape by Moonlight	3.	441	Mr. Tomline
Winter Landscape, Afternoon	3.	481	Marquis of Bute
Winter Landscape, smaller	3.	481	Marquis of Bute
Landscape by Moonlight	4.	62	National Gallery
Sunset on Dutch Canal	4.	90	Marquis of Hertford
Dutch Village, Moonlight	4.	134	Lord Overstone
Village on Canal, Moonlight	4.	134	,,
Moonlight on frozen Canal	4.	138	,,
Wide Canal frozen over, 1643	4.	139	,,

	VOL. & PAGE	OWNER
VAN DER NEER, Artus—*continued*		
Canal with Houses	4. 149	Earl of Caledon
Canal with Houses, Sportsman	4. 166	Earl of Shaftesbury
Small Moonlight Landscape	4. 192	H. T. Hope
Moonlight Scene on Canal	4. 195	G. Field
Sunset on a Canal	4. 195	,,
Broad frozen Canal, Sledge and Skater	4. 195	,,
Sea Coast and a Windmill	4. 208	Mr. Henderson
Evening Sun over a Canal	4. 210	Mr. Henderson
Wide Canal, frozen, Villages, etc.	4. 283	Sir C. Eardley
Dutch Town with Gables, etc.	4. 291	J. Sanders
Frozen Canal, Figures, etc.	4. 307	J. Morrison
Broad Canal, Moonlight	4. 320	Lord Enfield
A Picture	4. 350	Vernon Harcourt
Rhine View in Guelders	4. 364	Earl of Normanton
A Moonlight Landscape	4. 367	,,
Moon behind Clouds, Water	4. 367	,,
Moonlight	4. 439	Earl of Wemyss
Moon over Canal	4. 454	Earl of Dunmore
A Fire by Moonlight	4. 476	W. W. Bardon
Moon behind Clouds, on Canal	4. 483	Matthew Anderson
Night Scene	4. 491	Mr. Fenderson
Day Scene	4. 491	Mr. Fenderson
Moonlight	4. 491	Archdeacon of Durham
VAN DER NEER, Eglon		
Gentleman and Lady with Music	2. 9	Buckingham Palace
Death of Cleopatra	2. 9	Buckingham Palace
Boy in blue Silk with a Drum	2. 44	Bridgewater House
Gentleman and Lady at Table, etc.	2. 117	H. T. Hope
Female washing her Hands	2. 253	F. Heusch
Girl with a Book seated before a Mirror	2. 292	C. Bredel
Gentleman and Lady at the Piano	2. 433	Windsor Castle
Page presenting golden Vessel to a Lady	3. 448	Fitzwilliam Museum
VAN DER POEL, Egbert		
Town of Breda, 1654	4. 207	Mr. Henderson
A Fire	4. 289	Joseph Sanders
A Fire	4. 459	M'Lellan Gallery
VAN DER SPELT		
A Wreath of Flowers	2. 71	Duke of Sutherland
VAN DER ULFFT, Jacob		
Roman Ruins	2. 123	H. T. Hope
Landscape, Men before a Wall	4. 146	Lord Overstone

	VOL. & PAGE		OWNER
VAN DER WERF, Adrian			
Lot and his Daughters	2.	9	Buckingham Palace
A Boy with a Guinea-Pig	2.	9	Buckingham Palace
St. Margaret and Dragon	2.	105	Lord Ashburton
A penitent Magdalen	2.	119	H. T. Hope
Incredulity of St. Thomas	2.	120	,,
Lot and his Daughters	2.	120	,,
Repose in Egypt	2.	168	Marquis of Westminster
One of Diana'a Nymphs	2.	308	Mr. Wombwell
The Fishmonger	2.	503	Orleans Gallery
The Egg Woman	2.	503	,,
The Judgment of Paris	2.	503	,,
Two Nymphs dancing to the flute of a Satyr	3.	263	Earl of Lonsdale
Christ and the Woman of Samaria	3.	264	Earl of Lonsdale
A Burgomaster and his Wife	3.	270	Edinburgh R.I.
Dalilah cutting off Samson's Hair	3.	288	M'Lellan Gallery
Adam and Eve expelled from Paradise	3.	396	Duke of Rutland
Venus and Cupid	4.	69	Earl of Yarborough
Lot and his Daughters	4.	438	Earl of Wemyss
VAN DER WEYDEN, Goswin			
Coronation of the Virgin	4.	226	Prince Consort
VAN DER WEYDEN, Roger			
Descent from the Cross	2.	55	Bridgewater House
Christ with a Globe	2.	161	Marquis of Westminster
An Ecce Homo	2.	459	Mr. Green
Adoration of the Kings	2.	459	Mr. Green
Descent from the Cross	3.	235	Liverpool R.I.
Virgin with the Child on her Lap	3.	251	Blundell Weld
Deposition from the Cross	4.	226	Prince Consort
Ecce Homo	4.	227	,,
Mater Dolorosa	4.	227	,,
The Entombment	4.	278	Sir C. Eardley
Virgin and Child (School of)	4.	286	Rev. Mr. Russell
Descent from the Cross, etc. (School of)	4.	314	Rev. Mr. Heath
VAN DE VELDE, Adrian			
Shepherd conversing with a Milkmaid	1.	406	Sir R. Peel
Herdsman, a Woman, and Cattle	1.	406	Sir R. Peel
Two Cows with a Goat	2.	15	Buckingham Palace
Seashore at Scheveningen	2.	15	,,
Small Herd of Cows, Sheep and Goats	2.	15	,,
Two Cows, Sheep and Goat	2.	16	,,
Huntsmen on Horseback	2.	16	,,

VAN DE VELDE, Adrian—*continued*

	VOL. & PAGE		OWNER
Woman and a Cow in a Landscape	2.	16	Buckingham Palace
Shepherd and Flock under Trees	2.	16	,,
Red Cow being milked	2.	46	Bridgewater House
Cattle Piece	2.	85	Earl de Grey
Cattle Piece	2.	85	Earl de Grey
Haymaking, 4 Men and 2 Women	2.	108	Lord Ashburton
Three Cows, Flock of Sheep, etc.	2.	108	Lord Ashburton
Four Cows and Sheep in Water	2.	120	H. T. Hope
Cows and Horses in Meadow	2.	120	H. T. Hope
Reddish Cow in Water, a Man and a Woman	2.	138	H. A. J. Munro
Cowherd washing Feet, Cow drinking	2.	138	H. A. J. Munro
La Fuite de Jacob, 1663	2.	159	Marquis of Hertford
Farm—Cows, Pigs, etc.	2.	168	Marquis of Westminster
Le Rendezvous de Chasse	2.	185	T. Baring
Flock of Animals, Hills behind	2.	201	R. S. Holford
A large Drawing	2.	204	,,
Smaller Drawing	2.	204	,,
Cow and Sheep by still Water	2.	243	H. D. Seymour
A Picture	2.	252	Henry Bevan
Reddish Cow drinking, 1670	2.	254	Mr. Heusch
Cattle, Man playing a Flute, 1671	2.	254	Mr. Heusch
Boat on a Canal, etc.	2.	274	Duke of Wellington
Three Cows and Grey Horse in a Meadow	2.	290	C. Bredel
Landscape with Horses, etc.	2.	433	Windsor Castle
His own Portrait with a Palette	3.	208	Lord Northwick
Landscape, Shepherds and Cows	3.	274	Edinburgh R.I.
Landscape, Woman on Donkey	3.	275	Edinburgh R.I.
Landscape, Cow being milked, 1670	3.	286	M'Lellan Collection
Landscape, Shepherdess and old Shepherd	3.	479	Marquis of Bute
Seven Cows at a Ford, etc.	4.	136	Lord Overstone
Red Cow lying behind a Brown one	4.	157	St. John Mildmay
Stately Man in Yellow, 1658	4.	162	A. Robarts
Landscape with Huntsmen	4.	180	Rev. Mr. Townshend
Cow, a Ram and Sheep, 1668	4.	194	G. Field
Cattle in a Meadow	4.	209	Mr. Henderson
A Dutch Canal with a Brown Horse, etc.	4.	212	Mr. Henderson
A Large Picture	4.	240	R. P. Nichols
Brown Cow drinking, a Woman washing her Feet	4.	292	J. Sanders
Two Sheep by the Stem of a Tree	4.	296	J. Walter
Ruins, a Woman on a Grey Horse	4.	308	J. Morrison
Cattle in a Landscape	4.	363	General Buckley

	VOL. & PAGE	OWNER
Landscape, Brown Cow and Sheep	4. 384	H. Danby Seymour
Coast at Scheveningen, etc.	4. 418	J. Chapman

VAN DE VELDE, Jesaias

A Landscape	2. 503	Orleans Gallery
A Landscape and Figures	2. 503	,,
The Campo Vaccino	2. 503	,,

VAN DE VELDE, William

Sea Piece	1. 358	National Gallery
Sea Piece	1. 358	National Gallery
Coasting Vessel, etc., 1657	1. 411	Sir R. Peel
Sea in a Calm	1. 412	,,
Coast Scene, four Figures bathing, 1661	1. 412	,,
Coast of Scheveningen with A. v. de Velde	1. 412	,,
A Dutch Coast, fishing Boat	1. 412	,,
View of the Texel in Rain and Wind	1. 412	,,
Violently agitated Sea	1. 412	,,
Coast Scene, Sea running high	1. 412	,,
Sea Coast in calm weather	2. 22	Buckingham Palace
Shore of a River, Yachts, etc.	2. 22	,,
An agitated Sea, Men-of-War	2. 22	,,
Fishermen putting off, 1671	2. 22	,,
Entrance to the Texel	2. 50	Bridgewater House
Man-of-War in rough Sea	2. 50	,,
Dutch Coast, Sea high, 1656	2. 51	,,
Mouth of the Brille	2. 51	,,
Coast, calm Sea	2. 51	,,
Naval Battle in 1666	2. 51	,,
Naval Battle (larger)	2. 51	,,
Calm Sea and Vessels	2. 95	Devonshire House
La petite Flotte	2. 111	Lord Ashburton
Agitated Sea, Boat with Red Sail	2. 122	H. T. Hope
Agitated Sea, Mainsail being lowered	2. 123	H. T. Hope
Quiet Sea with Vessels	2. 131	Baron L. Rothschild
Smooth Sea, Vessel in foreground	2. 139	H. A. J. Munro
Two Vessels in fresh Breeze	2. 139	,,
An agitated Sea	2. 139	,,
A Storm	2. 139	,,
Quiet Sea, large Vessels	2. 160	Marquis of Hertford
A quiet Sea (small)	2. 160	Marquis of Hertford
A Calm, Pier and Vessels	2. 187	T. Baring
Quiet Sea, Vessel firing Cannon	2. 188	T. Baring
Quiet Sea, two Boats in foreground	2. 203	R. S. Holford
A Calm at Sea	2. 252	Henry Bevan
Quiet Sea, three Vessels in foreground	2. 256	Mr. Heusch
Calm Sea, numerous Vessels	2. 262	J. Morrison

	VOL. & PAGE	OWNER
VAN DE VELDE, William—*continued*		
Sea Piece, numerous Vessels	2. 281	Sir A. Rothschild
Quiet Sea, 2 Men on a Pier	2. 291	C. Bredel
A quiet Sea	2. 297	Wynn Ellis
A quiet Sea	2. 297	Wynn Ellis
Quiet Sea with Vessels	2. 312	Earl of Listowel
A Sea Fight	2. 312	Earl of Listowel
A Naval Battle	2. 316	Earl Brownlow
Small Sea Piece	2. 335	Sir Henry Bunbury
A smooth Sea	2. 336	George Field
A fresh Breeze	2. 336	James Gray
Vessels in a River	2. 344	Dulwich Gallery
View of the Texel	2. 345	Dulwich Gallery
A Sea Piece	2. 364	Hampton Court
Several Pictures	2. 414	Hampton Court
A Harbour, with A. van de Velde	2. 422	H. Labouchere
View of the Zuyder Zee	2. 453	Richard Forster
Agitated Sea, large Ship	2. 453	Richard Forster
Agitated Sea, a Yacht	3. 142	Earl of Radnor
Coast in brisk Gale	3. 142	Earl of Radnor
Small, rough Sea	3. 154	Earl of Pembroke
Small, calm Sea	3. 154	Earl of Pembroke
A quiet Sea	3. 164	Marquis of Lansdowne
A calm Sea, Man-of-War, etc.	3. 165	Marquis of Lansdowne
A quiet Sea	3. 170	Earl of Suffolk
Calm Sea, Boats in foreground	3. 209	Lord Northwick
A Sea Fight with burning Ship	3. 209	,,
Quiet Sea, several Vessels	3. 209	,,
Quiet Sea, Vessel firing Cannon	3. 209	,,
Mouth of a River, 2 Fishermen	3. 260	Earl of Lonsdale
A slightly agitated Sea	3. 264	Earl of Lonsdale
Smooth Sea, fishing Boats	3. 275	Edinburgh R.I.
Sea Piece, Ship of War firing	3. 287	M'Lellan Gallery
Sea Piece, Ship of War firing a Gun	3 290	,,
Sea Piece, numerous Vessels	3. 291	,,
A quiet Sea	3. 303	Duke of Hamilton
Small Sea Piece, Vessel firing a Gun	3. 311	Earl of Hopetoun
Sea Piece with Vessels	3. 313	Duke of Buccleuch
Sea Piece with Vessels	3. 332	Meynall Ingram
Sea Piece with Vessels	3. 332	,,
One of Admiral Tromp's Victories	3. 333	,,
Sea Piece with Sunbeam	3. 336	Charles Wynn
A Heavy Storm, with Sunbeam	3. 347	Duke of Devonshire
A calm Sea, Ship firing a Gun	3. 347	,,
A Storm, sunny lighting	3. 349	,,
Two large Sea Pieces	3. 390	Oakover Hall

	VOL. & PAGE	OWNER
Dark Sea with Clouds	3. 395	Duke of Rutland
Slightly agitated Sea, Vessels	3. 397	,,
Calm Sea, Vessel firing a Gun	3. 399	,,
A Picture	3. 428	Joseph Muskett
Large Sea Piece, Vessels	3. 430	A. Fountaine
Small Sea Piece, Vessel firing a Gun	3. 430	A. Fountaine
A Storm at Sea	3. 442	Mr. Tomline
Naval Battle, a Ship on fire	3. 481	Marquis of Bute
A Calm Sea, Vessel firing a Gun	4. 90	Marquis of Hertford
Fresh Breeze at Sea, fishing Boats	4. 90	Marquis of Hertford
Coast Scene, Man-of-War	4. 109	J. Morrison
Calm Sea, Vessels with Troops	4. 133	Lord Overstone
Three Fishing Smacks at Anchor	4. 137	,,
Sea with fresh Breeze	4. 146	,,
Sea-shore at Scheveningen, 1659	4. 151	Earl of Caledon
A quiet Sea, Vessel firing a Gun	4. 156	St. John Mildmay
Calm Sea, a manned Boat	4. 164	A. Robarts
Sea Coast, Boat and 2 Men	4. 179	Rev. Mr. Townshend
A calm Sea, 3 Men on Shore	4. 196	G. Field
A calm Sea, Shore in the Foreground	4. 199	J. Tulloch
An agitated Sea	4. 209	Mr. Henderson
A quiet Sea, Man-of-War firing a Gun	4. 237	Earl of Harrington
Agitated Sea, a Fleet in distance	4. 237	Earl of Harrington
A calm Sea, Boat and 3 Figures	4. 283	Sir C. Eardley
A calm Sea, Man-of-war, etc.	4. 319	Lord Enfield
A calm Sea with Vessels	4. 330	Sir T. Sebright
Embarkation of Charles II	4. 350	Vernon Harcourt
Agitated Sea, Vessels by a Pier	4. 354	Lord Folkestone
A good Sea Piece	4. 363	General Buckley
Calm Sea, Coast and Pier	4. 364	Earl of Normanton
A fresh Breeze, fishing Boats	4. 365	Earl of Normanton
A Picture	4. 374	Sir W. Knighton
A calm Sea, Coast to left	4. 385	H. D. Seymour
A Sea Piece	4. 404	Joseph Gillott
A quiet Sea, Gun being fired	4. 424	Earl of Burlington
A Sea Piece, Gun being fired	4. 427	Rev. Mr. Staniforth
Slightly agitated Sea, a Cloud	4. 438	Earl of Wemyss
Ships in Distress	4. 443	Sir H. Campbell
View from Shore, light Breeze	4. 443	Sir H. Campbell
A calm Sea, Boat and Fishermen	4. 476	W. W. Bardon
A Calm, Gun being fired	4. 514	Duke of Portland
A Calm, several Boats	4. 514	Duke of Portland

VAN DIEST, Adrian

	VOL. & PAGE	OWNER
A Storm	4. 366	Earl of Normanton
A misty Distance	4. 366	Earl of Normanton

VANDYCK, Sir Anthony

	VOL. & PAGE	OWNER
Gevartius	I. 351	National Gallery
Three Figures (half length)	I. 352	,,
St. Ambrose and Theodosius	I. 352	,,
Study of Horses	I. 352	,,
Three half Figures	I. 394	Duke of Northumberland
A young Man, one hand seen	I. 400	Sir R. Peel
The Crucifixion	I. 415	,,
Rinaldo in the lap of Armida	I. 415	,,
Thirty-seven small Portraits	I. 415	Duke of Buccleuch
Christ healing the Lame	2. 3	Buckingham Palace
Virgin and Child and St. Catherine	2. 3	,,
Virgin and Child	2. 3	,,
Charles I on a Horse and Sir T. Norton	2. 3	,,
Man in Black with Book	2. 4	,,
Three Horsemen	2. 4	,,
Virgin and Child	2. 40	Bridgewater House
A Man	2. 40	Bridgewater House
Lord Arundel seated	2. 69	Duke of Sutherland
Man in Black in a Chair	2. 69	,,
An Astronomer in a furred Mantle	2. 69	,,
Three Children	2. 84	Earl De Grey
Lords John and Bernard Stuart	2. 84	,,
Countess of Southampton	2. 85	,,
Rachel, Countess of Southampton	2. 85	,,
Other Portraits	2. 85	,,
Adoration of the Shepherds	2. 85	,,
Charles I	2. 85	,,
Henrietta Maria	2. 85	,,
Madame Kirk	2. 85	,,
Charles Mallory	2. 85	,,
A Bishop of Ghent	2. 86	Duke of Norfolk
Margaret, Countess of Carlisle	2. 94	Devonshire House
Rubens, in sepia	2. 94	,,
Vandyck, in sepia	2. 94	,,
Two other Portraits	2. 94	,,
Infant Moses on the banks of the Nile	2. 94	,,
Virgin with the Child on her Lap	2. 102	Lord Ashburton
John, Count of Nassau	2. 103	,,
One of the Children of Charles I	2. 103	,,
Charles I, with lace, in black	2. 103	,,
Henrietta Maria, with lace, in white	2. 103	,,
The Virgin and Child	2. 114	H. T. Hope
Horsemen galloping and trotting	2. 130	Baron L. Rothschild
Henrietta Maria	2. 151	Marquis of Lansdowne
Female Portrait in black Dress	2. 151	Marquis of Lansdowne

	VOL. & PAGE	OWNER
Philip Le Roy	2. 157	Marquis of Hertford
Wife of Philip Le Roy	2. 157	,,
A female Portrait	2. 158	,,
Virgin and Child and St. Catherine	2. 165	Marquis of Westminster
Three Saints in ecstasy and two Angels	2. 182	T. Baring
Marchesa Balbi	2. 200	R. S. Holford
Scaglia	2. 200	,,
St. Martin dividing his Cloak	2. 200	,,
Beheading a Saint	2. 200	,,
A male Portrait (called Grotius)	2. 225	R. Ford
A Portrait from Stowe	2. 239	Marquis of Breadalbane
Henrietta Maria, three-quarters	2. 242	H. D. Seymour
Middle-aged Man in ruff	2. 261	J. Morrison
Infant Christ and St. John	2. 262	J. Morrison
Armida enamoured of Rinaldo	2. 264	Sir C. Eastlake
Charles I on Horseback	2. 277	Duke of Wellington
A Virgin and Child	2. 281	Sir A. Rothschild
Six small Pictures in sepia	2. 286	Duke of Bedford
A General of the Jesuits	2. 295	Wynn Ellis
Two Children	2. 295	Wynn Ellis
Achilles and Daughters of Lycomedes	2. 312	Earl of Listowel
Woman in black silk	2. 315	Earl Brownlow
Le Clerc	2. 315	,,
Anton Triest	2. 315	,,
St. Sebastian, in brown (chiaroscuro)	2. 315	,,
Sketch for Crucifixion	2. 315	,,
Philip, 5th Earl of Pembroke	2. 342	Dulwich Gallery
Countess of Pembroke	2. 342	,,
General in rich Armour	2. 342	,,
Mrs. Lemon, half length	2. 356	Hampton Court
Charles I on Horseback	2. 357	,,
Cupid and Psyche	2. 360	,,
Henry, Count Le Berg	2. 426	Windsor Castle
Charles I and Henrietta Maria, etc.	2. 426	,,
Duchess of Richmond	2. 426	,,
Thos. Killigrew and T. Carew	2. 427	,,
Henrietta Maria, in white	2. 427	,,
Venetia, Lady Digby	2. 427	,,
George and Francis Villiers, 1635	2. 427	,,
Prince Thomas of Carignan, 1634	2. 427	,,
Henrietta Maria, profile	2. 427	,,
Beatrice de Cusancs	2. 428	,,
Children of Charles I, 1637	2. 428	,,
3 Heads of Charles I	2. 428	,,
Henrietta Maria, full face	2. 428	,,
Lucy, Countess of Carlisle	2. 428	,,

		VOL. & PAGE		OWNER
VANDYCK, Sir Anthony—*continued*				
Sir Kenelm Digby	2.	428		Windsor Castle
Charles II when a Boy	2.	428		,,
His own Portrait	2.	429		,,
Henrietta Maria, full length	2.	429		,,
Prince Charles and Brother and Sister	2.	429		,,
Mary, Countess of Dorset	2.	429		,,
Charles I on a grey Horse	2.	429		,,
A Man, called Snellinck	2.	429		,,
Arthur, 1st Lord Capel	2.	454		Earl of Clarendon
Lady Capel	2.	454		,,
James, Duke of Richmond	2.	454		,,
Thomas, Earl of Arundel	2.	455		,,
James, 7th Earl of Derby and Wife	2.	455		,,
Henry, Count de Berg	2.	455		,,
Lucius, 2nd Lord Falkland	2.	455		,,
William, Marquis of Hertford	2.	455		,,
Infant Don Ferdinand the Cardinal	2.	456		,,
Sir John Minnes	2.	456		,,
George, Earl of Kinnoul	2.	456		,,
William, Lord Grandison	2.	456		,,
Henrietta Maria, with a Glove	2.	456		,,
Algernon, 10th Earl of Northumberland	2.	456		,,
William, Marquis of Newcastle	2.	457		,,
Catherine, Lady Aubigny	2.	457		,,
Philip, 4th Earl of Pembroke	2.	457		,,
Sir Thomas Ailesbury	2.	457		,,
Lady Ailesbury	2.	457		,,
3 Children of Charles I, 1635	2.	457		,,
Charles I on a dun-coloured Horse	2.	457		,,
Lord Goring	2.	458		,,
Earl of Portland	2.	458		,,
Charles I and Family	2.	469		Charles I
Charles I on Horseback	2.	470		,,
Charles I on yellow Horse	2.	470		,,
Five Children of Charles I	2.	470		,,
Henrietta Maria in white	2.	470		,,
His own Portrait	2.	470		,,
Duchess of Richmond	2.	470		,,
Mary de Medicis in a Chair	2.	470		,,
Princess of Pfalzburg	2.	470		,,
Nicholaus Laniere	2.	470		,,
Charles Maurice Rupert	2.	470		,,
Count Henry van du Borcht	2.	470		,,
A Musician with a Gold Chain	2.	470		,,

	VOL. & PAGE		OWNER
Lady Shirley	2.	470	Charles I
Old Man's Head	2.	470	,,
Procession of Knights of the Garter	2.	470	,,
Virgin and Child and Joseph	2.	470	,,
Charles I on Horseback	2.	470	,,
Charles I on dark-brown Horse	2.	483	,,
Children of Charles I	2.	483	,,
Henrietta Maria	2.	483	,,
Henrietta Maria in profile	2.	483	,,
Henrietta Maria in white silk	2.	483	,,
Charles II as a Boy in Armour	2.	483	,,
Prince and Princess of Orange	2.	483	,,
Woman in a Blue Dress	2.	483	,,
Venetia, Lady Digby	2.	483	,,
Sir Kenelm Digby	2.	483	,,
Sons of the Duke of Buckingham	2.	483	,,
Mrs. Margaret Leman	2.	483	,,
A Madonna	2.	483	,,
Christ and St. John as Children	2.	483	,,
Cupid and Psyche	2.	483	,,
A red Spaniel	2.	483	,,
Frans Snyders	2.	500	Orleans Gallery
Charles I, Wife and Children	2.	500	,,
Charles I (full length)	2.	500	,,
Duke of York	2.	500	,,
Portrait of an Englishman	2.	500	,,
An English Nobleman	2.	500	,,
Wife of the above	2.	500	,,
A Widow of rank	2.	500	,,
Princess of Pfalzberg	2.	500	,,
Wife of Frans Snyders	2.	500	,,
John, Duke of Nassau, and Family	3.	16	Earl Cowper
Duke of Lennox	3.	24	Earl of Darnley
Lords Bernard and John Stuart	3.	24	Earl of Darnley
Charles I (half length)	3.	29	Duke of Norfolk
Henrietta Maria	3.	30	,,
Henry, Earl of Arundel	3.	30	,,
Thomas, 2nd Duke of Norfolk	3.	30	,,
James, Lord Mowbray	3.	30	,,
Thomas, Earl of Arundel, and Wife	3.	30	,,
Thomas, Earl of Arundel, and Son	3.	31	,,
Henry Howard	3.	31	,,
Algernon, Earl of Northumberland	3.	33	Petworth
Sir Charles Percy	3.	34	,,
Anne, Lady Rich	3.	34	,,

	VOL. & PAGE		OWNER
VANDYCK, Sir Anthony—*continued*			
Mrs. Porter	3.	34	Petworth
Henry, Lord Percy of Alnwick	3.	34	,,
Mountjoy, Earl of Newport	3.	34	,,
Thomas, Earl of Strafford	3.	34	,,
Henry, 9th Earl of Northumberland	3.	34	,,
William, Prince of Orange, as a Child	3.	35	,,
Sir Robert Shirley and Wife	3.	40	,,
Lady (whole length)	3.	40	,,
Lady (whole length)	3.	40	,,
Dorothy, Countess of Sunderland	3.	43	,,
Lucy, Countess of Carlisle	3.	43	,,
Dorothy, Countess of Leicester	3.	43	,,
Elizabeth, Countess of Devonshire	3.	43	,,
A Lady	3.	43	,,
Henrietta Maria (whole length)	3.	122	Duke of Marlborough
Saturn holding Cupid	3.	122	,,
Mary, Duchess of Richmond	3.	123	,,
Duchess of Buckingham	3.	123	,,
Catherine, Countess of Chesterfield	3.	123	,,
Charles I and Sir T. Morton	3.	129	,,
Charles I	3.	129	,,
Henrietta Maria	3.	129	,,
Earl of Strafford and his Secretary	3.	130	,,
Female Portrait	3.	134	J. Morrison
Female Portrait	3.	134	J. Morrison
Philip, Earl of Pembroke, and Family	3.	153	Earl of Pembroke
Charles I in Armour	3.	153	,,
Henrietta Maria	3.	154	,,
Philip, Earl of Pembroke (young)	3.	154	,,
Three Children of Charles I	3.	154	,,
Duke of Epernon	3.	154	,,
Mary, Duchess of Richmond	3.	154	,,
Virgin and Child	3.	186	J. P. Miles
Lady in Armour as Minerva	3.	191	Mr. Harford
A young Man	3.	212	Earl of Warwick
Wife of Frans Snyders	3.	213	,,
Lady Brooke	3.	213	,,
Henrietta Maria (whole length)	3.	213	,,
Duke of Alba, 1630	3.	213	,,
Charles I with Glove	3.	214	,,
David Ryckaert	3.	214	,,
Antonio de Zuniga	3.	214	,,
Robert, Earl of Warwick	3.	214	,,
Prince Maurice	3.	219	Earl of Craven

	VOL. & PAGE	OWNER
Prince Rupert	3. 219	Earl of Craven
Princess of Orange	3. 219	,,
First Earl of Craven	3. 219	,,
Duke of Richmond and Dog	3. 219	,,
Family of de Wael	3. 222	Howard Galton
Portrait of Rubens	3. 225	Mr. Martin
Henrietta Maria	3. 227	Lord Lyttelton
Several old Replicas	3. 227	Lord Lyttelton
A Charity	3. 261	Earl of Lonsdale
Earl of Dorset	3. 264	Earl of Lonsdale
The Lomellini Family	3. 268	Edinburgh R.I.
A Gentleman in Armour	3. 268	,,
Martyrdom of St. Sebastian	3. 268	,,
A Male Head	3. 286	Glasgow College
Charles I	3. 290	M'Lellan Gallery
Henrietta Maria	3. 290	,,
Henrietta Maria	3. 291	,,
A Woman seated	3. 292	Sir A. Campbell
A Knight holding a Sword	3. 293	Sir A. Campbell
William, Earl of Denbigh	3. 297	Duke of Hamilton
Duchess of Richmond	3. 297	,,
Charles I on Horseback	3. 297	,,
Princess of Thalsburg	3. 298	,,
Duke of Hamilton	3. 308	,,
Duchess of Hamilton	3. 308	,,
Head of a Monk	3. 308	,,
Clara Isabella Eugene	3. 310	Earl of Hopetoun
Christ as Ecce Homo	3. 310	,,
A Man (whole length)	3. 311	,,
Duke of Monmouth (young)	3. 313	Duke of Buccleuch
Henrietta Maria	3. 314	Duke of Buccleuch
Frans Snyders	3. 319	Earl of Carlisle
Lord Holland	3. 332	Meynell Ingram
St. Francis	3. 333	Meynell Ingram
Infant Bacchus and Tiger	3. 336	Charles Wynn
Three Children of Earl of Strafford	3. 338	Earl Fitzwilliam
Earl of Strafford and his Secretary	3. 338	,,
Henrietta Maria	3. 338	,,
Rinaldo and Armida	3. 338	,,
Earl of Strafford in Armour	3. 339	,,
Earl of Strafford in Armour	3. 340	,,
Archbishop Laud	3. 340	,,
Henrietta Maria in Blue Silk Dress	3. 340	,,
Arabella, Countess of Strafford	3. 340	,,
Earl of Strafford	3. 342	W. V. Wentworth

	VOL. & PAGE		OWNER
VANDYCK, Sir Anthony—*continued*			
Vandyck in a Hat	3.	342	W. V. Wentworth
Earl of Devonshire	3.	364	Duke of Devonshire
Countess of Devonshire	3.	364	,,
Lady Wharton	3.	364	,,
Lady Rich	3.	364	,,
Arthur Goodwin	3.	364	,,
Romulus and Remus, called Rubens	3.	386	Earl of Shrewsbury
Abraham with three Angels	3.	387	Earl of Shrewsbury
A Male Portrait (half length)	3.	399	Duke of Rutland
William, Duke of Newcastle	3.	406	Marquis of Exeter
Rachel, Daughter of the Earl of West-moreland	3.	410	Earl of Westmoreland
James, Duke of Richmond	3.	410	Earl of Westmoreland
Duke d'Aremberg	3.	420	Earl of Leicester
Duke of Richmond	3.	420	Earl of Leicester
A Man	3.	429	A. Fountaine
Several Pictures	3.	439	Lord Hastings
His own Portrait	3.	441	Mr. Tomline
Dædalus and Icarus	3.	458	Earl Spencer
George, Earl of Bristol, etc.	3.	458	,,
Rubens in Black Dress	3.	458	,,
Penelope, Countess Spencer	3.	458	,,
Ann, Countess of Bedford	3.	458	,,
Lady E. Thimbleby and Lady Rivers	3.	458	,,
William, Duke of Newcastle	3.	459	,,
Rachel, Countess of Southampton	3.	459	,,
Two Admirals of Brudenell Family	3.	460	Duke of Buccleuch
Daughter of the Duke of Buckingham	3.	460	Duke of Buccleuch
Lord Holland	3.	462	Glendon Hall
Countess of Pembroke	3.	462	,,
Head of old Man	3.	462	,,
Francis, 4th Earl of Bedford	3.	464	Duke of Bedford
Ann, Countess of Bedford	3.	464	,,
Duchess of Ormond	3.	464	,,
Aubertus Miræus	3.	464	,,
Daniel Mytens	3.	464	,,
Wife of Mytens	3.	464	,,
William, Viscount Stafford	3.	475	Marquis of Bute
Sketch for the Crucifixion	4.	70	Earl of Yarborough
Young Man in Black Dress	4.	86	Marquis of Hertford
Lady in Black and Yellow	4.	86	,,
Charles I	4.	87	,,
Henrietta Maria	4.	87	,,
Male Figure in Black	4.	98	T. Baring

	VOL. & PAGE	OWNER
Infant Christ and St. John	4. 109	J. Morrison
Male Portrait with Moustache	4. 110	J. Morrison
Marchesa Spinola and Child	4. 151	Earl of Caledon
Man in Black, white Collar	4. 163	A. Robarts
St. Rock entreating Christ for plague-stricken	4. 185	W. Russell
Charles I, 1636	4. 235	Earl of Harrington
Henrietta Maria	4. 235	,,
Continence of Scipio	4. 235	,,
Virgin and Child	4. 237	,,
Virgin and Child (Child at Breast)	4. 238	,,
A Daughter of Charles I	4. 238	,,
Study of a grey Horse	4. 241	R. P. Nichols
Count de Berg	4. 262	Duc D'Aumale
Female in Black and White	4. 263	Duc D'Aumale
Earl of Strafford in Armour	4. 271	Earl of Jersey
A family Picture	4. 276	Sir C. Eardley
Lady with 4 Children	4. 277	Sir C. Eardley
Charles I in Armour	4. 309	J. Morrison
Two Ladies seated, Orange Branch	4. 310	J. Morrison
Thomas, Duke of Cleveland and Family	4. 322	Lord Enfield
Earl of Strafford	4. 325	Lord Enfield
Figure of Christ	4. 327	Sir T. Sebright
Charles I in Black with Star	4. 328	Sir T. Sebright
Francis, 4th Earl of Bedford, 1636	4. 334	Duke of Bedford
Anne, Countess of Bedford	4. 334	,,
Charles I (whole length)	4. 334	,,
Lady Herbert in White	4. 334	,,
Aubertus Miræus	4. 334	,,
Henrietta Maria	4. 334	,,
Percy, Earl of Northumberland	4. 334	,,
Duchess of Orleans	4. 334	,,
Earls of Bristol and Bedford	4. 334	,,
Anne, Countess of Bedford	4. 334	,,
Christ with the Globe	4. 334	,,
Daniel Mytens and his Wife	4. 335	,,
A male Portrait	4. 335	,,
M. de Mallery	4. 335	,,
His own Portrait	4. 336	,,
A male Portrait	4. 336	,,
Male Portrait in Armour and Red Dress	4. 338	Knole
Frances, Countess of Dorset	4. 339	Knole
Henrietta Maria in White	4. 347	Vernon Harcourt
David Ryckaert (copy)	4. 355	Lord Folkestone
Gaston, Duke of Orleans	4. 360	,,

	VOL. & PAGE		OWNER
VANDYCK, Sir Anthony—*continued*			
Countess of Chesterfield	4.	362	Lord Folkestone
Countess of Monmouth	4.	362	Lord Folkestone
Princess Mary	4.	364	Earl of Normanton
Richard, Earl of Pembroke	4.	375	Kingston Lacy
Charles I	4.	375	,,
Henrietta Maria	4.	375	,,
Three Children of Charles I	4.	375	,,
Sir John Balace	4.	375	,,
Lady Balace (Miss Bankes)	4.	375	,,
Betrayal of Christ	4.	395	Lord Methuen
James, Duke of Richmond	4.	396	Lord Methuen
Virgin with Child on Parapet	4.	408	Smith Barry
The Virgin in Glory	4.	411	,,
Sir William Temple	4.	412	,,
Young Man in Black Dress	4.	425	Earl of Burlington
Whole length male Portrait	4.	436	Duke of Buccleuch
Two Youths	4.	437	Duke of Buccleuch
Don Livia Odescalchi	4.	443	Sir Hugh Campbell
Lady in Black with a Child	4.	445	Lord Kinnaird
Boy in White	4.	445	Lord Kinnaird
Henrietta Maria	4.	457	Earl of Dunmore
Perseus and Andromeda	4.	457	Earl of Dunmore
Repose in Egypt, Angels Dancing	4.	459	M'Lellan Gallery
Lord Lindsay in Armour	4.	462	Lord Douglas
Charles I (*copy*)	4.	463	,,
Earl of Strafford	4.	463	,,
James I in black Armour	4.	463	,,
Henrietta Maria in Yellow	4.	463	,,
Lady Paulett	4.	463	,,
Lord Banning	4.	463	,,
Duke of Buckingham in White	4.	464	,,
Earl of Holland	4.	464	,,
Mrs. Howard	4.	464	,,
Two Women	4.	464	,,
St. Jerome in a Landscape	4.	480	Matthew Anderson
Virgin and Child with Magdalen	4.	505	Earl of Yarborough
Rinaldo and Armida	4.	511	Duke of Newcastle
Charles I on Horseback	4.	512	Duke of Portland
Sir Hugh Middleton	4.	512	,,
Sir Kenelm Digby	4.	513	,,
William of Orange as a Child	4.	513	,,
Archbishop Laud	4.	513	,,
A Child upon a Bed	4.	514	,,
An Antwerp Senator	4.	514	,,

	VOL. & PAGE	OWNER
Earl of Strafford	4. 515	Duke of Portland
Charles I and Horse (*copy*)	4. 516	Lord Galway
Entombment (*copy*, after Titian)	4. 516	,,
William, 1st Duke of Bedford	4. 517	,,
Catherine, Duchess of Buckingham and Children	4. 517	,,
Thomas, 8th Earl of Pembroke	4. 517	,,
David Ryckart in fur Cap	4. 518	Earl of Hardwicke
Woman in Black Dress	4. 519.	,,
Male Portrait in Armour	4. 519	,,
Lady standing with Yellow Fan	4. 519	,,
Henderakas du Booys	4. 520	,,
Wife of Henderakas du Booys	4. 520	,,

VANDYCK, Philip

Two Girls at a Window	2.	118	H. T. Hope
Young Man and Woman at a Window	2.	253	F. Heusch

VAN EYCK, Jan

The Painter and his Wife	1.	316, 348	National Gallery
A Male Portrait	1.	317	,,
Man in Fur and Red Turban	1.	348	,,
Virgin and Child, seven Joys (in relief)	2.	78	S. Rogers
Man in Red Dress, 1462	2.	78	S. Rogers
St. Jerome, called A. Dürer	2.	182	T. Baring
Mass of St. Gregory	2.	237	Lord Ward
A Man	2.	269	Miss Rogers
A Woman	2.	269	Miss Rogers
Adoration of the Kings	2.	459	Mr. Green
Himself and his Brother Hubert	2.	500	Orleans Gallery
Philip le Bel (school of)	3.	33	Petworth
Annunciation, etc.	3.	39	Petworth
Virgin holding Child on a Parapet (School)	3.	205	Lord Northwick
Christ blessing	3.	205	,,
Adoration of the Kings	3.	206	,,
Virgin and Child	3.	249	Blundell Weld
Adoration of the Kings (School of)	3.	251	,,
John Baptist getting Water (School of)	3.	254	,,
Virgin and Child (School of)	3.	282	Mr. Dennistoun
Presentation of the Virgin in the Temple	3.	348	Duke of Devonshire
Consecration of Thomas à Becket	3.	349	Duke of Devonshire
Virgin and Child in Blue	3.	386	Earl of Shrewsbury
Virgin and Child and St. Barbara	3.	406	Marquis of Exeter
Virgin and Child, seven Joys (in relief)	4.	97	T. Baring

	VOL. & PAGE		OWNER

VAN EYCK, Jan—*continued*

Virgin and Child, etc.	4.	190	A. Beresford Hope
Infant swathed, and Virgin (School)	4.	316	Rev. Mr. Heath
Virgin on stone Bench, and			
Child (School)	4.	316	Rev. Mr. Heath
St. Francis receiving the Stigmata	4.	389	Lord Heytesbury
Virgin and Child enthroned	4.	394	Lord Methuen

VAN GOYEN

Landscape	1.	357	National Gallery
Circular Tower and Cattle on a Canal	2.	70	Duke of Sutherland
A Picture	2.	95	Devonshire House
View of Nimwegen	2.	167	Marquis of Westminster
Canal with steep Bank	2.	240	Lord Colborne
A Marine Piece	2.	270	Miss Rogers
Shore of a Dutch Canal	2.	270	Miss Rogers
View of a Dutch Canal	2.	284	Duke of Bedford
A Landscape	3.	36	Petworth
A quiet Sea	3.	222	Howard Galton
Canal with Vessels and a Village	3.	250	Blundell Weld
View of a Dutch Canal	3.	300	Duke of Hamilton
Village on a Canal	3.	322	Earl of Carlisle
A Coast with a Boat	3.	388	Earl of Shrewsbury
View of Scheveningen	3.	480	Marquis of Bute
A Landscape	4.	170	Lord Wensleydale
View of a Dutch Canal	4.	208	Mr. Henderson
Grand Trees and 4 Figures	4.	238	Earl of Harrington
Sea Piece	4.	283	Sir C. Eardley
View of a Dutch Canal	4.	283	Sir C. Eardley
Dutch Canal	4.	439	Earl of Wemyss
Dutch Canal	4.	439	Earl of Wemyss
Figures on a frozen Stream	4.	483	Matthew Anderson

VAN HARP

A Picture	2.	42	Bridgewater House

VAN HELMONT, Matthew

A Market	3.	334	Meynall Ingram

VAN HEMESSEN, Jan

Adoration of the Kings	4.	230	Prince Consort
Parable of the Unjust Steward	4.	281	Sir C. Eardley

	VOL. & PAGE		OWNER

VAN HERP, Gerritz

Monks at a Convent	1.	356	National Gallery
A Cow Stall	3.	337	Charles Wynn
Two rich Pictures	3.	478	Marquis of Bute
A Church with Dirk van Delen	4.	149	Earl of Caledon

VAN HOVE

Maidservant listening to a Concert	4.	177	Rev. Mr. Townshend

VAN HUCHTENBURGH, Jan

Battle Piece	1.	357	National Gallery

VAN HUYSUM, Jan

Fruit Piece	2.	52	Bridgewater House
Fruit Piece, 1723	2.	52	Bridgewater House
Flower Piece, 1731	2.	112	Lord Ashburton
Fruit Piece, 1732	2.	112	Lord Ashburton
Bouquet of Roses, etc.	2.	124	H. T. Hope
Grapes, Melon, Peaches, etc., 1730	2.	124	H. T. Hope
Fruit and Flowers	2.	169	Marquis of Westminster
Fruit and Flowers	2.	203	R. S. Holford
Vase with Flowers	2.	203	R. S. Holford
Basket of Fruit and Flowers	2.	256	Mr. Heusch
Flowers	2.	263	J. Morrison
Flowers in a Vase	2.	309	Mr. Wombwell
Fruit and Flower Piece	2.	345	Dulwich Gallery
Flower Piece	2.	345	Dulwich Gallery
Flowers in a glass Vessel	2.	422	H. Labouchere
Landscape	3.	209	Lord Northwick
Flower Piece	3.	286	Glasgow College
Bouquet of Flowers	4.	105	J. Morrison

VAN KESSEL

Landscape, Tree in foreground	4.	99	T. Baring

VAN MOL

A Wedding Dance	2.	501	Orleans Gallery

VAN MUSSCHER, Michiel

Painter preparing his Palette	2.	184	T. Baring
Man looking in a Glass	4.	165	A. Robarts

VAN ORLEY, Bernard

Neptune and Amphitrite	2.	94	Devonshire House
Emperor Charles V on a grey Horse	2.	270	Miss Rogers

K K

	VOL. & PAGE		OWNER
VAN ORLEY, Bernard—*continued*			
Calling of St. Matthew	2.	432	Windsor Castle
St. Jerome writing	3.	206	Lord Northwick
Virgin and Child	3.	206	„
Virgin and Child under Canopy	3.	236	Liverpool R.I.
Infant Christ and St. John	3.	262	Earl of Lonsdale
Virgin and Child and St. John	3.	392	Lord Scarsdale
Anne of Cleves	3.	456	Earl Spencer
Christ and Magdalen	4.	229	Prince Consort
Holy Family near a Fountain	4.	229	„
Portrait of a Woman	4.	229	„
Virgin and Child and 2 Saints	4.	229	„
Mary Magdalen	4.	268	Duke of Northumberland
Portrait of a Woman	4.	365	Earl of Normanton
Virgin and Joseph adoring the Child	4.	385	H. D. Seymour
VAN OS, Jan			
A Picture	2.	52	Bridgewater House
A Flower Piece	2.	124	H. T. Hope
Fruit Piece	2.	124	H. T. Hope
Bouquet of Flowers in a Vase	2.	238	Lord Ward
Fruit	2.	238	Lord Ward
Flower Piece	3.	210	Lord Northwick
Flower Piece	3.	210	Lord Northwick
Fruit in a Vase	4.	208	Mr. Henderson
Flower and Fruit Piece	4.	510	Duke of Newcastle
VAN SCHENDEL			
Greengrocer Woman by Candlelight	2.	191	T. Baring
VAN SHUPPEN, Peter			
Lady, Gentleman playing a Guitar	3.	241	Liverpool R.I.
VAN SOMER, Paul			
Christian IV of Denmark	2.	357	Hampton Court
Lord Bacon (half length)	3.	17	Earl Cowper
Thomas Earl of Arundel	3.	30	Duke of Norfolk
Duke of Buckingham	3.	171	Earl of Suffolk
James I	3.	219	Earl Craven
Anne of Denmark	3.	219	„
Prince Henry	3.	219	„
Sir Thomas Lyttelton	3.	227	Lord Lyttelton
Louis Duke of Richmond	4.	362	Lord Folkestone
Elizabeth Wriothesley	4.	426	Earl of Burlington
Sir Walter Raleigh	4.	464	Lord Douglas

	VOL. & PAGE		OWNER
VAN STRY			
A Picture	2.	52	Bridgewater House
VAN TOL, Dominic			
A Picture	2.	52	Bridgewater House
Schoolmaster and Scholars	2.	117	H. T. Hope
Old man counting Money	2.	118	,,
A Cook at a Window	2.	118	,,
A Girl plucking a Pink	2.	184	T. Baring
A Kitchen	2.	503	Orleans Gallery
A Girl with a Pink	3.	207	Lord Northwick
Woman selling Fish, etc.	4.	162	A. Robarts
A Hermit	4.	439	Earl of Wemyss
VAN TULDEN, Theodor			
Battle of the Amazons	3.	223	Howard Galton
VAN UDEN, Lucas			
Landscape	2.	94	Devonshire House
Landscape, reflection on Water	3.	35	Petworth
Landscape, figures by Teniers	3.	341	W. V. Wentworth
Landscape, figures by Teniers	3.	350	Duke of Devonshire
A Landscape, called Rubens	3.	400	Duke of Rutland
Landscape, figures by Teniers	3.	480	Marquis of Bute
Landscape	4.	148	Earl of Caledon
Small Landscape	4.	148	,,
Landscape, Group of Trees	4.	148	,,
House with Trees	4.	268	Duke of Northumberland
Landscape	4.	358	Lord Folkestone
Landscape, with a Repose in Egypt	4.	459	McLellan Gallery
by Van Balen			
A Village, figures by Teniers	4.	510	Duke of Newcastle
VAN UTRECHT, Adrian			
Poultry	3.	393	Lord Scarsdale
VANVITELLI, Gasparo			
Roman Buildings	3.	250	Blundell Weld
VAN VLIET, Heinrich			
Interior of a Church	4.	297	J. Walter
Interior of a Church, 1669	4.	362	Lord Folkestone
VARGAS, Luis de			
St. John in the Wilderness	2.	498	Orleans Gallery
Virgin and Child in Glory	3.	380	W. Davenport Bromley

	VOL. & PAGE	OWNER
VAROTARI Alessandro (Il Padovanino)		
Mars and Venus	3. 132	Duke of Marlborough
Cupid and Psyche	3. 132	„
Apollo and Daphne	3. 132	„
Pluto and Proserpine	3. 132	„
Hercules and Dejanira	3. 132	„
Vulcan and Ceres	3. 132	„
Bacchus and Ariadne	3. 132	„
Jupiter and Juno	3. 132	„
Neptune and Amphitrite	3. 132	„

These pictures, engraved as " Loves of the Gods," are said to be by Titian, but Dr. Waagen gives the name of Varotari as the painter.

	VOL. & PAGE	OWNER
VASARI, Giorgio		
St. Mark the Evangelist	2. 176	T. Baring
St. Luke the Evangelist	2. 176	T. Baring
Poets of Italy, Dante, Petrarch, etc.	2. 499	Orleans Gallery
Susanna in the Bath	2. 499	Orleans Gallery
Three Apostles	3. 237	Liverpool R.I.
Christ on Mount of Olives	4. 64	Lord Elcho
The Italian Poets, Dante, etc.	4. 185	William Russell

	VOL. & PAGE	OWNER
VECCHIA, Pietro della. *See* **Pietro della Vecchia, p. 148.**		
A Picture	1. 417	Earl of Malmesbury
A Company of Soldiers	2. 61	Duke of Sutherland
Binding up a wounded Finger	2. 152	Marquis of Lansdowne
Portrait of a Smith	2. 347	Dulwich Gallery
The Nativity	4. 67	Earl of Yarborough
Adoration of the Kings	4. 68	Earl of Yarborough

	VOL. & PAGE	OWNER
VELASQUEZ		
Philip IV hunting	1. 317, 347	National Gallery
Adoration of the Shepherds	1. 317, 347	National Gallery
Duke of Olivarez	2. 40	Bridgewater House
His own Portrait	2. 40	Bridgewater House
A Horseman addressed by a Beggar, etc.	2. 67	Duke of Sutherland
St. Charles Borromeo and Clergy	2. 67	Duke of Sutherland
His own Portrait and Count Olivarez	2. 151	Marquis of Lansdowne
Pope Innocent X	2. 151	„
Landscape with Figures	2. 151	„
Landscape with Figures	2. 151	„
A Royal Personage	2. 156	Marquis of Hertford
Philip IV when a Boy	2. 172	Marquis of Westminster
An Officer in Armour with Marshal's Staff	2. 199	R. S. Holford

	VOL. & PAGE		OWNER
Queen Maria, 2nd Wife of Philip IV	2.	223	Richard Ford
Queen Isabella, 1st Wife of Philip IV	2.	223	,,
Conde Duque Olivares	2.	223	,,
Pope Innocent X	2.	242	H. D. Seymour
A Male Portrait with a Sword	2.	245	Joseph Neeld
The old Alamada of Seville	2.	259	G. A. Hoskins
A Head	2.	260	W. A. Mackinnon
A Head	2.	260	W. A. Mackinnon
Philip IV on an Andalusian Horse	2.	267	Miss Rogers
The Water Seller	2.	276	Duke of Wellington
Pope Innocent X	2.	277	,,
His own Portrait	2.	277	,,
A youthful Cardinal	2.	294	Wynn Ellis
Landscape, Country People, and Cattle	2.	294	Wynn Ellis
Two Men in Peasant Costume	2.	311	Earl of Listowel
Philip IV (young) on Horseback	2.	345	Dulwich Gallery
Philip IV in red Dress and white Sleeves	2.	345	Dulwich Gallery
Philip IV	2.	357	Hampton Court
Queen of Philip IV	2.	357	Hampton Court
The Finding of Moses	2.	498	Orleans Gallery
Lot and his Daughters	2.	498	Orleans Gallery
A Man with a white Collar	3.	42	Petworth
Adrian Pulido Pareja	3.	141	Earl of Radnor
His own Portrait	3.	141	Earl of Radnor
Two Gentlemen on Horseback	3.	164	Marquis of Lansdowne
A Lady seated holding Fan, and Dwarf	3.	164	Marquis of Lansdowne
A female Saint in Ecstasy	3.	179	J. P. Miles
Philip IV on Horseback	3.	184	J. P. Miles
A Landscape with a Hunt	3.	204	Lord Northwick
A sleeping Man, Girl pointing	3.	204	Lord Northwick
A young Man with Moustachios	3.	212	Earl of Warwick
The Infant Don Ferdinand on horseback	3.	221	Howard Galton
A Spanish General (School of)	3.	240	Liverpool R.I.
Philip IV (whole length)	3.	297	Duke of Hamilton
Two Children in elegant dresses	3.	322	Earl of Carlisle
Man with Features like a Negro	3.	325	Earl of Carlisle
Annunciation to the Shepherds	3.	380	W. Davenport Bromley
Duchess of Ossuna	3.	435	Earl of Orford
A male Portrait (whole length)	3.	465	Duke of Bedford
Pope Innocent X	3.	484	Marquis of Bute
An Infant of Spain in Grey Dress	4.	80	Marquis of Hertford
An Infanta of Spain in Black	4.	81	,,
Don Balthasar of Spain	4.	81	,,
A Lady in Black with Gloves and Fan	4.	81	,,

	VOL. & PAGE		OWNER
VELASQUEZ—*continued*			
Don Balthasar of Spain	4.	93	Marquis of Westminster
Philip IV on a brown Horse	4.	96	T. Baring
A stately Man in black Dress	4.	181	Earl Stanhope
A young Man with plaited Collar	4.	208	Mr. Henderson
A stately Château in a Garden, etc.	4.	321	Lord Enfield
Admiral Pareja (whole length)	4.	333	Duke of Bedford
Adrian Pulido Pareja, etc.	4.	359	Lord Folkestone
Juan de Pareja	4.	361	Lord Folkestone
A Picture	4.	374	Sir W. Knighton
Las Meniñas (sketch)	4.	381	Kingston Lacy
A Cardinal	4.	381	,,
Philip IV in Black with Paper	4.	382	,,
" Los Borrachos " (sketch)	4.	387	Lord Heytesbury
A male Head	4.	393	Lord Arundel
Cupid in open Air and dead Birds	4.	410	Smith Barry
A Man of middle Age with Paper	4.	438	Earl of Wemyss
Conde Duca Olivarez on a white Horse	4.	444	Earl of Elgin
Seven Peasants leading an Ox	4.	455	Earl of Dunmore
Peter Alcantara	4.	471	Duke of Northumberland
Head of a Boy	4.	475	W. W. Bardon
A Cardinal in an Armchair	4.	476	W. W. Bardon
A Spanish Officer	4.	502	Earl of Yarborough
VENETIAN SCHOOL			
Holy Family	4.	408	Smith Barry
Holy Family	4.	408	Smith Barry
VENETO, Bartolommeo			
A young Man in Costume of Calza	4.	60	National Gallery
VENUSTI, Marcello			
Holy Family, Child asleep	2.	151	Marquis of Lansdowne
The Crucifixion, with the Virgin and St. John	3.	184	J. P. Miles
Christ bound to a Pillar, after Del Piombo	3.	188	Mr. Harford
Christ driving Moneychangers	3.	305	Duke of Hamilton
Descent from the Cross	3.	382	Earl of Shrewsbury
Christ on the Mount of Olives	4.	456	Earl of Dunmore
Holy Family, Child asleep	4.	482	Matthew Anderson
VERBOECKHOVEN, Eugene			
A Cow lying down and Sheep	2.	191	T. Baring
Flock of Sheep taking Refuge	2.	329	Mr. Oppenheim
An Ass and 2 Sheep	4.	176	Rev. Mr. Townshend
An Inn, Woman giving Drink, etc.	4.	176	Rev. Mr. Townshend

	VOL. & PAGE	OWNER

VERBOOM

A wooded Hill, Figures by A. van de Velde	2. 187	T. Baring
A Wood with House in it	4. 321	Lord Enfield
Landscape, Buildings and Water	4. 425	Earl of Burlington

VERELST

Young Girl making a Dog sit up	3. 163	Marquis of Lansdowne

VERKOLIE, Jan

A family Picture, Man in Wig, etc.	3. 460	Duke of Buccleuch
Gentleman and Lady and Page	3. 477	Marquis of Bute

VERNET, Horace

Four Pictures of Battles	2. 157	Marquis of Hertford
Napoleon on Horseback	2. 284	Duke of Bedford
Mounted Shepherd on a grey Horse	4. 84	Marquis of Hertford
Scene in Algiers, 10 Arabians in a circle	4. 85	,,
French Soldiers storming a Gateway	4. 85	,,

VERNET, Joseph

A Sea Piece	1. 346	National Gallery
A quiet Sea	2. 284	Duke of Bedford
An agitated Sea	2. 284	Duke of Bedford
In the Neighbourhood of Rome	2. 348	Dulwich Gallery
Three Landscapes	3. 171	Lord Arundel
Sea Piece with morning Mist	3. 185	J. P. Miles
A Sea Coast	3. 191	Mr. Harford
A Sea Piece	3. 191	Mr. Harford
View of a Harbour	3. 205	Lord Northwick
A Picture	3. 290	M'Lellan Gallery
A Sea Cave near Sorrento	3. 294	Sir A. Campbell
A Landscape	3. 313	Duke of Buccleuch
Misty Morning on the Sea	3. 386	Earl of Shrewsbury
A Storm at Sea	3. 421	Earl of Leicester
View of Tivoli	3. 421	Earl of Leicester
Sea Piece with stranded Boat	4. 68	Earl of Yarborough
Large Picture	4. 158	St. John Mildmay
Port of Genoa	4. 158	St. John Mildmay
A Stream surrounded by Hills	4. 209	Mr. Henderson
A Sea Coast, Figures bathing	4. 385	H. D. Seymour
Tempest on Sea Coast	4. 392	Lord Arundel
Calm Sea by Moonlight	4. 392	Lord Arundel

	VOL. & PAGE		OWNER
VERNET, Joseph—*continued*			
Storm at Sea	4.	424	Earl of Burlington
Sea Piece	4.	424	Earl of Burlington
Landscape	4.	436	Duke of Buccleuch
Effect of Storm on a Coast	4.	445	Earl of Elgin
VERONESE, Alessandro (A. Turchi)			
Joseph and Potiphar's Wife	2.	33	Bridgewater House
Diana and Endymion	3.	20	Earl of Darnley
A Patron Saint with a Devotee	3.	176	Mr. Vivian
Flight into Egypt, Virgin on an Ass	4.	351	Vernon Harcourt
VERONESE, Paul			
Consecration of St. Nicholas	1.	334	National Gallery
Europa	1.	334	National Gallery
Christ with Disciples at Emmaus	2.	60	Duke of Sutherland
A Man on his Knees worshipping, etc.	2.	61	,,
Cupid held up by Venus, etc.	2.	61	,,
Christ driving out the Moneychangers	2.	87	Earl of Yarborough
Adoration of the Kings	2.	90	Devonshire House
Legend of St. Maurice	2.	90	Devonshire House
Christ on the Mount of Olives	2.	100	Lord Ashburton
Paul Veronese with Vice and Glory	2.	113	H. T. Hope
Hercules led by Wisdom	2.	113	H. T. Hope
Venus seated with Cupid	2.	134	H. A. J. Munro
Leda with the Swan	2.	134	H. A. J. Munro
Baptism of Christ	2.	179	T. Baring
Female Portrait with a pointed Cap	2.	197	R. S. Holford
Mars and Venus	2.	244	Joseph Neeld
St. Gregory with Hands clasped	2.	265	Sir C. Eastlake
St. Jerome reading	2.	265	Sir C. Eastlake
Woman taken in Adultery	2.	293	Wynn Ellis
Cardinal giving Benediction	2.	346	Dulwich Gallery
The Annunciation	2.	356	Hampton Court
St. Catherine before an Altar	2.	360	Hampton Court
Finding of Moses	2.	482	Charles I
Faith with Cup and Cross	2.	482	,,
Diana and Actæon	2.	482	,,
Leda with the Swan on white Bed	2.	482	,,
Death of Adonis	2.	498	Orleans Gallery
Judgment of Solomon	2.	498	,,
Christ with the Disciples at Emmaus	2.	498	,,
Leda with the Swan	2.	498	,,
Mars and Venus and Cupid	2.	498	,,

	VOL. & PAGE		OWNER
Wisdom accompanies Hercules	2.	498	Orleans Gallery
P. Veronese between Virtue and Vice	2.	498	,,
Finding of Moses	2.	498	,,
Europa carried off by Jupiter	2.	498	,,
Mars and Venus	2.	498	,,
Mars disarmed by Venus	2.	498	,,
Cupid showing a Man a Woman sleeping	2.	498	,,
Allegorical, called Respect	2.	499	,,
Allegorical, called Disgust	2.	499	,,
Allegorical, called Happy Love	2.	499	,,
Allegorical, called The Faithless	2.	499	,,
Mercury and Horse	2.	499	,,
Le Respect	3.	20	Earl of Darnley
L'Amour Heureux	3.	20	,,
Le Dégoût	3.	20	,,
L'Infidélité	3.	20	,,
Triumph of Bacchus	3.	20	,,
A Flight into Egypt	3.	171	Earl of Suffolk
A Great Feast (sketch)	3.	171	Earl of Suffolk
Magdalen washing the Feet of Christ	3.	172	Colt Hoare
Entry of Christ into Jerusalem	3.	185	J. P. Miles
Dead Christ on the Lap of the Virgin	3.	189	Mr. Harford
Marriage of Cana (? *copy*)	3.	248	Blundell Weld
Party of Men and Women	3.	265	Earl of Lonsdale
Venus and Adonis	3.	274	Edinburgh R.I.
Europa on the Bull	3.	290	M'Lellan Gallery
A Picture	3.	312	Lord Cranstoun
A Picture	3.	314	Captain Stirling
The Tribute Money	3.	341	Earl Fitzwilliam
Mary Magdalen washing the Feet of Christ	3.	384	Earl of Shrewsbury
Portrait of a Woman	3.	384	Earl of Shrewsbury
Christ and Mother of Sons of Zebedee	3.	404	Marquis of Exeter
Mercury transforming Aglauros	3.	447	Fitzwilliam Museum
Female with Foot on a Ball, etc.	3.	483	Marquis of Bute
Marriage of St. Catherine	3.	483	,,
Two Pictures of Figures	3.	483	,,
Adoration of the Kings	4.	60	National Gallery
Christ driving out the Moneychangers	4.	70	Earl of Yarborough
Perseus and Andromeda	4.	79	Marquis of Hertford
Catherine Cornaro	4.	101	R. S. Holford
A Buffet, Party at a Meal	4.	201	J. Tulloch
The Virgin enthroned, with a Book	4.	345	Earl Cowper
Baptism of Christ	4.	386	Lord Heytesbury
Finding of Moses	4.	386	Lord Heytesbury

	VOL. & PAGE	OWNER
VERONESE, Paul—*continued*		
A Male Portrait (whole-length)	4. 412	Smith Barry
Triumph of Truth	4. 420	Jacob Fletcher
The repentant Magdalen	4. 421	Jacob Fletcher
Male Saint with Palm Branch, etc.	4. 446	Lord Kinnaird
Baptism of Christ	4. 451	W. Stirling
Martyrdom of St. Catherine	4. 457	Earl of Dunmore
Magdalen kneeling, and 3 Angels	4. 469	Duke of Northumberland
Virgin and Child	4. 469	Duke of Northumberland
Marriage of Cana (sketch)	4. 476	W. W. Bardon
Susanna and the Elders	4. 502	Earl of Yarborough
Rebecca and Eleazar at the Well	4. 502	,,
Emperor Augustus and Sybil, etc.	4. 503	,,
The Annunciation	4. 503	,,
Venus seated in a Landscape, extracting Thorn	4. 503	,,
Repentant Magdalen and Angel	4. 520	Earl of Hardwicke
VERRIO		
Copies of Raphael's Cartoons	4. 491	Archdeacon of Durham
VERROCCHIO, Andrea		
St. John blessing Chalice	3. 375	W. Davenport Bromley
Virgin and Child, Baptist and Angel	3. 434	Earl of Orford
Virgin adoring Child	4. 72	Alexander Barker
Virgin and Child with Saints	4. 93	Marquis of Westminster
VERSCHURING, Henrik		
Landscape with Houses, called Wouvermans	3. 310	Earl of Hopetown
VICTORS, Jan		
Tobit and his Father, Mother, etc.	2. 42	Bridgewater House
Tobit blaming his Wife, etc.	3. 476	Marquis of Bute
View of a Village, Figures	4. 290	J. Sanders
VILLEGAS, Pedro de, De Mormoleja		
St. Francis with the Stigmata	3. 380	W. Davenport Bromley
St. Sebastian	3. 380	W. Davenport Bromley
VINCENZO, de S. Geminiano		
Virgin and Child enthroned, etc.	4. 300	Higford Burr
VINCI, Leonardo da		
Christ and 4 Doctors	1. 319	National Gallery
Virgin and Child and St. Ann	1. 391	Royal Academy
The Last Supper (*copy*)	1. 392	Royal Academy

	VOL. & PAGE		OWNER
Angel lifting Covering from Christ	2.	98	Lord Ashburton
Christ and St. John as Children	2.	99	Lord Ashburton
Head from Vierge des Rochers	2.	194	R. S. Holford
Virgin and Child and 2 Saints	2.	231	Lord Ward
Mona Lisa (*copy*)	2.	243	H. D. Seymour
La Belle Ferronnière (*copy*)	2.	243	H. D. Seymour
St. Catherine	2.	260	W. A. Mackinnon
Mona Lisa	2.	314	Earl Brownlow
St. John the Baptist pointing	2.	482	Charles I
A Smiling Girl with Flowers	2.	482	,,
Socrates, on whom his Wife rides	2.	482	,,
A Female Head	2.	499	Orleans Gallery
A Female Portrait, " La Colombine "	2.	499	Orleans Gallery
Flora	3.	134	Lord Dillon
La Vierge aux Rochers	3.	168	Earl of Suffolk
A Holy Family, on parchment	3.	172	Colt Hoare
Christ giving Benediction	3.	182	J. P. Miles
Virgin holding the Child, who is standing	3.	196	Lord Northwick
Christ as a Boy	3.	348	Duke of Devonshire
Bust of a Youth	3.	350	Duke of Devonshire
Virgin holding Child in her Arms	3.	377	W. Davenport Bromley
Vierge au bas relief (*copy*)	3.	447	Fitzwilliam Museum
Lucretia	3.	462	Glendon Hall
Virgin on the Lap of St. Anne	4.	69	Earl of Yarborough
Leda with the Swan	4.	75	Alexander Barker
A Picture	4.	166	W. Davenport Bromley
Female, Wreath of Flowers in her Hair	4.	305	J. Morrison
Virgin seated, Child seated next her	4.	326	Sir T. Sebright
Battle of the Standard	4.	329	Sir T. Sebright
The Holy Family	4.	343	Countess of Warwick
A Female Head (School)	4.	439	Earl of Wemyss
St. Sebastian	4.	444	Earl of Elgin
La Columbine	4.	446	Lord Kinnaird
Woman with Fillet on Forehead (School)	4.	447	Lord Kinnaird
Virgin holding the Child, Benediction	4.	456	Earl of Dunmore
Christ (School of)	4.	504	Earl of Yarborough

VINCKEBOOM, David

Landscape, Scripture History	2.	260	W. A. Mackinnon
Landscape	3.	225	Mr. Martin
Landscape, figures by Rothenhammer	3.	288	M'Lellan Gallery
A Picture	3.	476	Marquis of Bute
A Fair	4.	268	Duke of Northumberland
Landscape, Flight into Egypt	4.	269	Duke of Northumberland
Landscape with a Cow	4.	458	M'Lellan Gallery

	VOL. & PAGE	OWNER
VIVARINI, Bartolommeo		
Virgin and Child, St. Paul and St. Jerome	4. 58	National Gallery
VOLTERRA, Daniel de		
Descent from the Cross	2. 499	Orleans Gallery
Christ lamented by His Disciples	3. 170	Earl of Suffolk
The Entombment	3. 188	Mr. Harford
Dead Christ in the Lap of the Virgin, etc.	4. 345	Earl Cowper
Francesco Albizzi	4. 397	Lord Methuen
Mater Dolorosa	4. 397	,,
Study for Fresco at Rome	4. 399	,,
VOSTERMANN, Jan		
Windsor Castle, 1674	2. 434	Windsor Castle
Windsor Castle	2. 434	Windsor Castle
VOUET, Simon		
Allegory of Peace	2. 499	Orleans Gallery

	VOL. & PAGE	OWNER
WATTEAU, Antoine—*continued*		
Triumph of Love	2. 245	Joseph Neeld
A Picture	2. 268	Miss Rogers
A Picture	2. 268	Miss Rogers
A Picture	2. 287	H. Labouchere
A Ball	2. 499	Orleans Gallery
Small Picture	3. 158	Marquis of Lansdowne
Small Picture	3. 158	Marquis of Lansdowne
Hunting Party at a Repast	3. 205	Lord Northwick
Ladies and Cavaliers listening to Music	4. 83	Marquis of Hertford
A Wood, 4 Ladies and a Gentleman, etc.	4. 83	,,
Wood with tall Stems, Figures	4. 83	,,
Pierrot in white dress, and Figures	4. 96	T. Baring
Landscape, Carriage and 3 grey Horses	4. 97	,,
Two smaller Pictures	4. 97	,,
Ladies and Cavaliers in open air	4. 101	R. S. Holford
Gentlemen and Ladies in a Garden	4. 146	Lord Overstone
Couple dancing Minuet	4. 158	St. John Mildmay
A Fête champêtre	4. 201	J. Tulloch
Grandmother at Spindle, Mother sewing	4. 214	Mrs. James
Gentlemen and Ladies in open air	4. 214	,,
Gentlemen and Ladies in open air	4. 214	,,
Group of 3 Ladies and Pierrot	4. 307	J. Morrison
Gentleman playing the Guitar	4. 311	J. Morrison
Man in Oriental dress, Girl dancing	4. 430	Lord Murray
Girl blowing a little Windmill	4. 430	Lord Murray
A Girl (in red Chalk)	4. 451	W. Stirling
WEBSTER, Thomas, R.A.		
The Dame School	1. 379	Marlborough House
Going to Church	1. 379	Marlborough House
Children going to School	2. 190	T. Baring
Children coming out of School	2. 190	T. Baring
A Picture	2. 258	George Young
A Village Choir	2. 299	J. Sheepshanks
Sickness and Health	2. 300	,,
Going to the Fair	2. 302	,,
Returning from the Fair	2. 302	,,
Reading the Scripture	2. 305	,,
Contrary Winds	2. 307	,,
The Joke (The Smile)	2. 349	E. Bicknell
The Frown	2. 350	,,
Good-night	2. 353	,,
Sick Girl in a Chair	4. 302	J. Morrison
The Concert	4. 417	S. Ashton

	VOL. & PAGE		OWNER
Recruiting	4.	419	J. Chapman
Sick Child at a Meal	4.	419	,,
Three Children at a Peep Show	4.	419	,,

WEENIX, Jan Baptista

	VOL. & PAGE		OWNER
A dead Hare	2.	23	Buckingham Palace
Figures among Roman Ruins	2.	71	Duke of Sutherland
A Picture	2.	95	Devonshire House
A Hare, Swan, Dog and Parrot	2.	124	H. T. Hope
Dead Stag	2.	124	,,
Dead Partridge	2.	124	,,
A dead Hare	2.	260	W. A. Mackinnon
The Revel	2.	503	Orleans Gallery
A Sea Port and numerous Figures	3.	122	Duke of Marlborough
A sleeping Girl and a Dog	3.	208	Lord Northwick
A seated Party, animated Heads	3.	222	Howard Galton
A Girl with a Dog	3.	223	Howard Galton
A Gentleman and Lady on Horseback	3.	387	Earl of Shrewsbury
A dead Hare	3.	434	Earl of Orford
A dead Hare	3.	449	Fitzwilliam Museum
Two dead Hares and 2 Birds, etc.	4.	90	Marquis of Hertford
Dead Hare, Pheasant, etc.	4.	147	Earl of Caledon
A Boy	4.	268	Duke of Northumberland
Dead Wolf, white Fox, etc.	4.	276	Sir C. Eardley
Dead Hare, 2 Partridges, etc.	4.	288	Edmund Foster
A Sea Port with Buildings	4.	297	J. Walter
Landscape and Rape of Sabines	4.	427	Rev. T. Staniforth
A Sea Port	4.	458	M'Lellan Gallery
Landscape, large Urn and dead Game, etc.	4.	508	Duke of Newcastle
Dead Hare and Basket of Fruit, etc.	4.	508	Sir J. Nelthorpe

WEST, Benjamin, P.R.A.

	VOL. & PAGE		OWNER
Death of General Wolfe	1.	366	Marlborough House
Orestes and Pylades	1.	366	,,
Cleombrotus banished, etc.	1.	366	,,
The Last Supper	1.	366	,,
Christ healing the Sick	1.	366	,,
Alexander the Great and Physician	2.	72	Duke of Sutherland
Death of General Wolfe	2.	173	Marquis of Westminster
Battle of La Hogue	2.	173	,,
William III passing the Boyne	2.	174	,,
Death of General Wolfe	2.	365	Hampton Court
Other Pictures	2.	365	Hampton Court
Virgin and Child and St. Joseph	3.	290	M'Lellan Gallery

	VOL. & PAGE	OWNER
WEST, Benjamin, P.R.A.—*continued*		
Agrippina and Ashes of Germanicus	3. 407	Marquis of Exeter
Lord Eardley	4. 281	Sir C. Eardley
Pictures	4. 374	Sir W. Knighton
WESTMACOTT, Sir Richard, R.A. (Sculptor)		
Boy surrounded by Bears	3. 38	Petworth
Socrates defending himself	3. 419	Earl of Leicester
WESTMACOTT, Richard, Junior (Sculptor)		
A young Satyr seated	3. 367	Duke of Devonshire
WIGMANA		
House in a Landscape	3. 263	Earl of Lonsdale
WILDENS, J.		
A Picture	2. 42	Bridgewater House
Landscape and Boar Hunt	3. 225	Mr. Martin
A Landscape	3. 480	Marquis of Bute
WILKIE, Sir David, R.A.		
The Blind Fiddler, 1806	I. 317, 376	National Gallery
The Village Festival, 1811	I. 376	Marlborough House
The Bagpipe Player, 1813	I. 376	„
The Wood Scene, 1822	I. 376	„
Reading the News, 1823	I. 376	„
The First Earring, 1835	I. 377	„
Peep of Day Boys' Cabin, 1836	I. 377	„
John Knox preaching	I. 414	Sir R. Peel
Blind Man's Buff	2. 25	Buckingham Palace
Penny Wedding, 1818	2. 25	Buckingham Palace
Two Men and 2 Women at Breakfast	2. 72	Duke of Sutherland
Woman and 4 Children before a House	2. 130	Baron L. Rothschild
Chelsea Pensioners (sketch)	2. 189	T. Baring
Rabbit on the Wall (sketch)	2. 189	„
Interior of Inn with 9 Figures	2. 189	„
Old Man writing Letter for 2 Girls	2. 189	„
Columbus and the Prior	2. 203	R. S. Holford
Sportsmen taking Refreshment	2. 229	Hon. E. Phipps
"Not at Home"	2. 229	Hon. E. Phipps
Parish Beadle	2. 241	Lord Colborne
Group of Bacchanalian Character	2. 257	George Young
Distraining for Rent (sketch)	2. 257	George Young

	VOL. & PAGE		OWNER
Highland Sportsman with a dead Stag	2.	268	Miss Rogers
Chelsea Pensioners	2.	273	Duke of Wellington
George IV (whole length)	2.	277	,,
William IV (whole length)	2.	277	,,
Lady Lyndhurst	2.	277	,,
Blind Man's Buff (sketch)	2.	291	C. Bredel
Four Card Players, etc.	2.	291	C. Bredel
Rabbit on the Wall	2.	298	Wynn Ellis
The Broken Jar	2.	300	J. Sheepshanks
Duncan Gray or the Refusal	2.	301	,,
The Errand Boy	2.	306	,,
Two Landscapes, painted with W. Mulready	2.	306	,,
William IV	2.	425	Windsor Castle
John Knox preaching (sketch)	3.	39	Petworth
Capuchin Monk and Priest	3.	161	Marquis of Lansdowne
Father playing with Child	3.	162	,,
Father piping to two Children	3.	164	,,
Village Politicians (sketch)	3.	223	Howard Galton
Queen Victoria (sketch)	3.	287	M'Lellan Gallery
George IV in Highland Costume	3.	313	Duke of Buccleuch
Parish Beadle	4.	62	National Gallery
The Highland Toilette	4.	92	Marquis of Hertford
Piper, dead Stag, etc.	4.	100	T. Baring
Napoleon and Pope Pius VII	4.	184	W. Marshall
Young Girl confessing to Priest	4.	303	J. Morrison
Reading the Will (sketch)	4.	373	Earl of Normanton
Spanish Mother	4.	374	Sir W. Knighton
Fourteen other Pictures	4.	374	Sir W. Knighton
Tam O'Shanter	4.	416	S. Ashton
The Rent Day	4.	417	J. Chapman
Highlander with Bagpipe and 2 Girls	4.	433	Gibson Craig
George IV	4.	435	Duke of Buccleuch

WILLIAMS, Penry

Girl with Tambourine	1.	380	Marlborough House
Peasants reposing	1.	380	Marlborough House

WILLIAMS

A Landscape, Evening	3.	428	Sir J. Boileau

WILLIAMS, H. W.

Temple of Minerva at Sunium	3.	271	Edinburgh R.I.

M M

WILSON, Richard, R.A.

	VOL. & PAGE		OWNER
Villa of Mæcenas at Tivoli	I.	367	Marlborough House
Landscape, Apollo and Diana	I.	367	„
Italian Landscape	I.	367	„
Italian Landscape	I.	367	„
Death of Niobe's Children	2.	53	Bridgewater House
Landscape	2.	53	Bridgewater House
Landscape	2.	75	S. Rogers
Landscape, Figures under Tree	2.	140	H. A. J. Munro
Landscape, a Waterfall, etc.	2.	140	„
Sion House on the Thames	2.	140	„
Small Landscape	2.	140	„
Rome with River and Hills	2.	140	„
Macbeth and the Witches	2.	173	Marquis of Westminster
Landscape, clear calm River	2.	173	Marquis of Westminster
His own Portrait with Palette	2.	226	Richard Ford
Thirty-four Landscapes	2.	226	Richard Ford
Rocks on Seashore, etc.	2.	268	Miss Rogers
A Composition	2.	291	C. Bredel
Niobe and her Children	2.	298	Wynn Ellis
Landscape with a Bridge	2.	298	„
Landscape, clear Water, Evening	2.	298	„
Landscape, 2 large Trees	2.	298	„
Tomb of Horatii and Curiatii	2.	353	E. Bicknell
Landscape, Volcano Crater	3.	7	W. Fuller Maitland
Rock and Castle, Sunrise	3.	17	Earl Cowper
Rock and Castle, still water	3.	38	Petworth
Landscape with still Water	3.	39	Petworth
Landscape, Girls bathing	3.	211	Lord Northwick
Niobe and her Children	3.	211	Lord Northwick
Large Landscape	3.	249	Blundell Weld
Large Landscape	3.	249	Blundell Weld
Italian Landscape	3.	274	Edinburgh R.I.
Wood Scene, Gleams of Light	3.	393	Lord Scarsdale
Large Landscape	3.	431	A. Fountaine
A Landscape	3.	460	Duke of Buccleuch
A Landscape	3.	462	Glendon Hall
A Landscape	4.	153	William Gladstone
View of Funchal in Madeira	4.	208	Mr. Henderson
Landscape with Bridge	4.	290	J. Sanders
Wooded Landscape with Water	4.	303	J. Morrison
View of Haddon Hall	4.	332	Duke of Bedford
Landscape, Water in middle distance	4.	365	Earl of Normanton
Landscape with a Church	4.	462	M'Lellan Gallery
View in South Wales	4.	478	John Anderson

	VOL. & PAGE		OWNER
Landscape with Piece of Water	4.	479	John Anderson
Landscape, Water, etc.	4.	480	Matthew Anderson
Landscape with Piece of Water	4.	511	Duke of Newcastle

WOHLGEMUTH, Michael

The Crucifixion	2.	463	Rev. Mr. Russell
Presentation in Temple (School of)	3.	235	Liverpool R.I.
Adoration of the Kings	4.	461	M'Lellan Gallery

WOOTTON, J.

Six Hunting Pieces	3.	173	Marquis of Bath

WOUVERMANS, Jan

Landscape and Animals	4.	209	Mr. Henderson

WOUVERMANS, Philip

An Ass upon a Hill	1.	407	Sir R. Peel
La Belle Laitière	1.	407	,,
A Stable	1.	407	,,
A Hay Harvest	1.	407	,,
A grey Horse, Man with bundle of Sticks	1.	408	,,
Landscape with sandy Hills	1.	408	,,
A Sea Shore	1.	408	,,
Two Horsemen and a Lady	2.	18	Buckingham Palace
A Horse Fair, Goat Carriage	2.	18	,,
Five Cavalry Soldiers halting	2.	18	,,
Farmer's Waggon attacked by Robbers	2.	18	,,
A hawking Party halting	2.	18	,,
Haymaking, Boat and Waggon	2.	19	,,
A Camp	2.	19	,,
Horsemen fighting on Hill	2.	19	,,
A Horse Market	2.	19	,,
A Tent with Horse being shod	2.	19	,,
Water, Boys bathing	2.	47	Bridgewater House
Horses watering at Foot of Bridge	2.	47	,,
Horsemen attacking Infantry	2.	47	,,
Le Ferme au Colombier	2.	109	Lord Ashburton
Man with Pack Horse and a Washer-woman	2.	109	,,
Landscape with Sunbeams	2.	109	,,
Gentleman and Lady on Horseback, etc.	2.	109	,,
A Landscape	2.	110	,,
Hunting Party halting by Inn	2.	121	H. T. Hope
Hawking Party halting by Inn	2.	121	H. T. Hope

	VOL. & PAGE		OWNER
WOUVERMANS, Philip—*continued*			
Falconers, Cavaliers, and Ladies	2.	130	Baron L. Rothschild
Landscape with grey Horse	2.	160	Marquis of Hertford
Landscape, Horses and Figures	2.	160	Marquis of Hertford
A Horse Fair	2.	168	Marquis of Westminster
A Horseman with Hounds, etc.	2.	186	T. Baring
An Inn with Tents near it	2.	186	T. Baring
Men and Women on Horseback	2.	202	R. S. Holford
Horses being laden near Sea Coast	2.	202	,,
A Halt before Tents	2.	202	,,
A Cart with a grey Horse	2.	202	,,
Tower on the Seashore	2.	202	,,
A Drawing	2.	205	R. S. Holford
Two Pictures	2.	239	Marquis of Breadalbane
Woman with Spindle before a House	2.	241	Lord Colborne
Woman and Child and Water-carrier	2.	247	Joseph Neeld
Landscape with Herdsman	2.	247	,,
A grey Horse upon a Hill	2.	247	,,
A Hunting Party by Piece of Water	2.	247	,,
Pictures	2.	252	Henry Bevan
Three Cavaliers watering Horses	2.	255	Mr. Heusch
A Seaport, Horses and Figures	2.	262	J. Morrison
Return from the Chase	2.	274	Duke of Wellington
Halt of Cavalry before a Booth	2.	274	Duke of Wellington
Figure on a brown Horse	2.	279	Earl of Carlisle
" Le Bouffon des Masseurs "	2.	282	Sir A. Rothschild
Hunting Party halting, Lady with Guitar	2.	282	Sir A. Rothschild
A Winter Landscape and Figures	2.	291	C. Bredel
Horses bathing	2.	291	C. Bredel
Landscape and Sandhills	2.	296	Wynn Ellis
Combat of Horsemen	2.	296	,,
A Stable	2.	296	,,
Two Horsemen conversing with Girl	2.	343	Dulwich Gallery
Woman shaking Fodder before Horse	2.	343	,,
Selling Fish at Scheveningen	2.	343	,,
A sandy Landscape, Cart and grey Horse	2.	343	,,
" Le Colombier du Maréchal "	2.	343	,,
" Petite Chasse à l'Oiseau "	2.	343	,,
Man and Wife on Horseback by Fountain	2.	422	H. Labouchere
Soldier's Life	2.	433	Windsor Castle
A high Road, Men and Cattle	2.	433	,,
Horsemen before Tavern	2.	434	,,
Departure for the Chase	2.	503	Orleans Gallery

	VOL. & PAGE		OWNER
Returning from the Chase	2.	503	Orleans Gallery
The Stable	2.	503	,,
Falconry	2.	503	,,
A Landscape	3.	159	Marquis of Lansdowne
Flat Landscape, Man on grey Horse	3.	163	Marquis of Lansdowne
Religious War and all its Terrors	3.	208	Lord Northwick
Hunting Party halting, Country House	3.	261	Earl of Lonsdale
Horsemen halting, Female Suttler	3.	262	,,
Four Horsemen halting at Smithy	3.	263	,,
A Landscape	3.	287	M'Lellan Gallery
A young black Boy	3.	287	,,
Grey and brown Horse under Tree	3.	288	,,
A barren Country, Huntsman on brown Horse	3.	303	Duke of Hamilton
A Stable with Horses	3.	310	Earl of Hopetown
A Stag Hunt	3.	313	Duke of Buccleuch
Horse being shod	3.	350	Duke of Devonshire
A Stag Hunt, with Water	3.	387	Earl of Shrewsbury
Hawking Party in hilly Country	3.	387	Earl of Shrewsbury
Horse being shod	3.	397	Duke of Rutland
A Battle Piece	3.	422	Earl of Leicester
Landscape, Hunting Dogs being fed	3.	441	Mr. Tomline
A Stable	3.	448	Fitzwilliam Museum
Horseman watering his Horse	3.	448	Fitzwilliam Museum
A Dancing Party	3.	462	Glendon Hall
Hunting Party halting before Inn	3.	480	Marquis of Bute
A Smithy in a Cavern, Horse being shod	4.	88	Marquis of Hertford
Large Landscape, sandy Hill	4.	89	,,
Horse Market	4.	89	,,
A Tent on the Seashore	4.	108	J. Morrison
Battle of Horsemen and Infantry	4.	133	Lord Overstone
Grey Horse, a Woman and a Man	4.	150	Earl of Caledon
Combat of Horsemen and Foot	4.	155	St. John Mildmay
Piece of Water and Bridge, etc.	4.	156	St. John Mildmay
A Farrier's Shop, Post Waggon	4.	164	A. Robarts
Horsemen in open Landscape	4.	182	G. C. Legh
Water with Boat and three Men	4.	193	G. Field
Conflict between Horse and Foot	4.	193	G. Field
A Smithy, with Vine Arbour	4.	199	J. Tulloch
Flat Country, Man on grey Horse	4.	210	Mr. Henderson
Man on grey Horse and Lady at Smithy	4.	236	Earl of Harrington
Man with grey Horse, Woman and Child	4.	239	Earl of Harrington
Large Picture, Group of Horsemen	4.	240	R. P. Nichols
A Picture	4.	240	,,
Landscape, Men and Animals	4.	240	,,

	VOL. & PAGE	OWNER
WOUVERMANS, Philip—*continued*		
Interior of a Court, grey Horse and Boy	4. 282	Sir C. Eardley
Interior of a Court, brown Horse tied up	4. 282	Sir C. Eardley
A small Landscape	4. 288	Edmund Foster
Seashore, numerous Figures	4. 296	J. Walter
A Picture	4. 338	Knole
A Man on grey Horse, Woman and Child	4. 339	Knole
Landscape with Sandhill, etc.	4. 366	Earl of Normanton
Pictures	4. 374	Sir W. Knighton
Tree and Tent, Soldier and *vivandière*	4. 423	Earl of Burlington
Hilly Landscape, grey Horse, restive	4. 423	Earl of Burlington
A Stag Hunt	4. 436	Duke of Buccleuch
Ruin, with Gateway, 2 Women and Children	4. 451	W. Stirling
Barren hilly Scene, Market Cart	4. 458	M'Lellan Gallery
Peasant's House, with a Horse	4. 471	Duke of Northumberland
Horsemen on a Road	4. 481	Matthew Anderson
Landscape, with Falcon Chase	4. 494	Lord Feversham
Landscape, with Stag Hunt	4. 510	Duke of Newcastle
A Hunting Party, blowing Bugle	4. 513	Duke of Portland
Horseman on a grey Horse, a Woman and Child with a dog	4. 522	Earl of Hardwicke
WYATT, Richard (Sculptor)		
The Infant Bacchus	3. 222	Howard Galton
Statue of a Fisher-boy	3. 341	Earl Fitzwilliam
WYCK, Thomas		
Interior of a House	3. 311	Earl of Hopetoun
WYLD, W.		
A Turk and 2 Boys (drawing)	2. 153	Marquis of Lansdowne
St. Paul's from the Thames „	4. 414	Mr. Cooke
Thames from the Banks „	4. 414	„
A hilly Landscape „	4. 414	„
Turks reposing „	4. 415	„
A Couple dancing „	4. 415	„
WYNANTS, Jan		
A Clay Hill	1. 409	Sir R. Peel
A Hill, House and Trees, etc.	1. 409	Sir R. Peel
Hilly Landscape, Hawking Party	2. 21	Buckingham Palace
Five Pictures, three painted with A. van de Velde and two with Lingelbach	2. 48	Bridgewater House
Two small Landscapes	2. 70	Duke of Sutherland

	VOL. & PAGE	OWNER
Landscape, Figures by A. van de Velde	2. 110	Lord Ashburton
A Cottage on rising Ground	2. 187	T. Baring
Landscape, Figures by A. van de Velde	2. 187	T. Baring
A Picture	2. 252	Henry Bevan
Falcon flying, and Dogs	2. 255	Mr. Heusch
Tree reflected in Water	2. 256	Mr. Heusch
Large Landscape with River	2. 258	George Young
Landscape	2. 262	J. Morrison
Two Horses, Boy angling	2. 292	C. Bredel
A Landscape	2. 292	C. Bredel
Hilly Landscape	2. 297	Wynn Ellis
Landscape, dead Tree, etc., 1675	2. 309	Mr. Wombwell
Landscape, Hunting Party by Lingel-bach	2. 309	Mr. Wombwell
Hilly Country, Farmhouses, 1663	3. 141	Earl of Radnor
Smaller Landscape	3. 142	Earl of Radnor
Water and Sandhill	3. 164	Marquis of Lansdowne
A Landscape	3. 209	Lord Northwick
A Landscape	3. 225	Mr. Martin
Sandbank, Gentleman and Lady	3. 287	M'Lellan Gallery
Landscape, 1669	3. 309	Earl of Hopetoun
Landscape	3. 313	Duke of Buccleuch
Landscape	3. 337	Charles Wynn
Large Landscape	3. 388	Earl of Shrewsbury
A Landscape	3. 396	Duke of Rutland
A Landscape	3. 397	Duke of Rutland
Dead Tree and piece of Water	4. 90	Marquis of Hertford
Two Men and Women with 4 Cows	4. 108	J. Morrison
Hill and clusters of Trees	4. 135	Lord Overstone
Dead Tree, Shepherd and Sheep	4. 145	Lord Overstone
High Road, Horseman attacked by Robbers	4. 154	St. John Mildmay
Dead Tree, Figures by Lingelbach	4. 162	A. Robarts
Landscape, Figures by Lingelbach	4. 165	A. Robarts
Sandhill, Shepherd and Shepherdess	4. 195	G. Field
A Landscape	4. 201	J. Tulloch
Hill with Trees and Water, 1670	4. 207	Mr. Henderson
Small Landscape	4. 209	,,
Sandhill, Horseman and Animals	4. 209	,,
Sandhill, Man and Woman on Horseback	4. 209	,,
Hilly Landscape, Cow, etc.	4. 212	,,
Road, with a Woman, Boy and Dog	4. 289	J. Sanders
Hilly Landscape, grey Horse and Cart	4. 289	J. Sanders
Trees and Buildings, Water	4. 295	J. Walter
Large Landscape	4. 355	Lord Folkestone

	VOL. & PAGE		OWNER
WYNANTS, Jan—*continued*			
Landscape, Sportsman and Dogs	4.	356	Lord Folkestone
House with a Tree next to it	4.	366	Earl of Normanton
A Landscape	4.	436	Duke of Buccleuch
A fine Oak, a Man conversing with a Woman, painted with Lingelbach	4.	442	Sir H. Campbell
Woman driving Sheep through an Archway, painted with A. van de Velde	4.	442	Sir H. Campbell
Landscape, Sportsman in Foreground	4.	477	W. W. Bardon
Landscape, a large Tree	4.	480	Matthew Anderson
WYTEWAEL, Joachim			
A Feast of the Gods	3.	224	Howard Galton

	VOL. & PAGE	OWNER
ZEEMAN, Remigius		
A Sea Coast	3. 224	Howard Galton
ZEITBLOOM, Bartholomew		
Christ on Mount of Olives (School of)	4. 461	M'Lellan Gallery
ZELOTTI		
Ceiling Fresco Picture	3. 314	Captain Stirling
ZENO di Verona		
Virgin and Child, St. John, etc.	3. 189	Mr. Harford
ZIMMERMANN, Albert		
Extensive Plain with Alps in the distance	4. 178	Rev. Mr. Townshend
ZINCKE, C. F.		
Miniatures	4. 512	Duke of Portland
ZOFFANY, J., R.A.		
A Family Scene, 2 Children dancing	4. 462	M'Lellan Gallery
ZORGH (Hendrick Rockes)		
Interior of a Kitchen	2. 336	James Gray
Peasants at a Table	4. 200	J. Tulloch
Peasants at a Table	4. 200	J. Tulloch
A Man and his Wife at Breakfast	4. 206	Mr. Henderson
Man and Wife playing Cards	4. 206	,,
Aged Alchemist at Window, 1643	4. 207	,,
ZUCCARELLI		
Europa and the Bull	2. 258	Sir C. Coote
Seven Landscapes	2. 429	Windsor Castle
Isaac and Rebecca	2. 429	,,
Finding of Moses	2. 429	,,
Two Landscapes	4. 425	Earl of Burlington
Near Verona	4. 502	Earl of Yarborough
Near Vicenza	4. 502	Earl of Yarborough
Two upright Landscapes	4. 508	Duke of Newcastle

N N

	VOL. & PAGE	OWNER
ZUCCHERO, Federigo		
Queen Elizabeth's Porter	2. 355	Hampton Court
Queen Elizabeth	2. 361	Hampton Court
A Picture	2. 482	Charles I
Portraits	3. 142	Earl of Radnor
Francis II, 1559	3. 151	Earl of Pembroke
Charles IX, 1560	3. 151	Earl of Pembroke
Earl of Essex (profile)	3. 215	Earl of Warwick
Thomas, Earl of Norfolk	3. 323	Earl of Carlisle
Earl of Essex	3. 342	W. V. Wentworth
Mary Queen of Scots	3. 346	Duke of Devonshire
Queen Elizabeth	4. 358	Lord Folkestone
Sir Walter Raleigh	4. 432	Gibson Craig
Lady Raleigh	4. 432	Gibson Craig
Young Man in silk dress	4. 502	Earl of Yarborough
Sir Walter Raleigh	4. 519	Earl of Hardwicke
ZUCCHI, Andrea		
Wall Paintings, 1767	4. 270	Earl of Jersey
ZURBARAN		
Kneeling Franciscan	1. 317, 348	National Gallery
Infant Christ in Lap of Virgin	2. 67	Duke of Sutherland
A Monk reading	2. 67	,,
Two Monks in white Robes	2. 67	,,
Her own Portrait (young)	2. 223	Richard Ford
A young Lady in red dress, etc.	2. 223	,,
A Magdalen in mourning	2. 223	,,
St. Francis with the Stigmata	2. 259	G. A. Hoskins
St. Justina	2. 259	G. A. Hoskins
The Flight into Egypt	2. 458	Earl of Clarendon
Head of John the Baptist	3. 204	Lord Northwick
St. Francis and St. Augustin	3. 313	Duke of Buccleuch
Virgin and Child in Glory, and Saints	4. 64	Lord Elcho
A Monk shaded by Cowl	4. 96	T. Baring
A Monk praying	4. 173	E. Cheney
A Monk with a Crucifix	4. 173	E. Cheney
St. Anthony of Padua	4. 238	Earl of Harrington
A Saint and 4 Fathers of the Church	4. 240	R. P. Nichols
St. Justa with a Pitcher	4. 382	Kingston Lacy
Two Pictures of Saints	4. 388	Lord Heytesbury
St. Francis in a dark space	4. 389	,,
A Saint with a Skull	4. 389	,,
Infant Christ on an Ass, and Joseph	4. 390	,,

	VOL & PAGE		OWNER
St. Stephen pointing to a Stone	4.	410	Smith Barry
St. Elizabeth in rich dress	4.	410	Smith Barry
Saints Justa and Ruffina	4.	449	W. Stirling
Virgin with a Crown on her Head	4.	450	„
Marriage of St. Catherine	4.	450	„

ZWENGAUER

Clear Lake with a Boat	4.	177	Rev. Mr. Townshend

OMITTED

CUYP, Albert

Landscape with Cattle	4.	332	Duke of Bedford

The Following are the Pictures Mentioned by Dr. Waagen in his Tour of 1835 (London, John Murray, 1838) and not Repeated in that of 1854, or in the Supplement of 1857.

	VOL. & PAGE	OWNER
AGI, Cordelle		
Virgin and Child	3. 118	Fonthill
ALBANO		
Mars and Venus and Cupid	1. 267	Duke of Devonshire
ANGELO, Michael		
The Annunciation	2. 297	Duke of Wellington
The Crucifixion, with the Virgin and		
St. John	3. 143	J. P. Miles
BACKHUYSEN, L.		
Dark Clouds over Sea	3. 127	Beckford, at Bath
A Picture	3. 148	W. Acraman
BAGNACAVALLO, Il (Bartolomeo Ramenghi)		
Virgin and Child, St. John, etc.	2. 189	Edward Solly
BAROCCIO		
Cardinal Baronius	1. 266	Duke of Devonshire
BARTOLOMEO, Fra		
Virgin and Child	2. 203	Sir Abraham Hume
BASAITI, Marco		
St. Jerome	3. 118	Fonthill

		VOL. & PAGE		OWNER
BASSANO, Giacomo				
Maries at the Foot of the Cross		1.	266	Duke of Devonshire
Landscape, Men and Cattle		3.	36	Sir Thomas Baring
BATONI, Pompeo				
Duke of Devonshire		3.	229	Duke of Devonshire
BELLINI, Giovanni				
Virgin and Child		2.	397	Lord Dudley
The Doge Vendramini		3.	117	Fonthill
Another Doge		3.	117	Fonthill
BERGHEM, N.				
A Ferry with Cattle		1.	270	Duke of Devonshire
Cattle at Waterside		1.	271	Duke of Devonshire
A Picture		2.	403	Mr. Antis
Sea-coast, embarking Fish		3.	126	Beckford, at Bath
A Picture		3.	148	W. Acraman
BOLTRAFFIO				
A young Girl		1.	250	Duke of Devonshire
BONIFACIO				
A Holy Family		3.	115	Fonthill
BORDONE, Paris				
Perseus armed by Minerva and Mercury	2.	193		Edward Solly
BOTH, Jan				
A Picture		2.	403	Mr. Antis
Philip baptising Eunuch		3.	107	Lord Methuen
Sunset, in Italy, Waterfall, etc.		3.	127	Beckford, at Bath
A Picture		3.	148	W. Acraman
BOTTICELLI, Sandro				
Birth of Christ		2.	125	Y. Ottley
BOURGUIGNON				
March of Cavalry		1.	268	Duke of Devonshire
Battle Piece		3.	95	Lord Methuen
Battle Piece		3.	95	,,
A Spanish Noble in profile		3.	97	,,
BRANDI, Giacinto				
St. Charles Borromæus		3.	99	Lord Methuen

	VOL. & PAGE		OWNER
BREUGHEL, Jan			
Two small Landscapes	3.	93	Lord Methuen
Landscape, Flowers by Rothenhammer	3.	116	Fonthill
Very small Picture	3.	116	Fonthill
BRILL, Paul			
The Tower of Babel	3.	116	Fonthill
BRONZINO, Angelo			
A young Woman	1.	192	National Gallery
Wife of Malatesta and Son	2.	195	Edward Solly
CANALETTO			
Canal Scene	2.	40	Lord Farnborough
Venice, Doge's Palace	3.	128	Beckford, at Bath
CARAVAGGIO, Michael Angelo da			
Angel with Tobit	3.	103	Lord Methuen
CARRACCI, Annibal			
Christ and St. Peter	1.	207	National Gallery
Holy Family in Landscape	1.	265	Mr. Wilkins
Christ bearing Cross, and Veronica	3.	37	Sir Thomas Baring
Landscape, Satyrs and Nymphs	3.	37	Sir Thomas Baring
Landscape, Mountains and Sea	3.	85	Marquis of Lansdowne
St. Matthew (sketch)	3.	105	Lord Methuen
A Boy blowing Bubbles	3.	105	Lord Methuen
Martyrdom of St. Stephen	3.	380	Earl of Darnley
The Toilet of Venus	3.	380	Earl of Darnley
CARRACCI, Ludovico			
Susannah and the Elders	1.	209	National Gallery
Bathsheba	3.	37	Sir Thomas Baring
CASTAGNO, Andrea del			
Dead Christ and Virgin	2.	125	Y. Ottley
CASTIGLIONE, Benedetto			
Noah entering the Ark	3.	95	Lord Methuen
Duchess of Mantua with Son asleep	3.	96	Lord Methuen
CHAMPAGNE, Philip de			
Theseus and Father's Sword	3.	42	Sir Thomas Baring

	VOL. & PAGE	OWNER
CIMABUE		
Annunciation	2. 124	Y. Ottley
CIVETTA (Henry de Bles)		
Virgin and Child	3. 183	Liverpool R.I.
CLAUDE		
A Sunset, 1674	3. 39	Sir Thomas Baring
Morning, with Mountains	3. 39	Sir Thomas Baring
Morning	3. 107	Lord Methuen
Evening, Sun on a Lake	3. 107	Lord Methuen
Sunset on Seashore	3. 115	Fonthill
Landscape, Christ and Magdalen	3. 125	Beckford, at Bath
CLOUET, François (Janet)		
Small Portrait (whole length)	2. 249	Duke of Sutherland
CONEGLIANO, Cima da		
Virgin and Child	2. 203	Sir Abraham Hume
CORREGGIO		
St. John the Baptist	1. 180	Windsor Castle
Vierge au Panier	1. 184, 198	National Gallery
Ecce Homo	1. 184, 194	„
Education of Cupid	1. 184, 198	„
Christ on Mount of Olives	1. 200	„
Christ on Mount of Olives	2. 295	Duke of Wellington
Virgin and Child and 2 Female Saints	3. 36	Sir Thomas Baring
A pale Man with sunken Eyes	3. 104	Lord Methuen
The Entombment	3. 144	J. P. Miles
CORTONA, Pietro da		
Erminia binding Tancred's Wounds	3. 103	Lord Methuen
A Female Saint and 2 Angels	3. 103	Lord Methuen
CUYP, Albert		
View of Dort	2. 206	Sir Abraham Hume
Three Cows in Landscape	2. 403	H. A. J. Munro
A Picture	3. 148	W. Acraman

	VOL. & PAGE	OWNER
DE LAAR, Pieter (Bamboccio)		
A Cattle Piece	3. 98	Lord Methuen
DE LORME, A.		
Piece of Architecture, 1640	3. 119	Fonthill
DE LOUTHERBOURG, P. J., R.A.		
The Fire of London, 1797	3. 46	Sir Thos. Baring
DE VLIEGER, Simon		
Scheveningen	2. 398	Lord Dudley
DOBSON, William		
Nurse of Queen Anne	3. 93	Lord Methuen
DOLCE, Carlo		
Our Saviour (*copy*)	1. 180	Windsor Castle
Magdalen with Skull	3. 38	Sir Thos. Baring
Mater Dolorosa	3. 38	,,
Virgin with Light from Child	3. 38	,,
St. Bruno	3. 97	Lord Methuen
Guardian Angel with a Boy	3. 105	Lord Methuen
DOMENICHINO		
St. Jerome and Angel	1. 211	National Gallery
Landscape, Finding of Moses	3. 37	Sir Thos. Baring
Landscape with Waterfall	3. 37	Sir Thos. Baring
DOSSI, Dosso		
Don Antonio de Leyva	3. 99	Lord Methuen
DUCCIO		
Crucifixion	2. 123	Y. Ottley
DURER, Albert		
St. Jerome in his Study	3. 42	Sir Thos. Baring
ELSHEIMER, Adam		
Angel and young Tobit	3. 124	Beckford, at Bath

	VOL. & PAGE	OWNER
FABRIANO, Gentil da		
Virgin on Throne and Angels	2. 126	Y. Ottley
FERRARI, Gaudenzio		
The Visitation of the Virgin	2. 194	Edward Solly
FIESOLE		
Entombment of Virgin	2. 124	Y. Ottley
Ascension of Virgin	2. 124	Y. Ottley
Mary and the Angel of Annunciation	3. 116	Fonthill
FOUQUET, Jean		
Virgin and Child and Worshippers	3. 116	Fonthill
FRANCIABIGIO		
Man with Gardener's Knife	1. 180	Windsor Castle
FRANCK, Frans		
Several small Pictures	3. 119	Fonthill
FUSELI, Henry, R.A.		
Numerous Pictures	2. 402	Mr. Knolls
GADDI, Taddeo		
Crucifixion	2. 124	Y. Ottley
GAROFALO, B.		
St. Augustine and Infant Christ	1. 193	National Gallery
Holy Family	3. 123	Beckford, at Bath
GHIRLANDAJO, Dominico		
Virgin embracing Infant	2. 126	Y. Ottley
GIORDANO, Luca		
Battle Piece	3. 101	Lord Methuen
Battle Piece	3. 101	Lord Methuen
GIORGIONE		
Virgin and Child enthroned	2. 192	Edward Solly
A Sybil	2. 193	,,
Death of Peter Martyr	2. 193	,,
Berni (Tuscan Poet)	3. 100	Lord Methuen
Guidobaldo, Duke of Urbino	3. 184	Liverpool R.I.

	VOL. & PAGE	OWNER
GIOTTO		
Dead Christ and Saints	2. 124	Y. Ottley
GRIFFIER, J.		
A Picture	3. 128	Beckford, at Bath
GRIMANI, Francesco		
Large Landscape	1. 267	Duke of Devonshire
GUERCINO		
Christ lamented by Angels	1. 211	National Gallery
Christ on Mount of Olives	1. 267	Duke of Devonshire
Marriage of St. Catherine	3. 102	Lord Methuen
Christ and Nicodemus	3. 105	Lord Methuen
A Female Head	3. 145	J. P. Miles
GUIDO		
Painting and Drawing, Two Women	1. 266	Duke of Devonshire
St. Cecilia	3. 38	Sir Thos. Baring
Baptism of Christ	3. 102	Lord Methuen
HOLBEIN, Hans		
Portrait of Stallhof, 1532	1. 178	Windsor Castle
Two Warriors	1. 269	Duke of Devonshire
Reckemar	2. 116	Hampton Court
Cloth of Gold	2. 117	Hampton Court
Sir Brian Tuke	3. 93	Lord Methuen
Francis von Taxis	3. 96	Lord Methuen
Bishop Gardiner	3. 128	Beckford, at Bath
HONDEKOETER, Melchior		
A Cock, Hens, and Ducks	3. 115	Fonthill
INGANNATI, Pietro degli		
Holy Family	3. 118	Fonthill

	VOL. & PAGE	OWNER
JORDAENS, J.		
Twelfth Night	1. 270	Duke of Devonshire
Holy Family	2. 183	Duke of Northumberland
LAIRESSE, Gerard		
Laban showing Leah and Rachel to Jacob	3. 44	Sir Thos. Baring
Judgment of Midas	3. 92	Lord Methuen
Judgment of Paris	3. 92	Lord Methuen
LANFRANCO		
A Dominican	3. 97	Lord Methuen
LAURI, Filippo		
A repose in Egypt	3. 105	Lord Methuen
LAWRENCE, Sir T., P.R.A.		
Duke of Wellington	2. 27	Sir R. Peel
Canning	2. 27	,,
Huskisson	2. 27	,,
Sir Robert Peel	2. 27	,,
LELY, Sir Peter		
The Painter playing on the Violoncello	3. 95	Lord Methuen
LIEVENS, Jan		
Raising of Lazarus	2. 402	Mr. Knolls
LIPPI, Filippo		
Wise Men's Offering	3. 124	Beckford, at Bath
LORENZETTI, Ambrogio		
Crucifixion	2. 123	Y. Ottley
LOTTO, Lorenzo		
His Family	2. 193	Edward Solly
Lot and his Daughters	3. 104	Lord Methuen
LUINI, Bernardino		
Virgin and Child and St. Sebastian	2. 194	Edward Solly

	VOL & PAGE		OWNER
MABUSE, Jean			
Virgin and Child under Canopy	3.	43	Sir Thos. Baring
The Mother of Henry VIII	3.	93	Lord Methuen
MARATTI, Carlo			
Pope Clement XI	I	267	Duke of Devonshire
MARTINI, Simon			
Ascension of the Virgin	2.	123	Y. Ottley
Annunciation	2.	123	Y. Ottley
MASACCIO			
Head of a Young Man	2.	124	Y. Ottley
MATSYS, Quentin			
Mary Magdalen	3.	94	Lord Methuen
MAZZOLINO, L.			
Holy Family	I.	193	National Gallery
Virgin and Child and Saints	3.	123	Beckford, at Bath
Woman taken in Adultery	3.	123	„
Wise Men's Offering	3.	123	„
METZU, Gabriel			
A Picture	3.	148	W. Acraman
MIEL, Jan			
Soldiers and Girl at a Tavern	3.	106	Lord Methuen
MIREVELDT, Michael			
A Man and his Wife	3.	115	Fonthill
MOLA, Pietro Francesco			
Mary Magdalen in the Desert	3.	38	Sir Thos. Baring
Landscape, Shepherd playing	3.	38	Sir Thos. Baring
A Man with a Beard holding a Book	3.	100	Lord Methuen
St. John in the Wilderness	3.	101	Lord Methuen
MORE, Sir Antonio			
A Man's Head	3.	100	Lord Methuen
MOUCHERON, Friedrick			
Two small Landscapes	3.	115	Fonthill

	VOL. & PAGE	OWNER
MURILLO		
Assumption of the Virgin	3. 41	Sir Thos. Baring
Girl lifting her Veil	3. 42	Sir Thos. Baring
NEEFS, Peter		
Piece of Architecture	3. 115	Fonthill
NETSCHER, Gaspar		
A Picture	3. 148	W. Acraman
NORTHCOTE, James, R.A.		
Romeo and Juliet	3. 45	Sir Thos. Baring
Richard of York and Mortimer	3. 45	Sir Thos. Baring
OLIVER, Peter		
Edward VI, after Holbein	1. 271	Duke of Devonshire
OPIE, John, R.A.		
Lady Grey and Edward IV	3. 45	Sir Thos. Baring
Antonius and King of Sicily	3. 45	Sir Thos. Baring
ORSI, Lelio da Novellara		
A Female Head	3. 143	J. P. Miles
OSTADE, Adrian Van		
Three Men and Child, 1658	3. 126	Beckford, at Bath
Six Persons round Table, 1663	3. 126	Beckford, at Bath
A Picture	3. 148	W. Acraman
OSTADE, Isaac		
Travellers and Musician	3. 107	Lord Methuen
PALMA, Giovane		
The Nativity	3. 99	Lord Methuen
PALMA, Vecchio		
Virgin and Child and Saints	3. 35	Sir Thos. Baring
Virgin and Child and Saint	3. 99	Lord Methuen

	VOL. & PAGE	OWNER
PATENIER, Joachim		
Wise Men's Offering	3. 124	Beckford, at Bath
PENNI, F.		
Man with a Book	3. 97	Lord Methuen
PERUGINO, Pietro		
Virgin and Child and St. John	3. 117	Fonthill
A Female Saint (School of)	3. 124	Beckford, at Bath
PESELLI, Pesello		
God holds Christ on the Cross	2. 125	Y. Ottley
PETERS, William, R.A.		
Falstaff in the Buck Basket	3. 45	Sir Thos. Baring
Beatrice	3. 46	Sir Thos. Baring
PINTURICCHIO		
St. Augustine baptised	2. 397	Lord Ward
St. Augustine teaching	2. 398	Lord Ward
PISANO, Giunta		
Crucifixion	2. 123	Y. Ottley
POELEMBURG, C.		
Landscape, with Nymphs	3. 98	Lord Methuen
Landscape, with Nymphs	3. 98	Lord Methuen
A Repose in Egypt	3. 115	Fonthill
A Picture	3. 128	Beckford, at Bath
POLIDORO, da Caravaggio		
Infant Jupiter and Goat	2. 120	Hampton Court
Jupiter and Juno	2. 120	,,
Birth of Diana and Apollo	2. 120	,,
POLLAJUOLO, Antonio		
Dead Christ in Lap of Virgin	3. 182	Liverpool R.I.
PORDENONE, Licinio		
Himself and his Family	2. 119	Hampton Court
A Man with a Music Book	2. 202	Sir Abraham Hume
Christ	3. 100	Lord Methuen

	VOL. & PAGE	OWNER
POUSSIN, Gaspar		
View of Tivoli	1. 265	Mr. Wilkins
Large Landscape	2. 40	Lord Farnborough
Landscape and Figures	3. 40	Sir Thos. Baring
Landscape, Thisbe and Pyramus	3. 40	,,
Landscape, dark Water	3. 40	,,
A Storm, and two Figures	3. 97	Lord Methuen
A dark Landscape	3. 98	Lord Methuen
Large Landscape	3. 125	Beckford, at Bath
A smaller Picture	3. 125	Beckford, at Bath
POUSSIN, Nicholas		
St. Peter and St. John healing	1. 265	Mr. Wilkins
Circular Landscape	1. 267	Duke of Devonshire
Landscape and Waterfall	3. 42	Sir Thos. Baring
Testament of Eudamidas	3. 105	Lord Methuen
PRETI, Matia		
Old Man playing Lute	1. 252	Duke of Devonshire
RAPHAEL		
Virgin enthroned	2. 188	Edward Solly
Virgin and Child and St. John	2. 200	Lord Gavagh
La Belle Jardinière	3. 18	Henry Leggatt
Holy Family (*copy*)	3. 19	Mr. Nossoc
Madonna di Casa Colonna (*copy*)	3. 20	Mr. Emerson
Madonna di Casa Colonna (*copy*)	3. 20	Mr. Coesvelt
Vision of Ezekiel (*copy*)	3. 34	Sir Thos. Baring
Lorenzo de Medici	3. 35	Sir Thos. Baring
St. Catherine	3. 122	Beckford, at Bath
REMBRANDT		
Man (half length)	1. 270	Duke of Devonshire
An Old Man	1. 270	Duke of Devonshire
Man with Hand on Bust of Homer, 1653	2. 205	Sir Abraham Hume
Catherine Hoograet, 1657	3. 25	Mr. Peacock
A Young Girl	3. 97	Lord Methuen
Old Rabbi in Turban	3. 101	Lord Methuen
REYNOLDS, Sir Joshua, P.R.A.		
Venus and Cupid	2. 26	Sir R. Peel
A sleeping Woman and Huntsman	2. 346	Royal Academy

	VOL. & PAGE	OWNER
Paul Cobb Methuen	3. 106	Lord Methuen
Mrs. Methuen	3. 106	Lord Methuen
Duchess of Devonshire and Child	3. 229	Duke of Devonshire

ROMANO, Giulio

Virgin and Child	3. 35	Sir Thos. Baring

ROSA, Salvator

Rocks on Shore, Fishermen	1. 267	Duke of Devonshire
Two Banditti near Rocks	3. 40	Sir Thos. Baring
Martyrdom of St. Lawrence	3. 100	Lord Methuen
Masaniello	3. 106	Lord Methuen

ROSELLI, Cosimo

Christ on the Cross	2. 125	Y. Ottley

RUBENS, Sir P. P.

Archduke Ferdinand at Nördlingen	1. 174	Windsor Castle
Ascension of the Virgin	1. 174	„
Pan pursuing Syrinx	1. 174	„
Man with a Falcon	1. 175	„
St. George and the Dragon	1. 175	„
Prairie de Lacken	1. 176	„
Going to Market	1. 176	„
Prodigal Son in Stable	1. 264	Mr. Wilkins
Discovery of Achilles with Women	2. 204	Sir Abraham Hume
Wise Men's Offering	2. 303	Marquis of Westminster
Philemon and Baucis	3. 44	Sir Thos. Baring
Cadmus and Minerva (sketch)	3. 44	Sir Thos. Baring
Man in white Ruff	3. 92	Lord Methuen
A Bacchanalian Scene (sketch)	3. 99	„
Murder of the Innocents	3. 102	„
David and Abigail	3. 103	„
Two Sketches	3. 381	Petworth
Landscape	3. 381	Petworth

RUYSDAEL, Jacob

Flat Country, Cows and Sheep	2. 205	Sir Abraham Hume
Extensive Plain, 1660	2. 398	Lord Dudley
A Wood on the Waterside	2. 401	F. Heusch
A Waterfall	3. 127	Beckford, Bath
A Picture	3. 148	W. Acraman

	VOL. & PAGE		OWNER
SACKTLEVEN, Hermann			
A Picture	3.	128	Beckford, at Bath
SARTO, Andrea del			
Male Portrait	1.	179	Windsor Castle
Man with Gardener's Knife	1.	179	Windsor Castle
Marriage of St. Catherine, after Correggio	3.	106	Lord Methuen
SCHIDONI			
Virgin praying, with Book	3.	85	Marquis of Lansdowne
SCHOREEL, Jan			
Lovers feasting	3.	97	Lord Methuen
SIRANI, Elizabeth			
Boy blowing Bubbles	3.	97	Lord Methuen
SNYDERS, F.			
A Fox chase	3.	95	Lord Methuen
Two Cats fighting	3.	95	Lord Methuen
SOGLIANI			
Adoration of Shepherds	2.	297	Duke of Wellington
STEEN, Jan			
Marriage at Cana	2.	397	Lord Northwick
Consequences of Intemperance	3.	125	Beckford, at Bath
STEENWYCK, Hendrik van			
Interior of a Church, 1611	3.	100	Lord Methuen
Piece of Architecture	3.	117	Fonthill
Very small Picture	3.	119	Fonthill
A Picture	3.	128	Beckford, at Bath
STROZZI, B. (Il Prete Genovese)			
St. Mark and St. John	3.	104	Lord Methuen
David and Solomon	3.	104	Lord Methuen
TADDEO DI BARTOLO			
Virgin and Child, etc.	2.	123	Y. Ottley

	VOL. & PAGE	OWNER
TEMPESTA (Pieter Molyn)		
A Storm	2. 398	Lord Dudley
TENIERS, David		
Two Pictures	2. 403	Mr. Antis
Two small Pictures	3. 105	Lord Methuen
A Picture	3. 148	W. Acraman
TINTORETTO		
Doge Francesco Donati	2. 203	Sir Abraham Hume
Vesalius	3. 97	Lord Methuen
The Crucifixion	3. 99	,,
The Last Supper	3. 99	,,
TITIAN		
Repose of the Holy Family	1. 264	Mr. Wilkins
Mary Magdalen	2. 202	Sir Abraham Hume
Landscape with Virgin and Child, etc.	3. 35	Sir Thos. Baring
A Man, front view	3. 36	Sir Thos. Baring
Virgin and Child and Tabernacle	3. 101	Lord Methuen
Mary Magdalen	3. 102	,,
Ferdinand Cortez	3. 104	,,
TURCHI, A. (L'Orbetto)		
Murder of the Innocents	3. 93	Lord Methuen
UGOLINO, da Siena		
Panels from St. Croce at Florence	2. 121	Y. Ottley
VAN BASSEN, Bartholomeus		
A large Picture	3. 115	Fonthill
VAN BLES, Heinrich (Civetta)		
St. John Preaching	3. 124	Beckford, at Bath
VAN DE CAPELLA		
Agitated Sea	3. 115	Fonthill

	VOL. & PAGE		OWNER
VAN DER NEER, Artus			
A Sunset	2.	40	Lord Farnborough
Skaters on Canal	3.	127	Beckford, at Bath
VAN DE VELDE, Adrian			
Frozen Canal, Skating 1668	2.	17	Sir R. Peel
VAN DE VELDE, William			
Agitated Sea and Ships	1.	271	Duke of Devonshire
Naval Battle	2.	206	Sir Abraham Hume
A Storm at Sea, 1673	2.	403	Mr. Antis
Sea Piece	3.	104	Lord Methuen
Naval Battle	3.	104	Lord Methuen
VANDYCK			
Thomas Killigrew and Dog	1.	270	Duke of Devonshire
Belisarius	1.	270	Duke of Devonshire
Woman in black Silk	2.	204	Sir Abraham Hume
Anton Triest	2.	205	,,
St. Sebastian	2.	205	,,
Crucifixion (sketch)	2.	205	,,
Cæsar Alexander Scaglia	3.	44	Sir Thos. Baring
Virgin and Child and 5 Saints	3.	98	Lord Methuen
A Charity	3.	103	Lord Methuen
VAN EYCK, Jan			
Virgin and Child and Apple	1.	268	Duke of Devonshire
Altar Piece at Ghent	3.	20	Mr. Aders
Virgin and Child and Architecture	3.	22	Mr. Aders
St. Jerome in Study (called Dürer)	3.	42	Sir Thos. Baring
Twelve Miniatures (School of)	3.	117	Fonthill
A Male Portrait (School of)	3.	118	Fonthill
Prayer book, Mary of Burgundy (School of)	3.	178	Sir John Tobin
Roman Breviary (School of)	3.	176	,,
The Bedford Missal (School of)	3.	175	,,
VAN EYCK, Margaret			
Virgin and Child and St. Catherine	3.	21	Mr. Aders
VAN HUYSUM, J.			
Bouquet of Flowers	3.	128	Beckford, at Bath

	VOL. & PAGE	OWNER
VAN KESSEL, F.		
Two small Pictures	3. 116	Fonthill
A Picture	3. 128	Beckford, at Bath
VAN ORLEY, Bernard		
Female Portrait	1. 270	Duke of Devonshire
Cleopatra	1. 270	Duke of Devonshire
VELASQUEZ		
A Spanish General	3. 41	Sir Thos. Baring
VERONESE, Paul		
Martyrdom of St. Peter called Giorgione	1. 207	National Gallery
Procession of Doge's Wife	1. 266	Duke of Devonshire
History of Judith (4 pictures)	3. 102	Lord Methuen
VERONESE SCHOOL		
A Pope receives Nosegay	3. 118	Fonthill
VINCI, Leonardo da		
Mona Lisa (*copy*)	2. 203	Sir Abraham Hume
VINCKEBOOM, D.		
Two Stags in a Forest	3. 119	Fonthill
A Picture	3. 128	Beckford, at Bath
WATERLOO, A.		
A rich Landscape	3. 127	Beckford, at Bath
WEENIX, Jan Baptista		
Young Man and Dog, 1650	3. 97	Lord Methuen
WEST, Benjamin, P.R.A.		
A Picture	3. 148	W. Acraman
WESTALL, R., R.A.		
A Picture	3. 148	W. Acraman
WILKIE, Sir David, R.A.		
A Picture, 1827	2. 291	St. James's Palace
Princess Doria washing Feet, 1827	2. 291	"
Maid of Saragossa, 1827	2. 291	"

	VOL. & PAGE	OWNER
WILKIE, Sir David, R.A.—*continued*		
Guerilla receiving Absolution, 1827	2. 291	St. James's Palace
Visit of George IV to Holyrood, 1829	2. 292	,,
Return of wounded Guerilla, 1830	2. 292	,,
WILSON, Richard, R.A.		
Landscape with broad River	2. 403	Mr. Antis
WOUVERMANN, P.		
A Picture	3. 148	W. Acraman
WYNANTS, J.		
A large Landscape	3. 127	Beckford, at Bath
ZACHTLEVEN, Herman		
View of a Ruin	1. 342	Orleans Gallery
View of a Ruin	1. 342	Orleans Gallery

INDEX TO THE PORTRAITS
MENTIONED BY DR. WAAGEN
IN 1854–1857

	VOL. & PAGE	OWNER
ALCANTARA, Peter		
Velasquez	4. 471	Duke of Northumberland
ALENCON, François, Duc d'		
Clouet	3. 25	Earl of Darnley
Clouet	4. 263	Duc d'Aumale
ALEXANDER, Emperor of Russia		
Unknown	2. 277	Duke of Wellington
ALEXANDER VI, Pope		
Titian	2. 481	Charles I
ALTHAM, Mr. (Cousin to Sir Ralph Bankes)		
S. Rosa	4. 378	Kingston Lacy
ALVA, Duke of		
Rubens	4. 362	Lord Folkestone
ANDILLY, Robert Arnaud d'		
Champagne	3. 459	Earl Spencer
ANDRARA, Don Andrea di		
Murillo	2. 180	T. Baring
ANGELO, Michael		
Del Sarto	3. 176	Mr. Vivian
Del Sarto	3. 443	Mr. Tomline
ANGERSTEIN, John Julius		
Lawrence	1. 380	Marlborough House
ANGUISCIOLA, Sofonisba		
Anguisciola	3. 456	Earl Spencer
Anguisciola	4. 449	W. Stirling
ANNE OF DENMARK		
Van Somer	3. 219	Earl of Craven
ANNE OF CLEVES		
Van Orley	3. 456	Earl Spencer
ANSLO, Rainer		
Rembrandt	3. 27	Earl of Ashburnham

	VOL. & PAGE	OWNER
ARAGON, Joanna of		
Raphael	3. 213	Earl of Warwick
AREMBERG, Duke d'		
Vandyck	3. 420	Earl of Leicester
ARETINO, Peter		
Tintoretto	2. 496	Orleans Gallery
ARIOSTO		
Titian	3. 19	Earl of Darnley
ARNAULD, Catherine Agnès		
Champagne	4. 263	Duc d'Aumale
ARPINO, Cavaliere d'		
Arpino	4. 336	Duke of Bedford
ARUNDEL, Henry, Earl of		
Vandyck	3. 30	Duke of Norfolk
ARUNDEL, Thomas, Earl of		
Vandyck	2. 69	Duke of Sutherland
Mytens	2. 86	Duke of Norfolk
Vandyck	2. 455	Earl of Clarendon
Van Somer	3. 30	Duke of Norfolk
Vandyck	3. 31	Duke of Norfolk
Rubens	3. 213	Earl of Warwick
Rubens	3. 323	Earl of Carlisle
AUBIGNY, Catherine, Lady		
Vandyck	2. 457	Earl of Clarendon
AUSTRIA, Emperor Francis of		
Lawrence	2. 425	Windsor Castle
AUSTRIA, Archduke Albert of		
Rubens	2. 436	Windsor Castle
AUSTRIA, Archduke Charles of		
Lawrence	2. 424	Windsor Castle
AYLESBURY, Lord		
Jansen	3. 170	Earl of Suffolk

	VOL. & PAGE	OWNER
BACCELLI, Madame		
Reynolds	4. 339	Knole
BACON, Lord		
Van Somer	3. 17	Earl Cowper
BALACE, Sir John		
Vandyck	4. 375	Kingston Lacy
BALBI, Marchesa		
Vandyck	2. 200	R. S. Holford
BALDWIN, Mrs.		
Reynolds	3. 160	Marquis of Lansdowne
BALTHASAR, Don		
Velasquez	4. 81	Marquis of Hertford
Velasquez	4. 93	Marquis of Westminster
BALTIMORE, Lord		
Vandyck School	3. 340	Earl Fitzwilliam
BANKES, Jerome		
Stanzioni	4. 378	Kingston Lacy
BANKES, Miss		
Vandyck	4. 375	Kingston Lacy
Lely	4. 380	Kingston Lacy
BANKES, Mrs.		
Romney	4. 380	Kingston Lacy
BANKES, Sir Ralph		
Lely	4. 380	Kingston Lacy
BANNING, Lord		
Vandyck	4. 463	Lord Douglas
BARBERINI, Cardinal Antonio		
Domenichino	4. 152	Lady Waldegrave
Maratti	4. 471	Duke of Northumberland
BASSANO, Giacomo		
Bassano	4. 335	Duke of Bedford

	VOL. & PAGE	OWNER
BASSANO, Leandro		
Bassano	4. 336	Duke of Bedford
BATHURST, Allen, Earl		
Lawrence	2. 425	Windsor Castle
BEDFORD, Francis, 4th Earl of		
Vandyck	3. 464	Duke of Bedford
Vandyck	4. 334	Duke of Bedford
BEDFORD, William, 5th Earl of		
Vandyck	3. 458	Duke of Bedford
"	4. 334	Duke of Bedford
"	4. 517	Lord Galway
BEDFORD, William, 1st Duke of		
Gainsborough	4. 331	Duke of Bedford
Nollekens	3. 352	Duke of Devonshire
BEDFORD, John, Duke of		
Reynolds	3. 464	Duke of Bedford
Gainsborough	3. 130	Duke of Marlborough
BEDFORD, Anne Carr, Duchess of		
Vandyck	3. 458	Earl Spencer
"	3. 464	Duke of Bedford
"	4. 334	"
"	4. 334	"
BEDFORD, Gertrude, Duchess of		
Reynolds	3. 464	Duke of Bedford
BENEDICT XIV, Pope		
Subleyras	2. 66	Duke of Sutherland
BENTIVOGLIO, Cardinal		
Maratti	4. 495	Earl of Harrington
BERG, Henry, Count de		
Vandyck	2. 426	Windsor Castle
"	2. 455	Earl of Clarendon
"	4. 262	Duc d'Aumale

	VOL. & PAGE	OWNER
BERGHEM, Nicholas		
Rembrandt	2. 166	Marquis of Westminster
BEZA		
Holbein	4. 356	Lord Folkestone
BIANCHINI, Bartholomew		
Francia	3. 199	Lord Northwick
BLUCHER, Prince		
Lawrence	2. 424	Windsor Castle
BOHEMIA, Frederick, King of		
Jansen	2. 364	Hampton Court
Honthorst	3. 219	Earl of Craven
BOHEMIA, Elizabeth, Queen of		
Honthorst	2. 358	Hampton Court
„	2. 455	Earl of Clarendon
„	3. 219	Earl of Craven
Jansen	4. 495	Earl of Harrington
BOOTH, Benjamin		
Reynolds	2. 225	Richard Ford
BOOTHBY, " Prince "		
Reynolds	3. 40	Petworth
BOOYS, Henderakas du		
Vandyck	4. 520	Earl of Hardwicke
BORGHESE, Pauline		
Campbell	3. 367	Duke of Devonshire
BORGIA, Cæsar		
Correggio	2. 490	Orleans Gallery
Titian	3. 140	Earl of Radnor
Titian	4. 360	Lord Folkestone
BOURBON, Isabella of		
Pareja	4. 66	Earl of Yarborough
BOURBON, Philip of		
Pareja	4. 66	Earl of Yarborough

	VOL. & PAGE	OWNER
BOURGUIGNON, Le		
Bourguignon	3. 333	Meynell Ingram
BOUVERIE, Hon. Edward		
Gainsborough	4. 362	Lord Folkestone
BOUVERIE, Jacob		
Reynolds	4. 355	Lord Folkestone
BOUVERIE, Hon. W. H.		
Gainsborough	4. 362	Lord Folkestone
BRAHE, Tycho		
Unknown	4. 520	Earl of Hardwicke
BRAMANTE (Architect)		
Romano	4. 293	J. Sanders
BRANDON, Duke of (Children of)		
Holbein	2. 471	Charles I
BRANDON, Lady Eleanor		
De Heere	3. 342	W. V. Wentworth
BRANDT, Catherine		
Rubens	2. 86	Duke of Norfolk
„	4. 450	W. Stirling
„	4. 483	Matthew Anderson
BRISTOL, George Digby, Earl of		
Vandyck	3. 458	Earl Spencer
Vandyck	4. 334	Duke of Bedford
BROOKE, Lady		
Vandyck	3. 213	Earl of Warwick
BROUNCKER, William, Viscount		
Lely	3. 227	Lord Lyttelton
BRUDENELL Family, Admirals of		
Vandyck	3. 460	Duke of Buccleuch
BRUNSWICK, Duke of		
Mytens	2. 367	Hampton Court

	VOL. & PAGE	OWNER
BRUNSWICK, Duchess of		
Kauffmann	2. 368	Hampton Court
BUCCLEUCH, Charles, Duke of		
Reynolds	3. 313	Duke of Buccleuch
BUCCLEUCH, Elizabeth, Duchess of		
Reynolds	3. 313	Duke of Buccleuch
Reynolds	4. 436	Duke of Buccleuch
BUCER, Martin		
Titian	3. 334	Meynell Ingram
BUCKINGHAM, George Villiers, 1st Duke of		
Honthorst	2. 360	Hampton Court
Jansen	2. 456	Earl of Clarendon
Van Somer	3. 171	Earl of Suffolk
Rubens	4. 272	Earl of Jersey
Vandyck	4. 464	Lord Douglas
BUCKINGHAM, George Villiers, 2nd Duke of		
Knupfer	2. 360	Hampton Court
BUCKINGHAM, Duke of (Sons of)		
Vandyck	2. 483	Charles I
BUCKINGHAM, Catherine, Duchess of (Wife of 1st Duke)		
Vandyck	3. 123	Duke of Marlborough
„	4. 277	Sir C. Eardley
„	4. 517	Lord Galway
BUNBURY, Lady		
Reynolds	2. 152	Marquis of Lansdowne
BURLEIGH, William Cecil, Lord		
Garrard	3. 408	Marquis of Exeter
BURLINGTON, Earl of		
Gainsborough	4. 426	Earl of Burlington
BUTE, John, Earl of		
Reynolds	3. 485	Marquis of Bute

	VOL. & PAGE		OWNER
BUTE, Mary, Countess of			
Reynolds	3.	485	Marquis of Bute
BUTTS, Dr.			
More	3.	6	W. Fuller Maitland
BUTTS, Mrs.			
More	3.	6	W. Fuller Maitland
CÆSAR, Julius			
Titian	3.	443	Mr. Tomline
CALDERON			
Cano	4.	104	H. Labouchere
CALCOTT, Lady			
Calcott	2.	152	Marquis of Lansdowne
CALVIN			
Holbein	4.	356	Lord Folkestone
CAMBRIDGE, Duke of			
Lawrence	2.	425	Windsor Castle
CAMDEN, Marchioness			
Reynolds	3.	459	Earl Spencer
CANNING, Rt. Hon. George			
Lawrence	2.	425	Windsor Castle
Chantrey	3.	352	Duke of Devonshire
Chantrey	4.	428	Rev. Mr. Staniforth
CANOVA			
Canova	3.	366	Duke of Devonshire
CANTECROIX, Beatrice de Cusance, Princess of			
Vandyck	2.	428	Windsor Castle
CAPEL, Arthur, 1st Lord			
Vandyck	2.	454	Earl of Clarendon

	VOL. & PAGE	OWNER
CAPEL, Lady		
Vandyck	2. 454	Earl of Clarendon
CAPELLO, Bartolommeo		
Moretto	4. 498	W. Drury Lowe
CAPELLO, Admiral Nicola		
Tintoretto	3. 346	Duke of Devonshire
Tintoretto	4. 454	Earl of Dunmore
CAREW, Thomas		
Vandyck	2. 427	Windsor Castle
CAREW, Sir Nicholas		
Holbein	3. 313	Duke of Buccleuch
Holbein	4. 435	Duke of Buccleuch
CARIGNAN, Prince Thomas of		
Vandyck	2. 427	Windsor Castle
CAREY, Lady		
Holbein	4. 361	Lord Folkestone
CARLISLE, Frederick, Earl of		
Reynolds	3. 323	Earl of Carlisle
CARLISLE, Lucy Percy, Countess of		
Vandyck	2. 428	Windsor Castle
Vandyck	3. 43	Petworth
CARLISLE, Margaret, Countess of		
Vandyck	2. 94	Devonshire House
CASTIGLIONE, Count		
Titian	2. 497	Orleans Gallery
CASTLEREAGH, Lord		
Lawrence	2. 425	Windsor Castle
CATHERINE HOWARD		
Holbein	3. 170	Earl of Suffolk
CATHERINE PARR		
Holbein	3. 462	Glendon Hall

	VOL. & PAGE		OWNER
CATHERINE II, Empress of Russia			
Unknown	3.	305	Duke of Hamilton
CAVENDISH, Lord George			
Nollekens	3.	352	Duke of Devonshire
CAVENDISH, Lord Richard			
Reynolds	2.	96	Devonshire House
Reynolds	4.	514	Duke of Portland
CENCI, Beatrice			
Guercino	2.	36	Bridgewater House
CHARLES I			
Vandyck	2.	3	Buckingham Palace
Mytens	2.	4	,,
Jansen	2.	4	,,
Vandyck	2.	85	Earl de Grey
Petitot	2.	97	Miss Burdett Coutts
Vandyck	2.	103	Lord Ashburton
,,	2.	277	Duke of Wellington
,,	2.	357	Hampton Court
,,	2.	426	Windsor Castle
,,	2.	428	,,
,,	2.	429	,,
,,	2.	457	Earl of Clarendon
,,	2.	469	Charles I
,,	2.	470	,,
,,	2.	470	,,
,,	2.	470	,,
,,	2.	483	,,
,,	2.	500	Orleans Gallery
,,	2.	500	Orleans Gallery
,,	3.	29	Duke of Norfolk
,,	3.	129	Duke of Marlborough
,,	3.	129	Duke of Marlborough
,,	3.	153	Earl of Pembroke
Jansen	3.	170	Earl of Suffolk
Rubens	3.	214	Earl of Warwick
Honthorst	3.	219	Earl of Craven
Vandyck	3.	290	M'Lellan Gallery
Vandyck	3.	297	Duke of Hamilton
Stone	3.	322	Earl of Carlisle
Jansen	3.	346	Duke of Devonshire
Vandyck	4.	87	Marquis of Hertford

R R

	VOL. & PAGE	OWNER
CHARLES I—*continued*		
Coques	4. 179	Rev. Mr. Townshend
Vandyck	4. 235	Earl of Harrington
Lely	4. 266	Duke of Northumberland
Vandyck	4. 309	J. Morrison
,,	4. 334	Duke of Bedford
,,	4. 375	Kingston Lacy
Mytens	4. 454	Earl of Dunmore
Vandyck	4. 463	Lord Douglas
Jansen	4. 498	W. Drury Lowe
Vandyck	4. 512	Duke of Portland
Mytens	4. 516	Lord Galway
Vandyck	4. 516	Lord Galway
CHARLES I, Children of		
Vandyck	2. 103	Lord Ashburton
,,	2. 428	Windsor Castle
,,	2. 457	Earl of Clarendon
,,	2. 470	Charles I
,,	2. 483	Charles I
Lely	3. 37	Petworth
Vandyck	3. 154	Earl of Pembroke
,,	4. 238	Earl of Harrington
,,	4. 375	Kingston Lacy
CHARLES II		
Petitot	2. 97	Miss Burdett Coutts
Vandyck	2. 428	Windsor Castle
,,	2. 429	Windsor Castle
,,	2. 483	Charles I
Dobson	3. 219	Earl of Craven
Lely	4. 234	Earl of Harrington
CHARLES V, Emperor of Germany		
Van Orley	2. 270	Miss Rogers
More	2. 432	Windsor Castle
Titian	2. 481	Charles I
,,	2. 484	Charles I
,,	2. 497	Orleans Gallery
,,	3. 440	Mr. Tomline
,,	4. 95	T. Baring
Rubens	4. 111	J. Morrison
Netherlandish School	4. 478	J. Anderson

	VOL. & PAGE	OWNER
CHARLES V, Wife of		
Titian	2. 481	Charles I
CHARLES IX of France		
Zucchero	3. 151	Earl of Pembroke
CHARLES V of France, Leonora, Sister of		
Clouet	4. 263	Duc d'Aumale
CHARLES IX, Queen of		
Clouet	4. 263	Duc d'Aumale
CHARLOTTE, Queen		
Reynolds	4. 266	Duke of Northumberland
CHATHAM, Lady		
Gainsborough	3. 443	Mr. Tomline
CHÂTILLON, Cardinal de		
Primaticcio	4. 261	Duc d'Aumale
CHESTERFIELD, Philip, Earl of		
Hoare	4. 495	Earl of Harrington
CHESTERFIELD, Catharine, Countess of		
Vandyck	3. 123	Duke of Marlborough
Vandyck	4. 362	Lord Folkestone
CHEVREUX, Duchesse de		
Netscher	4. 237	Earl of Harrington
CHILD, Mr.		
Reynolds	4. 273	Earl of Jersey
CHILD, Mrs.		
Reynolds	4. 273	Earl of Jersey
CHRISTIAN IV of Denmark		
Van Somer	2. 357	Hampton Court
CLANWILLIAM, Lord		
Lawrence	2. 72	Duke of Sutherland

	VOL. & PAGE	OWNER
CLANWILLIAM, Countess of		
Reynolds	3. 26	Earl of Darnley
CLARA, Eugenia Isabella		
Pourbus	2. 367	Hampton Court
Vandyck	3. 310	Earl of Hopetoun
CLARENDON, Edward Hyde, Earl of		
Lely	2. 457	Earl of Clarendon
CLARENDON, Anne Hyde, Countess of		
Netscher	4. 237	Earl of Harrington
CLEMENT VII, Pope		
Titian	2. 32	Bridgewater House
Titian	2. 497	Orleans Gallery
Piombo	3. 303	Duke of Hamilton
Piombo	4. 62	Lord Elcho
CLEVE, Philipes de, Sr. de Ravenstein		
Pourbus	2. 73	Duke of Sutherland
CLEVELAND, Thomas Wentworth, Duke of		
Lely	4. 339	Knole
Vandyck	4. 322	Lord Enfield
CLEVELAND (Poet)		
Dobson	2, 53	Bridgewater House
CLIVE, Lord		
Reynolds	2. 53	Bridgewater House
COLBERT, Jean Baptist		
Champagne	4. 335	Duke of Bedford
COLE, Lady Frances		
Reynolds	3. 26	Earl of Darnley
CONDÉ, Prince de		
	4. 264	Duc d'Aumale
COPPENOL, Lieven Van		
Rembrandt	2. 103	Lord Ashburton

	VOL. & PAGE		OWNER
CORNARO, Catherine			
Veronese	4.	101	R. S. Holford
CORNBURY, Henry Lord			
Lely	2.	454	Earl of Clarendon
COSMO I			
Bronzino	3.	302	Duke of Hamilton
COSMO I, Isabella, Wife of			
Bronzino	3.	302	Duke of Hamilton
COTTERELL, Sir Charles			
Dobson	1.	394	Duke of Northumberland
COUTTS, Miss Burdett			
Unknown	2.	97	Miss Burdett Coutts
CRAVEN, William, Earl of			
Vandyck	3.	219	Earl of Craven
CROFT, Mr.			
Reynolds	4.	330	Sir T. Sebright
CROFT, Mrs.			
Reynolds	4.	330	Sir T. Sebright
CROMWELL, Thomas, Lord			
Holbein	3.	152	Earl of Pembroke
Holbein	4.	464	Lord Douglas
CROMWELL, Oliver			
Walker	3.	216	Earl of Warwick
Walker	3.	342	W. V. Wentworth
Unknown	3.	436	Earl of Orford
Walker	4.	450	W. Stirling
CUMBERLAND, William, Duke of			
Reynolds	2.	424	Windsor Castle
CUYP, Albert			
Cuyp	4.	336	Duke of Bedford

	VOL. & PAGE	OWNER
DARBY, Miss Elizabeth (lady with letter)		
Reynolds	3. 40	Petworth
DARNLEY, Lord		
De Heere	2. 363	Hampton Court
DENNY, Sir Anthony		
Holbein	3. 139	Earl of Radnor
Holbein	4. 355	Lord Folkestone
DERBY, James, 7th Earl of		
Vandyck	2. 455	Earl of Clarendon
DESCARTES		
Mignard	3. 323	Earl of Carlisle
Unknown	4. 440	Earl of Wemyss
DEVONSHIRE, Earl of		
Vandyck	3. 364	Duke of Devonshire
DEVONSHIRE, Duke of		
Lawrence	3. 325	Earl of Carlisle
Unknown	3. 352	Duke of Devonshire
Unknown	3. 366	,,
DEVONSHIRE, Georgiana, Duchess of		
Reynolds	2. 96	Devonshire House
Reynolds	3. 352	Duke of Devonshire
DEVONSHIRE, Christiana, Countess of		
Vandyck	3. 364	Duke of Devonshire
DE WAEL, Family of		
Vandyck	3. 222	Howard Galton
DIGBY, Sir Kenelm		
Oliver	2. 96	Miss Burdett Coutts
Vandyck	2. 428	Windsor Castle
Vandyck	4. 513	Duke of Portland
DIGBY, Venetia, Lady		
Oliver	2. 96	Miss Burdett Coutts
· Vandyck	2. 427	Windsor Castle
,,	2. 483	Charles I
,,	4. 513	Duke of Portland

	VOL. & PAGE	OWNER
DOBSON, William		
Dobson	1. 394	Duke of Northumberland
Dobson	4. 341	Knole
DOLCE, Carlo		
Dolce	4. 357	Lord Folkestone
DONATI, Doge Francesco		
Tintoretto	2. 314	Earl Brownlow
DORIA, Andrea		
Piombo	4. 498	W. Drury Lowe
DORSET, Earl of		
Vandyck	3. 264	Earl of Lonsdale
DORSET, John, 3rd Duke of		
Reynolds	4. 338	Knole
DORSET, Frances, Countess of		
Vandyck	4. 339	Knole
DORSET, Mary, Countess of		
Vandyck	2. 429	Windsor Castle
DOUGLAS, Margaret, Duchess of		
Reynolds	4. 463	Lord Douglas
DOW, Gerard		
G. Dow	1. 355	National Gallery
Rembrandt	4. 336	Duke of Bedford
DU QUESNOY (Sculptor)		
N. Poussin	3. 16	Earl Cowper
DÜRER, Albert		
Dürer	3. 298	Duke of Hamilton

	VOL. & PAGE	OWNER
EARDLEY, Lord		
West	4. 281	Sir C. Eardley
Battoni	4. 284	Sir C. Eardley
EARDLEY, Lady		
Reynolds	4. 281	Sir C. Eardley
EARDLEY, Sir Culling		
Röting	4. 281	Sir C. Eardley
EBOLI, Princess		
Titian	2. 497	Orleans Gallery
EDWARD VI		
Holbein	2. 431	Windsor Castle
„	3. 36	Petworth
„	3. 140	Earl of Radnor
„	3. 152	Earl of Pembroke
„	3. 301	Duke of Hamilton
„	3. 407	Marquis of Exeter
More	3. 429	A. Fountaine
Unknown	3. 436	Earl of Orford
Holbein	4. 67	Earl of Yarborough
Holbein	4. 269	Duke of Northumberland
ELISON, Rev. John		
Rembrandt	3. 432	Rev. Mr. Colby
ELISON, Mrs. John, 1634		
Rembrandt	3. 432	Rev. Mr. Colby
ELIZABETH, Queen		
Unknown	2. 361	Hampton Court
Zucchero	2. 361	Hampton Court
Holbein	2. 472	Charles I
Garrard	3. 407	Marquis of Exeter
More	3. 429	A. Fountaine
Garrard	4. 269	Duke of Northumberland
Zucchero	4. 358	Lord Folkestone
EPERNON, Duke of		
Vandyck	3. 154	Earl of Pembroke
ERASMUS		
Holbein	2. 363	Hampton Court
Holbein	2. 364	Hampton Court

	VOL. & PAGE		OWNER
Pens	2.	430	Windsor Castle
Holbein	2.	471	Charles I
Pens	2.	474	Charles I
Holbein	3.	138	Earl of Radnor
„	4.	356	Lord Folkestone
„	4.	464	Lord Douglas

ESSEX, Earl of

More	2.	87	Earl of Yarborough
Gorzius	3.	210	Lord Northwick
Zucchero	3.	215	Earl of Warwick
Zucchero	3.	342	W. V. Wentworth
Garrard	3.	408	Marquis of Exeter
More	4.	64	Earl of Yarborough

FALKLAND, Lucius Cary, Lord

Vandyck	2.	455	Earl of Clarendon

FANE, Mr.

Reynolds	3.	411	Earl of Westmoreland

FANE, Lady Rachel

Vandyck	3.	410	Earl of Westmoreland

FARNESE, Alessandro

Susterman	3.	269	Edinburgh R.I.

FAURA, Francisco de

Espinosa	4.	382	Kingston Lacy

FEDE, Lucretia

Sarto	3.	382	Earl of Shrewsbury

FERDINAND, Infant Cardinal Don

Vandyck	2.	456	Earl of Clarendon
Velasquez	3.	221	Howard Galton
Rubens	3.	458	Earl Spencer
Crayer	4.	449	W. Stirling

FERRARA, Duke Alfonso of

Dossi	2.	196	R. S. Holford
Tintoretto	2.	496	Orleans Gallery
Tintoretto	3.	320	Earl of Carlisle

S S

	VOL. & PAGE	OWNER
FISCHER (the Composer)		
Gainsborough	2. 369	Hampton Court
FISHER, John, Bishop of Rochester		
Holbein	3. 210	Lord Northwick
FISHER, Kitty		
Reynolds	2. 152	Marquis of Lansdowne
FITZWILLIAM, Earl		
Reynolds	3. 339	Earl Fitzwilliam
Lawrence	3. 339	Earl Fitzwilliam
FITZWILLIAM, Countess		
Reynolds	3. 339	Earl Fitzwilliam
FLAXMAN, J., R.A.		
Jackson	2. 152	Marquis of Lansdowne
Jackson	2. 335	Lady Dover
Essex	4. 112	J. Morrison
FLEMING, Lady		
Reynolds	4. 495	Earl of Harrington
FOIX, Gaston de		
Giorgione	2. 491	Orleans Gallery
FORMANN, Helena		
Rubens	2. 435	Windsor Castle
Rubens	3. 126	Duke of Marlborough
FORNARINA, La		
Raphael	3. 443	Mr. Tomline
FOX, Charles James		
Nollekens	3. 352	Duke of Devonshire
FRANCIS I of France		
Clouet	2. 236	Lord Ward
Titian	3. 441	Mr. Tomline
FRANCIS I (Leonora, 1st wife of)		
Clouet	2. 363	Hampton Court
Clouet	4. 263	Duc d'Aumale

	VOL. & PAGE	OWNER
FRANCIS II of France		
Clouet	2. 363	Hampton Court
Zucchero	3. 151	Earl of Pembroke
Janet	3. 457	Earl Spencer
FREDERICK THE GREAT		
Pesne	2. 368	Hampton Court
FROBENIUS, Joannes		
Holbein	2. 363	Hampton Court
Holbein	2. 471	Charles I
GAGE, Lord		
Gainsborough	4. 282	Sir C. Eardley
GALILEO		
Sustermans	4. 397	Lord Methuen
GARRICK, David		
Reynolds	2. 152	Marquis of Lansdowne
„	4. 233	General Fox
„	4. 336	Duke of Bedford
„	4. 341	Knole
„	4. 370	Earl of Normanton
GELDERN, Prince Adolphus of		
Rembrandt	3. 308	Duke of Hamilton
GENTZ, M. Von		
Lawrence	2. 413	Hampton Court
Lawrence	2. 425	Windsor Castle
GEORGE IV		
Wilkie	2. 277	Duke of Wellington
Lawrence	2. 425	Windsor Castle
Wilkie	3. 313	Duke of Buccleuch
Lawrence	4. 338	Knole
Wilkie	4. 435	Duke of Buccleuch
GERBIER, Sir Balthasar		
Dobson	1. 394	Duke of Northumberland
Rubens	2. 437	Windsor Castle

	VOL. & PAGE	OWNER
GERMAIN, Lord George		
Gainsborough	4. 338	Knole
GEVARTIUS		
Vandyck	1. 351	National Gallery
GHENT, Bishop of		
Vandyck	2. 86	Duke of Norfolk
GILLY, Mr.		
Lely	4. 380	Kingston Lacy
GLOUCESTER, Duke of		
Lely	3. 340	Earl Fitzwilliam
Lely	3. 378	W. Davenport Bromley
GLOUCESTER, Maria Duchess of		
Reynolds	4. 152	Lady Waldegrave
Reynolds	4. 348	Vernon Harcourt
GOLDSMITH, Oliver		
Reynolds	4. 336	Duke of Bedford
Reynolds	4. 341	Knole
GONSALVI, Cardinal		
Lawrence	2. 425	Windsor Castle
Lawrence	3. 193	Mr. Harford
Thorwaldsen	3. 366	Duke of Devonshire
GOODWIN, Arthur		
Vandyck	3. 364	Duke of Devonshire
GORDON HEADS		
Reynolds	1. 365	Marlborough House
GORING, Lord		
Vandyck	2. 458	Earl of Clarendon
GRAHAM, Hon. Mrs.		
Gainsborough	4. 434	Robert Graham
GRANBY, Marquis of		
Reynolds	3. 41	Petworth

	VOL. & PAGE	OWNER
GRANDISON, William, Lord		
Vandyck	2. 456	Earl of Clarendon
GREGORY, Pope		
Titian	3. 125	Duke of Marlborough
GRESHAM, Sir Thomas		
More	2. 246	Joseph Neeld
Holbein	4. 272	Earl of Jersey
GREY, Lady Jane		
Holbein	4. 364	Earl of Normanton
GRIFFINDORP, Hans Van		
Cranach	2. 469	Charles I
GRIGNON, Madame de		
Petitot	4. 213	Mr. Henderson
GRIMALDI, Marchesa Maria Princess		
Rubens	4. 375	Kingston Lacy
GRITTI, Doge		
Titian	2. 481	Charles I
GROTIUS, Hugo		
Vandyck	2. 225	Richard Ford
Rubens	3. 171	Lord Arundel
GUASTO, Marquis del		
Titian	2. 414	Hampton Court
Titian	2. 481	Charles I
GUERCINO		
Guercino	4. 336	Duke of Bedford
GUILDFORD, Sir Henry		
Holbein	2. 362	Hampton Court
Holbein	2. 430	Windsor Castle
GUISE, Henry, Duc de		
Pourbus	3. 457	Earl Spencer

	VOL. & PAGE	OWNER
GUSMAN, Don		
Mytens	2. 368	Hampton Court
GWYN, Miss		
Reynolds	4. 372	Earl of Normanton
GWYN, Nell		
Lely	4. 463	Lord Douglas
GYSSET		
Holbein	2. 500	Orleans Gallery
HALS, Franz		
Hals	4. 335	Duke of Bedford
HAMILTON, James, Marquis of		
Mytens	2. 355	Hampton Court
Vandyck	3. 308	Duke of Hamilton
Mytens	3. 311	Earl of Hopetoun
HAMILTON, Duke and Duchess of		
Reynolds	3. 220	Howard Galton
HAMILTON, Sir William		
Reynolds	1. 365	Marlborough House
HAMILTON, Duchess of		
Vandyck	3. 308	Duke of Hamilton
HAMILTON, Emma, Lady		
Romney	1. 369	Marlborough House
Romney	4. 104	H. Labouchere
Reynolds	4. 371	Earl of Normanton
Romney	4. 372	Earl of Normanton
HANDEL		
Denner	4. 341	Knole
HARCOURT, Simon Earl		
Reynolds	4. 352	Vernon Harcourt

	VOL. & PAGE		OWNER

HARCOURT, Mary, Countess of
| Reynolds | 4. | 349 | Vernon Harcourt |

HARCOURT FAMILY
| Reynolds | 4. | 348 | Vernon Harcourt |

HARDENBERG, Prince
| Lawrence | 2. | 425 | Windsor Castle |

HARDWICKE, Earl of
| Lawrence | 4. | 518 | Earl of Hardwicke |

HARDWICKE, Philip, 2nd Lord
| Reynolds | 4. | 523 | Earl of Hardwicke |

HARFORD, Mr.
| Lawrence | 3. | 193 | Mr. Harford |

HARFORD, Mrs.
| Lawrence | 3. | 191 | Mr. Harford |

HARRINGTON, 1st Earl of
| Reynolds | 4. | 496 | Earl of Harrington |

HARRINGTON, Jane, Countess of
| Reynolds | 4. | 236 | Earl of Harrington |
| Reynolds | 4. | 495 | Earl of Harrington |

HEATHFIELD, Lord
| Reynolds | 1. | 365 | Marlborough House |

HENRIETTA, Maria
Vandyck	2.	85	Earl de Grey
"	2.	103	Lord Ashburton
"	2.	151	Marquis of Lansdowne
"	2.	427	Windsor Castle
"	2.	427	"
"	2.	428	"
"	2.	456	Earl of Clarendon
"	2.	470	Charles I
"	2.	483	"
"	2.	483	"
"	2.	483	"
"	3.	30	Duke of Norfolk

	VOL. & PAGE		OWNER
HENRIETTA, Maria—*continued*			
Vandyck	3.	122	Duke of Marlborough
,,	3.	129	Duke of Marlborough
,,	3.	154	Earl of Pembroke
,,	3.	213	Earl of Warwick
,,	3.	227	Lord Lyttelton
,,	3.	290	M'Lellan Gallery
,,	3.	291	M'Lellan Gallery
,,	3.	314	Duke of Buccleuch
,,	3.	338	Earl Fitzwilliam
,,	3.	340	Earl Fitzwilliam
,,	4.	87	Marquis of Hertford
Coques	4.	179	Rev. Mr. Townshend
Vandyck	4.	235	Earl of Harrington
,,	4.	334	Duke of Bedford
,,	4.	347	Vernon Harcourt
,,	4.	375	Kingston Lacy
Mytens	4.	454	Earl of Dunmore
Vandyck	4.	457	Earl of Dunmore
Vandyck	4.	463	Lord Douglas
Mytens	4.	516	Lord Galway
HENRY VII			
Remée (after Holbein)	2.	413	Hampton Court
Torregiano	4.	269	Duke of Northumberland
HENRY VII, Children of			
Mabuse	2.	364	Hampton Court
,,	2.	472	Charles I
,,	3.	152	Earl of Pembroke
,,	4.	358	Lord Folkestone
,,	4.	395	Lord Methuen
HENRY VIII			
Holbein	2.	241	Henry Danby Seymour
,,	2.	362	Hampton Court
,,	2.	366	,,
,,	2.	413	,,
,,	2.	432	Windsor Castle
,,	2.	471	Charles I
,,	2.	471	,,
,,	2.	472	,,
,,	3.	41	Petworth

T T

	VOL. & PAGE	OWNER
HONTHORST, Gerard		
Honthorst	3. 219	Earl of Craven
HOOGH, Catherine		
Rembrandt	2. 336	Edmund Higginson
HOWARD, Mrs.		
Vandyck	4. 464	Lord Douglas
HOWARD, Henry		
Vandyck	3. 31	Duke of Norfolk
HUDDESFORD, Mrs. (called Hudspath)		
Reynolds	4. 479	J. Anderson
HUMBOLDT, Alexander Von		
Pickersgill	4. 303	J. Morrison
HUMBOLDT, William Von		
Lawrence	2. 425	Windsor Castle
HUNTER, Dr.		
Reynolds	3. 283	Glasgow College
ILCHESTER, Countess of		
Reynolds	2. 153	Marquis of Lansdowne
INCHBALD, Mrs.		
Reynolds	4. 371	Earl of Normanton
INNOCENT X, Pope		
Velasquez	2. 151	Marquis of Lansdowne
"	2. 242	H. Danby Seymour
"	2. 277	Duke of Wellington
"	3. 484	Marquis of Bute
IRVINE, Charles Ingram, 9th Viscount		
Reynolds	3. 333	Meynell Ingram
IRVINE, Viscountess		
Reynolds	3. 333	Meynell Ingram

	VOL. & PAGE	OWNER
ISTRIAS, Count Capa d'		
Lawrence	2. 425	Windsor Castle
JAMES I		
Van Somer	3. 219	Earl of Craven
Vandyck	4. 463	Lord Douglas
JAMES II		
Petitot	2. 97	Miss Burdett Coutts
JAMES, King of Scotland		
Holbein	3. 482	Marquis of Bute
JANSEN, Cornelius		
Jansen	4. 356	Lord Folkestone
JENKINSON, Lady		
Lely	4. 380	Kingston Lacy
JENKINSON (afterwards Earl of Liverpool)		
Reynolds	3. 485	Marquis of Bute
JOHNSON, Dr. Samuel		
Reynolds	2. 72	Duke of Sutherland
"	4. 106	James Morrison
"	4. 341	Knole
JULIUS II, Pope		
Raphael	1. 324	National Gallery
"	2. 494	Orleans Gallery
"	3. 184	J. P. Miles
Romano	3. 383	Earl of Shrewsbury
KEMBLE, J. P.		
Lawrence	1. 380	Marlborough House
KILLIGREW, Mrs. Anne		
Lely	3. 128	Duke of Marlborough

	VOL. & PAGE	OWNER
KILLIGREW, Thomas		
Vandyck	2. 427	Windsor Castle
KINNOUL, George, Earl of		
Vandyck	2. 456	Earl of Clarendon
KIRK, Madame		
Vandyck	2. 85	Earl de Grey
KNELLER, Sir Godfrey		
Kneller	4. 335	Duke of Bedford
KRATZER, Nicholas		
Holbein	4. 516	Lord Galway
LAMBERT, General		
Walker	4. 522	Earl of Hardwicke
LANFRANCO		
Lanfranco	4. 335	Duke of Bedford
LANIERE, Nicholaus		
Vandyck	2. 470	Charles 1
LANSDOWNE, 1st Marquis of		
Reynolds	3. 166	Marquis of Lansdowne
LANSDOWNE, 2nd Marquis of		
Lawrence	2. 153	Marquis of Lansdowne
LANSDOWNE, Marchioness of		
Lawrence	3. 166	Marquis of Lansdowne
LAUD, Archbishop		
Vandyck	3. 340	Earl Fitzwilliam
Vandyck	4. 513	Duke of Portland
LE CLERC		
Vandyck	2. 315	Earl Brownlow
LEICESTER, Earl of, Children of		
Lely	3. 460	Duke of Buccleuch

	VOL. & PAGE	OWNER
LEICESTER, Dorothy Percy Countess of		
Vandyck	3. 43	Petworth
LELY, Sir Peter		
Lely	4. 361	Lord Folkestone
LEMAN, Mrs. Margaret		
Vandyck	2. 483	Charles I
LENNOX, Duke of		
Vandyck	3. 24	Earl of Darnley
LEO X, Pope		
Raphael	3. 420	Earl of Leicester
LE ROY, Philip		
Vandyck	2. 157	Marquis of Hertford
LE ROY, Madame		
Vandyck	2. 157	Marquis of Hertford
LETITIA, Madame		
Canova	3. 365	Duke of Devonshire
LINDSAY, Lord		
Vandyck	4. 462	Lord Douglas
LINLEY, Miss		
Reynolds	4. 462	M'Lellan Gallery
LINLEY, William		
Lawrence	2. 348	Dulwich
LIVERPOOL, Earl of		
Lawrence	2. 425	Windsor Castle
LOMELLINI FAMILY		
Vandyck	3. 268	Edinburgh R.I.
LONG, Lady Tilney		
Reynolds	4. 362	Lord Folkestone
LOUIS XII		
Fouquet	2. 422	H. Labouchere

	VOL. & PAGE	OWNER
LOUIS XIV		
Kneller	2. 368	Hampton Court
LOUIS XIV, Queen of		
Petitot	4. 264	Duc d'Aumale
LOUIS XV		
Rigaud	3. 434	Earl of Orford
Rigaud	4. 263	Duc d'Aumale
LOWTHER, Sir William		
Reynolds	4. 422	Earl of Burlington
LOYOLA, Ignatius		
Rubens	3. 214	Earl of Warwick
LUTHER, Martin		
Cranach	2. 469	Charles I
Holbein	3. 139	Earl of Radnor
Cranach	3. 219	Earl of Craven
Cranach	3. 407	Marquis of Exeter
Holbein	4. 360	Lord Folkestone
LYNDHURST, Lady		
Wilkie	2. 277	Duke of Wellington
LYTTELTON, Sir Thomas		
Van Somer	3. 227	Lord Lyttelton
MACCHIAVELLI		
Titian	3. 214	Earl of Warwick
McGILL, Miss		
Gainsborough	3. 26	Earl of Darnley
MAINWARING, Sir Thomas		
Vandyck	3. 130	Duke of Marlborough
MALLORY, Charles		
Vandyck	2. 85	Earl De Grey
Vandyck	4. 335	Duke of Bedford

	VOL. & PAGE	OWNER
MANTUA, Brother of the Duke of,		
Rubens	2. 477	Charles I
MANTUA, Marchioness of		
Titian	2. 481	Charles I
MARGARET, Queen (Wife of James IV of Scotland)		
Holbein	3. 482	Marquis of Bute
MARGARET OF VALOIS		
Holbein	3. 236	Liverpool R.I.
MARLBOROUGH, Charles, Duke of		
Reynolds	3. 130	Duke of Marlborough
MARLBOROUGH, John, Duke of		
Kneller	4. 495	Earl of Harrington
MARLBOROUGH, Sarah, Duchess of		
Kneller	3. 122	Duke of Marlborough
Kneller	4. 433	Gibson Craig
MARY I		
De Heere	2. 421	H. Labouchere
Unknown	2. 431	Windsor Castle
More	2. 473	Charles I
More	3. 323	Earl of Carlisle
Holbein	3. 456	Earl Spencer
More	3. 464	Duke of Bedford
More	4. 65	Earl of Yarborough
Holbein	4. 119	C. S. Bale
More	4. 336	Duke of Bedford
More	4. 337	Duke of Bedford
MARY II		
Netscher	4. 358	Lord Folkestone
MARY, Princess		
Vandyck	4. 364	Earl of Normanton
MAURICE, Prince		
Vandyck	3. 219	Earl of Craven

	VOL. & PAGE	OWNER
MAXIMILIAN I, Emperor		
Unknown	2. 335	Sir Charles Burrell
Dürer	3. 210	Lord Northwick
Unknown	3. 334	Charles Wynn
MAZARIN, Cardinal Hippolito		
Del Piombo	1. 333	National Gallery
Champagne	4. 263	Duc d'Aumale
MEDICI, Alessandro de		
Pontormo	2. 232	Lord Ward
MEDICI, Cardinal de		
Titian	3. 42	Petworth
MEDICI, Catherine de		
Rubens	3. 126	Duke of Marlborough
Clouet	3. 322	Earl of Carlisle
MEDICI, Gaston de		
Pontormo	3. 302	Duke of Hamilton
MEDICI, Giuliano de		
Romano	4. 466	Duke of Northumberland
MEDICI, Mary de		
Vandyck	2. 470	Charles I
Rubens	4. 362	Lord Folkestone
MELANCHTHON		
Cranach	3. 219	Earl of Craven
METTERNICH, Prince		
Lawrence	2. 425	Windsor Castle
MIDDLETON, Sir Hugh		
Vandyck	4. 512	Duke of Portland
MIDDLETON, Lady		
Lely	4. 380	Kingston Lacy
MILAN, Christine, Duchess of		
Holbein	3. 29	Duke of Norfolk

	VOL. & PAGE	OWNER
MILTON, John		
Dobson	3. 221	Howard Galton
MINNES, Sir John		
Vandyck	2. 456	Earl of Clarendon
MIRABELLA, Davilla, Marquis of		
Vandyck	3. 214	Earl of Warwick
MIRÆUS, Aubertus		
Vandyck	3. 464	Duke of Bedford
Vandyck	4. 334	Duke of Bedford
MIRANDOLA, Pico di		
Giorgione	2. 491	Orleans Gallery
MIREVELDT, Michael		
Mireveldt	4. 335	Duke of Bedford
MONK, General		
Unknown	2. 97	Miss Burdett Coutts
MONK, Mrs. D.		
Reynolds	3. 26	Earl of Darnley
MONMOUTH, Duke of		
Vandyck	3. 313	Duke of Buccleuch
MONMOUTH, Countess of		
Vandyck	4. 362	Lord Folkestone
MONTAGU, John, 2nd Duke of		
Gainsborough	3. 313	Duke of Buccleuch
Gainsborough	4. 436	Duke of Buccleuch
MONTAGU, Duchess of		
Gainsborough	3. 313	Duke of Buccleuch
Gainsborough	4. 436	Duke of Buccleuch
MONTANSIER, Julie d'Angennes, Duchess of		
Mignard	3. 459	Earl Spencer
MONTESPAN, Duchess of		
Boucher	2. 128	Alexander Barker

U U

	VOL. & PAGE	OWNER
MORE, Sir Antonio		
More	2. 327	Society of Antiquaries
More	3. 457	Earl Spencer
MORE, Sir John		
Holbein	3. 152	Earl of Pembroke
MORE, Sir Thomas		
Holbein	2. 471	Charles I
"	3. 252	Blundell Weld
"	3. 334	Charles Wynn
"	4. 464	Lord Douglas
MORTON, Countess of		
Lely	3. 128	Duke of Marlborough
MOSAICO, Don Francesca del		
Titian	3. 19	Earl of Darnley
MOWBRAY, James Howard, Lord		
Vandyck	3. 30	Duke of Norfolk
MURILLO, B. E.		
Murillo	3. 42	Petworth
Murillo	4. 336	Duke of Bedford
Tobar	4. 450	W. Stirling
MYTENS, Daniel		
Vandyck	3. 464	Duke of Bedford
Vandyck	4. 335	Duke of Bedford
MYTENS, Mrs.		
Vandyck	3. 464	Duke of Bedford
Vandyck	4. 335	Duke of Bedford
NAPOLEON I		
David	3. 298	Duke of Hamilton
Colossal Bust	3. 365	Duke of Devonshire
Wilkie	4. 184	W. Marshall
NASSAU, Count of		
Titian	3. 177	Mr. Vivian

	VOL. & PAGE	OWNER
NASSAU, John, Count of		
Vandyck	2. 103	Lord Ashburton
Vandyck	3. 16	Earl Cowper
NAVAGERO, Andrea		
Titian	2. 313	Earl Brownlow
NELSON, Lord		
Reynolds	4. 372	Earl of Normanton
NESBITT, Mrs.		
Reynolds	2. 229	Hon. E. Phipps
NESSELRODE, Count		
Lawrence	2. 425	Windsor Castle
NEVILL, Lady Dorothy		
Jansen	3. 408	Marquis of Exeter
NEWCASTLE, William Cavendish, Duke of		
Vandyck	2. 457	Earl of Clarendon
„	3. 406	Marquis of Exeter
„	3. 459	Earl Spencer
NEWPORT, Montjoy Blount, Earl of		
Vandyck	3. 34	Petworth
NEWPORT, Diana Russell, Lady		
Lely	2. 455	Earl of Clarendon
NICHOLAS, Emperor		
Rauch	3. 352	Duke of Devonshire
NORFOLK, Thomas Howard, Earl of		
Holbein	3. 323	Earl of Carlisle
NORFOLK, Thomas, 3rd Duke of		
Holbein	2. 86	Duke of Norfolk
Holbein	2. 430	Windsor Castle
Vandyck	3. 30	Duke of Norfolk
Holbein	3. 323	Earl of Carlisle
„	3. 30	Duke of Norfolk
„	4. 358	Lord Folkestone

	VOL. & PAGE	OWNER
NORFOLK, Duchess of		
Lawrence	3. 30	Duke of Norfolk
NORMANTON, Earl of		
Lawrence	4. 369	Earl of Normanton
NORMANTON, Countess of		
Lawrence	4. 372	Earl of Normanton
NORTHUMBERLAND, Algernon, 10th Earl of		
Vandyck	2. 456	Earl of Clarendon
„	3. 33	Petworth
„	4. 334	Duke of Bedford
NORTHUMBERLAND, Henry Percy, 9th Earl of		
Rembrandt	3. 33	Petworth
Vandyck	3. 34	Petworth
NORTHUMBERLAND, Jocelyn, 11th Earl of		
Lely	3. 33	Petworth
Lely	3. 323	Earl of Carlisle
NORTHUMBERLAND, Hugh, 1st Duke of		
Barry	4. 266	Duke of Northumberland
NORTHUMBERLAND, Duke of		
Lawrence	4. 266	Duke of Northumberland
NORTHUMBERLAND, 1st Duchess of (called Queen Charlotte in error)		
Reynolds	4. 266	Duke of Northumberland
NORTHUMBERLAND, Anne Cecil, Countess of		
Vandyck	3. 33	Petworth
O'BRIEN, Nelly		
Reynolds	2. 160	Marquis of Hertford
Reynolds	4. 91	Marquis of Hertford
ODESCALCHI, Don Livio		
Vandyck	4. 443	Sir Hugh Campbell

	VOL. & PAGE	OWNER
ŒCOLAMPADIUS		
Holbein	3. 140	Earl of Radnor
Cranach	3. 219	Earl cf Craven
Holbein	3. 342	W. V. Wentworth
Holbein	4. 356	Lord Folkestone
OLIVARES, Duc d'		
Velasquez	2. 151	Marquis of Lansdowne
Velasquez	2. 223	Richard Ford
Rubens	3. 308	Duke of Hamilton
Velasquez	4. 181	Earl Stanhope
Velasquez	4. 444	Earl of Elgin
OMAI		
Reynolds	3. 323	Earl of Carlisle
ORANGE, Henry Frederick, Prince of		
Jordaens	2. 94	Devonshire House
Mireveldt	4. 266	Duke of Northumberland
Vandyck	2. 483	Charles I
ORANGE, William, Prince of (William III)		
Vandyck	3. 35	Petworth
ORANGE, William the Silent, Prince of		
Du Jardin	4. 183	G. C. Legh
ORANGE, Prince of		
Mireveldt	4. 354	Lord Folkestone
Mireveldt	4. 355	,,
Ravesteyn	4. 358	,,
ORANGE, Maurice, Prince of		
Mireveldt	3. 333	Meynell Ingram
ORANGE, Princess of		
Vandyck	3. 219	Earl of Craven
ORLEANS, Gaston, Duke of		
Vandyck	4. 360	Lord Folkestone
ORLEANS, Henrietta, Duchess of		
Petitot	2. 97	Miss Burdett Coutts
Vandyck	4. 334	Duke of Bedford

	VOL. & PAGE	OWNER
ORMONDE, Mary, Duchess of		
Vandyck	3. 464	Duke of Bedford
OSSUNA, Duchess of		
Velasquez	3. 435	Earl of Orford
OTHO, Emperor		
Titian	2. 313	Earl Brownlow
OUVAROFF, General		
Lawrence	2. 425	Windsor Castle
PALLIOTTI, Count		
Gennari	3. 385	Earl of Shrewsbury
PALMERSTON, Lady		
Hoppner	4. 346	Earl Cowper
PARACELSUS		
Rubens	3. 124	Duke of Marlborough
PAREJA, Adrian Pulido		
Velasquez	3. 141	Earl of Radnor
„	4. 333	Duke of Bedford
„	4. 359	Lord Folkestone
PAREJA, Juan de		
Velasquez	4. 361	Lord Folkestone
PARMA, Duke of		
Titian	3. 313	Duke of Buccleuch
Velasquez	3. 322	Earl of Carlisle
Titian	4. 436	Duke of Buccleuch
PARMA, Margaret of		
Titian	3. 215	Earl of Warwick
PAUL III, Pope		
Titian	3. 203	Lord Northwick
Titian	4. 468	Duke of Northumberland

	VOL. & PAGE		OWNER
PAUL V, Pope			
Bronzino	3.	382	Earl of Shrewsbury
Guido	4.	397	Lord Methuen
PAULETT, Lady			
Vandyck	4.	463	Lord Douglas
PAUSIAS			
Rubens	2.	164	Marquis of Westminster
PELHAM, Mrs.			
Reynolds	4.	68	Earl of Yarborough
PELLICORNE, Jan			
Rembrandt	2.	158	Marquis of Hertford
PELLICORNE, Jan, Wife of			
Rembrandt	2.	158	Marquis of Hertford
PEMBROKE, Philip, 5th Earl of			
Vandyck	2.	342	Dulwich
„	3.	153	Earl of Pembroke
„	3.	154	Earl of Pembroke
„	2.	457	Earl of Clarendon
PEMBROKE, Henry, 10th Earl of			
Reynolds	4.	370	Earl of Normanton
PEMBROKE, Richard Weston, Earl of			
Vandyck	4.	375	Kingston Lacy
PEMBROKE, Thomas Herbert, 8th Earl of			
Vandyck	4.	517	Lord Galway
PEMBROKE, William, 1st Earl of			
Holbein	3.	152	Earl of Pembroke
PEMBROKE, Countess of			
Vandyck	2.	342	Dulwich
„	3.	408	Marquis of Exeter
„	3.	462	Glendon Hall
PEMBROKE, Elizabeth, Countess of			
Reynolds	4.	371	Earl of Normanton

	VOL. & PAGE	OWNER
PERCY, Henry, Lord		
Vandyck	3. 34	Petworth
PERCY, Sir Charles		
Vandyck	3. 34	Petworth
PETER THE GREAT		
Kneller	2. 356	Hampton Court
A Bronze	3. 352	Duke of Devonshire
PFALZBURG, Princess of		
Vandyck	2. 470	Charles I
Vandyck	2. 500	Orleans Gallery
PHILIP II, of Spain		
Velasquez	1. 347	National Gallery
More	2. 362	Hampton Court
More	2. 473	Charles I
Titian	2. 497	Orleans Gallery
More	3. 134	Lord Dillon
Titian	3. 299	Duke of Hamilton
Titian	3. 346	Duke of Devonshire
Medallion	3. 367	Duke of Devonshire
More	3. 429	A. Fountaine
,,	3. 457	Earl Spencer
,,	3. 464	Duke of Bedford
Titian	4. 181	Earl Stanhope
More	4. 337	Duke of Bedford
Giordano	4. 386	Lord Heytesbury
PHILIP II, Third wife of		
More	3. 206	Lord Northwick
PHILIP II, Isabella, wife of		
More	3. 378	W. Davenport Bromley
PHILIP III, Margaret of Austria, wife of		
Pantoja	4. 449	W. Stirling
PHILIP IV, of Spain		
Velasquez	2. 172	Marquis of Westminster
,,	2. 267	Miss Rogers
,,	2. 345	Dulwich
,,	2. 345	Dulwich
Rubens	2. 435	Windsor Castle

	VOL. & PAGE	OWNER
Velasquez	3. 184	J. P. Miles
"	3. 297	Duke of Hamilton
"	4. 96	T. Baring
"	4. 382	Kingston Lacy
Rubens	4. 449	W. Stirling

PHILIP IV, of Spain, Maria, 2nd wife of

Velasquez	2. 223	Richard Ford
Velasquez	2. 357	Hampton Court

PHILIP IV, of Spain, Isabella, 1st wife of

Velasquez	2. 223	Richard Ford

PHILIP LE BEL

Van Eyck School	3. 33	Petworth

PIOMBO, Sebastian del

Del Piombo	1. 333	National Gallery
Il Rosso	4. 467	Duke of Northumberland

PITT, William

Lawrence	2. 337	Miss Wilbraham
Gainsborough	4. 373	Earl of Normanton
Gainsborough	4. 372	Earl of Normanton
Bust	4. 492	Lord Feversham

PIUS VII, Pope

Lawrence	2. 425	Windsor Castle
Wilkie	4. 184	W. Marshall

PIUS IX, Pope

Bust	3. 366	Duke of Devonshire

PLATOFF

Lawrence	2. 424	Windsor Castle

PLAYFAIR

Chantrey	4. 434	Mr. Playfair

POLE, Cardinal

Del Vaga	3. 455	Earl Spencer

POMPADOUR, Madame de

Boucher	4. 432	Gibson Craig

X X

	VOL. & PAGE		OWNER
POPE, Alexander			
Jervas	2.	152	Marquis of Lansdowne
Richardson	3.	227	Lord Lyttelton
Kneller	4.	348	Vernon Harcourt
PORDENONE			
Giorgione	2.	491	Orleans Gallery
PORTER, Mrs.			
Vandyck	3.	34	Petworth
PORTLAND, 1st Earl of			
Vandyck	2.	458	Earl of Clarendon
Mytens	4.	331	Duke of Bedford
PORTLAND, William, Duke of			
Reynolds	4.	515	Duke of Portland
POZZO, Chevalier del			
Unknown	2.	499	Orleans Gallery
PRETENDER, Young			
Petitot	2.	97	Miss Burdett-Coutts
PRUSSIA, King of			
Lawrence	4.	425	Windsor Castle
QUEENSBERRY, Marchioness of			
Reynolds	3.	313	Duke of Buccleuch
QUEENSBERRY, Duchess of			
Dobson	3.	313	Duke of Buccleuch
QUEENSBERRY, Duke of			
Dobson	3.	313	Duke of Buccleuch

	VOL. & PAGE	OWNER
RADNOR, James, 2nd Earl of		
Reynolds	4. 355	Lord Folkestone
RADNOR, Anne, Countess of		
Gainsborough	4. 354	Lord Folkestone
Reynolds	4. 362	Lord Folkestone
RALEIGH, Sir Walter		
Zucchero	4. 432	Gibson Craig
Van Somer	4. 464	Lord Douglas
Zucchero	4. 519	Earl of Hardwicke
RALEIGH, Lady		
Zucchero	4. 432	Gibson Craig
RECKEMAR		
Holbein	2. 363	Hampton Court
REMBRANDT		
Rembrandt	1. 354	National Gallery
„	2. 158	Marquis of Hertford
„	4. 335	Duke of Bedford
REYNOLDS, Sir Joshua, P.R.A.		
Reynolds	1. 366	Marlborough House
„	2. 348	Dulwich
„	4. 292	J. Sanders
„	4. 311	J. Morrison
„	4. 336	Duke of Bedford
„	4. 341	Knole
„	4. 371	Earl of Normanton
„	4. 496	Earl of Harrington
RICH, Anne Cavendish, Lady		
Vandyck	3. 34	Petworth
RICH, Johanna de Blois, Lady		
Vandyck	3. 364	Duke of Devonshire
RICHARD III		
Unknown	4. 432	Gibson Craig
RICHMOND, Lodowick Stuart, Duke of		
Van Somer	4. 362	Lord Folkestone

	VOL. & PAGE		OWNER
RICHMOND, James Stuart, Duke of			
Vandyck	2.	454	Earl of Clarendon
,,	3.	219	Earl of Craven
,,	3.	410	Earl of Westmoreland
,,	3.	420	Earl of Leicester
,,	4.	396	Lord Methuen
RICHMOND, Mary Herbert, Duchess of			
Vandyck	3.	123	Duke of Marlborough
,,	3.	154	Earl of Pembroke
,,	3.	297	Hampton Court
Lely	3.	323	Earl of Carlisle
RICHMOND, Frances, Duchess of			
Vandyck	2.	426	Windsor Castle
Vandyck	2.	470	Charles I
RIDLEY, Miss			
Lawrence	4.	379	Kingston Lacy
RIVERS, Catherine, Countess			
Vandyck	3.	458	Earl Spencer
RIZZIO, David			
Mola	3.	422	Earl of Leicester
ROBINSON, Sir John			
Kneller	3.	476	Marquis of Bute
ROBINSON, Mrs.			
Reynolds	2.	229	Hon. E. Phipps
Gainsborough	4.	91	Marquis of Hertford
ROCKINGHAM, Charles, Marquis of			
Reynolds	3.	338	Earl Fitzwilliam
Reynolds	4.	522	Earl of Hardwicke
ROCKINGHAM, Earl of, Family of			
Hogarth	3.	339	Earl Fitzwilliam
RUBENS, Sir P. P.			
Vandyck	1.	416	Duke of Buccleuch
Unknown	1.	416	Duke of Buccleuch
Vandyck	2.	94	Devonshire House

	VOL. & PAGE	OWNER
Rubens	2. 435	Windsor Castle
Vandyck	3. 225	Mr. Martin
Vandyck	3. 458	Earl Spencer
Rubens	4. 335	Duke of Bedford

RUPERT, Prince

Lely	2. 430	Windsor Castle
Vandyck	2. 470	Charles I
Honthorst	3. 154	Earl of Pembroke
Vandyck	3. 219	Earl of Craven
Honthorst	3. 219	Earl of Craven
Lely	3. 340	Earl Fitzwilliam

RUSSELL, Lady Caroline

Reynolds	4. 331	Duke of Bedford

RUSSELL, John

Holbein	4. 331	Duke of Bedford

RUSSIA, Emperor Alexander of

Lawrence	2. 425	Windsor Castle

RUSSIA, Empress of

Rauch	3. 352	Duke of Devonshire

RUYTER, Admiral De

Jansen	4. 515	Duke of Portland

RYCKAERT, David

Vandyck	4. 355	Lord Folkestone
"	4. 518	Earl of Hardwicke
"	3. 214	Earl of Warwick

SACCHINI

Reynolds	4. 341	Knole

SANVITALE, Count

Parmigiano	3. 176	Mr. Vivian

SAVORGNANO, Marchese di

Titian	4. 378	Kingston Lacy

	VOL. & PAGE	OWNER
SAVOY, Duke of, Grandfather of More	2. 473	Charles I
SAVOY, Duke of, Grandmother of More	2. 473	Charles I
SAXONY, Frederick, Duke of Holbein Cranach	2. 199 4. 97	R. S. Holford T. Baring
SAXONY, John the Constant, Elector of Cranach	4. 97	T. Baring
SAXONY, George, Elector of Cranach	3. 219	Earl of Craven
SAY AND SELE, Lady Reynolds	4. 282	Sir C. Eardley
SCAGLIA Vandyck	2. 200	R. S. Holford
SCALIGERO, Giulio Cesare Carracci	4. 470	Duke of Northumberland
SCANDERBEG Giorgione	4. 394	Lord Methuen
SCHINDLERIN, Madame After Reynolds Reynolds	2. 351 4. 340	E. Bicknell Knole
SCHWARZENBERG, Prince Lawrence	2. 424	Windsor Castle
SCOTS, Mary, Queen of Clouet Zucchero Janet De Heere	2. 363 3. 346 3. 457 4. 357	Hampton Court Duke of Devonshire Earl Spencer Lord Folkestone
SCOTT, Sir Walter Smith Gordon	4. 173 4. 453	E. Cheney W. Stirling

	VOL. & PAGE	OWNER
SEYMOUR, Jane		
Holbein	3. 464	Duke of Bedford
SHAKESPEARE, William		
Unknown	2. 53	Bridgewater House
,,	3. 216	Earl of Warwick
,,	3. 339	Earl Fitzwilliam
SHERIDAN, Mrs.		
Gainsborough	2. 348	Dulwich
Reynolds (called Mrs. Billington		
in error)	3. 160	Marquis of Lansdowne
SHIRLEY, Sir Robert		
Vandyck	3. 40	Petworth
SHIRLEY, Lady		
Vandyck	3. 40	Petworth
Vandyck	2. 470	Charles I
SIDDONS, Mrs.		
Lawrence	1. 381	Marlborough House
Reynolds	2. 172	Marquis of Westminster
Reynolds	2. 348	Dulwich
Lawrence	2. 351	E. Bicknell
Gainsborough	4. 435	Mrs. Mair
SIDNEY, Sir Henry		
More	3. 41	Petworth
SIDNEY, Maria, Lady		
More	3. 41	Petworth
SIDNEY, Sir Philip		
Velasquez	3. 342	W. V. Wentworth
SIX, Burgomaster		
Rembrandt	2. 335	Lady Dover
SMITH, Sir Sidney		
Lawrence	4. 478	J. Anderson
SNYDERS, Franz		
Vandyck	2. 500	Orleans Gallery
Vandyck	3. 319	Earl of Carlisle
Snyders	3. 443	Mr. Tomline

	VOL. & PAGE	OWNER
SNYDERS, Mrs.		
Vandyck	2. 500	Orleans Gallery
Vandyck	3. 213	Earl of Warwick
Snyders	3. 443	Mr. Tomline
SOCRATES		
Da Vinci	2. 482	Charles I
SODERINI, Cardinal		
Bronzino	4. 456	Earl of Dunmore
SOMERSET, Edward Seymour, Duke of		
Holbein	4. 269	Duke of Northumberland
SOMMERS, Will		
Holbein	3. 456	Earl Spencer
SOUTHAMPTON, Thomas, Earl of		
Oliver	4. 119	C. S. Bale
SOUTHAMPTON, William Fitzwilliam, Earl of		
Holbein	3. 449	Fitzwilliam Museum
SOUTHAMPTON, Countess of		
Vandyck	2. 85	Earl de Grey
SOUTHAMPTON, Rachel, Countess of		
Vandyck	2. 85	Earl de Grey
Vandyck	3. 459	Earl Spencer
SPALATRO, Archbishop of		
Tintoretto	3. 346	Duke of Devonshire
SPELMAN, Sir Henry		
Ravesteyn	4. 519	Earl of Hardwicke
SPENCER, Georgiana, Countess		
Gainsborough	4. 348	Vernon Harcourt
SPENCER, Penelope Wriothesley, Countess		
Vandyck	3. 458	Earl Spencer
SPENCER, Lord Charles		
Reynolds	3. 130	Duke of Marlborough

	VOL. & PAGE	OWNER
SPENCER, Lady Charlotte		
Reynolds	3. 130	Duke of Marlborough
SPINOLA, Marquis of		
Vandyck	1. 416	Duke of Buccleuch
Rubens	3. 213	Earl of Warwick
Rubens	4. 519	Earl of Hardwicke
SPINOLA, Marchesa		
Vandyck	4. 151	Earl of Caledon
Rubens	4. 375	Kingston Lacy
STAFFORD, William Howard, Viscount		
Vandyck	3. 475	Marquis of Bute
STAFFORD, Granville, Marquis of		
Reynolds	4. 349	Vernon Harcourt
STAFFORD, Mr.		
Lely	4. 380	Kingston Lacy
STANHOPE, Hon. Fitzroy		
Reynolds	4. 236	Earl of Harrington
STANHOPE, Hon. Francis		
Reynolds	4. 236	Earl of Harrington
STANHOPE, Hon. Leicester		
Reynolds	4. 236	Earl of Harrington
STANHOPE, Hon. Lincoln		
Reynolds	4. 236	Earl of Harrington
STEEN, Jan		
Steen	4. 336	Duke of Bedford
STERNE, Laurence		
Reynolds	2. 152	Marquis of Lansdowne
STIRLING, Helen		
Raeburn	4. 453	W. Stirling
STOKESBY, Dr., Bishop of London		
Holbein	2. 431	Windsor Castle

	VOL. & PAGE	OWNER
STRAFFORD, Thomas Wentworth, Earl of		
Vandyck	3. 34	Petworth
„	3. 130	Duke of Marlborough
„	3. 338	Earl Fitzwilliam
„	3. 339	„
„	3. 340	„
„	3. 342	W. V. Wentworth
„	4. 271	Earl of Jersey
„	4. 325	Lord Enfield
„	4. 463	Lord Douglas
„	4. 515	Duke of Portland
STRAFFORD, Arabella, Countess of		
Vandyck	3. 340	Earl Fitzwilliam
STRAFFORD, Thomas, Earl of, Children of		
Vandyck	3. 338	Earl Fitzwilliam
STUART, Lord Bernard		
Vandyck	2. 84	Earl De Grey
Vandyck	3. 24	Earl of Darnley
STUART, Lord John		
Vandyck	2. 84	Earl De Grey
Vandyck	3. 24	Earl of Darnley
SUNDERLAND, Dorothy, Countess of		
Lely	3. 24	Earl of Darnley
Vandyck	3. 43	Petworth
SURREY, Henry, Earl of		
Strote	3. 30	Duke of Norfolk
SUTHERLAND, Duchess of		
Lawrence	2. 72	Duke of Sutherland
SWEDEN, Christina, Queen of		
Bourdon	2. 487	Orleans Gallery

	VOL. & PAGE	OWNER
TASSO, Torquate		
Allori	3. 282	Mr. Dennistoun
TAVISTOCK, Marquis of		
Reynolds	3. 130	Duke of Marlborough
Reynolds	4. 331	Duke of Bedford
TAVISTOCK, Marchioness of		
Reynolds	4. 333	Duke of Bedford
Reynolds	4. 334	Duke of Bedford
TAYLOR, Mr.		
Jansen	4. 361	Lord Folkestone
TCHERNICHEFF, General		
Lawrence	2. 425	Windsor Castle
TELL, William		
Rembrandt	3. 406	Marquis of Exeter
TEMPLE, Sir William		
Vandyck	4. 412	Smith Barry
TENIERS, David		
Teniers	4. 335	Duke of Bedford
THALSBURG, Princess of		
Vandyck	3. 298	Duke of Hamilton
THIMBLEBY, Lady Elizabeth		
Vandyck	3. 458	Earl Spencer
THOMSON, James		
Aikman	3. 227	Lord Lyttelton
TICHFIELD, Marquis of		
Reynolds	4. 512	Duke of Portland
TINTORETTO		
Tintoretto	4. 336	Duke of Bedford
TITIAN		
Piombo	1. 417	Earl of Malmesbury
Titian	2. 481	Charles I
Titian	2. 484	Charles I

	VOL. & PAGE	OWNER
TITIAN—*continued*		
Tintoretto	2. 496	Orleans Gallery
Titian	2. 497	Orleans Gallery
Titian	4. 335	Duke of Bedford
TORNABUONI, Maria		
Ghirlandajo	4. 497	W. Drury Lowe
TOWNSHEND, The Ladies		
Reynolds	1. 365	Marlborough House
TRIESTE, Anthony, Senator of Ghent		
Vandyck	2. 315	Earl Brownlow
TURENNE, Marshal		
Rembrandt	3. 16	Earl Cowper
TUSCANY, Alessandro, Duke of		
Pontormo	2. 232	Lord Ward
TUSCANY, Cosmo I, Duke of		
Bronzino	2. 195	R. S. Holford
TUSCANY, Leonora de Toledo, Duchess of		
Bronzino	2. 195	R. S. Holford
Bronzino	2. 269	Miss Rogers
Domenichino	3. 170	Earl of Suffolk
URBINO, Guidobaldo, Duke of		
Unknown	3. 238	Liverpool R.I.
VAN DER BORCHT, Count Henry		
Vandyck	2. 470	Charles I
VANDYCK, Sir Anthony		
Vandyck	2. 94	Devonshire House
„	2. 429	Windsor Castle
„	2. 470	Charles I
Rubens	2. 484	Charles I
Vandyck	3. 441	Mr. Tomline
Vandyck	4. 336	Duke of Bedford

	VOL. & PAGE	OWNER
VAN EYCK, Jan		
Van Eyck	1. 348	National Gallery
VAN EYCK, Jan, Wife of		
Van Eyck	1. 348	National Gallery
VAN HOOFT		
Rembrandt	2. 315	Earl Brownlow
VAUGONA, Marquess		
Titian	2. 481	Charles I
VAUX, Lady		
Holbein	2. 361	Hampton Court
VECCHIO, Violante		
Giorgione	4. 361	Lord Folkestone
VEGA, Lope de		
Cano	4. 520	Earl of Hardwicke
VELASQUEZ		
Velasquez	2. 151	Marquis of Lansdowne
VERNON, Robert		
Pickersgill	1. 381	Marlborough House
VERONESE, Paul		
Cagliari	4. 336	Duke of Bedford
VESALIUS, Andrea		
Titian	4. 335	Duke of Bedford
VESPASIAN, Emperor		
Titian	2. 497	Orleans Gallery
VICTORIA, Queen		
Wilkie	3. 287	McLellan Gallery
VILLIERS, Lord Francis		
Vandyck	2. 427	Windsor Castle
VILLIERS, Lord George		
Vandyck	2. 427	Windsor Castle

	VOL. & PAGE	OWNER
VILLIERS, Lady		
Vandyck	3. 460	Duke of Buccleuch
VITELLIUS, Emperor		
Titian	2. 497	Orleans Gallery
WALDEGRAVE, Three Ladies		
Reynolds	4. 152	Lady Waldegrave
WALDEGRAVE, Mr.		
Reynolds	4. 152	Lady Waldegrave
WALES, Henry, Prince of		
Van Somer	3. 219	Earl of Craven
WALPOLE, Sir Robert		
Reynolds	4. 152	Lady Waldegrave
WALSINGHAM, Sir Francis		
More	2. 199	R. S. Holford
WALTERS, Lucy		
Lely	3. 313	Duke of Buccleuch
WARHAM, Archbishop		
Holbein	1. 429	Lambeth Palace
WARWICK, Robert Rich, Earl of		
Vandyck	3. 214	Earl of Warwick
WARWICK, Countess of		
Vandyck	3. 408	Marquis of Exeter
WELLINGTON, Duke of		
Lawrence	2. 424	Windsor Castle
Campbell	3. 313	Duke of Buccleuch
Simpson	4. 372	Earl of Normanton
Campbell	4. 435	Duke of Buccleuch
Bust	4. 492	Lord Feversham
WENTWORTH, Lady Anne		
Lely	3. 338	Earl Fitzwilliam

	VOL. & PAGE	OWNER
WENTWORTH, Lady Arabella		
Lely	3. 338	Earl Fitzwilliam
WESTMORELAND, 8th Earl of		
Reynolds	3. 411	Earl of Westmoreland
WESTMORELAND, 9th Earl of		
Reynolds	3. 411	Earl of Westmoreland
WESTMORELAND, Countess of		
Lawrence	3. 411	Earl of Westmoreland
WHARTON, Jane, Lady		
Vandyck	3. 364	Duke of Devonshire
WILKIE, Sir David, R.A.		
T. Phillips	1. 381	Marlborough House
WILLIAM III		
Netscher	2. 8	Buckingham Palace
,,	4. 372	Earl of Normanton
,,	4. 512	Duke of Portland
Vandyck	4. 513	Duke of Portland
WILLIAM IV		
Wilkie	2. 277	Duke of Wellington
Lawrence	2. 425	Windsor Castle
WILMOT, Sir Eardley		
Reynolds	4. 281	Sir C. Eardley
WOODLEY, Mrs.		
Reynolds	4. 379	Kingston Lacy
WOODWARD		
Reynolds	3. 33	Petworth
WORSLEY, Sir Richard		
Reynolds	4. 66	Earl of Yarborough
WRIOTHESLEY, Lady Elizabeth		
Van Somer	4. 426	Earl of Burlington

LIST OF OWNERS MENTIONED BY DR. WAAGEN

In many instances the same name appears several times on one page. They are only given once in this index.

The names of the more important Houses, by which many of the collections are known, are also given in the following index.

The owners mentioned in the Portrait Index are not included in this list, as they already appear under the painters.

Acraman, W. (sold at Christie's, 1842). 277, 278, 280, 285, 286, 289, 291, 293, 294.

Aders, Mr. 292.

Aldermaston. *See* Higford Burr.

Allerton. *See* Fletcher, Jacob.

Alnwick. *See* Northumberland, Duke of.

Althorpe. *See* Spencer, Earl.

Alton Towers. *See* Shrewsbury, Earl of.

Amherst, Earl. *See* Knole.

Anderson, John (Coxlodge Hall). 2, 21, 28, 48, 59, 96, 106, 130, 134, 141, 172, 191, 212, 266, 267.

Anderson, Matthew (Jesmond Cottage, Newcastle). 8, 15, 20, 29, 39, 48, 50, 51, 53, 72, 87, 103, 115, 116, 122, 123, 124, 126, 133, 135, 139, 155, 157, 159, 173, 179, 185, 189, 191, 194, 201, 203, 212, 217, 228, 230, 232, 246, 248, 254, 267, 270, 272.

Antiquaries, Society of. 124.

Antis (? Artis), Mr.—Collection of Richard Artis, sold at Christie's, 17th May 1851. 278, 291, 292, 294.

Apethorpe. *See* Westmoreland, Earl of.

Appledurcombe. *See* Yarborough, Earl of.

Apsley House. *See* Wellington, Duke of.

Arundel, Lord (Wardour Castle). 29, 44, 58, 90, 129, 141, 154, 167, 169, 172, 178, 183, 194, 201, 206, 212, 220, 254, 255.

Arundel Castle. *See* Norfolk, Duke of.

Ashburnham, Lord (Ashburnham Place) —portions sold at Christie's, July 1850 and July 1901. 47, 165, 209.

Ashburnham, Hon. Mr. 192.

Ashburton, Lord (Piccadilly)—portions sold at Christie's, June 1872, July 1905; residue sold at Melchet Court, Sept. 1911. 7, 14, 18, 27, 28, 30, 42, 46, 50, 55, 57, 58, 75, 81, 83, 89, 91, 112, 120, 124, 127, 134, 138, 140, 151, 164, 180, 186, 196, 202, 208, 213, 217, 229, 233, 234, 235, 238, 249, 256, 259, 267, 271.

Ashton, Samuel (Manchester). 26, 34, 40, 41, 45, 61, 62, 66, 87, 88, 96, 126, 149, 150, 195, 201, 207, 224, 262, 265.

Bale, C. Sackville (71 Cambridge Terrace)— dispersed at Christie's in May 1881. 19, 20, 27, 32, 36, 37, 44, 59, 67, 78, 91, 93, 137, 139, 144, 146, 150, 151, 161, 165, 192, 199, 209, 215, 218, 221, 224, 261.

Balgowan. *See* Graham, Robert.

Bankes, E. G. *See* Kingston Lacy.

Barbers' Hall. 91.

Bardon, W. W. (? Burdon). 8, 11, 72, 80, 88, 110, 121, 130, 157, 167, 189, 201, 203, 212, 232, 237, 254, 258, 272.

100, 103, 105, 106, 108, 111, 116, 126, 127, 133, 135, 147, 163, 167, 174, 176, 201, 204, 205, 223, 225, 261, 262, 263, 264, 265, 266.

Marshall, William (85 Eaton Square). 26, 38, 40, 43, 61, 107, 130, 224, 265.

Martin, Joseph John (Ham Court). 4, 19, 47, 52, 61, 93, 123, 148, 153, 177, 183, 188, 210, 214, 227, 231, 243, 259, 264, 271.

Methuen, Lord (Corsham Court)—sold at Christie's, May 1899. 2, 3, 9, 21, 33, 35, 38, 43, 45, 55, 56, 60, 62, 65, 66, 67, 74, 77, 78, 82, 109, 111, 113, 116, 148, 149, 150, 157, 163, 178, 185, 193, 200, 205, 217, 225, 246, 248, 260, 278, 279, 280, 281, 282, 283, 284, 285, 286, 287, 288, 289, 290, 291, 292, 293.

Mildmay, Humphrey St. John (46, Berkeley Square)—sold at Christie's, June 1893. 8, 11, 15, 19, 51, 56, 59, 87, 90, 110, 140, 176, 188, 199, 203, 228, 230, 234, 237, 255, 262, 269, 271.

Miles, J. P. (Leigh Court)—dispersed at Christie's in June 1884, and May 1899. 1, 9, 10, 12, 25, 31, 33, 37, 43, 54, 56, 58, 65, 84, 90, 93, 103, 109, 117, 119, 129, 144, 151, 153, 156, 162, 174, 177, 183, 193, 205, 220, 242, 253, 254, 255, 257, 259, 277, 280, 283, 286.

Mills, Mr.   79.

Morrison, James (Basildon Park). 1, 2, 7, 8, 10, 11, 15, 19, 36, 38, 40, 46, 48, 57, 58, 59, 61, 62, 66, 79, 82, 85, 87, 88, 89, 90, 91, 133, 139, 140, 144, 145, 147, 151, 152, 153, 154, 156, 157, 158, 159, 166, 167, 168, 170, 171, 174, 181, 183, 184, 187, 188, 201, 203, 209, 210, 211, 218, 221, 223, 224, 229, 230, 232, 234, 235, 237, 239, 242, 245, 249, 259, 261, 262, 265, 266, 268, 269, 271.

Munro, H. A. J. (Novar)—dispersed at Christie's in March 1859, March 1860, June 1861, May and Dec. 1867, Dec. 1876, June 1877, April and June 1878, Feb. 1879, and March 1880. 1, 3, 7, 14, 17, 19, 24, 28, 30, 36, 41, 44, 46, 53 55, 58, 62, 67, 75, 83, 88, 90, 115, 127, 128,

138, 141, 143, 150, 152, 155, 158, 161, 164, 168, 174, 180, 187, 192, 193, 195, 196, 202, 213, 215, 217, 223, 228, 231, 234, 235, 256, 261, 266, 280.

Murray, Lord.   79, 80, 145, 262.

Muskett, Joseph.   94, 237.

Narford.   *See* **Fountaine, A.**

National Gallery.   *See also* **Marlborough House**.   3, 7, 8, 9, 11, 12, 13, 15, 18, 20, 22, 28, 29, 30, 35, 42, 45, 49, 53, 55, 57, 60, 65, 67, 71, 72, 73, 75, 76, 77, 78, 81, 82, 84, 91, 94, 101, 103, 111, 112, 115, 117, 122, 127, 141, 142, 143, 146, 148, 152, 155, 161, 163, 164, 166, 174, 176, 180, 184, 192, 200, 201, 204, 207, 211, 214, 217, 221, 231, 235, 238, 247, 248, 249, 252, 254, 255, 256, 257, 258, 260, 264, 265, 274, 279, 280, 281, 282, 283, 285, 293.

Naylor, John.   2, 3, 40, 41, 45, 61, 104, 109, 118, 201, 224.

Neeld, Joseph (Grittleton).   19, 32, 46, 49, 50, 53, 61, 65, 73, 75, 81, 83, 87, 91, 99, 108, 120, 122, 124, 135, 140, 143, 146, 156, 158, 165, 176, 181, 187, 191, 192, 195, 196, 202, 209, 218, 228, 231, 253, 256, 261, 262, 268.

Nelthorpe, Sir John, Bart. (Scawby).   20, 94, 104, 106, 116, 130, 158, 173, 179, 189, 204, 263.

Newcastle, Duke of (Clumber Park).   22, 33, 39, 52, 57, 68, 69, 72, 85, 94, 126, 149, 155, 167, 185, 189, 199, 212, 222, 246, 250, 251, 263, 267, 270, 273.

Newhall.   *See* **Buckley, General.**

Nichols, R. P. (25 Maida Hill, West)—sold at Christie's in April 1875.   55, 68, 84, 126, 130, 184, 192, 194, 222, 234, 245, 269, 274.

Norfolk, Duke of (Arundel Castle).   4, 71, 91, 92, 106, 109, 122, 131, 180, 205, 238, 241, 250.

Normanton, Earl of (Somerley).   8, 15, 17, 19, 23, 27, 38, 43, 45, 48, 50, 56, 63, 72, 79, 81, 85, 91, 94, 97, 102, 106, 109, 117, 125, 130, 133, 135, 143, 145,

25, 46, 50, 51, 52, 53, 62, 75, 83, 87, 90, 105, 117, 145, 168, 181, 187, 202, 208, 228, 229, 231, 261, 264.

Playfair, Mr. (Scotch architect).   35, 161, 174, 213.

Portland, Duke of (Welbeck).   11, 13, 20, 23, 25, 32, 39, 41, 55, 66, 80, 87, 88, 94, 95, 96, 100, 108, 130, 134, 135, 137, 147, 155, 163, 167, 172, 173, 185, 189, 194, 199, 204, 217, 222, 231, 237, 246, 247, 270, 273.

Raby Castle.   *See* **Cleveland, Duke of.**

Radnor, Earl of (Longford Castle).   *See also* **Folkestone, Lord.**   37, 43, 49, 54, 84, 92, 99, 122, 128, 148, 153, 156, 177, 183, 220, 236, 253, 271, 274.

Ravensworth, Lord.   29, 69, 155, 157, 158, 189.

Rawdon, Colonel.   168, 202.

Robarts, Abraham (Hill Street, Berkeley Square).   8, 15, 16, 18, 38, 42, 48, 53, 60, 63, 79, 82, 90, 102, 115, 121, 130, 139, 140, 159, 184, 188, 198, 203, 211, 228, 230, 234, 337, 245, 249, 251, 269, 271.

Rock (Northumberland).   162, 183.

Rogers, Samuel—dispersed at Christie's in April 1856.   9, 10, 17, 29, 36, 44, 55, 59, 66, 71, 75, 77, 83, 109, 119, 155, 161, 164, 168, 180, 191, 192, 215, 217, 247, 266.

Rogers, Miss.   8, 9, 17, 21, 23, 52, 56, 69, 73, 75, 78, 81, 105, 108, 109, 119, 122, 128, 133, 144, 150, 152, 168, 181, 195, 205, 209, 218, 223, 230, 231, 247, 248, 249, 253, 262, 265, 266.

Rossie Priory.   *See* **Kinnaird, Lord.**

Rothschild, Sir Anthony.   47, 79, 128, 139, 181, 209, 236, 239, 268.

Rothschild, Baron Lionel.   46, 51, 55, 79, 134, 140, 186, 187, 208, 213, 229, 235, 238, 264, 268.

Royal Academy.   3, 137, 161, 213, 258, 288.

Russell, Rev. John Fuller (Eagle House, Enfield)—dispersed 18th April 1885.   8,

9, 18, 26, 49, 60, 67, 68, 71, 77, 99, 118, 119, 192, 200, 201, 207, 225, 233, 267.

Russell, William (38 Chesham Palce)— sold at Christie's in March 1863 and December 1884.   50, 57, 104, 123, 145, 170, 184, 196, 205, 245, 252.

Rutland, Duke of (Belvoir Castle).   10, 14, 21, 29, 37, 38, 43, 48, 54, 58, 60, 62, 72, 93, 107, 108, 129, 139, 149, 153, 156, 157, 158, 166, 170, 184, 188, 195, 196, 203, 210, 213, 229, 231, 233, 237, 244, 251, 269, 271.

St. James's Palace.   293, 294.

Sanders, Joseph (Taplow House).   15, 17, 19, 59, 63, 67, 72, 76, 117, 126, 133, 149, 159, 171, 175, 176, 178, 188, 196, 204, 205, 222, 232, 234, 258, 261, 266, 271.

Sanderson, Richard.   47, 128, 140, 151, 187.

Scarsdale, Lord (Keddleston Hall).   1, 10, 31, 37, 48, 54, 56, 65, 69, 75, 77, 82, 84, 99, 102, 113, 118, 123, 156, 199, 203, 205, 250, 251, 266.

Scawby.   *See* **Nelthorpe, Sir J.**

Scottish Academy.   63.

Sebright, Sir Thomas (Beechwood).   11, 21, 32, 43, 77, 82, 84, 96, 130, 145, 147, 154, 163, 171, 178, 185, 192, 193, 199, 237, 245, 259.

Serlby.   *See* **Galway, Lady.**

Seymour, Henry Danby (Knoyle House).   8, 18, 19, 28, 36, 48, 68, 73, 87, 91, 94, 111, 118, 124, 149, 152, 154, 161, 168, 174, 189, 193, 223, 225, 230, 234, 235, 237, 239, 250, 253, 255, 259.

Shaftesbury, Earl of.   232.

Sharpe, Mr.   126.

Sheepshanks, J. (presented to South Kensington Museum in 1857).   26, 39, 40, 41, 45, 59, 61, 62, 68, 73, 95, 103, 104, 108, 109, 127, 163, 174, 201, 205, 223, 224, 225, 261, 262, 265.

Sherrington, Mr. (Yarmouth).   45.

Shrewsbury, Earl of (Alton Towers)— dispersed by Christie in 1857, 1861, and